Foreign Policy Restructuring

Studies in International Relations

Charles W. Kegley, Jr.,
and
Donald J. Puchala, General Editors

Foreign Policy Restructuring
How Governments Respond to Global Change

Edited by

Jerel A. Rosati
Joe D. Hagan
Martin W. Sampson III

University of South Carolina Press

Copyright © 1994 by the University of South Carolina

Published in Columbia, South Carolina, by the
University of South Carolina Press

Manufactured in the United States of America

Library of Congress Cataloging-in-Publication Data

Foreign policy restructuring : how governments respond to global
    change / edited by Jerel A. Rosati, Joe D. Hagan, Martin W. Sampson
    III.
        p.   cm.—(Studies in international relations)
    Includes bibliographical references and index.
    ISBN 0–87249–976–6 (acid-free paper)
    1. International relations. 2. World politics—1945– 3. United
States—Foreign policy—1945– I. Rosati, Jerel A., 1953– .
II. Hagan, Joe D. III. Sampson, Martin W., 1943– . IV. Series:
Studies in international relations (Columbia, S.C.)
JX1395.F624   1994
327.1′01—dc20   93–50575

To our families

Contents

Preface

The world is in a period of great turbulence and change, which has only intensified with the end of the cold war. The dramatic changes in recent years include the collapse of communism and Soviet power in Eastern Europe, the disintegration of the Soviet Union, the development of a bloody ethnic conflict in the former Yugoslavia, the difficult reintegration of East Germany into a unified Germany, the further integration of the European Community, the destruction of Iraqi military power, the rise of the Palestinian Intifada, the dismantling of apartheid in South Africa, and the growth of democratization in Asia and Latin America. Most profound was the "new thinking" in Soviet foreign policy associated with Mikhail Gorbachev's policies of perestroika and glasnost and its catalytic role in ending the rule of communism throughout Eastern Europe and, ultimately, in ending the cold war. It is in this context of continuing global change that a volume on foreign policy change is timely and significant.

With this in mind, there are several important reasons why scholars and students of foreign policy and international relations should find this book of interest. First, foreign policy is increasingly important in understanding the dynamics of continuity and change in world politics. Clearly, attempts to understand world politics solely as a result of underlying global forces are inadequate due to the fact that these global changes not only have produced significant shifts in foreign policy, but are a result of reorientations in foreign policy. Foreign policy per se not only carries greater importance, it also seems less predictable than a decade ago. In order to better understand continuity and change over time, this book presents a variety of approaches to explain why governments restructure their foreign policies. In this respect, it is intended to act as a stimulant to the evolving study of international relations and foreign policy. This is an important endeavor because progress on this scholarly front contributes to a more powerful understanding of the dynamics of world politics in general as the turn of the century approaches.

Second, this book directly addresses the question of change in foreign policy, an intellectually significant and increasingly prevalent topic which has been neglected in the systematic study of foreign policy. During the 1960s and 1970s, scholars heeded a call to promote a "science" of international relations and foreign policy. Yet, for all the energy and resources devoted to the comparative study of foreign policy during this time, little attention was given to the study of foreign policy change. Since the 1970s, however, different types of inquiry in international relations have converged on questions of foreign policy, and the scholarly foundation is now in place for students in the field to address change as well as continuity in the study of foreign policy. Today, there is a growing recognition that change as well as continuity must be examined in order to understand foreign policy in its entirety. This volume represents an effort to offer different perspectives for studying and understanding foreign policy change and restructuring. It is meant to represent and reinforce the work of others who are also engaged in the same scholarly enterprise. Ultimately, it is hoped that this volume contributes to stimulating the study as well as enhancing the comprehension of foreign policy change.

Third, this book demonstrates the growing maturity and potential of the study of foreign policy. The chapters present a rich body of knowledge and thought about continuity and change in foreign policy drawing on numerous theoretical approaches, literatures, and intellectual traditions within foreign policy and international relations. Among these are bargaining theory, decision-making theory, development theory, leadership orientations and domestic politics, political adaptation, political economy, rational choice, and structural analysis. They also offer a sophisticated synthesis of the dynamics of politics, recognizing the interplay of governmental, domestic, and international sources of foreign policy change, with concern for the historical context in which they occur. The resulting chapters, hence, both address and provoke numerous questions about change and foreign policy. They demonstrate that the study of foreign policy and international relations has generated considerable breadth and depth in theoretical knowledge which can contribute to an improved understanding of the dynamics of continuity and change in foreign policy.

Finally, this book is intended to be appealing and comprehensible to the specialist in foreign policy as well as the general student of international relations. The introductory chapter provides an overview of the study of foreign policy change and raises the major questions underlying the entire volume. The subsequent chapters each highlight a particular theoretical perspective, yet are organized so that each chapter flows from the work found in the preceding chapters. The concluding chapter discusses the implications derived from the previous chapters in addressing the major questions and the implications for the future study of foreign policy restructuring. To maximize overall coherence and unity, each chapter is preceded by editorial comments which provide a summary of the chapter, its contribution to the study of foreign policy change in the context of the larger volume, and a brief biosketch of the authors in order to better inform the reader about the writer's background and perspective.

The idea for this project began in 1988 at the ISA convention in St. Louis when Joe Hagan broached the idea of editing a volume on foreign policy change to Martin Sampson and Jerel Rosati. At the time, Hagan was the chair of the Foreign Policy Analysis Section of ISA, Sampson was the chair-elect, and Rosati was the previous chair of the section. Together, these authors were interested in the topic of foreign policy change and restructuring and shared the sentiment that ever-increasing research activity in the topic, especially among younger scholars, made this an opportune moment to develop a volume on the subject. An edited volume was thought to be an appropriate way to communicate significant theoretical and empirical research throughout the scholarly community on the study of change in foreign policy and international relations.

This book was developed at the University of South Carolina and we owe a special thanks to those who have been instrumental in bringing this project to fruition. Donald Puchala as director of the Institute of International Studies at the University of South Carolina was most generous in making it possible for the editors to meet together and push the project forward. Darin Van Tassell, David Hurt, Robert Shaw, Pete Steen, and, especially, Roger Moore, all Ph.D. candidates at the University of South Carolina, provided crucial support in bringing the manuscript to final form. Roger Coate also has been an invaluable friend and colleague in this regard. Sandra Hall, Becky Deaton, Lori Joy, and the secretarial staff of the department of Government and International Studies at the University of South Carolina were always there to provide assistance. Finally, those involved from the University of South Carolina Press have always been quite helpful and supportive. Naturally, the editors take full responsibility for any sins of commission or omission in the final product.

Foreign Policy Restructuring

Part I

Introduction

Chapter 1

The Study of Change in Foreign Policy

Jerel A. Rosati, Martin W. Sampson III, and Joe D. Hagan

Jerel Rosati, Martin Sampson, and Joe Hagan provide an overview of the study of change in foreign policy. As an introduction to the topic, they discuss the significance of understanding foreign policy change for world politics, consider why the study of foreign policy change has been neglected in the study of international relations, and review the few early efforts addressing foreign policy change and restructuring. They then examine the varied approaches to the study of foreign policy change offered in the subsequent chapters, discussing their theoretical relationship to earlier efforts and exploring their contributions to an improved understanding of the dynamics of world politics. In particular, they highlight the questions that are raised and addressed by the authors about change and foreign policy. The editors conclude by offering this volume as a basis to enhance understanding and stimulate research in foreign policy change and restructuring.

At the end of the 1980s, it became increasingly obvious that the world was experiencing considerable turbulence and change. Among some of the more profound changes were the rise of Mikhail Gorbachev, "perestroika," and "glasnost" in the Soviet Union, the collapse of communism in Eastern Europe and the Soviet Union, the unification of Germany, the continued integration of the European Community, the development of the Palestinian intifada, the easing of apartheid in South Africa, and the growth of democratization in Asia, Africa, and Latin America. To this one could add the rise of Japan in the world economy, the changing role of OPEC in the global politics of oil, the Iranian Revolution and the revival of Islam, and the rise and decline of the revolutions in El Salvador and Nicaragua. The list grows constantly. Decades of behavior patterns in different parts of the world have altered rapidly to produce a torrent of radical changes. While these changes were responsible for significant shifts in foreign policy they were concurrently a function of shifts in foreign policy.

In addition to David Hurt, Roger Moore, Pete Steen, and Darin Van Tassell, we would like to thank Mike Link and Jeff Morton for their helpful comments.

Most momentous was the fundamental change in Soviet foreign policy and its catalytic role in ending the rule of communism throughout Eurasia and, ultimately, in ending the cold war.

These global changes have evoked considerable speculation about the future of world politics. Some speak optimistically of a post–cold war environment and a new world order where government foreign policies face new opportunities and constraints. At the same time, in the post–cold war environment many conflicts continue and old ethnic and national rivalries have reappeared throughout the former Soviet Union and Eastern Europe. Many, in fact, fear that a post–cold war world will be one of greater instability throughout the international political economy. The American success in the Persian Gulf War has also triggered hopes and fears of a restored American hegemony throughout the world. In each case, the continually changing global environment has necessitated fundamental reassessments, and the implications are perhaps greatest for foreign policy.

In order to understand international developments of the past, present, and future one must attempt to comprehend change in general and foreign policy change in particular. How will governments respond to these global changes? What is foreign policy change? When and why does it occur? How does it affect world politics? The purpose of this volume is to provoke thought and to suggest some answers to these questions. Although a few earlier efforts have been made to understand foreign policy change, scholars of international relations for the most part have neglected its study. This volume is intended to stimulate the study and enhance the understanding of foreign policy change and restructuring.

The specific purpose of this introductory chapter is to provide an overview of the study of foreign policy change. First, it seeks to answer why the study of foreign policy change has been in large part neglected by scholars of international relations, including those who focus on the study of foreign policy. Then the few efforts that have been conducted to understand foreign policy change and restructuring are reviewed. This is followed by a brief discussion of the relationship between the earlier works and the studies offered in this volume. Finally, general questions about foreign policy change raised by the contributions of this volume are addressed so as to better understand foreign policy and world politics. In this way this introductory chapter sets the context for a deeper analysis into the process of foreign policy change offered by the subsequent chapters.

The Neglect of Foreign Policy Change

During the 1960s and 1970s, scholars heeded a call to promote a "science" of international relations and foreign policy (Snyder, Bruck, and Sapin 1962; Rosenau 1966). This resulted in, among other pursuits, the rise of the comparative study of foreign policy or, as it was commonly called, comparative foreign policy (McGowan and Shapiro 1973; Rosenau 1968, 1975). Yet, for all the energy and resources devoted to the systematic and comparative study of foreign policy during this time, little attention was given to the study of foreign policy change. As Kal Holsti (1982, 2) made quite clear over a decade ago, although "foreign policy reorientation is certainly no new phenomenon in international politics," its systematic study has basically been ignored. Most of the systematic foreign policy research and literature, with an occasional exception, has had very little to do with change. Why has the study of foreign policy restructuring been such a backwater among contemporary scholars of international relations? Why is it that the study of foreign policy change has begun to receive some serious attention only since the 1980s?

An evaluation of Robert Gilpin's central purpose in writing *War and Change in World Politics* (1981) helps to explain the neglect of foreign policy change by scholars of international relations and foreign policy. As he makes clear, a similar inattention to the study of international political change during the 1960s and 1970s motivated him to write *War and Change*. At the time, Gilpin argued that there were five reasons why international political change was not treated as an important topic by most international relations scholars. More than a decade later, those same five reasons seem to explain the failure of most contemporary students of international relations and foreign policy to address the study of foreign policy change as well (see also Holsti 1982, 8–12).

First, Gilpin argued that international relations was a young discipline and that the development of any science naturally proceeds from analyzing order to analyzing change. "Until the statics of a field of inquiry are sufficiently well developed and one has a good grasp of repetitive processes and recurrent phenomena, it is difficult if not impossible to proceed to the study of dynamics" (Gilpin 1981, 4). Unfortunately, much of science consists of static analysis. According to Wilbur Moore (1968, 365) in the *International Encyclopedia of the Social Sciences,* "Paradoxically, as the rate of social change has accelerated in the real world of experience, the scientific disciplines dealing with man's actions and products have tended to emphasize orderly interdependence and static continuity."[1] The same can be said for the study of foreign policy—scholars have emphasized continuous patterns of foreign policy, as opposed to restructuring in foreign policy over time. This is best illustrated in the study of U.S. foreign policy where attention has focused on the continuity of the policy of containment since the end of World War II (see, e.g., Gaddis 1982; Kegley and Wittkopf 1987). Consequently, upon reviewing the comparative study of foreign policy, James Caporaso, Charles Hermann, Charles Kegley, James Rosenau, and Dina Zinnes (1987, 42) came to the following conclusion, "Unfortunately, political scientists [and by this they would include international relations and foreign policy scholars] spend so much time learning how to describe . . . they are often baffled by dynamics. This is probably why they are so much better at postulating hypotheses that relate variables to each other . . . than they are at building theories."[2]

Second, according to Gilpin the rise of behavioralism resulted in the decline of grand theory which damaged the search for a general theory of international order and change. "The more recent emphasis on so-called middle-range theory, though valuable in itself, has had the unfortunate consequence of diverting attention away from more general theoretical problems" (Gilpin 1981, 5). Instead, as Kal Holsti (1971, 171) noted, "the major preoccupations of theorists during the past decade have been to explore specific problems, to form hypotheses or generalizations explaining limited ranges of phenomena, and particularly, to obtain data to test those hypotheses." A similar movement away from grand theory occupied students of foreign policy. Rosenau's (1966) pretheory and the study of decision-making (see, e.g., Snyder, Bruck, and Sapin 1962; Allison 1971) were among the more popular fields of foreign policy inquiry. Elements of Rosenau's pretheory served as the basis for the comparative study of foreign policy along the lines noted by Holsti. Decision-making theory heavily influenced the study of U.S. foreign policy where the focus became the role of the president, the foreign policy bureaucracy, and the governmental process as the determinants of policy. Such commitment to middle-range theory resulted in a proliferation of research into more narrow questions and microphenomena, analysis not conducive to the broader study of foreign policy change. Students of governmental decision-making and U.S. foreign policy, for example, tended to ignore how political leaders acquired, as well as lost, their policy positions over time, how their beliefs were formed, and how governmental institutions evolved. Hence, political leaders and government institutions were usually treated as operating in relative isolation from society and the world.

For Gilpin, Western bias was a third reason contributing to the neglect of the study of change. "For a profession whose intellectual commitment is the understanding of the interactions of societies, international relations as a discipline is remarkably parochial and ethnocentric. It is essentially a study of the Western state system, and a sizable fraction of the existing literature is devoted to developments since the end of World War II" (Gilpin 1981, 5). For Gilpin this bias was primarily the result of the dominance of the United States and American scholarship since World War II. The same situation exists in the study of foreign policy. American scholars and, for the most part, students of U.S. foreign policy have had a disproportionate amount of influence on the larger study of foreign policy. Not surprisingly, these students have been preoccupied with explaining the cold war policies of the great powers in the contemporary post–World War II era (see, e.g., Korany 1974, 1983). This narrow focus in terms of foreign policy actors, scope, and time was reinforced by the rise of behavioralism and the decline of grand theorizing, contributing to a general neglect of foreign policy change.

"A fourth reason for neglect of the theoretical problem of political change is the widespread conviction of the futility of the task. Prevalent among historians, this view is also held by many social scientists" (Gilpin 1981, 5). Rarely, for example, did diplomatic historians go beyond the standard historical chronology and narrative account of foreign policy to offer theoretical explanations for continuity and change in foreign policy. A similar attitude also seemed predominant among scholars and students of foreign policy, including leading proponents of the comparative study of foreign policy. For example, although he no longer subscribes to this position, James Rosenau (1968, 324) once argued that "those whose aspirations for foreign policy theory include the capacity to explain and predict systemic coherence and collapse are bound to be thwarted. The fantasy is enticing and the aspiration is worthy, but neither can ever be realized."

The final reason inhibiting the development of a theory of political change for Gilpin was the existence of a conservative bias in Western social science due to ideology and emotion. "Most academic social scientists have a preference for stability or at least a preference for orderly change" (Gilpin 1981, 6). American scholars of international relations were heavily affected by the cold war years, anticommunism, and the realist tradition (see Vasquez 1983). The close relationship between politics and scholarship also can be clearly seen in the study of foreign policy, especially U.S. foreign policy. The almost exclusive concentration on the role of governmental decision-making in U.S. foreign policy acquired scholarly legitimacy during the height of the cold war—a time of perceived national emergency, when "high" national security policy was dominant and there was a tremendous increase in presidential power. In a sense, it may have seemed natural to focus on the president and the national security bureaucracy during the 1950s and 1960s because it was a time of foreign policy consensus within American society and a time of great wealth in U.S. resources and power. Yet, it was the societal and global context that ultimately had given rise to the increased prerogatives for the president and an expanded foreign policy bureaucracy (see Hodgson 1976; Rosati 1993).

These five mutually reinforcing reasons contributed to the neglect of the study of international political change. Yet, by the 1970s and, especially, the 1980s, the study of international change became the predominant focus of international relations scholars symbolized by Gilpin's *War and Change*. Over the last two decades the discipline of international relations has become more mature and moved beyond a narrow preoccupation with explaining international order. Grand theoretical concerns have been restored in a post–positivist era; interest in the third world, north-south relations, and history have grown in Western scholarship; the necessity of grappling with international change has been recognized; and greater ideological diversity has emerged among Western social scientists (see, e.g., Alker and Biersteker 1984; Lapid 1989; Puchala 1990). The result has been an explosion of competing theories to explain the "dynamics" of world politics: strategic hegemonic stability theory, long cycles theory, world systems theory, dependency theory, interdependence theory, international regimes theory, and so on.

A similar process appears to be unfolding in the study of foreign policy. The field of foreign policy is maturing and has expanded beyond the narrow methodological and intellectual straitjacket that dominated during the sixties. In the study of foreign policy, including U.S. foreign policy, knowledge has grown and diversity of inquiry has proliferated, providing a sufficient foundation for more dynamic analysis. The epistemological and methodological bases of inquiry have become more diverse and eclectic. Greater scholarly pluralism has resulted since the Vietnam War and the decline of the cold war in both the study of international relations and foreign policy. Students of foreign policy are beginning to address larger questions in their work and to search for "new directions" (see, e.g., Hermann, Kegley, and Rosenau 1987).[3] Therefore, as with the study of international political change, developments may be in place that allow for a growing recognition that change as well as continuity must be examined in order to understand foreign policy in its entirety.

Early Efforts at Foreign Policy Change and Restructuring

Although ignored for the most part, foreign policy change did receive some attention in the 1970s beginning with the work of Rosenau. During the 1980s it received more attention in the foreign policy work of Kal Holsti, Kjell Goldmann, and Charles Hermann, as well as in some of the literature in international political economy. It is these early efforts, sparse yet important, that provide an introduction to foreign policy change and restructuring.

Rosenau and Political Adaptation. An early effort pertinent to the study of foreign policy change is collected in *The Study of Political Adaptation* (1981) by James Rosenau, a set of essays that were predominantly written and published throughout the seventies. Rosenau's (1981a, iii) study of political adaptation is premised on the assumption that "our understanding of politics can be deepened and broadened by treating political phenomena as forms of human adaptation." According to Rosenau, "the political organism is always experiencing both continuities and change, and thus it is always in motion, slipping behind, moving ahead, holding fast, or otherwise adjusting and changing in response to internal developments and external circumstances." Therefore, "to analyze how the adjustments are made, the changes sustained, and the continuities preserved is to engage in the study of political adaptation" (Rosenau 1981, 1–2). Although the nation-state is the main actor whose adaptation is probed, Rosenau (1981, iv) makes the observation that "there are good reasons to believe that comprehension of political parties, legislatures, cabinets, revolutionary movements, international organizations, and a host of other political actors can be enlarged by treating them as adaptive entities." The study of political adaptation represented Rosenau's major effort to develop a general theory of foreign policy in a world of interdependence and transnationalism (see Smith 1983).

Specifically, Rosenau posits that foreign policy is essentially a mechanism for the nation-state to adapt to changes in its environment. Thus, governments, in order to survive and move toward their goals, have to balance the internal tensions and external demands to which they are subjected or risk failure and possibly disintegration. Changes in foreign policy are most likely to occur "when developments at home give rise to new needs and wants with respect to their environments, or when developments abroad give rise to potential threats to their essential structures'' (Rosenau 1981, 42). Ultimately, ''the connection between the adaptive behavior of a society and the consequences of that behavior for its essential structures exists primarily in the minds of foreign policy decision makers,'' who act to minimize costs and maximize opportunities based on their images of the world around them (Rosenau 1981, 50).

Rosenau laid out four possible patterns of foreign policy adaptation in response to the domestic and international constraints faced by policymakers: preservative adaptation (responsive to both external and internal demands and changes), acquiescent adaptation (responsive to external demands and changes), intransigent adaptation (responsive to internal demands and changes), and promotive adaptation (unresponsive to both internal and external demands and changes). According to Rosenau (1981, 59), ''while the myriad foreign policy behaviors of a society at a given moment may be unrelated and even contradictory,'' they tend to have an overall coherence in terms of one of the four underlying orientations in response to change at home and abroad. Each of these foreign policy orientations have different implications for foreign policy continuity and change, although this was not addressed at great length since it was not the focus of inquiry for Rosenau. Instead, Rosenau concentrated on how governments adapted to internal and external demands and to changes in a world of interdependence and transnationalism in order to ensure the success and survival of the state.

Holsti and Foreign Policy Restructuring. A significant step forward was taken by Kal Holsti in his *Why Nations Realign: Foreign Policy Restructuring in the Postwar World* (1982). The volume consists of a set of essays by Holsti and others (1982, ix), which had ''as its genesis an interest in an aspect of foreign policy which has received little attention in the theoretical literature, namely, foreign policy change.'' Holsti's (1982, x) purpose was to ''confirm that foreign policy change is a subject worthy of systematic analysis'' and to generate refinements, discussion, and debate ''about the nature of the international system and the theory of foreign policy.''

Holsti emphasized an examination of the changes in the patterns of foreign policy behavior over time. His specific focus was to better understand foreign policy restructuring—that is, ''the dramatic, wholesale alteration of a nation's pattern of external relations'' (Holsti 1982, ix). Such change usually involved both patterns of partnerships and types of activity (in geographic and functional sectors). ''We thus distinguish normal foreign policy change, which is usually slow, incremental and typified by low linkages between sectors . . . and foreign policy restructuring, which usually takes place more quickly, expresses an intent for fundamental change, is non-incremental and usually involves the conscious linking of different sectors'' (Holsti 1982, 2). Holsti identified twelve types of foreign policy restructurings that can be undertaken by a nation-state over time. These are subsumed under four ideal types of foreign policies: isolation, self-reliance, dependence, and nonalignment-diversification. He developed a framework to explain foreign policy restructuring based on the role of external factors, domestic factors, background historical and cultural factors, and factors within the policymaking process.

The key question Holsti addressed was why foreign policy restructuring occurs? Based on a cursory review of the foreign policy cases that might qualify for all of the twelve restructuring types, Holsti tentatively concluded that foreign policy restructuring appears to be more prevalent among smaller, developing countries, suggesting that "the developed countries are more 'satisfied' in the basic pattern of their foreign relations than are the developing states, or that the costs of restructuring are inordinately high for industrial countries" (Holsti 1982, 7). In order to elucidate and assess the value of his framework, foreign policy restructuring during the post–World War II years was examined in six cases involving developed and developing countries, major powers and small states, democracies and authoritarian regimes: Bhutan (from isolation to dependence, 1958 to 1962), Burma (from nonalignment to isolation, 1958 to 1962), Canada (from dependence to diversification, 1972 to 1978), Chile (an abortive attempt, 1970 to 1973), China (from dependence to self-reliance to isolation to diversity, 1959 to 1976), and Tanzania (from dependence to diversification, 1967 to 1977).

Holsti (1982, 198) concluded that "from the point of view of foreign policy theory, we regrettably cannot explain why some states restructure their foreign policies while others, facing similar domestic and external problems, do not." Nevertheless, Holsti (1982, 199) was able to "suggest that certain conditions, particularly dependence, vulnerability, perceptions of weakness and massive external penetration, *predispose* some governments to restructure their foreign policies and that sometimes the major residues of dependence and interdependence are seen as threats which, in turn, compel governments to build moats and create more 'distance' between themselves and their mentors." Therefore, the main instigator of foreign policy change was economic vulnerability or, more generally, the existence of a nonmilitary threat. This was especially the case for smaller and developing states, demonstrating the importance of nationalism. Under these conditions, foreign policy restructuring "is basically an attempt to assert autonomy, to control transnational processes, to destroy the residues of colonialism, to escape from the embrace of a hegemon" (Holsti 1982k, ix–x).

Holsti also found that foreign policy restructuring is easier to proclaim than carry out. "Despite the serious commitments of leaders to change their role and partners in the international or regional systems, the results are often meager, the costs often very high" (Holsti 1982, x). Holsti concluded by offering the following two generalizations. First, "foreign policy restructuring by relatively peripheral states which choose orientations that do not threaten the perceived security interests of bloc leaders or other hegemons are thus likely to succeed without generating high levels of conflict." Second, when foreign policy restructuring involves the strategic interests of great powers it is likely to "exacerbate international tensions and to result in a variety of coercive, punitive and violent responses by former hegemons" (Holsti 1982,

218). Although *Why Nations Realign* was an initial effort and highly suggestive, it represented a significant step forward in the study of foreign policy change and restructuring, especially as it applied to the foreign policies of smaller, developing, and more peripheral states.

Goldmann and Foreign Policy Stabilization. In the late 1980s, Kjell Goldmann focused on the study of foreign policy change in *Change and Stability in Foreign Policy: The Problems and Possibilities of Détente* (1988). The study is an extension of Goldmann's interest in reconciling the tension between two patterns of political action in order to understand the process of détente. On the one hand, nation-states "are under pressures to adapt to changing conditions in their environment. On the other hand, they have a tendency to stick to their previous policies" (Goldmann 1988, 3–4). How did these contradictory tendencies affect the process of détente in U.S.-Soviet relations since the late 1960s and into the future? This was of great importance for Goldmann because "the question of change and stability in foreign policy is vital for peace and security. In order to improve relations between long-standing adversaries it is necessary to destabilize their mutual policies of enmity. Once this has been achieved, the task is to stabilize their emerging policies of amity" (Goldmann 1988, xv).

Goldmann laid out a "theoretical sketch" of foreign policy stabilization as a means to address whether foreign policy is likely to endure or change. "Its core is an inventory of what will be called the 'stabilizers' of foreign policies, that is, of phenomena tending to inhibit change in foreign policy even when there is a pressure for change" (Goldmann 1988, xv). Goldmann describes thirteen administrative, political, cognitive, and international stabilizers which counteract dynamic elements including environmental change, negative feedback, and shifts in leadership and the policymaking process, thus impeding change. Goldmann goes on to discuss two foreign policy patterns based on the interaction of the thirteen stabilizers over time: a process of stabilization and a process of destabilization. The theoretical sketch is used to provide an informed understanding of the process of détente in U.S.-Soviet relations during the seventies.

The strength of Goldmann's framework lies in its catalogue of the ways in which stability could be undermined and foreign policy could undergo change. At the same time, Goldmann (1988, 62–69) acknowledges that it is no more than "a checklist of questions to ask" to help explain change and stability in foreign policy or forecast the future of a policy. Therefore, "the theoretical sketch is offered as a basis for further research" and "to pave the way for the improvement of foreign policy theory" (Goldmann 1988, xv).

Hermann and Foreign Policy Redirection. The contemporary work of Charles Hermann (1990) also investigates the study of foreign policy change. As Hermann (1990, 4) points out, "Changes that mark a reversal or, at least, a profound redirection of a country's foreign policy are of special interest because of the demands their adoption poses on the initiating government and its domestic constituents and because of their potentially powerful consequences for other countries. Wars may begin or end. Economic well-being may significantly improve or decline. Alliances may be reconfigured. Sometimes the entire international system is affected." In order to understand such change, Hermann views foreign policy in terms of four graduated levels of change: adjustment changes (in the level of effort and scope of recipients), program changes (in means and instruments), problem/goal changes (in the ends and purposes), and international orientation change (in its global role and activities). For Hermann, "major foreign policy redirection" includes the last three types of change—that is change in means, ends, or overall orientation.

Hermann, in order to illuminate the conditions that promote foreign policy redirection, reviews four areas of scholarship from different academic fields on domestic political systems, bureaucratic decision-making, cybernetics, and learning approaches. Based on the review of the literature, he suggests that there are four different sources of foreign policy change: leader driven, bureaucratic advocacy, domestic restructuring, and external shocks. Ultimately, Hermann argues that foreign policy redirection comes about through a decision process. In other words, intervening between the agents of change and actual foreign policy change is decision-making where the "decision process itself can obstruct or facilitate change" (Hermann 1990, 13). This requires that the decision process receive close examination in order to understand the process of foreign policy change. Specifically, Hermann discusses the possibilities and requirements for change in each of seven stages in the decision process, offering numerous propositions along the way.

Hermann's (1990, 20) purpose is "to join the ranks of those urging attention to the conditions giving rise to major changes in foreign policy." His major contribution is to highlight the role of the decision process for foreign policy change. As he states, "We need a perspective that views major change not as a deterministic response to large forces operative in the international system, but rather as a decision process. Of course, major shifts in international political and economic systems can pose significant requirements for the modification of foreign policy. But policymakers can either anticipate these international changes, respond just in time, or only after suffering dramatic consequences. Furthermore, policymakers can act as agents of change in the absence of any overwhelming systematic force" (Hermann 1990, 13). Unlike the other efforts reviewed above, however, Hermann's concept of foreign policy redirection encompasses more minor shifts (in means and instruments) in the conduct of day-to-day foreign policy and his emphasis on the decision process limits much of his analysis to what he calls self-correcting change—that is, "change that occurs when the existing government elects to move in a different policy direction" (Hermann 1990, 5).

International Political Economy and Foreign Economic Policy Change. Recent work within neorealism and international political economy has generated studies which have direct relevance for better understanding foreign policy change. Students of U.S. foreign economic policy, in particular, have addressed the question of continuity and change through the development of a common theoretical framework based on the interplay of three explanatory approaches: (global) system-centered, society-centered, and state-centered explanations (Ikenberry, Lake, and Mastanduno 1988). Illustrations of this theoretical orientation to the study of continuity and change in the history of U.S. foreign economic policy can be found in the work of David Lake and John Ikenberry.

Lake uses this framework to explain the movement in U.S. trade strategy away from protectionism and toward free trade in *Power, Protection, and Free Trade: International Sources of U.S. Commercial Strategy, 1887–1939* (1988). In his words (Lake 1988, 3), "Rapid and dramatic changes occurred in American trade strategy in the period 1887–1939. After the Civil War and before 1887, the United States was a relatively passive and highly protectionist nation-state. Tariffs were high, nonnegotiable, and nondiscriminatory." However, by 1945 the United States "shed the last vestiges of its nineteenth-century strategy" and "had emerged as an active world leader strongly supportive of universal free trade." What explained this transition in trade strategy?

Lake's (1988, 3) "central proposition is that the national trade interests, political choices, and ultimately trade strategies of individual countries are fundamentally shaped and influenced by the constraints and opportunities of the international economic structure." Changes in the international political economic environment, and a country's position within it, are fundamentally responsible for changes in trade policy. At the same time, society-centered and state-centered explanations determined "how the constraints and opportunities of the international economic structure are communicated or translated into national trade strategies" (Lake 1988, 3). Lake found that where the executive tended to be more responsive to demands and opportunities of the international economic system, the legislature was more responsive to domestic or societal forces where protectionist interests often prevailed. Therefore, although U.S. trade policy moved away from protectionism and toward free trade from 1887 to 1939, it was a much slower and sporadic process than predicted by neorealism and the theory of hegemonic stability, consisting of starts, stops, and retrenchment along the way.

Ikenberry uses a similar framework for explaining U.S. oil policy during the twentieth century in *Reasons of State: Oil Politics and the Capacities of American Government* (1988). Unlike Lake, however, Ikenberry finds that in response to changes in the international political economy of oil and to occasional oil shocks during the twentieth century, the existence of strong societal forces and weak state institutions heavily constrained the U.S. government from having more than a minimal role in American oil policy. As explained by Ikenberry (1988, 197), "the fragmented character of executive institutions and the limited scope of direct and selective U.S. government involvement in the economy, especially in the energy area, were shaped at particular historical junctures in the political and economic development of the United States. . . . Unlike its European counterparts, however, the American state became involved in the economy and in the energy area after, rather than before, the establishment of large private enterprises." Hence, the traditional

American reliance on the market where "the state remained on the periphery of business enterprise, primarily as a peace keeper and a regulator" (Ikenberry 1988, 197).

Energy and oil crises during the two world wars and the years preceding the Korean War, according to Ikenberry, presented opportunities for change. They, in fact, generated institutional experiments aimed at developing new state capabilities, but the new arrangements did not take root, for "powerful private groups, working through Congress, blocked the expansion of federal responsibilities" (Ikenberry 1988, 197). The "failure of earlier attempts at institutional transformation," Ikenberry (1988, 193) pointed out, "limited later possibilities for change." Even in response to the oil shocks of the seventies, Ikenberry found that "state institutions do not simply flex to the needs of the moment or to the wishes of executive officials who command those institutions." Instead, "the established arrangements of business and government limited the state to a minimalist role. National energy goals were thus pursued within a fragmentary institutional structure, one that conferred little coordinated planning capacity on executive policy makers and provided few instruments with which to shape private behavior" (Ikenberry 1988, 197). Thus, where Lake explained the restructuring of U.S. trade policy over time, Ikenberry found and explained the prevalence of continuity in U.S. oil policy. More importantly, both works demonstrate that understanding continuity and change requires the integration of system, society, and state-centered explanations of foreign policy.

Although these works represent initial efforts, the study of foreign policy change remains largely an unexplored area of great significance and promise as a tool to enhance the understanding of the dynamics of world politics. As seen above, there have been developments in the study of foreign policy change. During the 1970s Rosenau moved beyond his earlier pretheoretical effort to study foreign policy adaptation and eventually to elucidate about theories of cascading interdependence (see, e.g., Rosenau 1984). The 1980s have produced works by Holsti, Goldmann, Hermann, Lake, and Ikenberry. Furthermore, other bodies of scholarship are growing which are relevant to the study of foreign policy change, such as theories of learning in foreign policy (see, e.g., Etheredge 1985; Breslauer and Tetlock 1991). These developments have occurred at a time when the general field of foreign policy has become more diverse in its research questions, theoretical approaches, analytical strategies, and epistemological foundations (see, e.g., Gerner 1991; 1991–92). As a result, the study of foreign policy change may now be in a position to "take off" during the nineties.

Linking Earlier and Present Efforts

Considering the overview of the existing literature and the chapters which follow in the present volume, what kinds of relationships and linkages are seen? Clearly, the sense of futility regarding the possibility of theoretical explanation that Gilpin cites as a reason for lack of interest in foreign policy change has given way to a sense that the theoretical study of change and continuity is possible and important as an intellectual avenue to an improved understanding of foreign policy and international relations. If the earlier orientation in the study of foreign policy was guided by an action/reaction mindset and a fixation on superpower politics, the current orientation recognizes that what Rosenau termed "adaptation" is an enormously important, complex, and widespread phenomena. Thus, one finds a variety of perspectives in this volume on foreign policy change. These approaches range from depictions of cycles to analyses of the effects of changing constraints on security policies of third world regimes to discussions of the tendency of certain policymaking processes to respond with certain characteristics. The intellectual foundations from which these perspectives draw also are diverse. Common among the chapters, however, is a sense that the intellectual foundation of foreign policy analysis has progressed so as to offer a vantage point for thinking about continuity and discontinuity in foreign policy. The diversity of these perspectives is in its own right a statement of optimism about the possibility of an improved comprehension of foreign policy change.

Whether or not these chapters differ with Gilpin's point about the ethnocentricity and parochialism of the discipline is a question that might, and probably should, generate debate. The volume's authors are virtually all North American social scientists. It is also a work that is for the most part concerned with foreign policy within the existing, Western-designed and generated nation-state system. It reflects, on the other hand, numerous currents of academic inquiry and is not vulnerable to accusations of a large power bias in the focus of its research. In that regard parts of the volume push ahead with aspects of Holsti's pioneering *Why Nations Realign*. Some of the chapters study policy change that pertains to Egypt, Ethiopia, Israel, South and North Korea, India, Israel, Libya, Pakistan, Somalia, and Taiwan, echoing Holsti's stress on the dynamism in foreign policy among states that are not hegemons. They also illustrate certain underlying properties, theoretical and substantive, that are generalizable to numerous other states. In other words, examining continuity and change in the foreign policies of a variety of states provides insights into the dynamics of foreign policy in general. At the same time, it is interesting that some of the chapters that refer to the United States do so in ways that suggest the politics of change in U.S. foreign policy may be somewhat idiosyncratic—perhaps reducing ethnocentricity and parochialism in this way as well.

Holsti's question concerning "why some and not others" restructure their foreign policies is a challenge to which this volume responds with some new ideas, yet does not ultimately resolve. In the following chapters there is tension between continuity and change, tension in the sense that change has an inverse relationship to stability and thus important insights regarding change are found in the study of stability. Concepts such as "webs of restraint" and "stabilizers," indications that no change occurred in settings where change is commonly thought to have occurred, or findings that change did occur where it was least expected are all important parts of the inquiry into the study of foreign policy change.

The volume does respond to the question Holsti posed more than a decade ago with numerous ideas and insights. There are arguments that juxtapose hegemons who have difficulty changing their policies with lesser powers that have more agile policy structures and will respond more rapidly and precisely to new circumstances. There are arguments that evaluate the kinds of constraints that affect foreign policy, the extent of changes in foreign policy when constraints change, and the form those policy changes might take. There are arguments that weigh evolutionary versus sporadic change. There are arguments that consider the implications of regime democratization, whether triggered from above or below, as they relate to shifts in foreign policy. These and other arguments of the following chapters do not imply, however, that the question Holsti posed is now well under control. The chapters, nonetheless, do present theoretical ideas and methodologies concerning foreign policy change that are applicable to settings beyond the historical context discussed in the chapter. The volume thus offers scope and points of departure for further consideration of when and why change occurs in foreign policy.

Much of the earlier work was concerned with change driven by domestic and international forces external to the state. Holsti, for example, notes that in many of the cases considered in his 1982 book economic deprivation seems to have been a motivating factor for foreign policy change. The Rosenau consideration of adaptation—like the work by Goldmann, Hermann, Lake, and Ikenberry—is premised on an assumption that domestic and global demands impact on polities in ways that require some kind of response. The subsequent chapters reflect the implications of this assumption in a variety of ways. They call for a more systematic assessment of a state's situational context, consider the role of the external environment in cycles of foreign policy change, and demonstrate how structures of the international environment create opportunities for clever leaders. They also address arguments that as the constraints in the environment change, states may respond in patterns that are quite similar to Rosenau's adaptations. But, they additionally offer some original ideas concerning the foreign policy implications of such adaptation processes. Again, the authors pursue these analyses in a variety of ways, which include both efficient mechanisms from a rational choice perspective and less precise mechanisms from institutional and domestic politics perspectives.

Current Questions and Contributions

This section clarifies in greater depth the key questions regarding foreign policy change and restructuring addressed in the following chapters. Together, the chapters raise and attempt to deal with significant questions concerning the study and dynamics of foreign policy:

1. What is foreign policy change and restructuring?

2. What are the sources of foreign policy change? What bodies of theoretical knowledge and thought contribute to an understanding of foreign policy change?

3. To what extent does the study of change and restructuring contribute to an understanding of foreign policy and international relations?

These questions should be of particular interest to scholars and students of foreign policy and international relations. Each of these general questions about foreign policy raised by the volume are briefly touched upon below.

What is Foreign Policy Change and Restructuring?   The study of foreign policy change forces students in the field to give greater thought about the phenomenon to be explained—foreign policy. One of the problems in the study of foreign policy has been the lack of attention to what it is that is being explained—the dependent variable. As Hermann (1978, 25) has noted, "One of the most remarkable features of the post–World War II study of foreign policy is the scant attention given to the general concept of foreign policy." Instead, most of the attention from students of international relations and foreign policy has focused on the sources of explanation (the independent and intervening variables) and to methodological questions (see, e.g., Ikenberry 1989; McGowan and Shapiro 1973; East, Salmore, and Hermann 1978; Vocke 1976). This neglect of the concept of foreign policy and what it is that is being explained may help to account for the lack of attention to foreign policy change. In addition, it has often contributed to pseudo-debates over which theoretical explanations of foreign policy are superior in that they assume, often incorrectly, identical dependent variables (see, e.g., Rosati 1987, 170–74).

The contributors offer definitions and insights into the concepts of foreign policy, change, and restructuring. As the earlier literature review makes clear, there is no consensus as to the concept and definition of foreign policy change. Rosenau speaks in terms of political adaptation; Holsti offers the concept of foreign policy restructuring as separate from change; Goldmann examines foreign policy stabilization and destabilization; Hermann suggests foreign policy redirection; while Lake and Ikenberry examine continuity and change in foreign policy only in a general sense as a function of other factors. All are interested in understanding foreign policy change, but offer different concepts and somewhat different understandings of foreign policy change.

In this volume, *foreign policy* is the broad, generic term which encompasses both *foreign policy continuity* and *foreign policy change,* where *foreign policy restructuring* represents more wholesale, comprehensive change along the lines suggested by Holsti. If one thinks of foreign policy change as a spectrum involving macro-change (restructuring) on one end and micro-change on the other, most of the contributors are interested in explaining macro level foreign policy change, that is, foreign policy restructuring. Yet, different contributors have different levels of generality and different levels of scope in mind in their study of foreign policy change.

The fact that each contributor focuses on a different facet of foreign policy in terms of time, space, and scope is inescapable, for the concept of foreign policy allows for as much diversity as the sources of foreign policy. This is to be expected in social science inquiry where scholars pursue different research programs. In some ways this reinforces a lack of consensus about the concept of foreign policy change. Yet, at the same time, there is considerable overlap in their language and understanding of change in foreign policy. More importantly, this provides a growing foundation for scholars to come to terms with the concept of foreign policy, as well as foreign policy change and restructuring.

In sum, students of foreign policy need to give greater thought to the general phenomena of foreign policy, to the delineation of the concept they are attempting to explain, and to the implications this has for the development of theory and the cumulation of knowledge about foreign policy. According to Hermann (1978, 25), the neglect of the concept of foreign policy "has been one of the most serious obstacles to providing more adequate and comprehensive explanations of foreign policy." It is hoped that this volume on foreign policy change can serve somewhat as a stimulus for students to wrestle with these larger questions about the study of foreign policy.

What are the Sources of the Politics of Foreign Policy Change? What Bodies of Theoretical Knowledge and Thought Contribute to an Understanding of Foreign Policy Change?   Are the sources of foreign policy change predominantly international, governmental, or domestic? All the contributors recognize the need to develop multicausal explanations of foreign policy and to engage in some degree of synthesis—that the foreign policies of governments are heavily constrained and influenced by domestic and international factors—while at the same time avoiding the pitfalls of some of the early theoretical frameworks of incorporating too many variables for study (see, e.g., Dessler 1991; Rosati 1987, chap. 7). The contents of the chapters, in other words, demonstrate that students of foreign policy have acquired a sophisticated understanding of the dynamics of politics, recognizing the complex interplay of governmental, domestic, and international sources of foreign policy. They recognize the inherent difficulties that have plagued scholars concerning the levels-of-analysis and agency-structure problems (see Dessler 1989; Singer 1961; Waltz 1959; Wendt 1987).[4] For as pointed out by Walter Carlsnaes (1992, 256), "As long as the agency-structure issue remains unresolved, the foreign policy analyst is unable to address a crucial aspect of empirical reality itself; that the policies of states are a consequence of, and can hence only be fully explained with reference to, a dynamic process in which both agents *and* structures causally condition each other over time. In short, as long as the metatheoretical issue discussed here resists a solution, the problematic nature of *explaining the dynamics of foreign policy change itself* remains unresolved. " In the language of Ikenberry, Lake, and Mastanduno (1988), foreign policy scholars increasingly recognize that system-centered explanations, society-centered explanations, and state-centered explanations all are necessary and must be integrated in order to build a comprehensive understanding of foreign policy. Such sophistication is a prerequisite in the development of a more comprehensive understanding of the politics and dynamics of foreign policy.

In order to provide the reader with a better understanding of the politics of foreign policy change, the subsequent volume is arranged so that each chapter flows directly from, and builds upon, the sources of change presented in previous chapters. In this respect, the initial chapters that attempt to synthesize international and domestic sources of the politics of foreign policy are followed by chapters that emphasize international sources of change and then by chapters that highlight domestic sources of foreign policy. Lastly, the concluding chapters attempt to provide a more balanced synthesis between international and domestic sources of change. This arrangement maximizes comprehension and cumulation for the reader and student of foreign policy restructuring.

The sophisticated and realistic understanding of the dynamics of politics presented here demonstrates that the study of foreign policy and international relations has generated a considerable breadth and depth in theoretical knowledge which contributes to a greater understanding of foreign policy change. Drawing on numerous theoretical approaches and literatures in different intellectual traditions within foreign policy and international relations, the chapters present rich sources of knowledge and thought about continuity and change in foreign policy. Among these are bargaining theory, decision-making theory, development theory, institutional analysis, organizational theory, political adaptation, political economy, rational choice, regimes and political oppositions, and structural analysis.

The contributors also offer different methodological approaches for empirically studying foreign policy and its implications for theory development, ranging from case studies to historical analysis to aggregate statistical analysis. This is consistent with the type of diversity that now permeates the study of foreign policy. Although such theoretical, substantive, and methodological diversity does make it difficult to achieve intersubjective consensus among scholars for the steady cumulation of knowledge over time (see Rosenau 1967; Kuhn 1962), it does allow for the kind of theoretical and methodological flexibility best associated with intellectual creativity, discovery, competitiveness, and growth in the breadth and depth of knowledge (see Hermann and Peacock 1987; Lapid 1989). This collective eclecticism is indicative of the progress and potential of a post–positivist era for generating alternative paths of political inquiry so as to better understand international relations and foreign policy.[5]

The chapters, in this respect, raise and attempt to address a number of significant questions. To what extent does the strength of a state, abroad and at home, affect the likelihood of foreign policy change? Is foreign policy change a function of rational choice? How does the situational context, such as a crisis, affect foreign policy? To what extent do such factors as the nature of the regime and the political opposition or the process of democratization and modernization play a role? Although usually constrained by the circumstances, what flexibility do leaders have in affecting and changing foreign policy? Does change tend to be an incremental and evolutionary process? Or does change tend to be a cyclical and dialectical process? Not only do the chapters raise and address these significant questions about the dynamics of continuity and change in foreign policy, they also raise important issues in a number of scholarly traditions.

To What Extent Does the Study of Change and Restructuring Contribute to an Understanding of Foreign Policy and International Relations? The volume offers explanations and insights concerning the evolution of foreign policy over time, which encompasses both continuity and change. Just as a greater comprehension of stability guides explanations of change, a better understanding of patterns of foreign policy change enhances the evaluation of patterns of foreign policy continuity. As Rosenau (1978, 372) has stated, "Change cannot be discerned or assessed unless it is analyzed in the context of previously constant—or continuous—behavior. There are no discontinuities without continuities to highlight them." All of the contributors, in fact, highlight the constraints to foreign policy change and many discuss the process of foreign policy continuity and incrementalism in some depth. The contributors, in other words, help one to better understand foreign policy continuity as a result of their efforts to explain foreign policy change.

A stronger comprehension of continuity and change in foreign policy also is clearly essential to better comprehension of the dynamics of world politics. As the introduction to this chapter noted, the world has been undergoing some significant changes. As the collapse of communism in the Soviet Union and Eastern Europe clearly indicate, foreign policies are affected by such global changes. At the same time, foreign policies help to give rise to such global changes. It is the interaction between governmental foreign policy and the global environment that effects the dynamics of world politics. Governments and their foreign policies will continue to play an integral interactive role into the future. Therefore, the study of foreign policy change is an important endeavor because progress on this scholarly front contributes to a more powerful understanding of the larger dynamics of world politics as the turn of the century approaches.

Change and the Future Study of Foreign Policy

Clearly, there is a need for scholarship to address the study of foreign policy change and restructuring. The important questions about foreign policy change and restructuring raised above can and should be addressed at this juncture because of the growth in the maturity of the foreign policy field. The time is ripe for studies of foreign policy to encompass change as well as continuity in their work. The scholarly foundation now exists for understanding the comprehensive dynamics of foreign policy.

By no means is it implied that this is "the" definitive volume on foreign policy change. Rather, many people throughout the study of international relations are now interested and engaged in scholarship which is directly, as well as indirectly, related to the study of foreign policy change. This volume is intended to provide a collection of some of those efforts. In this respect, it represents an effort to offer different perspectives for approaching and understanding foreign policy change. It is meant to represent and reinforce the work of others who are engaged in the same scholarly enterprise—to stimulate the study and enhance the comprehension of foreign policy change. It is also designed to raise as many questions as it addresses about the dynamics of foreign policy.

Ultimately, readers must judge the value and worth of the chapters and the volume in coming to their own conclusions. Obviously, different scholars will arrive at different conclusions for a variety of different reasons. Hopefully, this volume will be seen as providing a serious foundation for students interested in the general study of foreign policy and, more specifically, foreign policy change and restructuring.

Notes

1. Likewise, Prigogine and Stengers (1984) argue about the history of modern science. As stated by Alvin Toffler in the foreword, "traditional science in the Age of the Machine tended to emphasize stability, order, uniformity, and equilibrium. It concerned itself mostly with closed systems and linear relationships in which small inputs uniformly yield small results" (Prigogine and Stengers 1984, xiv).
2. Likewise, according to Theodore Lowi (1972, 11) in his review of the study of political science. "Political disorder does not favor political scientists; it deranges their theories and cracks their time-honored assumptions. . . . The somber fact of the matter was that, on most of the fundamental questions underlying disorder, the discipline of political science simply did not have anything to say one way or another."
3. This is even beginning to be the case among American diplomatic historians. See Hogan and Paterson (1991).
4. For a discussion of the agency-structure problem from a Marxist perspective, see Callinicos (1988). Fernand Braudel (1972) points to another problem area involving time. He makes an interesting distinction between different levels or types of time throughout history: "short-term" time of immediate individuals, events, and daily life; "medium-term" time involving decades in which history often oscillates cyclically; and "long-term" time embracing hundreds of years where history is slow-moving and appears virtually static.
5. For a more pessimistic view, see Ferguson and Mansbach (1988, 1991).

Chapter 2

Foreign Policy Restructuring
and the Myriad Webs of Restraint

Thomas J. Volgy and John E. Schwarz

In this chapter, Thomas Volgy and John Schwarz discuss the importance of studying foreign policy change, the concept of foreign policy restructuring, and the major constraints to foreign policy change. They define foreign policy restructuring as major, comprehensive change in the foreign policy orientation of a country as manifested through behavioral changes in a nation's interactions with other actors in world politics. Despite profound changes in the global political climate and agenda which may necessitate foreign policy changes, Volgy and Schwarz highlight the existence of five major "webs of restraint" that significantly impede a nation's ability and willingness to fundamentally restructure its foreign policy: bureaucratic, regime, resource, global, and regional. As they argue, the recognition that governments tend to adopt stable foreign policy structures and are inhibited from radically altering these structures is a precondition for the development of a better understanding of the requirements and likelihood of foreign policy change. In this way, Volgy and Schwarz provide the reader with a conceptual and theoretical base from which to analyze foreign policy restructuring, emphasizing continuity and limits to change, while at the same time treating change as an integral part of foreign policy.

Thomas J. Volgy is associate professor of political science at the University of Arizona and was formerly mayor of Tucson between 1987 and 1991. He received a Ph.D. in political science from the University of Minnesota in 1972 and a B.A. in political science from Oakland University in 1967. His research interests include comparative foreign policy analysis, defense policy, mass media effects on political culture, and U.S. economic and social policy. He is coauthor of The Forgotten Americans: Thirty Million Working Poor in the Land of Opportunity *and his work has appeared in many journals, including* Harvard Business Review, Journal of Conflict Resolution, American Journal of Political Science, Journal of Politics, *and* World Politics. *He is currently working on a book on foreign policy restructuring within a systemic perspective. John E. Schwarz is professor of political science at the University of*

Arizona. He received a Ph.D. in political science from Indiana University in 1967 and a B.A. from Oberlin College in 1961. His research interests include comparative and international politics in Western Europe. He is the author of America's Hidden Success: A Reassessment of Public Policy from Kennedy to Reagan *and his work has appeared in* American Political Science Review, Journal of Politics, World Politics, *and other journals.*

Introduction

Within one short year, Cuban foreign policy lurched from submissive support of the United States to a close working relationship with the Soviet Union. Likewise, the Chinese heaped public scorn on "the running dogs of imperialism" and then, within a period of months, reestablished relations with the United States. President Anwar Sadat of Egypt, having spent a lifetime fighting the Israelis, made a dramatic overture to Tel Aviv and soon found himself at the Knesset. The Burmese, having contributed a statesman as secretary general to the United Nations and having actively participated in regional and global affairs, suddenly turned inward and drastically reduced their involvement in foreign affairs. More recently and most notably, Mikhail Gorbachev, as the leader of the "evil empire," staked his political future on a sweeping restructuring of the system under the policies of "perestroika" and "glasnost." These generated both fundamental domestic changes and radical "new thinking" in Soviet foreign policy. The cases above represent only a few of the dozens of instances (Holsti 1977; Hughes and Volgy 1970; Volgy and Kenski 1976) of states dramatically changing the direction of their foreign policies. Taken together, they constitute examples of a phenomenon involving fundamental and comprehensive change in foreign policy orientation, over a very short period of time.

For those who are accustomed to witnessing incremental or limited changes in foreign policies, these fundamental policy shifts are seen as deviant occurrences in international politics and often appear as "outliers" in the analysis of foreign policy. These sudden shifts stand apart from the incremental nature of most changes and are thus often shunted aside in the testing of hypotheses and evaluation of theory. As Rosenau (1978, 371) has observed: "In our search for recurring patterns—for constancies in the external behavior of nations—we tend to treat breaks in patterns as exceptions, as nuisances which complicate our task."

Yet, by treating such instances as deviant cases, one ignores the underlying commonalties which may cause their occurrence. By concentrating on the unique properties of an Iranian or an Ethiopian foreign policy reorientation, one fails to develop the conceptual, empirical, and theoretical tools that could eventually allow students of international politics to identify, measure, and comprehend the causes of such changes. Part of the reason for the lack of attention to the phenomenon of fundamental foreign policy shifts stems from the belief that the actual numbers of cases of fundamental foreign policy change have been too few to allow scholars, who practice their craft with complex methodologies, to apply to this phenomenon the tools used to study other aspects of international politics.

Yet, an assumption of too few cases may not be warranted. For example, in the Latin American sub-system, the primary emphasis on "deviant actors" has centered around four cases of idiosyncratic deviations from U.S. hegemony since World War II (Guatemala in 1954, Cuba since 1959, the Dominican Republic in 1965, and Nicaragua from 1978). However, empirical research (Volgy and Kenski 1976), focusing on a twenty year period, has identified forty-two additional cases of fundamental foreign policy changes for Latin American states.

Apart from their frequency and the intrinsic value of understanding why and how such fundamental changes occur, why should one be concerned with such phenomena? At the nation-state level of analysis, it is clear that fundamental restructurings in foreign policy have often led to greater conflicts and uncertainties between nations most affected by major departures from the status quo. Thus, a better understanding of why and how such changes occur will both account for, and perhaps predict, the broader turmoil often created by foreign policy restructurings.

At a more macro level of analysis, the answer may lie in the fundamental changes ongoing in the international system itself. Global international politics have witnessed profound change and turmoil over the last two decades. The rise of Japan and other economic actors (and the rise *and* fall of groups such as the Organization of Petroleum Exporting Countries, or OPEC), the diminution of control over global affairs by the two superpowers, the disintegration of the former Soviet Union, and the growing salience of economic, ecological, security, and developmental issues constitute just a small sample of major, global changes requiring fundamental restructurings in the foreign policy orientations of many, if not most nation-states. The ability to judge whether and how such changes will occur depends on a clear comprehension of the conditions that facilitate or impede the ability *and* the willingness of foreign policymakers to engage in more than incremental adjustments to their policies.

The purpose of this chapter is to examine a number of constraints that affect the likelihood of fundamental foreign policy changes. Drawn from the general literature in international politics, several conceptual and theoretical issues are addressed below in order to highlight a range of factors that may inhibit or facilitate the occurrence of basic foreign policy changes among nations. Such a review should produce a better understanding of both continuity and change in the study and practice of foreign policy.

The Concept of Foreign Policy Restructuring

Two sets of earlier efforts have sought to address the topic of major foreign policy change in a comparative perspective. Volgy and colleagues have identified the conceptual nature of this change as "distance" between nations and their respective hegemons operating in geographically distinct sub-systems (Hughes and Volgy 1970; Volgy and Kenski 1976, 1982). Empirically, these authors identify distance changes as changes in direction, linked to cold war orientations.

Holsti's (1977, 1983) approach to major foreign policy change is focused on a different type of research question: to what extent can nations successfully break away from patterns of dependency? The emphasis here on successful change leads to conceptual formulations based on intentions and attitudes/ opinions as well as behaviors. In addition, what for Holsti may be one unsuccessful case of restructuring (e.g., Hungary in the mid-1950s) is for Volgy and his colleagues two cases of restructuring (Hungary in 1956, and again in 1957), requiring two different kinds of explanations for their occurrence.

Combining elements of these two approaches, *foreign policy restructuring* is defined here as a major, comprehensive change in the foreign policy orientation of a nation, over a relatively short period of time, as manifested through behavioral changes in a nation's interactions with other actors in international politics. Using this definition, the concept of foreign policy restructuring implies a series of properties that can be used to identify and compare cases of foreign policy restructuring in international politics.

First, with respect to the type of change in behavior, the definition implies that restructuring occurs when there is a multidimensional change in behavior. Major change occurs when "processes that are normally independent of each other become intertwined and must undergo modification" (Rosenau 1978, 372). Restructuring refers to a basic, comprehensive change in foreign policy orientation and the notion of multidimensionality recognizes the complexity of such behavior. A fundamental change in foreign policy should reveal itself through the covariation of change over several dimensions of behavior that do not typically covary. For example, in 1960 had Castro of Cuba denounced the U.S. government and lavished praise on the Soviet Union (change in verbal behavior), shifted the pattern of Cuban imports (change in trade) from North American to Eastern European states, but maintained patterns of voting affiliation with the United States in the U.N. General Assembly (no change in organizational activity) and even increased Cuban embassies and legations with U.S. allies (diplomatic behavior), the multidimensional covariation requirement would have been absent in Cuban foreign policy restructuring. In fact, Cuban foreign policy behavior changed in all four of these dimensions, moving in tandem away from the United States and toward the Soviet Union.

Second, the definition focuses strictly on the behavioral manifestations of change. It ignores Holsti's "intentions" since the policymaker may not actually perceive certain actions as a case of deliberate restructuring of foreign policy. Not requiring evidence of intentions on the part of policymakers also allows for the identification of situations when the decision-maker is forced to change direction without having the desire to do so.

Third, the definition is inclusive enough to accept at least two broad types of policy restructuring: changes in direction and changes in participation. Directional changes may involve reductions in dependency relations (France, 1964), changes in alliance partners (Albania, 1960), or movements from alliance relationship to self-reliance (Iran, 1978); these are changes involving shifts in the direction of policy. Major changes are participatory when nations dramatically increase or decrease their degree of involvement in international politics, regardless of changes in direction (e.g., Burma since the early 1970s). This chapter focuses predominantly on directional changes.

Fourth, the definition suggests a temporal dimension for a set of behaviors to qualify for an actual restructuring. Unlike incremental adjustments, restructuring implies major change occurring within a relatively short time span. However, the time period is not specified here since any cut-off value is somewhat arbitrary. It is assumed that such time periods would vary across sub-systems with fundamentally different characteristics (for a similar argument, see Holsti and Sullivan 1969; Volgy and Kenski 1976). For example, it is plausible to assume that nations with extensive resources and the ability to mobilize those resources can effectuate fundamental changes faster than nations with limited resources.

Fifth, the definition implies some threshold value to the quantity of change necessary to constitute a restructuring. Radical change implies a departure from incremental adjustments to existing policies. For example, common sense suggests that the introduction of a small contingent of U.S. Marines in Lebanon during the early 1980s represented a change in U.S. foreign policy. However, it is not at all clear whether such change is so great as to constitute an actual restructuring in U.S. foreign policy toward Lebanon, and especially toward the Middle East. In fact, the threshold values needed to identify an actual restructuring can be empirically measured on the basis of historical observations of the mean rates of changes in behavior exhibited by nations over time.

The Webs of Restraint

Global politics in the post–World War II era are characterized by complexity and linkage. For instance, developments in communications technology today allow for the instantaneous transmission of cultural and political messages to virtually any place in the world. Bankers in New York or Ottawa may be ruined by riots in the face of economic reforms in Mexico. People in Paris are killed as a result of decisions made in Beirut. Children in Tokyo describe nightmares about Russian and American decision-makers pulling the triggers that lead to a global holocaust.

In fact, it has become trivial to claim that the affairs of the globe are complex and increasingly interrelated since even the most powerful nations lack the capacity to insulate themselves from these global trends. While it may sometimes be necessary to change the thrust of a nation's foreign policy under these circumstances, such restructuring is difficult at best. Any theory seeking to account for dramatic changes in the foreign policy orientations of nations must seek first to understand those forces which "inhibit" major, fundamental changes in the foreign policies of nations.

With respect to factors inhibiting major change, there exist five major barriers confronting foreign policymakers. Although there are some exceptions, decision-makers must confront bureaucratic, regime, resource, global, and regional "webs" which enmesh and restrict their abilities to effectuate fundamental changes in the direction of their foreign policies.

The Bureaucratic Web

The bureaucratic "web" is amply demonstrated by decision-making theory and by the range of decisional models developed in the literature that account for the process by which nations translate domestic and foreign pressures and demands into foreign policy activity. For most nations with an active foreign policy orientation, the task of monitoring the complexities of their regional or global environment is not possible without a fairly complex foreign policy bureaucracy. However, governing with a complex bureaucracy, presidents and kings alike find themselves enmeshed in governments in which various departments and agencies compete for scarce resources needed to carry out their functions. Bureaucrats, charged with representing their own turf, offer the policymaker competing and often contradictory views of what is happening, why it's important, and what should be done about it. Only rarely can a leader shift from balancing these competing sources of information and interests to fundamentally restructuring the course of the nation's affairs. Thus, most models of decision-making that focus on complex political systems point to decisional processes which either perpetuate previous decisions or, at most, create incremental departures from previous decisions.

For example, the standard operating procedures framework of the organizational model is so rigid that the possibility of forcing bureaucracies to change may require extreme forms of political coercion, or catastrophes which may eventually lead to revisions of those procedures. The bureaucratic model is more fluid and suggests a greater probability for change, but it describes a complex web within which actors duel with each other for additional influence and resources. The dynamics of such competition make bureaucracies impediments to changes in the direction of policy, particularly since such changes could negatively affect existing patterns of influence.

It is only Allison's (1969) rational model which holds significant promise for fundamental change, yet that model fails to meet two critical tests of validity. First, it reifies the decisional group as an individual actor in direct contradiction to the bureaucratic and organizational models. Second, it focuses on decision-makers as if they respond solely to foreign policy concerns, with little or no consideration being given to domestic issues, problems, or consequences for their foreign policy decisions. Yet, precisely because the combination of these two elements limits the actual flexibility of decision-makers to radically alter their orientations, the reality of Allison's model comes into question. Perhaps it is too farfetched to argue that Allison's rational model is no more than a framework for public rationalization of decisions by policymakers. More likely, the rational model probably has more utility for personalistic regimes than for centralized or pluralistic regimes, particularly when these latter types are active in international politics (for an alternative view, see Bueno de Mesquita 1981).

Other models of decision-making, even those designed to explain changes in policies, further underscore the difficulty of engaging in major policy change. Incremental models, quagmire models, group-think models, and satisficing models all point to the enormous pressures placed on decision-makers in minimizing conflict among competing actors in the decisional process, maintaining fragile coalitions, and reorganizing bureaucratic procedures when new approaches are adopted to deal with complex and unpredictable forces in the international environment.

The empirical research on decision-making tends to reinforce these generalizations. Brecher's study (1975) of Israeli policymakers highlights the range of barriers to be surmounted in the formulation of policy, even in small states. Brunck and Minehart's (1983) analysis attests to the degree to which even major personnel changes have only incremental effects on basic decisions involving the use of resources in industrialized nations. Even Henry Kissinger (1979), who as both presidential advisor and secretary of state attempted to fundamentally restructure the course of U.S. foreign policy, repeatedly points to how he struggled with the State Department in attempting to effectuate these changes, and often lost.

The literature on decision-making leads to pessimistic conclusions regarding the prospects for fundamental changes in foreign policy. Yet, it should also be noted that the vast majority of this literature is based on experiences derived from either the United States or other nations most active in international politics. Thus, the majority of modeling and hypothesis testing has been done with a sample of nations that are most intricately enmeshed in both the international and domestic webs.

Nevertheless, decision-making theory is still useful in the sense that it can illuminate the impediments to major policy changes, and specify the times and places where the web weakens. Since it is not impossible to break through the bureaucratic web, any theory of foreign policy restructuring must focus on conditions under which this web does not exist, or conditions under which its effects can be minimized.

The Regime Web

The type of regime in which decisions occur may further strengthen or weaken webs of restraint against major policy changes. For example, not all types of political regimes create similar bureaucratic filters: personalistic regimes may translate domestic pressures differently from pluralistic or centralized regimes (Sullivan 1976). Foreign policy restructuring should be easier to achieve in nations where foreign policies are formulated without the trappings of complex bureaucracies, such as in states controlled by a single leader or a small, ruling coalition. Such changes are more likely to occur in the Uganda of Idi Amin or the Libya of Qadhdhafi than in the France of Charles DeGaulle, or the Soviet Union of Gorbachev (e.g., Hermann, Hermann, and Hagan 1987).

Democratic regimes may constitute a very difficult web of restraint for policy restructurings. For example, there is evidence to indicate that in general, democracies engage in cooperative behaviors more than do nondemocratic states (Sullivan 1976). Additionally, one of the few studies of comparative foreign policy restructuring brings into sharp relief the problems associated with fundamental policy change in democratic systems. Holsti and Sullivan's analysis (1969) of Chinese and French deviations from alliance partners in the 1960s underlines the enormous difficulties faced by pluralist nations attempting to disengage from an existing policy direction. While the Chinese deviation was thorough and multidimensional, the French change was highly limited, constrained by the multitude of anchorings to differing domestic constituencies.

However, in pluralistic as well as centrist systems there are several ways that the bureaucratic web can be overcome. Changes in regimes (e.g., Hagan 1989a) that weaken the bureaucracy or foster ambiguity in the roles assigned to key actors in the decisional group (C. Hermann 1987) create major breaks in the web, and thus provide greater opportunities for fundamental changes in policy. Regime changes produced by domestic turmoil (e.g., revolution) or elite instability (e.g., coups d'état) may rip the fabric of the web in similar ways. Foreign policy restructurings were clearly preceded by such regime changes in Cuba, Chile, Hungary, and Iran and similar outcomes have occurred in virtually all ex-Warsaw Pact nations.

Leadership changes alone, even when accompanied by substantial changes in the personalities and ideological leanings of leaders, still encounter bureaucratic webs which reduce the ability of the new leaders to effectuate the changes they desire. Without doubt, changes of leadership and key personnel at the advent of the Mitterand and Reagan administrations were important for their respective nations' foreign policies; yet, both leaders found it difficult to fundamentally alter the course of their nations' policies over relatively short periods of time. The argument here is not that leadership change is not important, but rather that the context in which leadership change occurs may be even more critical in determining whether new leaders can achieve fundamental departures from the status quo. Thus, it may be that leadership changes are associated with foreign policy restructuring in nations with small foreign policy bureaucracies (e.g., Volgy and Kenski 1982), while leadership changes are less likely to result in policy restructurings when such changes occur in nations with democratic regimes and complex bureaucracies (e.g., Volgy and Schwarz 1989; Brunck and Minehart 1983).

Of course, foreign policy restructurings do occur even in complex, pluralistic regimes. DeGaulle's break from the North Atlantic Treaty Organization (NATO) in the 1960s, and the British entry into the Common Market in the early 1970s are but two of several instances of foreign policy restructurings in

Western Europe. Neither the complexities of democratic politics nor the webs of complex bureaucracies were able to arrest such changes. Therefore, further analysis is required to determine what factors can overcome the complex array of forces which otherwise restrict fundamental policy changes. Apart from the presence of a bureaucratic web, there are other considerations within the domestic environment which clearly impede the prospects for fundamental policy change. Not the least important is the issue of the amount of actual resources available to foreign policymakers with which to institute such changes.

The Resource Web

Altering the course of relations with other states in the international system may require substantial risks and outlays of resources. Given this consideration, national attribute theory (e.g., Sullivan 1976) can be of great utility in accounting for the conditions under which nations successfully alter, or become motivated to alter, the direction of their foreign policies. Beneath this apparently deterministic approach, which seeks to link attributes to foreign policy behavior, there lurks at least three distinct explanations of interstate behavior.

The first explanation posits that patterns of attributes create necessary, albeit insufficient, conditions which help to determine the "ability" of nations to act, react, or adapt to certain internal or external problems. For example, several investigators have reported significant correlations between the attribute of size (e.g., the absolute amount of resources potentially available within a nation) and certain forms of conflict behavior (Sullivan 1976). Clearly, foreign policy activity is costly with respect to the use of available resources, and the more decision-makers lack such basic resources, the more they are restrained from engaging in certain types of foreign policy activities. Given the costs involved in restructuring the entire foreign policy orientation of a state, restructuring behavior should be even more constrained by the relative availability of resources.

A second theoretical strain which emerges from an analysis of national attributes focuses on resources not as constraints on behavior, but rather as determinants of goal orientation in foreign policy. In this context, patterns of attributes of nations constitute a shorthand method with which to gauge satisfaction with the international status quo, and the degree to which nations are willing to take risks to alter that status quo. Consider the persistent finding that while the absolute amount of resources (i.e., size) of states is correlated with patterns of conflict in foreign policy behavior, measures of wealth are negatively correlated with those conflict behaviors that have highly serious consequences for interstate relations (e.g., severance of relations). In fact, Rummel's correlations between size and conflict are virtually all positive, while his measures of wealth and involvement in large-scale conflict are consistently negative when the relationships are statistically significant (e.g., Sullivan 1976).

These findings are obviously relevant to analyses of foreign policy restructuring. Nations with greater resources can be divided based on their satisfaction or dissatisfaction with the international structure. States which are relatively satisfied with the status quo (higher on wealth measures) are less likely to engage in fundamental changes to their own foreign policies, and are unlikely to pursue those changes which could jeopardize the stability of the global web from which they benefit. Conversely, nations that measure high on resources, but low on wealth (able to act but deriving little benefit from the international status quo) would be more likely to risk engaging in fundamental foreign policy restructuring (see East 1972 for a similar argument). It is interesting to note in this context that each of the three wealthiest nations in Western Europe engaged in foreign policy restructuring about twice over two decades (Volgy and Schwarz 1989), while some nations in Latin America, even though severely constrained by the United States, restructured their foreign policies at least four times during a similar period (Volgy and Kenski 1976).

While such resource webs contain formidable obstacles to policy change, they are not necessarily impervious to change. This leads to a third theoretical strain within national attribute theory in which attribute webs can be altered in at least two forms: disruption or enhancement. In one case, the potential for foreign policy activity can be altered due to a massive infusion of additional resources available to decision-makers (enhancement). Conversely, conditions can occur within the nation which substantially limit the ability of decision-makers to utilize existing resources for foreign policy purposes (disruption). Both conditions lead to a weakening of the domestic web constraining decision-makers from engaging in fundamental changes to their policies.

Enhancement of resources occurs in various forms. For example, Sylvan (1976) found that in the Asian sub-system, a massive infusion of military transfers corresponded to significant changes in foreign policy orientations for nations in the region, even years after receiving these resources. In a similar vein, the massive infusion of petrodollars in the Middle East may have significantly changed the foreign policy orientations of several nations.

Disruption to existing resources may also bring foreign policy change, but here the analysis becomes a bit more complex. For example, a substantial amount of research focuses on the relationship between types of domestic socio-political conflict and changes in foreign policy behavior. However, the findings are often contradictory, and seem to vary with two other attributes: type of government and availability of resources. With respect to type of government, democracies beset by internal socio-political conflict may be more constrained in their external activities as additional resources are mobilized for domestic problems. Conversely, in personalistic systems, socio-political instability may trigger the search for external scapegoats, thus altering the foreign policy orientation of the state. However, the absolute amount of resources available for foreign policy activity may mediate the relationship between internal conflict and foreign activity. Vengroff (1976) found that the relationship between domestic conflict and foreign policy activity was far stronger for resource-poor nations (e.g., sub-Saharan Africa) than for nations with greater amounts of resources.

The Global Web

In addition to bureaucratic, regime, and resource webs, there are global structures, rules, norms, regimes, and organizations which typically tend to create predictability for international actors and ultimately enmesh foreign policymakers in a set of global webs (Haas 1970). These global constraints serve to further reduce the flexibility of nations to engage in fundamental policy changes. Yet, it is important to point out that nations in international politics conduct their affairs under one of two environmental conditions: either under the constraints and rules operating within a specific type of international system, or during relatively rarer periods, under conditions of greater flexibility when international systems are undergoing transformation. Therefore, the type of global system existing at any point in time may restrict or enhance the flexibility of states and their decision-makers to change the direction of their foreign policies.[1]

Under conditions of bipolarity, for example, the rules of behavior for system members create substantial rigidity for individual actors. Deviation from bloc leadership is seldom tolerated since the hegemon will seek to exercise tight control over its alliance partners. Interalliance conflict is omnipresent since there is a tendency to view the system under zero-sum conditions; conflicts between individual members of opposing alliances run the risk of embroiling both poles in the conflict. In this context, certain types of foreign policy restructurings are unlikely to occur. While nations may reduce or enhance their participation in international politics, or restructure their relations to move closer to the dominant hegemon in their alliances, the risks of changing alliance partners or of disassociating from either of the two poles are nearly prohibitive. Seldom will partnership changes or moves toward diversity occur under such conditions.

Of course, partnership changes may still occur under such conditions, but they will require unusual circumstances and are rarely successful. In the mid-1950s, restructurings did take place in both the Eastern European (e.g., Hungary) and Latin American sub-systems (e.g., Guatemala), but hegemonic response was swift and the initial change in foreign policy direction was quickly reversed. Under bipolar conditions, autonomous activity may be thwarted even for more powerful partners. Note how quickly the United States stopped the attempt by the United Kingdom and France to assist Israel in 1956 and thus alter the balance of military relations in the Middle East when those states sought to act without the concurrence of the hegemon.

Conditions of multipolarity increase the flexibility of all actors. States run fewer risks in deviating from hegemonic leadership. It is possible to lose alliance members without the fear that the opposing alliance will automatically gain those members. The ideological glue which helps to bind together the alliances in a bipolar situation is significantly weaker under multipolar conditions. As a result, the prospect that an interalliance conflict between two states will spread to all alliance members is significantly reduced. In fact, in multipolar systems the frequency of war occurrence is greater than in bipolar systems, although the intensity of wars and the number of actors involved in wars is greater under conditions of bipolarity than multipolarity (Small and Singer 1982).

The prospects for foreign policy restructuring of all types are thus greatly enhanced in the multipolar system as compared to the bipolar system. States are freer to alter their involvement with global politics. Deviations from alliance leadership do not incur risks so prohibitive as to discourage actors from switching partners or to diversify significantly their foreign policy orientations. Even in the rigid hierarchical sub-system of Eastern Europe of the 1960s, several major departures from hegemon leadership occurred without retribution or sanctions on the part of the Soviet Union (Hughes and Volgy 1970). Likewise, in the 1960s the French decision to change direction toward greater policy diversity was met with unhappiness in Washington, but the U.S. response was far milder than the response to independent French initiatives in the 1950s. Of course, states are not completely free of hegemonic control in altering the direction of their policies under multipolar conditions. The response of the United States to the Dominican Republic in 1965 and similar actions on the part of the Soviet Union toward Czechoslovakia in 1968 are but two examples of the resistance of alliance leaders to bloc members' attempts to change policy direction. Nevertheless, those actions were of a qualitatively different sort than their counterparts in the 1950s (Franck and Weisband 1972).

Arguably, structural condition of the 1950s is best characterized by conditions of bipolarity, while that of the 1960s approached the condition of multipolarity (for an alternative view, see Rapkin, et al. 1979). It is far more difficult to characterize the state of the international system since 1970. However, looking at the "rules" of the system (e.g., Kissinger 1979; Franck and Weisband 1972), it is possible to classify the structural arrangements of the 1970s as consisting of two parts: a loose bipolar arrangement covering Latin America, Eastern Europe, and perhaps Western Europe (albeit in the midst of transformation); and a balance of power structure (Kaplan 1957) covering the other sub-systems in international politics.

Under this type of bipolar/balance-of-power arrangement, several consequences should arise for the prospects of foreign policy restructuring. With respect to the bipolar element in Eastern Europe, Latin America, and perhaps Western Europe, conditions should continue to approximate the "loose" bipolar era noted earlier. Sanctions should continue for major deviations from hegemonic leadership. Clearly, pressures placed on Poland in the 1970s, or overt and covert actions by the United States toward Grenada and Nicaragua in the 1980s resembled in some ways a continuation of sanctions on the part of hegemons toward deviating partners in their critical sub-systems. At the same time, resistance to tight hegemonic control in such spheres, particularly when these bipolar norms are in transformation, might appear more likely than in the previous periods. In fact, since the balance of power component requires an active participation of the hegemon in regions outside of the bipolar sphere, restructuring strategies by nations in Latin America and Eastern Europe may become a method of signaling to hegemons that insufficient attention and resources are being allocated to their region (Volgy and Kenski 1982).

The balance of power component of the system provides the greatest opportunities for changes in policy direction. Alliance commitments become less rigid. Actors search for greater advantage by shifting partners to gain access to vital economic and/or military resources not available under previous arrangements. As greater uncertainties in the system gradually replace ideological concerns, actors search for more power to deal with this increased unpredictability. The dramatic shifts in Egyptian foreign policy direction toward accommodation with Israel and the shifts in coalitions of Middle Eastern states on the heels of the Iran-Iraq War constitute ready examples of the options available to states under the flexibility of system-wide norms.

East's work (1972) on the effects of inconsistencies between system-wide norms, which confer prestige on actors, and the distribution of global resources indicates they have a significant relationship to conflict and war in the system. Presumably, those actors who are insufficiently accorded status seek to change global conditions. Thus, one systemic consideration which may hold relevance for foreign policy restructuring revolves around the degree to which systemic norms are inconsistent with the global distribution and control of resources. Individual actors are less likely to be constrained by global considerations and would be more likely to seek changes to the direction of their foreign policies when they encounter such inconsistencies or when such norms are undergoing transformation.

Consider the relative congruence between system-wide norms and resources in the 1950s and the 1960s. In the international system of the 1950s, both global norms and global resources tended to mirror Kaplan's (1957) bipolar system. In the 1960s, and particularly toward the second half of that decade, global norms tended to reflect global conditions akin to Kaplan's multipolar system, yet there is no evidence for multipolarity with respect to the distribution of global resources (Rapkin, et. al. 1979). One would expect that such incongruence between norms and resources would weaken the restraining effect of the global web on actors interested in restructuring the direction of their foreign policies.

In much of the international systems literature, the distribution of global resources is often conceptualized as a single dimension, equating the distribution of resources with military capabilities. Yet, what happens in the system when control of military resources no longer reflects control over economic resources? Consider the system of the 1970s and 1980s. Key actors such as Japan and Saudi Arabia and a bevy of multinational corporations controlled substantial amounts of global economic resources. These actors do not register significantly on measures of military capabilities, yet have profound effects on the foreign policies of other actors. This issue is best illustrated by the United States and the Soviet Union, which, combined, controlled well over 65 percent of global military and economic resources in the 1950s. By the 1980s the same two actors still controlled a slim majority of military capabilities but held no more than one third of global economic capabilities. Such systemic diversification in global resources points to further weakening of the global web, and opportunities for actors to change their foreign policy orientations.

Fluctuations in systemic polarization (Rapkin, et. al. 1979) also may have profound consequences for foreign policy restructuring. Periods of high conflict between superpowers are likely to tighten the global web as major actors seek support and increase the costs for deviation from their leadership. Conversely, during periods of low conflict, greater flexibility is created for nations to deviate from hegemonic leadership. Of particular interest may be periods of major transition from high to low conflict episodes in the system, such as the ending of the cold war. During such times, actors heretofore caught in the global conflict may seek to distance themselves from global hegemons as the intensity of the struggle abates. In a similar manner, systemic disturbances to global resources may force resource-dependent nations to reconsider their foreign policy directions. This would be especially the case in systems which permit greater degrees of flexibility among alliance partners. The "oil shocks" of the early 1970s illustrate one example of such resource disturbances.

The Regional Web

In addition to global considerations, foreign policy-makers also find themselves trapped in a regional web of forces which may restrict their ability to change the direction of their policies. Factors which may determine the effects of this web include: the degree of regional integration, the intensity of regional conflict, the existence of a dominant hegemon in the region, and the degree of competition between hegemons in the region.

There is a vast amount of literature in international politics which focuses on the meaning, salience, and effects of regional integration on member states (Sullivan 1976; Puchala 1981). For the purpose of this chapter, the integration process becomes a unique web of arrangements which restrict the flexibility of member nations to redirect their foreign policies. Integration is a slow, incremental process in which member nations share an increasingly significant volume of transactions and cooperative arrangements. The cost of disengaging from such arrangements may not be prohibitive, but it involves a degree of risk-taking which would be warranted only under highly unusual circumstances. Thus, states involved in regions with a high level of integration would be far less likely to engage in restructuring than nations operating in regions with fairly low levels of integration.

At the same time, it may be plausible to argue that when integration attempts reach some level of "critical mass," nations outside of the integration process become more willing to fundamentally change their foreign policy orientations in order to gain benefit from these integration efforts. For example, with the proposed dissolution of many European Economic Community (EEC) barriers, and in spite of major concerns regarding some of the socio-political implications for member nations, other European states have been looking at the EEC with new interest. Discussions occurring in Eastern Europe, Scandinavia, and Austria indicate the possibility of fundamental foreign policy restructurings in the European region. At the same time, such changes clearly do not occur solely in the context of integrationist pressures. Both domestic policy issues *and* fundamental changes at the system level between the two superpowers allow for the weakening of other constraints and make directional changes toward EEC member states more feasible.

A second major consideration revolves around the duration and intensity of ongoing conflicts in a region. The foreign policies of Middle Eastern states or the states of Southeast Asia differ from those of South America or Africa by the extent to which they are embroiled in long-standing conflicts which threaten basic national security interests. Under such conditions, nations become highly vulnerable to shifts in the balance of military relations in the region and directional changes may be necessitated by border conflicts or shifts in the policies of allies and antagonists. Balance theory (Sullivan 1976) is particularly useful in highlighting the dynamics leading to foreign policy restructuring when critical actors begin to reexamine their involvement in ongoing regional conflicts.

International regions or sub-systems also differ with respect to whether they are free of dominance by one or more hegemons (Gochman and Maoz 1984). In the sub-systems of South America, Central America, and Eastern Europe, the dominance of a single hegemon during the cold war mitigated against the freedom to redirect foreign policy activity. Conversely, the regional web has been less constrictive in sub-Saharan Africa or the Middle East where no such dominant hegemon posed the threat of major sanctions against changes in policy direction.

Regions can be classified as well according to the degree of competition between hegemons in a region. In the Middle East, or in Southeast Asia, rife with hegemonic rivalry, substantial opportunities exist for actors to shift partners in ongoing conflicts. However, as hegemons increase their own stakes in such conflicts, the costs of a shift in a regional actor's loyalties increase greatly. Under such circumstances, directional changes may be confined to those types of episodes in which regional actors sever ties altogether with former hegemonic partners. Illustrative of this trend was Egypt's total severance of relations with the Soviet Union as a precondition to a directional shift toward Israel and the United States.

Conclusion

Overall, the combination of domestic, systemic, and regional webs provides significant impediments to a substantial change in the foreign policy orientation of a nation. At the same time, these various perspectives also indicate conditions under which these webs can be sufficiently weakened to allow decision-makers to restructure the course of their affairs, should they desire to do so. Therefore, a comprehensive explanation of restructurings should address not only the impediments to such changes, but also the conditions which might motivate foreign policy actors to try to overcome the webs of restraint surrounding their foreign policies.

The Western European experience perhaps provides the most obvious evidence of the extent to which nations are likely to change through mostly incremental adjustments to their foreign policies, unless the domestic political calculus creates unusual stimuli for taking major policy risks. The Western European context is a fascinating site for the analysis of policy change, since it is a laboratory within which explanations of restructurings are examined under the most difficult of conditions as these democracies are enmeshed in virtually all the webs of restraint discussed above. Perhaps nowhere else in international politics (except possibly the United States and Canada) are both domestic and external webs of restraint as strong as in this region. A previous analysis of foreign policy restructurings (Volgy and Schwarz 1991) has shown that, over a twenty year period, only twelve cases had occurred out of 220 opportunities for foreign police restructuring among Western European states. Three states (Great Britain, France, and West Germany) accounted for seven of the twelve cases. Furthermore, fundamental differences accounted for the causes of policy changes between small and large democracies. Small democracies in Europe engaged in restructurings exclusively in response to large exogenous disturbances (i.e., the oil shocks of 1973 and 1980), while the larger democracies changed foreign policy orientations almost exclusively in response to domestic political problems and pressures. In the absence of highly unusual political stimuli, decision-makers in both small and large democracies were loath to take the types of risks associated with fundamental changes to their foreign policy orientations. However, the experiences in Western Europe are clearly not typical of foreign policy restructurings in other sub-systemic contexts. A broader comprehension of when and why sudden transformations in policy direction will occur necessitates a greater diversity of regional and national contexts.

For example, changes in Western European governments, or even major ideological changes accompanying new elites to positions of power, do not seem to stimulate fundamental policy shifts in these democracies (Brunck and Minehart 1983). However, in the Latin American context, it is the phenomenon of elite turnover in the form of coups d'état which is strongly associated with foreign policy restructurings (Volgy and Kenski 1982). Furthermore, while in the Middle East, turnover of critical policymaking elites does not seem to be predictive of restructurings in foreign policy, that is not the case in Eastern Europe (Volgy 1993). Such differences are probably linked to various regional factors as well as national attributes, regime dynamics, and bureaucratic webs which help determine the extent to which policy changes can be effectuated by governments. Therefore, much work remains to be done before one can effectively identify the relative salience of both webs of restraint and various motivating factors which may lead decision-makers to engage in fundamental alterations to their foreign policies.

At no time since the start of the cold war has there been a greater opportunity to pursue a clearer understanding of foreign policy restructurings. Regime webs of restraint have been ripped apart in the former Soviet Union, German Democratic Republic (GDR), Yugoslavia, and Czechoslovakia, as well as Hungary, Poland, Romania, Bulgaria, and Albania. In their wake, bureaucratic webs have been torn apart, as has the fabric of foreign policy orientations toward the cold war and the region. The global web today is stretched if not broken by the elimination of cold war norms, which in turn have helped to create conditions for internal change within Eastern Europe. In turn, existing foreign policy orientations in Western Europe, among the superpowers and in the sub-systems of Asia, Middle East, and Latin America, are all undergoing intense scrutiny.

Clearly, in the new republics emerging from the former Soviet Union, and as well throughout Eastern Europe, critical webs of restraint have been broken, and as a consequence, substantial restructurings in foreign policy orientation are occurring. At the same time, the webs of restraint for other major actors— be it in Western Europe, the United States, or China—are still operative. To what extent will these actors be able to fundamentally alter the course of their foreign policies to adapt to such momentous changes in global politics? The theoretical orientation of this chapter suggests that the responses of the larger democracies will be of incremental adaptations to this new global environment, unless domestic political circumstances trigger unusual risk-taking behavior among policymaking elites (Volgy and Schwarz 1991).

The 1990s also offer opportunities for testing the importance of external stimuli to foreign policy restructurings. There is very limited evidence from both Western Europe and Latin America to indicate that the changing circumstances of the global environment do matter, in that they create the context for greater flexibility in foreign policies. Can such external changes alone trigger foreign policy restructuring without any accompanying domestic stimuli such as severe economic problems or worries about political continuity? The oil crisis of 1973, at least for the smaller nations of Western Europe, seems to indicate that external stimuli may spark fundamental change, but only for certain types of nations (Volgy and Schwarz 1991). For larger nations, it still remains unclear as to what levels of global changes are necessary before nations such as the United States, France, West Germany, or Great Britain are willing to take the risks involved in fundamentally reorienting the course of their foreign policies.

The 1990s should constitute an interesting period in which comparative foreign policy scholars will be able to test the extent of their knowledge regarding major foreign policy change. Equally important, it will provide an opportunity for scholars to realize the intellectual gaps that exist relative to the

study of foreign policy restructuring and to develop a more powerful understanding of this crucial phenomenon.

Notes

1. International systems theory seeks to identify different "states" of the international system, the structural conditions operating within different states, the rules
   by which actors operate within those systemic conditions, and the range of conditions under which such systems continue (equilibrium) or change (system transformation). Discussion of different types of international systems—such as
   hegemonic, bipolar, multipolar, or balance of power systems—focuses on the
   specific structural arrangements in global politics with respect to at least two
   distinct dimensions: the degree to which global resources are controlled by one or
   more actors in the system (e.g., the number of poles, and tight versus loose
   polarity), and the sets of rules or norms which help to identify how actors will
   behave in the global system (where the rules of the system may range from broad
   norms to more specific regimes that actors implicitly accept; see Kaplan 1957;
   Franck and Weisband 1972; Young 1986).

Part II

Theoretical Perspectives

Chapter 3

Explaining State Responses
to International Change
The Structural Sources
of Foreign Policy Rigidity and Change

David Skidmore

David Skidmore provides a general overview concerning which types of countries are most likely to restructure their foreign policies in response to international change and which are most likely to resist foreign policy change. He draws upon realist and institutional theories of foreign policy to form an integrated model of foreign policy restructuring in which a country's ability to adjust its foreign policy to changes in the global environment is a function of both international and domestic constraints. A country which has a strong centralized state domestically, yet a weak position internationally, is more likely to restructure its foreign policy than one which is decentralized and subject to strong societal interests at home, yet enjoys hegemonic power abroad. This is illustrated by examining Great Britain at the turn of the century and the United States after World War II as declining hegemonic nations with weak, decentralized states slow to restructure their foreign policies in the face of a changing international environment. Skidmore, like Volgy in the previous chapter, focuses his analysis of declining hegemons on the international and domestic constraints to foreign policy restructuring, emphasizing that foreign policy is often rigid and slow to change. Yet, by combining realist theory, which predicts policy adjustment to international change, with institutional models, which predict domestic resistance to policy adjustment, Skidmore provides the reader with the basis to explain both the historical resistance to foreign policy restructuring and the degree of change which takes place in foreign policy over time.

David Skidmore is assistant professor of political science at Drake University. He received a Ph.D. in political science from Stanford University in 1989 and a B.A. in political science from Rollins College in 1979. His research interests include the study of U.S. foreign policy, domestic constraints on the conduct of foreign policy, and international political economy. He is the coauthor of International Political Economy: The Struggle for Power and Wealth, *the coeditor of* The Limits of State Autonomy: Societal Groups and

Foreign Policy Formulation, *and his work has appeared in journals such as* Political Science Quarterly.

How should hegemonic states respond to declining power? Indeed, how do states generally deal with international change? Does state responsiveness to external change vary across cases in predictable ways? These are important questions about which there is disagreement in the relevant literature. This chapter offers a model of state response to international change which encompasses apparently contradictory theoretical alternatives. The model suggests that states differ in their abilities to adapt to international change depending upon their particular combinations of international power and domestic state strength. This analysis exposes in bold relief the special problems that hegemonic powers experience in coping with relative decline and international change, as compared with more modestly endowed states.

The dependent variable—state response—can be pitched at various levels of abstraction. At the highest level, a state may either resist or adjust to international change. Resistance is the refusal to alter policies which have become poorly suited to cope with the new opportunities and constraints posed by a changed international environment. Adjustment, by contrast, involves policy changes designed to render state behavior more consistent with present or emerging international opportunities and constraints.[1] The choices facing declining hegemons, in particular, can be described less abstractly. The loss of relative power leads to a growing gap between resources and commitments. A strategy of resistance reinforces this tendency by stubbornly binding a hegemon to the defense of previous commitments while neglecting measures which might stimulate accelerated resource growth. A strategy of adjustment, in the context of decline, entails policy changes designed to close or narrow the gap between resources and commitments by either curtailing commitments, increasing resources, or both.

Existing theories about the relationship between international change and state response are typically pitched at the highest levels of abstraction. They offer predictions, sometimes implicitly, about how states in general should respond to international change, without distinguishing among various types of states or the nature of their position in the international system. Two alternative models of policy response can be identified: the first, an evolutionary model springing from realist theory, predicts policy adjustment; the second, a sporadic model drawn from an institutional framework, predicts resistance or, at a minimum, considerable lags in adjustment.

Neither of these models, however, is adequate to predict the policy responses of all types of states. The argument below posits that each applies under differing circumstances, depending upon the various combinations of state strength and international power characteristic of the case in question. Hegemonic powers, particularly those with weak states, will be apt to resist the implications of international change and declining power. Their behavior will follow the sporadic pattern of policy change predicted by institutional models. States combining modest power abroad and state strength at home, on the other hand, are more likely to carry out appropriate policy adjustments in response to international change, just as realist theory would lead one to expect. Following a description of the causal factors inducing resistance to foreign policy restructuring, the utility of this framework will be demonstrated in an analysis of the delayed British and American responses to hegemonic decline during different historical periods.

Models of Policy Response: Evolutionary Versus Sporadic

The concepts of adjustment and resistance allow one to distinguish between broadly different strategic orientations toward situations of decline. As Robert Gilpin (1981) suggests, hegemonic powers face increasingly difficult resource tradeoffs over time as the proliferating costs of consumption and protection (or defense) crowd out productive investment.[2] A strategy of adjustment uses policy change as an instrument for redressing this imbalance by shifting resources toward investment, while a strategy of resistance aggravates the dilemmas of decline by defending the very domestic and international commitments which continue to rob resources from investment.

Adjustment confronts policymakers with difficult choices. Although, in principle, a gap between resources and commitments can be narrowed by increasing resources while protecting existing commitments, there are practical obstacles to this path. In the short run, increased resources in support of commitments abroad can only be attained by increasing the extractive activities of the state at home (i.e., higher taxes or borrowing). Given the costs this will impose on societal groups, such a course may entail political risks. In the long run, increased resources can be obtained by shifting resources from consumption to investment, using natural resources more efficiently and promoting technological innovation. These measures, however, may be difficult to implement and, since the results may be long in materializing, do little to overcome the immediate consequences of a gap between resources and commitments. Shedding commitments offers a quicker means of narrowing the gap, although not without costs. Since commitments are made in order to defend actual or potential sources of benefit, shedding commitments will increase net benefits only if the costs avoided as result of shedding the commitment exceed the benefits to be preserved through its defense. Before commitments are actually abandoned, hegemonic powers are likely to seek less expensive ways of meeting them. This can be accomplished, for instance, by shifting burdens to allies or substituting, where possible, less expensive economic or diplomatic means of leverage for relatively expensive military forms of protection. Where these efforts fail or prove inadequate, then some degree of retrenchment must form part of a strategy of adjustment. Retrenchment is likely to begin with peripheral commitments, where benefits are marginal and costs are excessive. If declining power persists, the number of commitments which can still be defended at a cost lower than the benefits at stake will shrink. In other words, growing numbers of commitments will come to be viewed as marginal in relation to the expense of maintaining them.

It should be noted that a strategy of adjustment is not always an appropriate response to declining power. Where the sources of decline are transitory and contingent rather than long-term and structural, far-reaching and relatively permanent adjustments in policy are likely to be unnecessary and undesirable. In such cases, a strategy of resistance is better suited to the circumstances. The discussion which follows, however, assumes circumstances involving long-term, structural decline where policy adjustments are likely to be necessary and appropriate.

In considering which strategic orientation a hegemon is likely to adopt, it quickly becomes apparent that two conditions must be met before a strategy of adjustment may emerge. The leaders of a hegemonic state: (1) must be sufficiently sensitive to environmental conditions to recognize the condition of decline, its sources, and its implications, and (2) must have the political freedom and capacity to manipulate policies in such a way as to manage a strategy of adjustment.

Realism, the reigning intellectual model within the discipline of international relations, assumes that these conditions are easily met. Because realism posits a tight linkage between environmental conditions and policy responses, it points logically to policy change of an evolutionary nature. Given the premises of realist theory, it is expected that state leaders adjust policies in an incremental and adaptive way to international change.[3]

Realism depicts states as if they were "unitary rational actors, carefully calculating costs of alternative courses of action and seeking to maximize their expected utility" (Keohane 1986, 165). In a realist world, states constantly adjust their policies in response to perceived changes in the international configuration of power and interests. Robert Keohane (1984, 167) explains that "the link between system structure and actor behavior is forged by the rationality assumption, which enables the theorist to predict that leaders will respond to the incentives and constraints imposed by their environments." The assumption of rationality, which Keohane (1984, 167) describes as "essential to the theoretical claims of structural realism," allows the analyst "to attribute variations in state behavior to variations in characteristics of the international system" rather than "the calculating ability of states." Realism excludes the influence of domestic politics on foreign policymaking institutions, assuming that little explanatory power is lost in the process.

According to realist theory, hegemons are not unique in their capacities to adjust to international change. They differ from other states only in the nature of the constraints they face during a period of declining power. In understanding the sources and implications of decline, therefore, it is possible to predict the likely policy responses of the hegemon without acquiring knowledge about the domestic or institutional context in which such decisions are to be made.

Hans Morgenthau explains that realists put themselves "in the position of a statesman who must meet a certain problem of foreign policy under certain circumstances, and we ask ourselves what the rational alternatives are from which a statesman may choose . . . and which of these rational alternatives this particular statesman . . . is likely to choose" (Morgenthau and Thompson 1985, 5). Keohane (1984, 163) refers to this method of analysis as "rational reconstruction."[4] This reasoning rests upon the notion that decisionmakers have virtually infinite flexibility in choosing among various policies. Realism posits that they are constrained only by the resources at their disposal and the environmental conditions they face.

Institutional approaches challenge this assumption. Contrary to realist theory, institutionalism treats the constraints on rational adaptation as severe and predicts, therefore, a sporadic rather than an evolutionary pattern of policy change. The suggestion that social change is more often discontinuous and abrupt than continuous and gradual has been championed by many authors in a variety of fields.[5] Among these, the work of Stephen Krasner is particularly relevant here. Borrowing from theoretical developments in the field of evolutionary biology (see Gould and Eldredge 1977), Krasner builds a model of policy change around the concept of "punctuated equilibrium." This model suggests that policies do not adapt incrementally over time in tandem with environmental conditions. Instead, policy change occurs only intermittently and often in large leaps (Krasner 1984, 240–44; see also Krasner 1989, 80–88).

Policies remain rigid due principally to the intransigence of institutions and the domestic structures in which they are embedded. The first source of rigidity is that policy change is costly, requiring the creation of new analytic models and organizational routines corresponding to altered realities. The intellectual and organizational costs which go into the creation of new policies mitigate against future change. Change is also rendered difficult because policies become enmeshed in domestic interests which have a stake in their perpetuation. Krasner (1976, 343) suggests that "state decisions taken because of state interests reinforce private societal groups that the state is unable to resist in later periods." Vested interests can use their political power to rob policymakers of the flexibility required to manage a process of steady, gradual adaptation.

As a result of these constraints, policies become "stuck," leading to a growing gap between static policies and changing external realities. The increasing dysfunctionality of existing policies eventually leads to a crisis which may finally succeed in shaking up domestic routines. As Krasner (1976, 341) puts it: "Once policies have been adopted, they are pursued until a new crisis demonstrates that they are no longer feasible. States become locked in by the impact of prior choices on their domestic political structures." Policies change only when crises impress upon policymakers the external costs of maintaining old policies and galvanize the state to challenge vested interests and adopt new policies more congruent with the existing international conditions.

Toward an Integrated Model of Policy Response

Despite appearances to the contrary, these contrasting models of state response can be reconciled with one another. When the assumptions underlying both evolutionary and sporadic theories of policy change are treated as variables rather than as givens, it is possible to show that each applies under different conditions. This allows one to account for the rather obvious fact that some states adapt well and readily to international change while others do not; an observation which neither theory, taken alone, is prepared to acknowledge or explain given their blanket predictions.

The implicit independent variables underlying both of the models described above are (1) the degree of external compulsion and (2) the degree of domestic constraint. Where external compulsion is high, policies are likely to adapt. Where external compulsion is low, policies are likely to remain rigid. Similarly, domestic conditions affect the likelihood and degree of policy rigidity. A strong state—one where authority is centralized and which can act relatively autonomously of domestic interests—is potentially capable of implementing policy change at relatively low domestic costs. A weak state will be too divided and encumbered by domestic interests to manipulate policies so easily.

Realist theory, in other words, is best suited to explaining the behavior of states characterized by modest power abroad and great strength at home. Policy adjustment to international change is most likely where international constraints are tight and domestic constraints are loose. Middle-level powers will come closest to meeting the condition of sensitivity to external change because they face a competitive and compelling set of international constraints, due to their limited international power. States which possess considerable strength and autonomy in relation to societal actors at home will come closest to meeting the condition of policy flexibility because they will have the capacity to act relatively free of domestic constraints when it becomes necessary to adjust external policies in response to international change. Realist theory should predict behavior well for states combining both characteristics of sensitivity and flexibility. A state will respond quickly and easily to international change when there are stronger incentives for the state to respond to international constraints than to domestic constraints.

An institutional approach, on the other hand, is much better suited to explain the behavior of states characterized by a combination of extensive power abroad and state weakness at home. Policy adjustment to international change will be difficult where international constraints are low and domestic constraints are high. Due to their power, hegemonic states, for example, are likely to be less well-attuned to underlying international changes and less compelled to respond to them. States characterized by domestic weakness in relation to their society, may, even if they recognize the desirability of foreign policy change, lack the capacity or domestic freedom to manipulate policies in response to external change. States characterized by both hegemonic power abroad and relative weakness at home will be most poorly suited to meet the requirements of sensitivity and flexibility. Under these conditions, which fit the assumptions underlying the sporadic model of policy change, incentives are biased in favor of policy rigidity or resistance to international change rather than adjustment. Despite the excessive external costs such a strategy entails, they can better afford to ignore international change than to ignore the vested interests or ideological constraints which favor existing policies.

Figure 3.1 illustrates the relationships discussed in the preceding paragraphs. In the next two sections, the structural sources of the differential capacities of states to adjust to international change are elaborated upon in greater detail.

International Constraints

The realist assumption that states are responsive to changes in their international environment and that policies evolve incrementally is based upon the image of an unforgiving international system in which mistaken choices are quickly punished. The ability of states to safeguard vital interests—such as territorial security, political independence, and economic prosperity—is placed in constant jeopardy by the anarchic, competitive nature of the international system. Realism likens international politics to a Darwinian process of natural selection. States failing to adapt to changes in the global distribution of power and interests soon discover their basic values and even their sovereignty are at risk. Such a world enforces, through constant feedback and external compulsion, a Realpolitik logic of power and maneuver upon participating states. In the words of Kenneth Waltz (1979, 106): "Structures encourage certain behaviors and penalize those who do not respond to the encouragement."

This model approximates, at least crudely, the realities facing middle-level

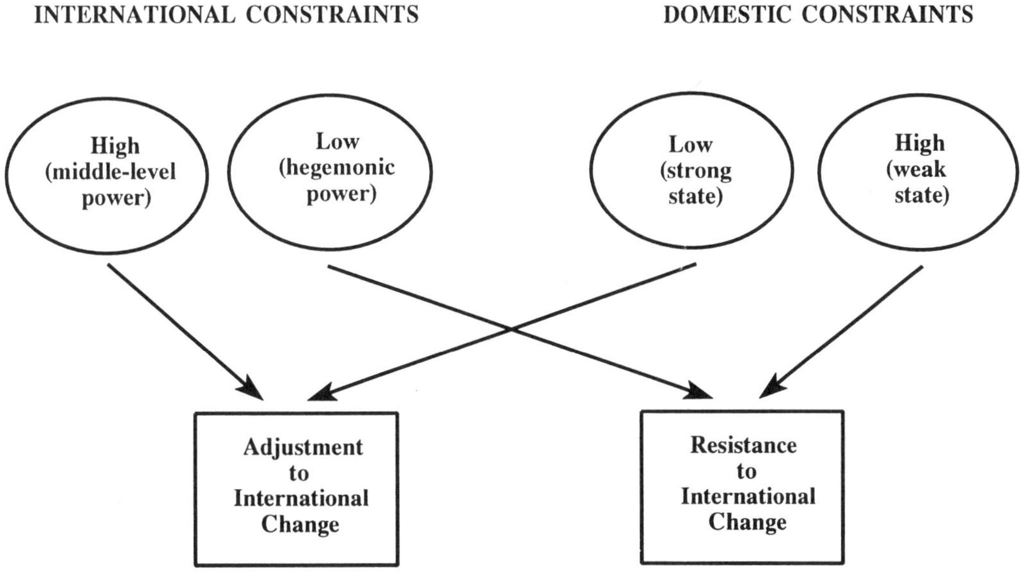

INTERNATIONAL CONSTRAINTS   DOMESTIC CONSTRAINTS

Figure 3.1   Predicting State Response to International Change

powers. Such states, as Keohane (1982, 70) has noted, "do not have the luxury of deciding whether or how fast to adjust to change. They do not seek adjustment. It is thrust upon them, because they are not powerful enough to control the terms through which they relate to the international [system]." Middle-level powers can ill afford to absorb the costs of defending policies and domestic structures which are poorly adapted to the international environment. The rapidly felt deleterious consequences of such policies quickly prompt a search for corrective adjustment. Day-to-day policies as well as basic institutional structures are affected by this adaptive process.

Traditional realist theory, which posits an evolutionary model of policy change, is likely to apply best under these conditions. If policies become rigid and fail to adapt, crises will emerge quickly, not after a long time lag. If the international system is itself in flux, then so too must be the state's policies for coping with it. An environment where policy change is the norm rather than the exception will prove inhospitable to the growth and maturation of vested interest groups. Even where state leaders are faced with a choice between serving their domestic or international interests, they will likely choose policies which favor international interests if the external threat is compelling.

Very powerful states, on the other hand, are likely to experience a quite different relationship to the international system. Due to their broad power, hegemonic states are largely free from many of the external constraints faced by middle-level powers. Basic interests such as independence, security, and prosperity require only a portion of their wide-ranging resources. As a consequence, changes in the international environment will not so readily compel changes in policy. The costs of resisting external incentives are more easily managed by hegemonic powers than middle-level powers. As Keohane observes, "Powerful countries can postpone adjustment; and the stronger they are, the longer it can be postponed" (Keohane 1982, 70; see also Rosenau 1981b, 174). Certainly, the costs of refusing to adapt policies appropriate to international change will eventually accelerate hegemonic decline. This process is, however, likely to be gradual with effects that may not become immediately apparent and costs that may be actively hidden by domestic groups who have developed vested interests in perpetuating old policies.

This unusual freedom from the competitive discipline which dictates the behavior of most states has two important effects on the choices of the elites in hegemonic states. First, hegemonic powers may choose to pursue ambitions beyond the reach of middle-level states. While middle-level powers must often struggle simply to defend their interests from external pressures, hegemonic states may seek to reshape their international environment in ways consistent with internally generated ideological preferences (Krasner 1978a, 340–42). Resources beyond those necessary to protect basic material interests may be externally deployed on behalf of an imperial vision. The extravagance of such ventures is hidden by the hegemon's ample economic, political, and military strength relative to other states.

Once the power of the hegemon has declined to the point where it begins to confront a more competitive environment similar to that experienced by other states, the costs of these far-reaching ideological goals may be felt more acutely. At this stage, it behooves the hegemon to begin shifting resources from imperial ambitions to the protection of more basic interests. An imperial ideology, however, can be difficult to shed once it has permeated the political culture of the dominant power. As will be suggested below, this is particularly likely to be the case if the resort to ideologically based appeals has been regularly utilized by officials in a domestically weak state to bolster the political legitimacy of their management of the nation's foreign policies.

Second, a state with the power and freedom to pursue foreign policies not closely conditioned by the international environment is much more likely to develop groups advocating particular policies which then act as the kind of domestic constraints on policy flexibility foreseen by institutionalists. Domestic groups with vested interests in the continuity of existing policies are most likely to succeed in forestalling policy adjustment to international change when the pursuit of increasingly maladaptive policies does not quickly lead to crisis. This is, of course, seldom the case for middle-level powers. Where a state's power is sufficient only to defend its basic interests, the making of policy is likely to be subordinate to the competitive discipline of the international system. If, by chance, state managers of a middle-level power do fail to make the appropriate policy adjustments, the result is unlikely to be a long period of policy rigidity but instead a quickly felt crisis which punishes the mistake and compels corrective action.

A country enjoying a surplus of power, on the other hand, may find it possible to absorb the costs of defending inappropriate policies and thereby delay a crisis. The leaders of a hegemonic state are likely to judge the pressures arising from vested interests more compelling than the international incentives for policy adaptation, particularly, as seems likely, if decline takes place gradually rather than quickly. Moreover, the longer policies remain rigid, the more dense the network of domestic interests which grow around them and eventually come to oppose their alteration.

It may be relevant here to recall Mancur Olson's (1982) argument that distributive coalitions—or groups organized to seek economic rents through collective action in the economic or political spheres—are more likely to proliferate in large nations than in small ones. This is due to the fact that such coalitions thrive only where they face little effective international competition; a condition more likely to be found in large states, where trade tends to account for a smaller proportion of economic output, than in small states. As distributive coalitions put their narrow interests ahead of those of the society as a whole, they tend to reinforce social rigidities and to oppose innovations which threaten to disrupt existing patterns of resource allocation. Since hegemons are usually characterized by large-scale domestic markets, as well as technological or organizational superiorities which yield cost advantages as compared with international rivals, they will face a less competitive international economic environment than rival states during the phase of hegemonic ascendence. These conditions favor the growth of distributive coalitions as well as the social, economic, and political rigidities to which they give rise.

While in the long run continuing external pressures may eventually lead to policy change, particularly if the failure to adapt results in one or more major crises, policy is likely to be dominated by the internal pressures for stability during the initial stages of decline. Unlike states which have always experienced the international environment as highly competitive, a declining hegemon will remain attached to patterns of behavior developed during its period of ascendance which are now inappropriate given altered realities. Founded upon intellectual and interest-based moorings, these policy patterns may loosen only slowly under the influence of external pressures.

Domestic Constraints

International power is, however, not the only variable affecting a state's capacity to respond flexibly to international change. As suggested above, hegemony contributes to policy rigidity by relaxing the external pressures on policymakers to respond to international change while also allowing the growth of ideological and interest group pressures for policy stability at home. Whether the latter sets of obstacles to adjustment prove decisive depends to a significant degree on the institutional strength and autonomy possessed by central decision-makers in relation to contending bureaucratic and societal forces. "Strong states" may be defined as those where decision-making authority is relatively concentrated in the hands of a few officials within the government and where decisions are made relatively autonomous of the influence of societal groups. "Weak states" are characterized by dispersed or shared authority and a lack of autonomy from societal influences.[6]

Why should state strength make a difference in the ability of a hegemon to adapt to decline? Conceptually, strong states loosely approximate the realist ideal of the state as a rational, unitary actor.[7] Strong states are better capable of formulating and implementing a consistent, rational, and appropriate strategy of adjustment to decline. Weak states, on the other hand, more closely share the characteristics posited by Krasner in his model of punctuated equilibrium, where it is assumed that domestic interests encumber the ability of central decision-makers to manage policy except during times of crisis. Thus the stagnating effects of hegemony on policy are conditioned in part by the domestic strength or weakness of the hegemonic state.

State weakness contributes to policy rigidity in several ways. It is more likely that continued attachment to an imperial ideology will become a source of policy rigidity during a period of decline if the hegemonic state suffers from domestic weaknesses. This stems from the fact that weak states are more dependent upon gaining widespread public legitimacy for their policies than are strong states. By definition, strong states experience relative autonomy from societal influences. They therefore have the capacity to pursue policies which are unpopular or poorly understood by the society at large. Lacking this autonomy, weak states are compelled to seek greater societal consensus behind their policies.

With reference to the United States, Alexander George (1980, 236) has stressed the importance of political legitimacy and the deference that its political leaders demonstrate toward the domestic environment when formulating U.S. policies. "In the absence of the fundamental consensus that policy legitimacy creates, it becomes necessary for the President to justify each action to implement the long-range policy on its own merits rather than as part of a larger policy design and strategy. The necessity for ad hoc day-to-day building of consensus under these circumstances makes it virtually impossible for the President to conduct a long range foreign policy in a coherent, effective manner."

This dependence upon public approval makes it difficult for officials in a weak state to pursue a rational, calculating, flexible, interest-based approach in dealing with the international environment. The need to acquire widespread policy legitimacy leads weak-state policymakers to rationalize favored policies in terms of popular cultural and ideological values which have broad societal appeal.[8] The pressures of legitimation may also lead to a reliance upon doctrine as a means of organizing policies around broad, principled, and easily explained rationales.[9] Political leaders may also resort to the exaggeration of threats and the oversell of solutions as mechanisms for bolstering legitimacy (Theodore Lowi 1979, 128–48). The manufacture or exaggeration of crises allows leaders to rally the public around their policies and helps to bypass elite opponents by isolating the latter politically and pushing decisions upward toward the apex of the state.[10] Each of these legitimacy-bolstering tactics biases foreign policymaking away from a rational, calculating approach of evaluating and coping with international change. As the legitimation process presses ideological values upon the nation's foreign policies, they become less an expression of national interest than a means by which national values are projected into the world.

Ideology, doctrine, and exaggeration/oversell also rob decisionmakers of future flexibility. Katarina Brodin (1972, 106, 108) argues that efforts to shore up support for present policies through the resort to broad foreign policy doctrines can "create commitments which serve as barriers against sudden or sharp changes of policy." Future decision-makers "[tend] to be tied down by the . . . commitments and public statements made by [their] predecessors." Similarly, Lowi (1979, 148) notes that "a great danger in oversell . . . is that the President's own flexibility may be further reduced at a later point when he may like the crisis to be over." Thomas Trout (1975, 280–81) best summarizes the overall effects of the vigorous pursuit of domestic legitimation on policy flexibility: "Because of legitimation, policy-makers tend toward relatively fixed positions which are extended to include broad areas of policy. This creates inertia with important consequences. If projected responses to specific conditions fall outside the scope of the available legitimative structure, . . . [then] the domestic costs of restructuring the image of the international situation may exceed foreign policy gains."

A highly ideological strategy of legitimation is most likely to be adopted by weak-state leaders where the state also possesses great power abroad. While the leaders of most states will find the international constraints on the pursuit of broad ideological goals too severe to allow them to resort to this sort of popular legitimation strategy, policymakers in a state combining domestic weakness with external strength will find such a strategy not only attractive and necessary from a domestic point of view, but feasible internationally as well due to the freedom afforded by the state's hegemonic status. Therefore, in the case of a state possessing both internal weakness and external strength, the exigencies of legitimation are all the more likely to lead to policies based upon simple declarative rationales and generalized ideological doctrines. Policies constructed and rationalized in this manner will be relatively insensitive to situational change or to differentiation across time and place. Public identification with the legitimative routines upon which the weak state becomes dependent produces a continuing ideological constraint on policy adjustment and change.

The accumulation of vested interests around old policies provides another source of policy rigidity. The interest group environment which influences present or future decisions is seldom autonomous of previous policies. If interest groups affect policy, it is equally true that policies affect the formation and strength of interest groups. Policy innovation reallocates resources among groups and generates new groups representing institutions involved in or affected by the implementation of the new policies. The interest groups which grow out of or become attached to existing policies can serve as powerful obstacles to policy change.

Weak states are especially prone to this sort of rigidity. They will be less capable of resisting the pressures brought by societal groups which lobby on behalf of old policies. They will also be vulnerable to bureaucratic resistance to change. Bureaucracies constitute institutional embodiments of past policies and, more often than not, may be expected to resist fundamental policy reform. Commenting on the obstacles to change and adaptation in U.S. foreign policy, Charles Hermann (1988, 262) points out that: "The Cold War provided a framework that for more than forty years served as a structure indicating to the U.S. government's foreign policy organizations what situations to monitor and what meaning to attach to problems that arose. These highly established search routines and interpretative processes may now become increasingly dysfunctional, not directing monitoring activities or situations that could pose new kinds of dangers or opportunities, or imposing an inappropriate Cold War definition on a detected problem."

Bureaucratic resistance proves more difficult to overcome in a weak state than in a strong state because weak-state bureaucratic institutions are given a greater grant of independence and autonomy from centralized control. Indeed, this problem is complicated by the fact that, as Hermann (1988, 258) suggests, highly independent bureaucratic organizations will "search for and sustain

public constituencies that support their general world view and specific interpretation of policy problems.''

In weak, hegemonic states, ideological and group pressures may interact in
complex ways and reinforce one another. If the leader of a weak state attempts
the wholesale adjustment of old policies as a response to declining power, he
or she may stimulate equally broad and comprehensive forms of ideological
and interest group resistance. Ironically, the popular ideological appeals once
used by the state to mobilize public support for previous policies may now be
used by the state's opponents to mobilize popular resistance to policy change.
Groups with vested interests in old policies are likely to depart from the usual
pattern of isolated, behind the scenes influence-wielding and instead seek to
build all-inclusive coalitions of interested parties which fight change through
broad-based ideological campaigns. Rather than disparate groups lobbying to
protect the narrow interests of their members, one may find more encompassing
associations of groups and individuals making public appeals based upon
grounds of national interest. These appeals will be addressed broadly, to linked
sets of issues, rather than narrowly, to single issues in isolation.

The hypothesis that weak states will be less responsive to the need for policy
adjustment in the face of hegemonic decline leads to two seemingly paradoxical
corollaries. First, although policy stability is often viewed as a sign of governmental strength while change is taken as an indicator of incoherence and
weakness, the institutionalist model developed above suggests that, under some
circumstances, just the opposite may be true. Policy stability or rigidity in the
face of external change often is indicative of a weak state unable to mobilize
the domestic political resources to respond appropriately to shifting environmental conditions. In a shifting international environment, policy change or
adjustment often signifies domestic political strength rather than weakness and
incoherence. Change requires a state strong enough to challenge the intellectual
and institutional forces which support the status quo.[11]

Second, the ambitiousness or scope of a declining hegemon's external
commitments or goals cannot be positively associated with the domestic
strength of the hegemonic state. If the above hypotheses are correct, it should
be the weak state, not the strong one, which pursues a more aggressive and
ambitious external agenda during a period of decline. A weak state will persist
in the pursuit of old policies which defend the status quo even if this results in
a net excess of costs over benefits. Only a strong state will be able to manage
the difficult politics of retrenchment.

Other Combinations of State Strength and International Power

The general theoretical argument advanced thus far can be adapted to
consider other combinations of state strength and international power. A state
may combine hegemonic power abroad with state strength at home or moderate
international power with domestic state weakness. While these hypothetical
cases do not generate entirely clear predictions of adjustment or resistance to

international change, some speculation is possible. A state possessing both hegemonic power abroad and great strength at home will experience few compelling constraints on its freedom from either the international or domestic spheres, which makes predictions about its behavior difficult. One may speculate, however, that while such states will pursue ambitious strategies abroad as ascendent hegemons, they will adjust to decline more quickly than hegemonic powers with weak states. International constraints will, as they tighten, come to outweigh the relatively low levels of domestic constraint. The situation is reversed for states characterized by modest power abroad and state weakness at home. Facing serious constraints from both their international and domestic environments, they may well vacillate between adjustment and resistance. The choice between these two strategies is likely to vary across issues and over time in response to subtle shifts in the relative strength of international and domestic constraints. Overall, responses to international change are likely to be inconsistent, incoherent, and ineffective.

What of small powers? In principle, they, like middle-level powers, experience strong incentives to adjust quickly to international change lest their failure to do so lead to serious negative consequences. In practice, however, small powers are unlikely to adjust readily due to failures of both capacity and will. Middle-level powers, while they may lack the surplus power necessary to pursue ambitious goals abroad or to postpone adjustment, nevertheless possess sufficient means to defend their sovereignty and independence, except under extreme circumstances. Small powers, on the other hand, can survive as separate entities only by sacrificing important elements of sovereignty. They often serve as only nominally independent satellites to larger powers. Their domestic political systems may be permeated by external forces. As a result, very weak nations do not calculate their own interests or deploy their own resources as autonomous actors. Larger powers not only constrain their policy choices but sometimes also influence who holds governmental power in such countries. Under such circumstances, the political elites of small powers may act less as defenders of their own nation's interests than as collaborators serving the interests of a dominating external power (Kahler 1984).

The ability of a small state to act independently is, of course, further undermined by domestic weakness. Yet where a small state is strong at home, one might expect opportunistic adjustment. Strong state elites, despite external weakness, have the domestic authority to mobilize available internal resources in occasionally successful efforts to exploit cracks in the edifice of external domination. The opportunities to do so will still depend heavily, however, upon international factors. Opportunistic small power elites are most likely to find the space to exercise independence if for instance their country is geographically removed from any great powers, the attention of nearby dominating powers is temporarily distracted by other pressing matters, or the issue at stake is peripheral to the dominant state's concerns.

The Cases of Great Britain and the United States

Evidence that the combination of hegemony abroad and state weakness at home will delay adaptive responses to declining power can be adduced from the case of turn-of-the-century Great Britain and, to a greater extent, from the case of the United States during the post–World War II period.

In his study of British foreign policy decision-making during the decades prior to World War I, Aaron Friedberg (1988, 290, 294) concludes that "Britain reacted to the early evidence of relative decline with a handful of partial, and only partially coordinated, measures . . . Even the nation's diplomacy . . . was largely ad hoc and opportunistic." While conceding that British efforts did, to a degree, succeed in narrowing the immediate gap between resources and commitments which plagued Britain's global posture, Friedberg (1988, 295) nevertheless argues that "the policies pursued at the turn of the century simply ignored or papered over serious underlying weaknesses in Britain's position or, in solving certain problems, created new and perhaps more dangerous ones." Options which might have more fully slowed British decline were either overlooked or rejected.

Friedberg focuses on British responses to decline in four areas of national power: industrial, financial, and land and naval forces. British leaders, with the exception of Joseph Chamberlain, largely ignored or explained away indices of the relative decline in British industrial and commercial power. Growing financial strains were met with partial and inadequate economizing measures. New taxes were too limited, and came after too great a delay, to place the country on a sound financial footing. The British responded more vigorously and successfully to the loss of naval supremacy; simultaneously modernizing the fleet and concentrating it in European waters. Yet, even here, officials did not fully face up to the consequences of naval redeployment for the security of the British empire. Finally, although the British did take steps to increase army efficiency after British troops performed poorly during the Boer War, officials resisted the introduction of conscription or other measures which might have better prepared the British army for a major war. Britain paid a heavy price for this oversight during the early stages of World War I.

Among the reasons Friedberg gives for the shortcomings of Britain's response to decline, two are pertinent to the present argument. Ideological presuppositions formed during and inherited from Britain's period of hegemonic ascendance desensitized British leaders to evidence of decline, even when manifested in the form of foreign crises. Ideology also distorted the debate concerning appropriate policy responses by ruling out potentially viable options when they either fit uncomfortably with traditional formulas or were deemed contrary to public sentiment and thereby politically unaffordable. The British clung to the notions of limited government, low taxes, free trade, a volunteer army, and the two-power naval standard long after changing circumstances dictated some reexamination of these cherished ideals.

The weakness of the British state also, according to Friedberg, served as a source of policy failure. Bureaucratic decentralization and fragmentation both impeded policy coordination and allowed vested interests the opportunity to inhibit threatening alterations in policy.[12] From this evidence, Friedberg (1988, 290–91) deduces more generally that "countries in which power is concentrated, both in the state and inside the national government, seem . . . to have a better chance of responding in a coordinated, centrally directed way to early inklings of relative decline. . . . The more widely distributed decision-making power is within a political system, the more likely it is that a nation's initial response to relative decline will be fragmented." Friedberg's treatment of the British case thus reinforces the proposition that hegemony and state weakness may serve as barriers to prompt adjustment in the face of international change.

The model also has the potential to shed light on various aspects of past and future American foreign policy.[13] Many, of course, have suggested that the United States during the post–World War II period has been characterized by each of the traits associated with policy rigidity and resistance—namely, hegemony and state weakness. This combination of traits may help account for the highly ideological character of American rhetoric and policies during the cold war period. According to this interpretation, the ideological content of U.S. foreign policy as well as associated characteristics such as heavy reliance upon doctrine, oversell, and moralism can be attributed to the pressures weak-state leaders experienced in seeking consensual legitimacy for America's new international leadership role as well as to the freedom afforded by its broad power to pursue particularly ambitious ideological goals. The combination of state weakness and hegemonic power, in other words, provided policymakers with both the internal incentive and the external opportunity to pursue an ideologically imbued foreign policy.

Alexander George (1980, 249–50) offers the foreign policy legacy of the Truman administration as an example of the way in which the efforts of U.S. policymakers to bolster legitimacy led to policy rigidity:

> In striving to attain policy legitimacy with Congress and the public for its Cold War policies the Truman Administration was led into a considerable rhetorical over-simplification and exaggeration of the Soviet threat, one that rested on a new "devil image" of the Soviets and a new premise to the effect that U.S.-Soviet conflict was a zero-sum contest. The struggle to maintain policy legitimacy for the Cold War led in time to considerable rigidification in the supporting beliefs and an unwillingness of American policy-makers to subject them to continual testing.

The Truman Doctrine, of course, best illustrates this phenomenon. In his famous speech to Congress, Truman justified aid to Greece and Turkey by declaring "it must be the policy of the United States to support free people who are resisting attempted subjugation by armed minorities or by outside pressures." In fact, however, the Greek communists had strong indigenous support, and they received little aid from the Soviet Union. Moreover, the civil war pitted communists not against democrats but against right-wing monarchists. Thus Truman's rhetoric bore little resemblance to the realities of the situation in Greece. According to Stephen Ambrose (1988, 79–86), George Kennan, among others, was "upset at the way in which Truman had seized the opportunity to declare a worldwide, open-ended doctrine, when what was called for was a simple declaration of aid to a single nation." Truman was preparing to use terms, Kennan later remarked, "more grandiose and more sweeping than anything that I, at least, had ever envisaged."

The universal scope of Truman's rhetoric was, however, quite deliberate. Policymakers believed that emphasizing the ideological aspects of the cold war played a crucial role in winning domestic legitimacy for their overall policies. Ambrose notes that Truman was unhappy with early drafts of the speech which he did not consider tough enough. Truman later recalled "I wanted no hedging in this speech. This was America's answer to the surge of expansion of Communist tyranny. It had to be clear and free of hesitation or double talk."

The purpose was, as Arthur Vandenberg put it, to "scare the hell out of the American people." Historian John Lewis Gaddis (1972, 350–51) quotes Clark Clifford, who characterized Truman's speech as "the opening gun in a campaign to bring people up to (the) realization that the war isn't over by any means." Gaddis himself calls the Truman Doctrine "a form of shock therapy: it was a last-ditch effort by the administration to prod Congress and the American people into accepting the responsibilities of . . . world leadership." Another historian, Marshall Shulman (1988, 23), sees this episode as a part of a more general pattern that had lasting consequences for U.S. foreign policy: "In the effort to loosen congressional purse strings to fund military programs, and the Marshall Plan, U.S. officials exaggerated and oversimplified the Soviet challenge as an ideologically driven effort to conquer the world. Anticommunism became the American ideology, the central principle of U.S. foreign policy."

Two examples among the many that could be cited, illustrate the argument that the demands of legitimation led to conscious distortions in the political rhetoric of American leaders throughout the cold war years. The author of a State Department memo written in 1951 argued that it was "necessary for the administration to oversimplify Soviet intentions in appealing to Congress and the people for support of the defense program" (May 1984, 226). During the Eisenhower administration, Secretary of State John Foster Dulles candidly explained "our people can understand, and will support, policies which can be explained and understood in moral terms. But policies merely based on carefully calculated expediency could never be explained and would never by understood" (Wander 1984, 344).

The resort to doctrine, universalism, moralism, and oversell as techniques for legitimizing America's cold war strategy proved largely successful. Yet this very success served to raise the domestic political costs facing future leaders who sought to fundamentally redirect U.S. foreign policies to bring them into alignment with changing international circumstances.

The material basis for America's ideologically ambitious foreign policy goals did not long endure. In Robert Gilpin's (1981, 173–74) words, "History affords no more remarkable reversal of fortunes in a relatively short period of time than the reversal the United States experienced in the decades following World War II."[14] With declining power came tighter external constraints, higher costs, and a growing gap between resources and commitments. These trends can be traced back to the late 1950s and early 1960s; a period when, as Robert Keohane (1982, 70) remarks, "the United States contracted the disease of the strong: refusal to adjust to change."

Vietnam punctured, at least for some, the myth of American omnipotence. In response, the Nixon, Ford, and Carter administrations each took partial steps toward the adjustment of traditional policies during the 1970s. As Kenneth Oye (1989, 4) suggests, "these Presidents narrowed the definition of American interests and commitments in peripheral regions, shifted some of the burdens of containment to China, Western Europe, and the Third World, and acted on limited areas of mutual interest with the Soviet Union, particularly through strategic arms control negotiations. . . . Their rhetoric was attuned to the politics of limits, and their actions were rooted in a strategy of adjustment."

Each presidential strategy, however, was frustrated in varying degrees by domestic politics. This was most evident during the Carter administration. Although support for cold war policies waned during the latter stages of the Vietnam War, surveys revealed increasing conservatism through the remainder of the seventies (see Schneider 1987). The latter part of the decade also saw a surge in activity by vested interest groups, such as the Committee on the Present Danger, on behalf of traditional policies and in opposition to adjustment (see Sanders 1983). Interest group opposition to reform was particularly evident on issues such as the Panama Canal and SALT II treaties and defense spending. Partially as a consequence of these trends, the Carter administration virtually repudiated its initial adjustment strategy before the end of Carter's term. Clearly, domestic structures which survived as legacies of the cold war period played a role in constraining America's strategic policy reassessment following a period of decline.

The Reagan administration gutted what little that remained of Carter's reforms and accelerated the shift toward an unambiguous strategy of resistance. This led to a growing gap between resources and commitments, as signaled by the emergence of large foreign trade and federal budget deficits in the 1980s. Paul Kennedy (1987b, 36) could therefore correctly observe, in 1987, that "the United States today has roughly the same enormous array of military obligations across the globe that it had a quarter century ago, when its shares of world GNP, manufacturing production, military spending, and armed forces personnel were much larger than they are now."

From a realist perspective, this is anomalous behavior. Realism cannot account for the surprising degree of rigidity in American policies. An institutionalist perspective that highlights the role of domestic constraints for a hegemonic but weak state, readily accounts for the difficulty U.S. foreign policy has experienced in adjusting to international change. Yet a strategy of resistance cannot eliminate, and may well exacerbate, growing external pressures for adjustment as decline. In the absence of policy change, it may lead to steady growth in the gap between resources and commitments. As Trout (1975) suggests, adjustment is most likely to emerge once the international costs of resistance come to exceed the domestic costs of policy change and reform. Therefore, resistance will eventually give way to some form of adjustment; whether managed or abrupt. The theoretical argument, in other words, predicts serious lags in adjustment, not permanent resistance. Interestingly, something of the sort seems to have occurred during the latter part of the Reagan era and the four years of the Bush administration when the United States once again undertook a number of tentative moves toward adjustment. These were largely ad hoc responses to unexpected international developments, such as the rise of Mikhail Gorbachev, and did not add up to a comprehensive or coherent strategy (see Oye 1987). Nevertheless, they point to the fact that a strategy of resistance cannot remain stable in the long run, principally because it runs counter to long-term trends in the international system.

Conclusion

A realist approach to international politics is inadequate to the task of understanding the dynamics of hegemonic decline and adaptation. Realism posits a close relationship between international change and policy response. By contrast, the theory in this chapter posits that adaptation to environmental change is conditioned by two key variables: external power and internal state strength. In particular, hegemonic powers characterized by state weakness at home are especially prone to policy rigidity during periods of declining power. For such states, the process of adapting to international change is not smooth or automatic. A model of sporadic policy change, informed by institutional analysis, applies best to such cases. Realist theory's prediction of evolutionary change remains superior, however, with respect to cases where modest power abroad is combined with state strength at home. The model thus encompasses both major existing theoretical alternatives by specifying the conditions under which each is likely to apply.

The resulting theory of state response to international change has the merit of parsimony. Yet this very trait may serve as a weakness from the standpoint of actual empirical research. Like most structural models, this one suffers from a lack of subtlety. While the distinctions between strong and weak states, or between hegemonic and normal powers, may prove analytically useful, they obviously remain too sweeping and overly simplified to capture accurately the actual range of empirical variation. Measurements of international power or domestic strength are further complicated not only by familiar problems of definition, but also by the fact that variation can occur across issue areas as well as countries. Similarly, the concepts of adjustment and resistance help to characterize broad policy orientations but do little to distinguish among more subtle and discrete policy options. Comparative research designed to test and refine the propositions suggested above must be sensitive to these sorts of problems.

Despite these pitfalls, the argument made here holds important general implications for how scholars might fruitfully go about studying foreign policy change. First, broad-based and long-term patterns of change and continuity can be best be studied through a contextual approach which locates the state at the intersection of two environments—the international and the domestic. As Theda Skocpol (1985) suggests, states are "Janus-faced" creatures with important interests in both internal and external order. Externally, states must cope with the problem of maintaining a balance between resources and commitments. Internally, states must strive to gain and maintain domestic legitimacy for their policies. States will vary in their ability to cope with and reconcile these twin sets of environmental demands depending upon their relative levels of power and state strength.[15]

Adopting this view suggests more attention be devoted to identifying changes in the environmental constraints confronting states, exploring the extent to which international and domestic demands complement or contradict one another, assessing the relative capacities of states to cope with these demands, and determining which sets of demands, if conflicts arise, are likely to prove the more compelling influences on policy. In other words, an approach is necessary which can accommodate the interaction of international and domestic forces in evaluating the long-term influence that these contextual constraints exert over foreign policy (see Gourevitch 1978). Unfortunately, existing approaches to the study of foreign policy seldom allow for this sort of contextual interaction. Realism suffers from a one-sided focus on the external determinants of policy. Institutionalist approaches suffer from a similar one-sided focus on the domestic determinants of policy. Decision-making theories typically confine their analysis to the immediate arena of decision—either ignoring or treating as exogenous (to be left, therefore, unexplained) constraints arising from the domestic or international realms.

A second analytical lesson is that there must be greater attention to the possible influence of past structures and policies on present choices. Realism assumes that policymakers are primarily influenced by contemporaneous evaluations of power and interests. The important question is: which option, from the available menu, best serves present interests? This ignores the possibility that past choices may become so embedded in bureaucratic organizations, vested interest groups, as well as intellectual outlooks and understandings that they place severe constraints on the choices realistically available to present policymakers. As Krasner (1989, 74) suggests, "prior institutional choices limit available future options."

This study contends that domestic structures are most likely to remain intransigent in the face of international change in cases where states combine external strength with internal weakness. Under these conditions, the optimal policy responses to external change will fall outside the limited scope of policy choices which are indeed politically feasible. It becomes important, where such circumstances exist, to distinguish between generative periods in history when structures and policies stabilize after a time of crisis and flux and stable periods when continuity is the norm. Ultimately, although the model developed focuses on foreign policy restructuring, the challenge of specifying the conditions under which change follows an evolutionary or a sporadic pattern remains an important, but too often neglected, theoretical task for all realms of political life.

Notes

1. Although the specific terminology varies, the following pieces each discuss, in some fashion or another, the choice between adjustment and resistance: Ikenberry (1986); Rosenau (1981); Oye (1987); Huntington (1987–88). On foreign policy change more generally, see Hermann (1990).
2. On the rise and decline of hegemonic powers, also see Kennedy (1987); Modelski (1978); Cipolla (1970); Olson (1982); Stein (1984).
3. It is important to note the existence of tensions between the analytic structure of realism and the normative dimensions of realist thought. Analytically, realism purports to explain state behavior as a function of externally imposed constraints. This assumption lies behind much of the systemic theorizing about international relations. States are depicted as functionally similar units driven by the rational pursuit of national interests in an anarchic world. Yet this analytic structure of realist theory is incompatible with the normative dimensions of realist thought.

   Normative realism holds that statesmen, because they are agents rather than principals, have a moral duty to maximize the power, security, and well-being of the nation they represent. The critical function of this school of thought has been to question actions, policies, and behavior which fail to maximize the national interest. The analytic and normative strands of realism stand in tension because the former asserts that states pursue their own national interests as a function of their participation in an anarchic international system, while the latter implicitly acknowledges that important deviations from realist standards of behavior are common.

   These tensions are evident not only across different realist thinkers but often in the work of single authors. See, for instance, Morgenthau and Thompson (1985, chap. 4, 7, 10, passim). I do not attempt to resolve this contradiction in realist thought. Instead, my purpose is limited to the demonstration that analytic realism is inadequate to explain the response of hegemonic states to the experience of decline. I am indebted to Stephen Krasner for urging that I address this point.
4. For an example of how this approach has been applied in practice to one aspect of American foreign policy, see Lake (1983).
5. See, for instance, Nisbet (1969, 272–304); Kuhn (1962); Skowronek (1982, chap. 10); Rosati (1988).
6. On strong and weak states, see Nettl (1968); as well as Katzenstein (1978) and Krasner (1978).

7. I say "loosely" because, given the serious psychological and organizational complexities of making decisions with reference to an often uncertain and complex international environment, no state, whether strong or weak, perfectly emulates a rational, unitary actor.

8. On the linkage between ideology and legitimation, see Trout (1985).

9. On the role of doctrine, see Brodin (1972).

10. Lowi links the frequent resort to oversell to state weakness and the pressures of legitimation.

11. For an original interpretation of U.S. foreign policy which also depicts state weakness as a source of policy rigidity, see Katznelson and Prewitt (1979).

12. Stephen Krasner makes a similar argument, suggesting that institutional rigidity and vested interests accounted for Great Britain's continued attachment to policies of free trade even after Britain's declining world economic position rendered such policies increasingly costly. According to Krasner (1976, 342), "Institutions created during periods of rising ascendancy remained in operation when they were no longer appropriate." In this particular case, the Bank of London and the powerful British financial community resisted more mercantilistic policies due to their heavy dependence on international financial flows and open trade.

13. The arguments outlined below are presented in much greater detail in Skidmore (1989). See also Skidmore (forthcoming).

14. See also Avery and Rapkin (1982); Calleo (1987); Kennedy (1987); Mead (1987). For dissenting views on the notion that U.S. power has undergone significant erosion, see Russett (1985); Strange (1987); Nye (1989); Gill (1986).

15. For two recent attempts to develop a theory of state action which takes into account the interaction of domestic and international structures, see Mastanduno, Lake, and Ikenberry (1989); Putnam (1988).

Chapter 4

Rational Choice and Foreign Policy Change
The Arms and Alignments of Regional Powers

Michael D. McGinnis

Michael McGinnis focuses his analysis on the restructuring of national security policies among regional rivals from a rational choice perspective. Changes in the arms acquisitions and alignments of regional rivals are analyzed as the consequence of the rational behavior of regimes seeking to maintain both external security and domestic support. Specifically, McGinnis develops a framework for explaining significant changes in regional power security policies as a result of a rational response to changes in three major constraints—the external threat from regional rivals, the arms transfer and alignment policies of the great powers, and the nature of each regime's domestic support structure. The utility of this rational choice approach to security policy restructuring is illustrated through case studies of regional rivalries between India and Pakistan, Ethiopia and Somalia, and North Korea and South Korea. Unlike the previous two chapters, which provide a general overview of foreign policy change, McGinnis focuses more specifically on the sources of continuity and change in the national security policies of regional powers. What Skidmore in the previous chapter expects to find among middle-power states, McGinnis's rational choice perspective does find in regional rivalries. In addition to providing a more sophisticated understanding of rational choice, this perspective also illustrates the range of interpretation possible in the study of foreign policy restructuring.

Michael D. McGinnis is associate professor of political science at Indiana University. He received a Ph.D. in political science from the University of Minnesota in 1985 and a B.S. in mathematics from Ohio State University in 1980. His research interests center on the application of game and other

I would like to thank John Aldrich, Brian Job, Raymond Duvall, Iliya Harik, Stephen Krasner, Mark Lichbach, Dina Spechler, Harvey Starr, John Williams, and the editors for their helpful comments at various stages of this project. The research reported here was partially supported by a Doctoral Dissertation Fellowship from the University of Minnesota Graduate School, and by a National Science Foundation Grant, SES–8810610. An earlier version of this chapter was presented at the 1986 Annual Meeting of the Midwest Political Science Association in Chicago. Naturally, none of these individuals or organizations are responsible for any errors of fact or interpretation.

rational choice models to the evolution of international order, particularly the combination of conflict and cooperation that sustains security rivalries lasting many decades. His work has appeared in articles published in American Journal of Political Science, American Political Science Review, Journal of Conflict Resolution, International Interactions, International Studies Quarterly, *and* Mathematical and Computer Modelling. *He is currently working on a book with John T. Williams on the dynamics of superpower rivalry.*

During the four decades of the cold war, regional powers exhibited a puzzling variety of behavior with regard to their relations to the superpowers. South Korea remained dependent on U.S. arms and support while North Korea played an elaborate balancing act between the Soviet Union and China. Although formally allied with the United States, Pakistan had to fend for itself in its wars against a nonaligned India with considerable access to Soviet arms. Israel maintained close but informal ties with the United States during a period in which Egypt changed patrons. Ethiopia and Somalia switched alignments in the space of a few months during the Ogaden War, yet Greece and Turkey remained allied to the same superpower despite recurrent regional tensions. Detailed, case-specific explanations can be offered for the security policies of each of these regional powers, but when taken as a whole the diversity of change and continuity in these policies defines a ''puzzle'' in the theoretical sense of Rosenau (1980). Are all these events instances of the same phenomenon? Evidence is presented for an affirmative answer, based on the idea that these policy patterns represent each state's rational pursuit of external security and domestic support.

The leaders of contemporary Third World states continue to face a volatile mixture of domestic unrest, regional conflict, and great power intervention. This chapter focuses on regional powers whose most pressing concern is the external security threat posed by a rival power within the same region. Regional rivals have a strong incentive to obtain arms imports and guarantees of military and diplomatic support from the more powerful and technologically advanced ''global powers.'' These powers are global in the sense that they have security interests that transcend any single region as well as the capability for military intervention in many regions. Conversely, regional powers are directly concerned only with local security threats, and they are incapable of intervening in other regions without assistance. For the purposes of this analysis, it is assumed that these global powers use access to their military resources as an incentive to obtain concessions on matters relevant to their own interests in the global competition, such as military bases. Since regional powers generally find these concessions costly in political terms, they must find some way to balance the benefits and costs of arms imports and political alignments. In short, regional powers strive to maintain an optimal balance between the benefits of increased security and the political costs expended to attain that security.

This analysis differs in fundamental ways from earlier applications of rational choice theory to regional conflicts. The classic models of Gillespie and Zinnes (1975, 1977) stress the efforts of the superpowers to use levels of foreign aid to control regional arms races (see also Baugh 1978). Here the viewpoint of the regional powers is adopted instead and the focus is on their efforts to use close relationships with the global powers to further their own self-interest. This analysis also differs from standard applications of rational choice theory to international relations. Economists focus on individuals as rational actors, and nearly all rational models in the international relations literature treat states as unitary rational actors. In order to study the combination of domestic and external threats typically confronting Third World states, this chapter investigates an alternative between these two extremes, namely, a unitary "regime" seeking to maintain its hold on power.

This theoretical perspective shares many similarities with the informal analyses of Weinstein (1972), who examines the interrelated goals of external security, economic development, and domestic political competition pursued by the leaders of less developed states, and David (1991), who emphasizes their efforts to balance external and internal security threats.[1] However, further development of these theoretical frameworks requires a more explicit specification of tradeoffs among these multiple goals.

This chapter summarizes this author's mathematical model (McGinnis 1985, 1990) of the security policies of rival regional powers and its implications concerning the consequences of changes in three types of constraints: the threat from the rival, the arms transfer and alignment policies of the global powers, and the nature of each regime's domestic support structure. The consequences of changes in these constraints are illustrated by discussing examples of significant changes in the arms acquisition and alignment policies of three pairs of regional rivals: India and Pakistan, Ethiopia and Somalia, and North and South Korea. The underlying causes of these enduring rivalries include border disputes, ethnic animosities, and challenges to the very legitimacy of the other state's continued existence, but in this chapter the focus is on explaining changes in their arms acquisition and alignment policies.

This analysis of the security policies of regional rivals has important implications for broader issues of continuity and change in foreign policy. In particular, it illustrates the use of rational choice theory to explain foreign policy restructuring. By interpreting foreign policy as the consequence of conscious choice on the part of some "decision-maker," rational choice theory draws attention to several fundamental questions. What is the nature of the "actor" making decisions about foreign policy? Which goals guide the choices made by that actor? What constraints exist, and how do they limit the range of feasible options? The answers to these questions set the context for analysis of change and continuity in policy choice.

Rationality and Foreign Policy Actors

Rational choice theory rests upon several fundamental principles. A rational actor selects the action it perceives most likely to bring about the outcome most preferred among the set of outcomes that are feasible given constraints on resources, time, and information. Utility is a theoretical construct used to summarize the preferences of actors among a set of outcomes, and expected utility combines these preferences with an actor's subjective assessment of the likelihood of each outcome. In short, a rational actor maximizes expected utility.

Many foreign policy analysts would find more familiar a definition in which a rational actor collects and evaluates information on all possible alternative options, estimates the conditional probability that each feasible outcome will result from selection of each option, calculates the expected costs and benefits of each outcome and thus the overall expected utility of each option, and then selects the one option that provides that actor with the highest value of expected utility (see, e.g., Allison 1971). However, this process definition does not capture the essence of the rational choice approach: rational actors optimize, but they do so *under constraints*. If a rational actor faces a limited decision time, or must expend costs in order to acquire or evaluate information, then such an exhaustive evaluation of all options would not be cost-effective. In other words, it would not be rational.

Two separable dimensions of rational choice analysis are often confused. First, rational choice models can be used normatively, as a prescription for a process of choice in decision situations that, ideally, involves all the steps discussed above (Raiffa 1968). Second, rational choice models can serve the theoretical purpose of providing explanations of human behavior. The use of rational models to explain behavior is often confused with a description of that behavior, but explanation and description are different intellectual tasks. Even if no specific individual follows the precepts of normative rational choice theory in making decisions, the rational choice approach provides a powerful theoretical lens that focuses attention on the aggregate consequences of the purposeful behavior of some set of optimizing agents or actors. For example, many useful economic theories typically assume individual households and firms are self-interested maximizers of utility and profit, respectively, and their analysis focuses on the consequences for the market as a whole.

Rational choice theory necessitates specifying the nature of the actors under consideration and the source of their preferences. Both of these tasks are problematic in applications to foreign policy. In this analysis, four different levels of abstraction—individual policymakers, governments (or ruling coalitions), regimes, and states—are distinguished. Most previous applications of rational choice models in the international relations literature treat a state as a unitary rational actor maximizing a collective utility function (see Snidal 1985). The concept of collective utility bears some similarity to the "national interest" prominent in the work of diplomatic historians and other traditional realists, who typically presume that a state's national interest derives from that state's position in the international hierarchy of power and from its geopolitical location. In balance of power models, for example, each state seeks to maximize its resource base (Niou, Ordeshook, and Rose 1989), and in rational models of arms races each state experiences disutility from increases in the rival's military capability and positive utility from increases in its own military capability (Brito 1972).

Rational models can be applied to the behavior of individual policymakers, but to do so would necessitate detailed information on that individual's policy preferences. For analysis pitched at that level of detail, it makes more sense to make use of all available information about the perceptions and beliefs of individual leaders (Herrmann 1988; Mefford 1987). Furthermore, any analysis of the policy outcomes that result from the interaction of rational individuals with different perceptions and interests must deal with the dilemmas identified by social choice theorists, who have demonstrated that any collective choice process can be manipulated to achieve different outcomes, depending on which actors control the agenda or are willing to misrepresent their preferences by voting strategically (Arrow 1963; see Riker 1982). Similar problems of preference aggregation occur for models of state policy as the result of shifting class coalitions or competition among interest groups. The alternative followed here is to postulate the existence of a common interest shared by all elite groups.

Although foreign policy decisions are ultimately taken by specific individuals acting in the name of the state, this does not mean that one must always examine the beliefs and behavior of individual leaders. Any individual who attains a position of major foreign policy responsibility will have been socialized through education and processes of political selection to pursue some set of common goals. Individuals differ in their perception of the national interest, but role expectations reinforce a sense of common interests.

If the national interest is interpreted as a baseline approximation of the preferences of the individual statesmen actually making the pertinent decisions, then the utility being maximized in foreign policy decisions includes individual fluctuations on this underlying collective utility. Under this interpretation, foreign policy optimizes a utility function including both systematic and stochastic (random) components. The systematic component is provided by the national interest, with all other factors, including idiosyncratic influences of individual personalities and the vagaries of agenda manipulation, treated as random. For example, policy changes resulting from the presence of new office holders can be attributed to random fluctuations around this shared national interest. Such changes need not be minor. However, to the extent that the systematic component dominates, it will prove useful to model state behavior as the choice of a unitary actor maximizing some common national interest or collective utility. This justification also clarifies the limits of rational choice analysis, for the presence of individual fluctuations implies that any such representation is approximate at best.

The concept of a geopolitics-based national interest does not suffice for the purposes of examining the security policies of regional rivals. The need to maintain sufficient domestic support to remain in power is an additional source of systemic influences on foreign policy. For this reason, this chapter focuses on a "regime" as a unitary rational actor rather than the state per se. This regime is an actor less all-encompassing than the realist concept of state, in that different domestic political structures within the same geographic/legal entity constitute different regimes within the same state. Any regime must have some support base, some set of influential or powerful groups or individuals willing to provide that regime with the resources (including the intangible resource of legitimacy) it needs to survive and implement its policies. If a state or regime fails to maintain national security it may be eliminated by external forces, but a loss of domestic support could lead to establishment of a new regime within the same state.[2]

Regime means something broader than the current government or ruling coalition. Changes in personnel that leave the fundamental domestic political structure intact are considered as changes of government within an existing regime. Just as two different regimes within the same state will share some of the same geopolitical concerns implied by that state's position in the international system but differ in their domestic support structure, any governmental coalition within an existing regime will share a commitment to maintaining the existing political system even though different governments will draw support from different combinations of domestic groups. Although different governments within the same regime may pursue different policies, all such governments are also likely to share some basic, common interests. This common "regime interest" is used as the basis for the rational choice model of foreign policy change discussed in this chapter.

In summary, this analysis posits a nested sequence of influences on foreign policy. Changes that seem significant at one level may actually be a continuation of existing trends when examined at a higher level of abstraction. The personalities of individual leaders may vary widely, but most leaders drawn from a given coalition of political parties are likely to share some important policy preferences. Although each of the political parties (or other groups) included in the ruling coalition will have its own distinct policy programs, all governments drawn from a given regime will share some basic similarities simply because they all draw their fundamental legitimation from the same domestic structures. Finally, different regimes may place more or less emphasis on domestic versus external security threats, but all regimes will share some basic geopolitical concerns. Different types of policy change are more effectively analyzed at different levels in this sequence, and changes in the security policies of regional rivals are best examined at the level of regimes as unitary rational actors.

This analysis is predicated on the assumption that changes in foreign policy goals attributed to changes in individual leaders or ruling coalitions can be interpreted as random (but not necessarily insignificant) fluctuations around a common "regime interest," which is based on domestic support structures and geopolitical concerns which act as the primary sources of continuity in foreign policy interests. This claim is controversial, and it contrasts most sharply with Rosenau's (1966) assertion that idiosyncratic factors are the primary determinant of the behavior of smaller states.[3] Idiosyncratic factors cannot be ignored, but the dominant explanatory factor is this fundamental tradeoff between external security and domestic support: while seeking to insure security from external threats each regime also tries to avoid undermining its domestic support structure.

Constraints and Policy Change

A realization of the inevitability of tradeoffs stands at the very heart of rational choice theory. By definition, a rational actor selects the feasible option that it believes will provide it with the highest expected utility. Thus, optimal outcomes are jointly determined by an actor's preferences, constraints, and beliefs about the consequences of its actions.[4] If a given rational actor changes its behavior, then something must have changed in order to make that actor prefer the newly selected alternative to the previously optimal action, and the only logical alternatives are changes in its preferences, constraints, or beliefs.

Since preferences are not directly measurable, it is impossible to test any assertion that an actor's behavior has changed because its preferences have changed. Thus, allowing preferences to change is generally considered taboo within the rational choice tradition (see Hogarth and Reder 1986). Economists typically presume that the efficiency of market processes allows analysts to ignore the effects of changing beliefs, since those actors whose behavior is driven by mistaken beliefs will eventually be driven out of the market by more efficient information processors. Processes of selection are unlikely to be so efficient in the realm of foreign policy. Indeed, the consequences of changes in a rational actor's beliefs are currently an area of active research, especially in terms of models of international crises (Morrow 1989; Powell 1990). However, since the effects of changes in information and beliefs can be evaluated only in the context of specific models, this analysis focuses on changes in the constraints facing regional rivals.

This focus on constraint change is standard practice in rational choice analyses. Economists typically relate behavioral changes to observable changes in constraints. For example, individual consumers buy more of a (normal) good when its price decreases or their overall budget expands. At the heart of economic analysis lies this simple idea of comparative statics: a rational actor's behavior can change only if its constraints have changed in such a way as to make the old choice infeasible or to expand the feasible set to include some allocation preferred over the old one (Silberberg 1978).

The constraints relevant to rational choice explanations of foreign policy change vary for actors at different levels of abstraction. In a model including constraints representing the idiosyncratic attributes of individual foreign policymakers, optimal policy outcomes could be expected to change whenever new office holders take power or whenever an individual changes his or her evaluation of the likely consequences of feasible options, whether based on new information or for some idiosyncratic reason. In a model of foreign policy determined by a ruling coalition the relevant constraints would include the voting (or other) strength of alternative coalition partners. Furthermore, in any model of policy competition among multiple actors it is difficult to attach meaning to specific outcomes, since outcomes can change for no discernable reason other than strategic manipulation (Riker 1982). Thus, for rational models of individual policymakers or governmental coalitions, there are far too many potential sources of change to catalog.

The only constraints in the standard realist model that matter are those external to the state and geopolitical in nature. Clearly, a state's geographic location rarely changes, but changes in alliance commitments can be seen as the political analogue to geographic proximity (Siverson and Starr 1990), and alliance configurations play an important role in Bueno de Mesquita's (1981) well-known expected utility model of war initiation decisions.

For regimes one important domestic constraint must also be considered— namely, the nature of its domestic support structure. A revolutionary transformation of domestic political structures imparts new domestic constraints on the post-revolutionary regime's ability to remain in power, but the new regime will share many of the same geopolitical ambitions of the pre-revolutionary regime. The classic example of continuity of national interest before and after a revolutionary regime transformation is the pursuit of access to warm-water ports by Czarist and Soviet regimes. To realists a revolution does not change the essential interests of a state, since the new leaders must share the same (or similar) geopolitical ambitions and concerns. In this interpretation the new regime faces different domestic constraints than its predecessor. In other words, pre- and post-revolutionary regimes share similar interests in maintaining external security and remaining in power, as well as similar geopolitical constraints, though they face fundamentally different domestic constraints.

In summary, policy changes by a rational regime can be attributed to changes in external or internal constraints. The importance of the latter category is most easily recognized after a revolutionary transformation of domestic political structures. For regional rivals the two most important types of external constraints include the magnitude of the security threat from the regional rival and the willingness of the global powers to transfer military or economic resources to that regional power. The remainder of this chapter examines changes in each of these three types of constraints in more detail.

Policy Tradeoffs

In this section the conceptualization of "regime interest" is clarified by explicating the set of interrelated tradeoffs confronting the foreign policymakers of regional rivals (see McGinnis 1985, 1990 for a more detailed representation of these tradeoffs).

Foreign policy involves a wide range of military, diplomatic, political, and economic activities, but analysts and practitioners alike persist in seeking regularity or consistency across policy areas. To the extent that policy consistency exists, changes in different policy areas are driven by common factors. As emphasized by Most and Starr (1984, 1989), rival states need not react in kind to each other's actions but can instead substitute one foreign policy instrument for another. It is widely acknowledged that arms and alliances are the two most important means by which states pursue national security (Morgenthau 1973, 181), and regional powers often obtain access to arms imports through a formal alliance (or more informal alignment) with one of the global powers. Thus, any analysis of the security policies of regional powers must consider relationships between changes in their arms acquisitions and political alignments.

Although military expenditures may have some beneficial effects on economic growth at low levels (Deger and Smith 1983; Looney 1989; Whynes 1979), any resources devoted to military purposes are not available for allocation to other desired goals. Imported weapons can offset these economic opportunity costs by providing "more bang for the buck." However, since suppliers sensitive to the dangers of escalation may restrict resupply during times of crisis or war, recipients are concerned about becoming dependent on the arms supplied by any one source (Catrina 1988). Buying from as many different sources as possible will minimize these dependency costs, since it is unlikely that all suppliers will curtail resupply efforts in unison. However, diversification is not without costs, because the weapons of different suppliers are rarely exactly compatible.

By becoming formally or informally aligned with a global power, a regional power can obtain increased access to arms as well as military and diplomatic support. Global powers frequently use arms transfers and aid as a reward for desired behavior on the part of other states, and they often subsidize purchases of their weapons through economic assistance programs.[5] Close military-security alignments may result in undesirable interference in a regional power's domestic affairs, but any regional power not aligned with one of the global powers may be effectively precluded from obtaining security guarantees, large quantities of weapons, or even small quantities of highly sophisticated weapons.

Global powers are primarily interested in matters directly pertaining to their own global competition, such as insuring continued access to export markets or oil and other strategic materials, obtaining bases and other facilities in geostrategically important areas (Fukuyama 1986; Harkavy 1982), or, more generally, countering any gains made by their global rivals in that region or in neighboring regions. Conversely, a regional power is primarily concerned with obtaining military resources that it can use in regional confrontations. There is no reason to expect that conflicts at these two levels necessarily coincide or reinforce each other. This inherent divergence in the concerns of regional and global powers provides an opportunity for mutually beneficial exchanges, in which a regional power offers concessions relevant to the global power competition in exchange for access to the military resources of the global powers. In other words, alignment concessions are "traded" for access to arms, aid, and allies, and global power "access policies" determine the amount of security benefits that a regional power receives for given levels of alignment concessions.

Benefits from these exchanges are unlikely to be distributed equally. Although regional powers can influence their level of access by making additional concessions or through such bargaining stratagems as threatening to switch alignment or buy arms from other suppliers, the overall contours of these "terms of trade" are primarily set by the global powers themselves, and for reasons exogenous to any specific regional rivalry system. Despite their limited success in past efforts to employ arms sales and foreign aid as a means of gaining influence (Rubinstein 1977, 1982), suppliers continue to justify arms sales and foreign aid in exactly these terms.

A regional power will react to the opportunities provided by global power access policies according to its assessment of the relative benefits and costs of alignment with each global power. One global power may offer access to more and better weapons on more generous economic terms. A regional power's concerns about falling under global power domination can be minimized by choosing the most geographically distant global power. Offering bases or other concessions to a global power can undermine the regime's domestic support if these concessions are seen as an unnecessary sacrifice of national autonomy, but these costs are ameliorated to the extent that a given global power is attractive to important elements of the regime's domestic support base. In sum, a rational regional power will, when choosing an alignment partner, prefer the most generous, geographically distant, and ideologically compatible global power. Since these criteria are unlikely to coincide in general, ideologically disparate global and regional powers may become aligned with each other. In other words, ideological compatibility influences but does not by itself determine the alignment and arms import decisions of regional powers (see also Walt 1987).

To further complicate matters, some regional powers may experience direct benefits from alignment, in addition to any contribution to its external security. Foreign powers may play a major role in providing the tangible resources a regime needs to remain in power. Global powers may also set an inspirational example or help establish an institutional structure (like a paramilitary force or a Marxist-Leninist party) through which the regime can exert its authority (MacFarlane 1985). The contribution of alignment to domestic security may result in net benefits rather than costs for some regimes, yet even alignment-seeking regimes may find themselves forced by national security considerations to become more closely aligned than they would otherwise prefer.

This argument reveals a hidden similarity between realist and dependency theory approaches to small state behavior. Whereas for realists, alliance choices are dictated by each state's search for increased security, dependency theorists insist that political alignments derive from asymmetric economic relationships of dependency. As Moon (1983, 321) summarizes, "a dependent relationship generates distortions in the social and political system of the weaker state which brings to power an elite whose interests, values, and perceptions have more in common with elites of the powerful nation than with the masses in their own country" (see also Galtung 1971). In an explicit comparison of dependency and realist-based bargaining models of small state behavior, Moon (1983) concludes his dependency model better explains U.N. voting behavior. However, this difference can be attributed to his inclusion of arms transfers only in the dependency model, even though arms transfers play a prominent role in bargaining between regional and global powers.

It is impossible to justify any clear distinction between a dependency and bargaining model, since bargainers can choose to incur greater or smaller dependency costs and dependent states have room to bargain (as long as they are not totally under the control of an external power). Convergence of economic interests may indeed make a given level of security alignment less distasteful, but no amount of convergence of economic interests will insure a similar convergence of the security interests of global and regional powers. Thus, economically dependent states should not be expected to always follow their patron's lead in political and security matters, because their security interests need not coincide. Both ideological and security concerns matter in alignment decisions, but neither is dominant in all circumstances.

In summary, regional powers confront a series of interrelated tradeoffs among the benefits and costs of military expenditures, arms imports, and political alignments. Each regional power can increase its security by obtaining access to the arms produced by a global power, and this access is facilitated by making political or military concessions to that global power. However, arms imports and political alignments also involve political costs. As a rational actor, each regional power must balance the costs and benefits it derives from allocation of its economic and political resources.

Explaining Changes in Arms Acquisitions and Alignments

Even without specification of a particular model one immediate implication is that different patterns of arms acquisitions and alignments will be optimal for regimes with different domestic support structures facing different levels of external threat in the context of different global power access policies. However, the relationship between overall patterns of foreign policy and these external and internal factors is extremely complex. Analysis is greatly facilitated by shifting the focus to *changes* in these policies, that is, by application of the logic of comparative statics.

As discussed earlier, changes in a rational regime's optimal security policy must be related to changes in one or more of the constraints it faces. In another study, comparative statics techniques are used to derive formal hypotheses relating changes in constraints to changes in the arms acquisitions and alignments of regional powers (McGinnis 1985, 1990). These hypotheses can be summarized as follows:

1. An increased security threat from the rival (or other threats exogenous to the regional rivalry system) can lead to increases in military expenditures, arms imports, and/or alignment concessions.

2. Changes in a global power's access policies that improve the "terms of trade" of access to military resources per alignment concessions can result in an increased reliance on arms transfers from that global power, an increase in alignment concessions, and a concomitant decrease in alignment with other global powers.
3. A significant transformation of a regional power's domestic support base away from the ideology of its global power patron makes continued alignment with that global power very unlikely, with alignment reversal the most natural result.

In the remainder of this chapter each of these relationships between constraint and policy changes is illustrated by discussing examples of significant changes in the arms acquisitions and alignments of the regional rivals India and Pakistan, Ethiopia and Somalia, and North and South Korea. Instead of providing a standard chronological description of each case, these theoretical relationships are highlighted by organizing discussion around the type of constraint change involved. Each of the specific policy changes discussed below is listed in table 4.1, along with the type of constraint change most relevant to an explanation of that policy change.

Changes in Threat Levels and Access Policies

Whenever one state in a region obtains access to some new weapons system, its neighbors usually seek similar or off-setting weapons systems from the same or alternative sources. Although rival states should be expected to react to any increase in the other's military capability, they need not react in kind (Most and Starr 1984, 1989). For example, in 1961 North Korea signed separate mutual defense treaties with both the Soviet Union and China, and its desire for these public affirmations of support has been attributed to a perceived increase in the security threat posed by the military regime that had just seized power in the South (Shinn 1973, 60; see Chung 1978, 56–57 for an alternative explanation). Furthermore, some changes in security policy can be attributed to security threats from sources other than their primary regional rival. For example, India fared poorly in its brief border war with China in 1962, and in response to this dramatic loss of its perceived security, India doubled its military expenditures during the years 1962 to 1963 (Stockholm International Peace Research Institute 1971, 474). Policy changes can also be taken in expectation of future threats, as in the Treaty of Peace, Friendship, and Cooperation India signed with the Soviet Union in 1971, a treaty widely interpreted as a quasi-military alliance directed against possible Chinese intervention in the upcoming Bangladesh War (Tahir-Kheli 1982, 39–40).

Budget constraints play a prominent role in economic applications of rational choice models, but the effects of this constraint are not very interesting in the present context.[6] Any increase in a state's economic resources will provide it with more money to spend on all its goals, including arms, but whether or not

Table 4.1. **Significant Changes in Arms Acquisitions and Alignments**

India-Pakistan

Pakistan	1954–55	U.S. alliances, Peshawar intelligence base	Access Policies
India	1962–63	Military budget doubled	Exogenous Threat
India	1965	Shift to emphasis on Soviet arms	Access Policies
Pakistan	1965–68	Diversify suppliers, expel U.S. from Peshawar	Access Policies
India	1971	Soviet Treaty of Friendship	Regional Threat
Pakistan	1980	Support Afghan rebels, U.S. aid increases	Access Policies

Ethiopia-Somalia

Ethiopia	1953	U.S. aid agreement, Kagnew intelligence base	Access Policies
Somalia	1963	Reliance on Soviet arms	Access Policies
Somalia	1974	Soviet Treaty of Friendship, Berbera base	Access Policies
Ethiopia	1976	First major Soviet arms purchase	Regional Threat, Access Policies, Domestic Support
Ethiopia	1977	U.S. arms embargo, vacate Kagnew base	Access Policies, Domestic Support
Somalia	1977	Renounce treaty, expel Soviets from Berbera	Access Policies
Ethiopia	1978	Soviet Treaty of Friendship, Dahlak base	Regional Threat, Access Policies, Domestic Support
Somalia	1980	U.S. aid, access to Berbera base	Access Policies

North Korea-South Korea

N. Korea	1961	Defense treaties with Soviet Union and China	Regional Threat
N. Korea	1962	Support Chinese position, no Soviet aid	Domestic Support
N. Korea	1965	Support Soviet position, little Chinese aid	Access Policies
N. Korea	1967	Major increase in military budget, "subversive" acts	Domestic Support
N. Korea	1969	Policy of "equidistance"	Access Policies
S. Korea	1971	Some U.S. troops withdrawn, increased military aid	Access Policies

the state will then spend proportionally more or less on domestic production of arms or imported arms cannot be determined in general. This is not to say that economics do not matter, for states with larger economic bases are more likely to develop an indigenous arms production capability. Although economic development may enable one regional power to meet much of its security needs through domestic production, these gains may be offset if its rival manages to obtain more sophisticated weapons from a global power.

The regional rivalry between India and Pakistan illustrates the consequences of unequal size.[7] In the 1950s India and Pakistan adopted dramatically different stances towards the global competition between the superpowers. Nehru's India played a leading role in the nonaligned movement, and began diversifying its arms purchases with its first Soviet arms purchase in 1955 (Chari 1979, 232). The smaller state of Pakistan was unable to match India on its own, and in 1954 to 1955 Pakistan joined the South East Asia Treaty Organization (SEATO) and the Baghdad Pact, granted the United States an intelligence base at Peshawar, and received extensive arms transfers and military aid. Pakistan was taking advantage of the opportunity presented by U.S. interest in regional security pacts, but this U.S.-Pakistan security relationship would prove a classic case of regional-global power misunderstanding. The United States saw Pakistan as one link in its worldwide containment strategy, but Pakistan was primarily interested in U.S. support for its confrontations with India (Tahir-Kheli 1982).

Not all global-regional power relationships are so ill-fated. In 1953 Ethiopia began receiving military aid and arms in return for granting the United States an intelligence and communications facility at Kagnew, thus instituting an enduring and mutually beneficial relationship (Ottaway 1982). Similarly, South Korea remained intimately dependent on U.S. support and arms, beginning with the quick U.S. response to the North Korean invasion in 1950 and maintained after the war through the 1953 Mutual Defense Treaty and the permanent stationing of some sixty thousand U.S. troops in South Korea. About a third of these troops were withdrawn beginning in 1971, with the South Koreans compensated by American financing of a major military modernization program. This change in emphasis was part of the Nixon Doctrine, intended to transfer more responsibility for Western defenses to powerful regional allies (Han 1983a).

This change in U.S. arms transfer policy is an example of access policies acting as exogenous constraints on the regional rivalry system. A global power more concerned about a given region will, in general, offer higher levels of access to states in that region than to states in other regions. Consider the security relationship between India and the Soviet Union. During the Indo-Chinese War of 1962 both the United States and the Soviet Union rushed aid to India, but the Western arms embargo on India and Pakistan in 1965 convinced India to concentrate on Soviet arms. Soviet willingness to offer very attractive terms to keep India as its only major noncommunist arms customer was a major factor contributing to India's successful development of a significant indigenous arms production capacity (Chari 1979; Singh 1984). Nonetheless, India continued to buy arms from Western suppliers as well as receive Western economic aid, and even the dramatic change to the Janata coalition resulted in only a minor shift in emphasis on importation of Western arms (Singh 1984, 715).

Global power access polices occasionally set severe limits on the feasible options of regional rivals, as when one global power refuses (for whatever reason) to sell a regional power any of its arms. At the time of its independence in 1960, Somalia had to contend with a preexisting relationship between the United States and Ethiopia. The United States and other Western powers refused Somalia access to the level of arms it wanted, for Somalia had made clear its intention to gain control over lands in Ethiopia, Kenya, and French Somaliland (now Djibouti) populated by ethnic Somalis. The Soviets proved willing to supply significant quantities of weapons to Somalia (*Keesing's Contemporary Archives* 1963, 1977), even though it made no significant alignment concessions at this time. Furthermore, the Somalis sought to limit their dependence on the Soviet Union by relying on Western sources to equip their police forces (Ottaway 1982, 57).

The relative access offered by global powers can change as a result of exogenous influences, especially as one global power seeks to redress a loss of its influence in a neighboring region. After expelling the Soviets in 1978 from the naval base at Berbera, Somalia offered this same base to the United States if it would provide arms and aid. The Carter administration declined, for fear of being seen as rewarding Somalia for its attack on Ethiopia that began the Ogaden War, but the same administration accepted a similar deal in 1980. This policy reversal was prompted not by Somali repentance but rather by widespread U.S. concern with its recent losses in Iran and the Soviet advance into Afghanistan (Petterson 1985).

Some regional powers can occasionally forestall threatened changes in its global patron's policies. President Carter's 1977 announcement that all U.S. troops would be eventually withdrawn from South Korea engendered opposition in South Korea and within the United States. This decision was never implemented but instead resulted in American financing of South Korean military modernization (Han 1983a, 215–16). More generally, some regional powers can improve their bargaining position by establishing a relationship with influential domestic groups within the global power (Keohane 1971; Park 1975).

Changes in global power access policies often seem arbitrary and unfair to the regional power recipients. The United States and other Western powers imposed an arms embargo on both India and Pakistan during their 1965 war over Kashmir. Ostensibly this was an even-handed approach, but Pakistan was considerably more dependent on Western arms than was India. Once Pakistan came to realize the limits of U.S. support, the low security benefits no longer offset the alignment costs and Pakistan expelled the United States from Peshawar in 1968. Pakistan then adopted an official policy of nonalignment,[8] getting arms from China and elsewhere, including significant levels of economic support from other Islamic states. United States-Pakistan relations remained sour until the Soviet intervention in Afghanistan in 1979 made the United States much more interested in a closer relationship. Pakistan's President Zia, after initially rejecting a modest aid package from the Carter administration as "peanuts," accepted a more generous aid program and allowed the support of Afghan rebels through Pakistan's territory (Wriggins 1987).

Transformation of Domestic Support Structures

The ideological component of U.S.-Soviet security competition in a cold war context implied that changes in a regime's domestic support structure can greatly complicate an ongoing regional-global power relationship. Consider the consequences of revolution in a regional power closely aligned with one of the global powers. No matter what the original impetus for revolutionary activity, a high priority for the new regime will be to distance itself from the policies of the previous regime, especially its dependence on foreign support. However, the regional rivalry will not, in general, have been mitigated by that revolution, and it may indeed be aggravated by the temptation revolutionary unrest often provides for external intervention. Thus, nonalignment may be undesirable because it would result in a lower level of military capability than that possessed by the pre-revolutionary regime, which had access to the arms and support of its global power patron. As a consequence, the new regime may find itself forced to accept the political costs of dependence and alignment in order to meet the continuing regional security threat. Given the costs associated with continued alignment with the same global power, however, the option most likely to be optimal for a post-revolutionary regime is to change its alignment to another global power.

A brief examination of Iran's transformation from a U.S. "client" to a nonaligned state illustrates the nature and limitations of this argument. In this case alignment reversal was not attractive to an Islamic regime that exhibited intense distaste of both the "Great Satan" United States and the "atheistic" Soviet Union that had occupied parts of Iran after World War II. Also, the Shah had built Iran's military capability to such a high level that the new nonaligned regime found its lower military capability sufficient to repulse the Iraqi attack (Segal 1988). Thus, alignment reversal did not occur because this case does not satisfy all the conditions implicit in the preceding argument about alignment reversal.

An example that more closely satisfies these conditions is post-revolutionary Ethiopia.[9] By 1976 Mengistu had emerged as the leader of a Marxist-Leninist regime sorely beset by internal unrest from several sources. Ethiopia tried to maintain access to U.S. arms and military aid, but also signed a major arms agreement with the Soviets in December 1976. Ethiopian alignment concessions to the United States were not repudiated until April 1977, when the United States vacated the Kagnew base. Despite reluctance to lose its close relationship with Ethiopia, the United States had become increasingly concerned about the policies undertaken by this radical regime (David 1979, 74–75).

The military situation deteriorated dramatically when the Somali army invaded in July 1977, producing a situation in which the Soviet Union was the predominant arms supplier to both sides. (The United States imposed an arms embargo on Ethiopia in September 1977 after earlier slowing deliveries of already purchased arms.) After an abortive effort at mediation, the Soviets shut off all arms supplies to Somalia in August 1977.[10] Somalia retaliated by abrogating their friendship treaty and ordering the Soviets out of the Berbera base in November 1977. Massive amounts of Soviet arms and aid and thousands of Cuban troops turned the tide in favor of the Mengistu regime (Porter 1984, 182–215), a relationship cemented by the November 1978 Treaty of Peace, Friendship, and Cooperation and Soviet naval access to the Dahlak Islands. This last change was driven by Soviet interests in obtaining some tangible reward for their assistance in saving the new Ethiopian regime.[11]

Each step in Ethiopia's alignment reversal demonstrates an attempt to obtain maximum military resources to deal with continuing domestic and external security threats, tempered by an ideological distaste for continued reliance on American assistance. A significant change in Ethiopia's domestic support structure coupled with a high security threat induced Ethiopia to shift to Soviet alignment. When the Soviets denied Somalia continued access to its military resources, the Somalis attempted, and later accomplished, a shift to the U.S. camp, but at a level of support too low to sustain direct confrontation. Although this case illustrates the importance of global power access constraints in shaping regional power behavior, global power policies clearly do not tell the whole story, as evidenced by the abject failure of a regional peace plan promoted by the Soviets.

Not all changes in regime can be profitably interpreted in this manner. Consider earlier events in the Horn of Africa. A brief period of improving relations within this region was disrupted by a military coup in Somalia in 1969. In 1974 this military regime obtained access to significantly higher levels of Soviet arms by signing a Treaty of Peace, Friendship, and Cooperation with the Soviet Union which included a significant concession allowing Soviet construction of a naval base at Berbera (Ottaway 1982, 41). Although this move might be attributed to the self-avowed "scientific socialism" of Siad Barre's regime, Somalia was too far from a Marxist-Leninist state for differential distaste for alignments to be a significant factor. This military regime may indeed have been more attracted to a military solution to the Ogaden problem (Ottaway 1982, 41), but the most convincing explanation for the timing of this exchange was the Soviet desire for a base in the area to offset their loss of access to Alexandria after Egyptian President Sadat's expulsion of Soviet advisors in 1972. Somalia simply took advantage of this opportunity to augment its military capability at the expense of Ethiopia.

Furthermore, political alignments between regional and global powers need not impose high costs to the regional power. India's 1971 Treaty of Peace, Friendship, and Cooperation with the Soviet Union approximated a military alliance directed against possible Chinese intervention, but it did not involve Soviet troops or bases (Tahir-Kheli 1982, 39–40). The Soviets have always accorded special treatment to India, which attaches high political costs to any alignment concessions that undermine its leadership role in the nonaligned movement.

Ideological Alignment and Domestic Legitimacy

In summary, all three categories of constraint change prove relevant in explaining these instances of significant change in the arms acquisitions and alignments of these three pairs of regional rivals. This same theoretical framework can be applied to nonsecurity issues, in particular, the ideological positions generally taken to define North Korea's changing alignment in the Sino-Soviet dispute.[12]

The North Korean regime of Kim il-Sung was originally established under Soviet occupation, and in 1950 U.S. leaders universally blamed Stalin for North Korea's invasion of South Korea. This attitude is epitomized in the acerbic comment attributed to Assistant Secretary of State Edward W. Barnett: "The relationship between the Soviet Union and the North Koreans is the same as that between Walt Disney and Donald Duck" (Stoessinger 1985, 61). Later historians attribute more of the responsibility for this attack to Kim il-Sung (Simmons 1975; Merrill 1989). In any event, during the war Chinese "volunteers" pushed U.S. and U.N. forces back from the Yalu River, and some Chinese troops stayed until 1958 to help in North Korean reconstruction, thus further distancing North Korea from direct Soviet control. Since that time North Korea has vacillated between these two communist powers, at times tilting closer to one but usually obtaining some arms and aid from both.

Although the intensely secretive nature of this regime makes it extremely difficult to obtain reliable information about even basic aspects of North Korean policies, there is a considerable degree of scholarly consensus on certain changes in these policies.[13] North Korea is consistently portrayed as closely siding with the Chinese position during 1962 to 1964, and the Soviets cut off all economic aid during these years (Zagoria 1983, 351). This "tilt" toward China is usually explained with reference to Khrushchev's de-Stalinization program. Close association with the Soviets during these years could have undercut the ideological legitimacy of Kim il-Sung's personal rule in North Korea; in the terms of the present analysis, siding with China involved lower alignment costs.

By 1965 North Korean relations with the Soviets had improved as China began its long preoccupation with the domestic upheaval of the Cultural Revolution. During these years no aid of any type was forthcoming from China, and so North Korea sought Soviet aid as the only viable alternative. However, Kim's earlier experiences with Soviet efforts to establish colonial control over North Korea inspired him to keep this alignment strictly limited (Zagoria 1983, 357–58). By 1969 Chinese-North Korean relations improved, and North Korea sought to maintain balance (or "equidistance") between its two neighboring communist powers. Although Hunter (1980) purports to discern a continuing pattern of regular swings in North Korean policy between the Soviet Union and China, none of these later moves involve any indications as clear as those of earlier periods (Ginsburgs and Kim 1977, 2).

Each supplier has provided only low levels of aid in recent years, which suggests that neither wants to encourage a repetition of North Korea's disruptive behavior, most noticeable in the late 1960s. North Korea significantly increased its military expenditures around 1967 and concurrently increased the quantity and intensity of its "subversive acts" directed against the South (Shinn 1973, 60–61). These acts included the construction of tunnels under the demilitarized zone (DMZ), the dispatch of a thirty-man commando squad sent to assassinate South Korean President Park, and the seizure of the USS Pueblo. Several interpretations of these efforts have been offered (Han 1983b, 159), but one common theme in these analyses is that Kim il-Sung was using external tension to tighten internal control in the North (Shinn 1973, 68). Despite a general realization that this aggressive policy was later reversed, there is no agreement as to when or why.

A consistent explanation for the various major and minor shifts in North Korea's ideological position is simply that "North Korea reacted to policies adopted by the Soviet Union and China on the basis of whether these policies were in its perceived interest or not" (Bernstein and Nathan 1983, 100). Thus, the theoretical perspective on military alignment outlined earlier proves equally relevant to explanations of the effects of ideological alignment on a regime's domestic legitimacy.

Summary of Case Studies

The last column of table 4.1 lists the type of constraint change most closely associated with each of the significant changes in arms acquisitions or alignments for the cases of regional rivalry discussed above. In some instances more than one constraint change is involved in the description, but only the type of change that constitutes the most important factor in each instance is listed. Before discussing the implications of this analysis, the patterns of change and continuity revealed in these case studies are recapitulated.

Throughout the period North Korea vacillated between the Soviet Union and China, this regime was apparently preoccupied with maintaining its domestic legitimacy. Meanwhile, South Korea obtained increased U.S. military aid as a result of various changes in U.S. access policy. The early South Asian pattern of Pakistani alignment with the United States and Indian nonalignment was upset by Western and Soviet efforts to improve their relations with India. In response Pakistan diversified its sources as best it could, while India developed an impressive military force based increasingly on indigenous production. Soviet intervention in Afghanistan temporarily moved the United States and Pakistan closer together, but many sources of tension continue to mar this relationship. Even more dramatic changes were apparent in the Horn of Africa. Somalia initially relied on Soviet arms supplies because of the close relationship between the United States and Ethiopia. A growing sense of mutual distaste gradually eroded this latter relationship after the Ethiopian revolution. During the Ogaden War the Soviets punished their Somali client for attacking their new Ethiopian client. As the United States and Somalia slowly developed a closer relationship, a remarkable reversal of alignments was completed.

More recently, internal unrest has resulted in the violent overthrow of both the Ethiopian and Somali regimes, and a recent upsurge in ethnic conflict in both India and Pakistan clouds their prospects for future stability. (Another war over Kashmir was apparently only narrowly averted in 1990.) Finally, fears of nuclear proliferation have complicated the evolving relationship between the two Korean regimes. Despite the end of the cold war, the underlying regional sources of these conflicts remain unresolved.

Implications

This chapter concludes by assessing the implications of this analysis for two basic questions about rational choice and foreign policy change. First, what does rational choice theory reveal about these cases of foreign policy change that analysts did not know (or would not fully appreciate) before? Second, what do these examples of foreign policy change reveal about rational choice theory?

With regard to the first question, the most important point is that a theoretical focus on tradeoffs among regional security concerns and economic and political costs brought a unity of explanation to cases that would otherwise have seemed entirely unrelated. With the somewhat ambiguous exception of India's reaction to continuing security threats from China, each of the significant changes in the arms acquisitions and alignments of these regional powers identified above can be explained as a natural consequence of changes in the three types of constraints identified earlier: security threats from their regional rival, global power access policies, and the transformation or manipulation of domestic support structures.

At first glance it may be difficult to believe that any single explanation could sufficiently encompass the diverse patterns of security policies of this disparate group of Third World states. No standard single-factor explanation is conceivable, since these six states run the gamut on all relevant political and economic attribute dimensions. They range from small, ethnically homogeneous Somalia to large, ethnically heterogeneous India; from the brutally poor states of Somalia and Ethiopia to the relatively prosperous newly industrializing country of South Korea; and they include such disparate political systems as communist North Korea and post-revolutionary Ethiopia, democratic India, authoritarian regimes and military dictatorships in Somalia, Pakistan, and South Korea, as well as the essentially feudal system that existed in imperial Ethiopia. The only attribute these states share in common is the persistence of regional rivalry.

The analysis reported here suggests that the diverse security policies adopted by these disparate regimes amount to different manifestations of the same underlying logic of regional security concerns filtered through differing political, economic, ideological, and arms supply constraints. Frankly, once these three cases have been examined as instances of a single phenomenon it becomes difficult to remember just how unique each case looks from a more traditional perspective.

In answer to the second question, these examples clarify the limitations of rational choice theory. A certain looseness of interpretation is inherent in the interconnected nature of arms acquisitions and political alignments, as well as the slippery logical basis of a regime as a unitary rational actor. More specificity could be imposed via precise utility functions and resource constraints, but any such models would necessarily be based on arbitrary restrictions. The complexity of foreign policymaking processes challenges analysts to develop indirect tests of more general models that incorporate the implications of policy substitutability and other subtle relationships (Most and Starr 1989; McGinnis 1991).

One surprising finding from this qualitative analysis is the relative absence of direct reactions to the rival's behavior. Of the twenty-one significant policy changes listed in table 4.1, only three are best explained by changes in the security threat posed by the rival. Furthermore, dramatic increases in one regional power's military capability are rarely followed by easily identifiable changes in the rival's polices. Two plausible explanations suggest themselves. First, since rival states often adopt very different arms acquisition and alignment policies, their reactions may take very different forms. For example, a relatively minor increase in one state's arms imports might suffice to counter a more dramatic increase in its rival's domestic arms production. As a consequence, only rarely are changes in both states' policies equally discernable. A second explanation is that rivalry is a pervasive and ever present aspect of the decision environment of these states that shapes their policies in more subtle ways than could be detected in this analysis.[14] By focusing solely on dramatic changes much of the reaction characterizing more normal circumstances may have been overlooked. In other words, this analysis may underestimate the importance of continuity in the security policies of rival states.

On the other hand, if these results indicate an undue emphasis on regional rivalry per se, then this theoretical framework may prove more broadly applicable than originally expected. Even in the absence of an enduring regional rivalry, the same factors of global power constraints and economic and political opportunity costs should shape the pursuit of more diffuse (or multilayered) security concerns by smaller states in general.

Integration of domestic, regional, and global conflict remains a challenging task for future research. More elaborate analyses could include persistent domestic security threats, as in India, Pakistan, and Ethiopia. Many of the changes in global power access policies identified in this analysis were driven by events in neighboring regions, including Soviet losses in Egypt and U.S. losses in Iran, and a more complete representation of the global rivalry between the superpowers would be needed to model these cross-regional effects. Another cross-regional connection is that Third World states such as Brazil and North Korea have each become important arms exporters in their own right. The general increase in weapons sources may limit the superpowers' ability to control future regional conflicts through restraints on shipments of spare parts and ammunition.[15]

These cases clearly demonstrate the significance of changes in global power access policies, which prove most influential in fully two-thirds of the examples listed in table 4.1. The cases discussed here also demonstrate that regional powers react to changes in their decision environment so as to best serve their own interests, consistent with a rational actor approach to the analysis of foreign policy change. Changes in constraints are necessarily the most important determinant of changes in the behavior of any rational actor, and it should hardly be surprising that *political* constraints such as those embodied in global power access policies prove so important to explanations of the behavior of the political actors examined here.

For too long foreign policy analysts have assumed that the foreign policies of smaller states are less comprehensible than those of great powers. This attitude was immortalized in British Foreign Secretary Lord Salisbury's exasperation at the assertive behavior of the newly independent Balkan states during the Congress of Berlin: "At Potsdam there are mosquitos—Here there are minor powers. I don't know which is worse" (Cecil 1921, 2:288). By identifying the basic logic underlying the diverse security policies of regional powers, the analysis presented here suggests a revision of the maxim that "the strong do what they can and the weak suffer what they must" (Thucydides 1982, 351). Regional powers manage to do the best they can for themselves, subject to a complex but understandable interplay of the constraints of external security and domestic politics and the opportunities provided by competition between the world's most powerful states. Even if all the world's major powers manage to cooperate in restraining arms transfers to volatile regions, the interests and activities of smaller powers could not be ignored.

Notes

1. For general conceptual frameworks for analyzing small power behavior, each very different from the others, see Buzan and Rizvi (1986); Clapham (1985); Kolodziej and Harkavy (1982); Handel (1981); Mares (1988); Razi (1988); Rothstein (1968); Shoemaker (1981); Singer (1972); Väyrynen (1984).
2. For related conceptualizations of the state's interrelated roles in domestic and international politics, see Mastanduno, Lake, and Ikenberry (1989); Putnam (1988); Tsebelis (1990).
3. See Korany (1983); Papadakis and Starr (1987); and Weinstein (1972) for critiques of the relevance of Rosenau's pre-theory to small state behavior.
4. Institutional or cognitive deviations from the rational model may also be involved; whether these "inefficiencies" invalidate the rational choice approach or merely provide additional constraints on rational behavior remains a matter of lively debate; see Hogarth and Reder (1986).
5. This presumption that global powers use arms transfers for political purposes is based on the "hegemonic" type of arms supplier discussed in Stockholm International Peace Research Institute (1971). Other suppliers (notably France) may provide fairly sophisticated weapons on a strictly cash basis, with no political

strings attached. For overviews of the arms trade, see Brzoska and Ohlson (1987) and Catrina (1988).

6. Economic constraints would play a more important role in, say, analysis of the arms acquisitions of OPEC members after the oil price increases in the 1970s.

7. My interpretation of the conflict between India and Pakistan is based on the analyses of Barnds (1972); Burke (1979); Choudhury (1975); Horn (1982); Tahir-Kheli (1982); Thomas (1983, 1986); and Ziring (1982).

8. Pakistan remained a member of SEATO until after its loss of East Pakistan in 1971 and of CENTO until its final dissolution after the Iranian Revolution in 1979, but neither of these alliances involved meaningful concessions on Pakistan's part. Also, the 1959 U.S.-Pakistan bilateral security agreement ostensibly remains in effect, albeit as an unratified executive agreement. Nonetheless, Pakistan's clearly distanced itself from the United States in the late 1960s. This example illustrates the dangers of strict reliance on any single indicator of alignment, since formal alliance membership alone would be misleading in this case.

9. On the regional sources of the Ethiopian-Somali conflict, see Zartman (1985, 71–117) and Touval (1972). For U.S. and Soviet roles in this region, see Ottaway (1982); Makinda (1987); and David (1979).

10. Analysts differ over whether the Soviets were willing to sacrifice Somalia to gain the larger and more influential Ethiopia as a client (Porter 1984, 182–215; Gavshon 1981, 258–85) or whether regional events simply prevented the Soviets from maintaining good relations with both states (Ottaway 1982, 161–74; Makinda 1987, 118–23).

11. This concession of the right to anchor dry-dock facilities off the Dahlak Islands may be considerably less than the Soviets sought to offset the loss of the Berbera base (Ottaway 1982, 149). Also, the Soviets were intent on convincing Mengistu to transform his regime into a Marxist-Leninist vanguard party, with questionable success (Makinda 1987, 183–88).

12. Sino-Soviet rivalry also involves security and territorial aspects, but North Korea has remained aloof from these nonideological aspects. Its precarious geographical position on the borders of both communist powers signifies the danger involved in any concrete concession that threatens the security of either of these states (Bernstein and Nathan 1983, 121).

13. My interpretation of North Korean foreign policies is based on the analyses of Bernstein and Nathan (1983); Chung (1978); Han (1983b); Koh (1984); Park (1984); Park, Koh, and Kwak (1987); Scalapino and Kim (1983); and Zagoria and Kim (1976).

14. This lack of explicit reaction is reminiscent of a similarly puzzling failure of statistical tests to detect reaction to external threats in generally accepted cases of arms races (Moll and Luebbert 1980; Russett 1983; Zinnes 1980; McGinnis 1991). For example, Williams and McGinnis (1988) argue that the superpower rivalry system is so pervasive that more indirect evidence must be examined.

15. Neuman (1986) argues that the United States and the Soviet Union maintained important advantages over other suppliers, and that they continued to use these advantages to influence their regional clients.

Chapter 5

Exploiting the Seams
External Structure and Libyan Foreign Policy Changes

Martin W. Sampson III

Martin Sampson focuses his analysis on the restructuring of foreign policy in a small state. Traditional scholarship in international relations assumes that small states have few meaningful foreign policy choices and that significant foreign policy restructuring in noncore states is largely derivative of structural forces in the global system. Sampson's assessment of Libyan foreign policy since its independence, however, leads him to express concerns akin to those of Skidmore and McGinnis and pose important questions regarding the limitations of conventional assumptions about foreign policy change in small states. Specifically, Sampson examines the policies of the King Idris era (1951 to 1969) and the early Muammar Qadhdhafi era (1969 to 1985). Besides finding that both eras provide examples of Libya playing a more significant role in international affairs than one would expect of a small state, Sampson also points to a larger issue concerning the predictability of foreign policy change in small states. According to Sampson, it is not that the international structure arguments are wholly incorrect; rather, it is that such arguments often presume a more limited scope for state policy choice than actually exists. In short, Sampson's analysis raises some insightful questions concerning the ability of states to exploit the seams of international structures which, when considered, generate a better understanding of the dynamics of foreign policy change.

Martin Sampson is associate professor in the Department of Political Science and director of International Relations at the University of Minnesota. He received a Ph.D in political science from Indiana University in 1979 and a B.A. from Cornell University in 1966. He spent five years in the Peace Corps, including three years in Libya. His research interests include the study of U.S. and comparative foreign policy and the politics of the Middle East. He is the author of International Policy Coordination: A Game Theoretic Study of OPEC and EACM, *and his work also has appeared in such journals as* Behavioral Science *and* Journal of Conflict Resolution. *His more recent work focuses on the role of culture in foreign policy and the foreign policy of Turkey.*

The author thanks Deborah Gerner, two anonymous reviewers, and Jerel Rosati for comments on earlier versions of this chapter.

"Libyan foreign policy" is a phrase that in many people prompts immediate thoughts of Muammar Qadhdhafi. Assessments of Libyan foreign policy change, of startling policy innovation, and of a foreign policy venturing in surprising directions accordingly would be expected to focus on Qadhdhafi's era, which began in 1969. Certainly it is after that 1969 change of leadership that Libya achieved an international reputation for an idiosyncratic foreign policy.

The following assessment of Libyan foreign policy change does not sustain this conventional wisdom. It argues that crucial foreign policy change occurred in the era of King Idris, who ruled Libya from 1951 to 1969, creatively establishing a foundation for a series of subsequent policy changes. Later initiatives drew upon the success of earlier changes, making the demarcation between the Idris and Qadhdhafi eras less clear than might be expected. Indeed, Libyan foreign policy displayed a pattern of unlikely continuities and innovative changes throughout the post-independence period, despite the dramatic change in leadership. Perhaps more startling, *both* the Idris era and the Qadhdhafi era are periods in which Libya played a more significant role in international affairs than one would expect of a country with Libya's resources, a puzzle that cannot be adequately addressed by consideration of only the Qadhdhafi era. This puzzle is of historical interest, but it also points to a larger puzzle concerning the predictability of foreign policy change and its content.

This chapter seeks to make two contributions. First, it offers an interpretation of Libyan foreign policy change between 1955 and the 1980s that finds commonalities among the apparently quite different foreign policies of King Idris and Muammar Qadhdhafi. This is a foreign policy history that might well be unimaginable to an observer who, for any number of *a priori* reasons well known in the international relations literature, assumes that small states have no meaningful foreign policy choices. While aspects of this history do indeed echo Holsti's findings in *Why Nations Realign,* other aspects of it are quite unique. The second concern of the chapter is that the Libyan case suggests some conceptually interesting questions about limitations in the usual understanding of the possible range of foreign policy change as understood in the international systems/structural literature. Accordingly, the discussion examines why the case is surprising from international systems/structural perspectives, asks what kinds of tactics the Libyan leadership used to produce such surprises, and, finally, draws some conclusions about certain kinds of explanations of foreign policy change. In this way one can better understand how small states can exploit the "seams" of international structures in the conduct of their foreign policy.

Systemic Structural Arguments and Libyan Foreign Policy

There is a genre of argument that construes significant foreign policy restructuring in noncore states as largely the effect of global systemic or structural forces, terms that for the purposes of this chapter can be used interchangeably.

Examples of the argument can be found in neorealist literatures, in world system approaches, in dependencia arguments, and elsewhere. Summarizing these perspectives, international structures basically determine foreign policy options for periphery states. As structural pressures build, the likelihood of foreign policy changes also rises, and eventually states shift and adjust to the obdurate realities that confront them. Understanding the international structure or system and its effects accordingly becomes the most useful focus for understanding foreign policy change in the periphery. Lesser states will have foreign policies that are narrowly derivative of prevailing structures and systems external to those states.

Although simplistic, global structural ideas of this kind have been persistently enticing analytic devices in foreign policy analysis. Certainly the external setting they attempt to delineate and understand is very important. By marginalizing the contours and local characteristics of decision-making processes, this perspective conveniently devalues information that is often unavailable to the analyst anyway. Thus, the approach has an attractive congruence between what many analysts distant from the situation can research and what the explanatory framework requires. Finally, this kind of argument is an apparently elegant strategy for the circumvention of an underlying and characteristic analytic difficulty in the study of foreign policy. That analytic difficulty stems from the massive array of foreign policy options available to an actor, especially when complexities such as timing, goals and combinations of multiple goals, differing levels of risks, and possibilities of coalitions are taken into consideration. Much of the apparent clarity in global structural arguments is possible because they avoid such complexities. They instead assume that weak states conform to the structures, especially strong core structures in the security or economic spheres of the international system determined on the basis of global distributions of resources or power. It is this expectation that sets up the surprises that one finds in studying the history of Libyan foreign policy.

As discussed below, from the perspective of international structural arguments, a volume on foreign policy change ought not to have chapters on countries like Libya, except as footnotes that vindicate the wisdom of the structural arguments. Certainly, Libya of the 1950s would presumably be derivative of the prevailing international structures and systems. Were such an expectation about Libya accurate, Libya would not have seen the pressures that spawned the rise of Qadhdhafi in the first place nor the petro-dollars from the West that have supported the flamboyance associated with Qadhdhafi's leadership.

Structural Expectations and the Idris Era of Libyan Foreign Policy

If one asks what prevailing structures confronted Libya at independence in 1951, a conventional answer would focus upon the postwar global structure that juxtaposed the United States, Britain, and Western Europe against the Soviet Union and China. In 1951 American/British predominance went unchallenged along the southern shore of the Mediterranean, and there were no Soviet bases anywhere in the Mediterranean. Between the 1950s and the 1970s, challenges to this structure would take the form of Nasserist Arab nationalism, Ba'athist Arab nationalism, and Soviet support for these movements. Between 1955 and 1967 the emergence of the superpower rivalry in the region resulted in some states of the Arab world maintaining diplomatic relationships with both superpowers. The outcome of the 1967 Arab-Israeli War ended that overlap, for the first time unambiguously polarizing the region along cold war lines. Many of the Arab regimes that dealt with Britain and Washington were monarchies; many of the regimes who found advantage in Soviet support were military regimes that described their coups and ensuing policies as revolutions. The military equipment, foreign aid, and general foreign policy orientation of each Arab state tended to reflect this bipolar structure.

The prevailing economic structure was also important, particularly the international oil regime. Some observers would see the political/military structure as the larger structure of metropole in which control of oil resources within the Middle East was embedded during the 1950s and 1960s. Others might ascribe the roots of the political/security structures to economic imperatives concerned with the control of the abundant and highly profitable Middle Eastern oil reserves. A third perspective might distinguish an oil regime that was in certain ways distinct from the political/security regime yet dominated by Western multinational companies and primarily concerned with the industrial, capitalist world. In anticipating Libyan foreign policy behavior, each of these perspectives would reach the same conclusion—namely that Libya, with no known oil reserves in 1951, was remarkably weak in relation to this global economic oil structure.

In the early 1950s there were certain clear features of this global structure that controlled the Middle East's petroleum resources and production. Throughout the region a small number of multinational oil companies had complete control of when and where to look for oil, how much oil to produce, what to charge for the oil, and how much of the proven reserves to report to authorities outside these companies. These companies were Exxon, Mobil, Texaco, Standard Oil of California (SOCAL), Gulf, Shell, British Petroleum (known in the early 1950s as Anglo-Iranian Oil Company), and the French Compagnie Francaise de Petroles (CFP). Except for the British Petroleum monopoly in Iran, for each Middle Eastern country there was a consortium that included two or more of these eight companies. For example, the Arabian American Oil Company (ARAMCO) consortium of Saudi Arabia was Exxon, Texaco, SOCAL, and Mobil; the Iraq Petroleum Company (IPC) consortium of Iraq was British Petroleum, Shell, CFP, and two American companies, Exxon and Mobil. In the mid-1950s a failed Iranian attempt to nationalize the British Petroleum operation in Iran led to a reorganization of the Iranian oil industry into a consortium including all eight of the companies plus a token share for smaller companies. The eight major companies then proceeded to use their Iran consortium as a mechanism for balancing or limiting Middle Eastern oil production so as to ensure that oil prices would remain at a profitable level (Blair 1976).

This system spread through the Middle East in the first three decades of the century as the oil-producing states gave concessions to these companies. While one could easily criticize the concessions as an unreasonable compromise of national sovereignty, the companies answered that early in the century none of the Middle Eastern countries had the engineering or marketing expertise to benefit from their own oil. The concessions at least generated some income for each of these states. The concessions also closed those states to other oil companies, multinational and otherwise, that sought access to the profitable oil fields.

The abortive nationalization effort in Iran between 1951 and 1953 and the subsequent use of the oil company consortium in Iran to limit overall production in the Middle East were a crucial demonstration of the structures that circumscribed Libya, which became independent in the same year that Iran attempted to gain control of its own oil. When the government of Iran declared in 1951 that it would market its own oil, the multinational companies responded with a boycott of Iranian oil and legal challenges to Iran's attempts to sell the oil. The result was the exclusion of Iranian oil from the market, economic stress in Iran, and a powerful lesson to other Middle Eastern states who considered the nationalization of foreign oil concessions. Except for BP, the companies may have welcomed the demise of Iranian oil production since the 1950s were a time during which these eight powerful oil companies worried about an oil "glut" or excess production which could drive prices down and undermine their profits. In that regard, for the seven companies not active in Iran during 1951, its nationalization attempt had been conveniently timed, and the return of Iranian production renewed worries about overproduction.

Upon independence Libya thus was faced with an oil production structure opposed to new oil production in the Middle East. One would expect that a structure strong enough to constrain the oil giants—such as Saudi Arabia, Iraq, and Iran—would ensure that Libya would not become an oil producer and exacerbate company concerns regarding overproduction of oil in the Middle East.

A few additional points underscore how weak Libya was vis-à-vis these global structures when it became independent in 1951. Libya was the first country to receive independence from the United Nations, in part because no nation made an internationally acceptable proposal to administer the former Italian colony as a protectorate or a trusteeship. The Libyan government began in 1951 with a frail organizational base, with little precedent of Libya as a coherent, self-governing nation, and with a leader whose credentials many Libyans viewed with misgivings. A sparsely populated and culturally uninfluential stretch of coast between Tunisia and Egypt plus a vast, much less populated hinterland, Libya also began its political existence with a staggering lack of economic resources. For example, its principal exports included iron from ruined World War II military equipment. Libya's lack of any sizeable resource base led one expert in development economics to remark that Libya was an economically hopeless nation, an extreme case that would have been invented to demonstrate the economically desperate end of the development continuum, had Libya not actually existed (Higgins 1953).

In 1951 Libya would seem to have been as dependent and powerless a country as one could imagine—a country that had few foreign policy choices and virtually no possibility of affecting the systems and structures of the outside world. This was not a country from which one would expect foreign policy innovation, or even a foreign policy that would have much impact.

The Idris Era Baseline Policy

With these comments about Libya's origins as a state and the then-prevailing international structures and systems, one can construct the likely expectations about the content of Libyan foreign policy in the 1950s. A consideration of structural arguments would lead one to expect the country to emphasize its strategic importance as a Mediterranean coastal state in order to receive a small amount of aid from that policy, and to persist as one of the more inconsequential states of the Arab world and the Mediterranean area. Economically, its promising geologic characteristics would mesh with the prevailing international oil structure on terms set by the major companies. To protect their monopoly over this oil, which was very cheap to produce and available in huge quantities, the multinational companies active elsewhere in the Middle East would have arranged to control Libyan oil production in the same fashion they controlled the oil industry in Saudi Arabia, Iraq, and the other countries of the Middle East. They would have established a "Libyan" consortium and secured a long-term concession from the Libyan government akin to the concessions they had elsewhere in the region. Exploration and production decisions would have been in the hands of the consortium. The consortium would then have announced that production of oil in Libya was not commercially feasible. This would guarantee that an already slack world oil market would not be further weakened by oil from Libya. For Libya, then, deference to the West would be the only foreign policy option, and cooperation on the military/security front would not open opportunities for oil production.

Initially, Libyan foreign policy followed the above scenario, particularly in regard to security policy. For the Libya of 1951 and 1952, foreign security policy was a more promising source of income than oil development. The Americans and British wanted military bases; the major oil companies wanted no more oil production in the Middle East; and Libya was so poor that other aspects of its foreign economic policy were irrelevant. In 1953 and 1954 King Idris signed military agreements with Britain and the United States (Wright 1982, 83–84; Deeb 1991, 30–32). The British operated military bases at Idris Airport and El Adhem, the latter close to a residence used by the King and perhaps affording him an implicit British protection from opponents to his regime. The United States obtained Wheelus Air Force Base which, by the late

1960s, had become the largest U.S. Air Force base outside the United States, except for Danang in South Vietnam. Ostensibly a base primarily concerned with training pilots in good flying weather, Wheelus was an excellent location that offered a support facility in the Southern Mediterranean for possible military action in the Arab world.

Libyan policy had other connections with British and American interests. Libyan acceptance of the Eisenhower Doctrine substantially raised the amount of assistance that the United States paid to Libya. In the late 1960s Libya signed a contract with Britain for a large air defense system that was reportedly intended primarily to protect Libya against incursions from Egypt, its neighbor to the East whose de facto leadership of Arab nationalism had led it to continually criticize Libya's cooperation with the Western alliance.

No aspect of Libyan policy in this regard is surprising or could be regarded as an exploitation of the seams inherent in an existing international structure. Indeed, in the later 1950s and into 1969 Libyan cooperation with British and U.S. policy represented one of the most clear-cut examples of the influence of the global structure on a periphery state's policy.

King Idris's 1955 Foreign Economic Policy Innovation

The above predictability and deference to existing international structures is not apparent in King Idris's agressive foreign economic policy innovation of 1955. The most important aspects of Libyan foreign economic policy pertained to the question of oil and Libya's treatment of powerful oil corporations. Libya pursued an improbable exploitation of weaknesses in the seams of the structure dominated by the powerful oil companies regulating the production of Middle Eastern oil. It was even more remarkable that this policy succeeded despite the glut of oil on the market in the 1950s.

The Libyan government chose not to play into the hands of this structure, as had Iran in 1951 when it attempted to nationalize its oil fields. Instead it produced an oil policy dramatically different from other such policies in the Middle East. Libya's 1955 Petroleum Law cleverly converted Libya's newcomer status from a weakness into a strength, and the eventual result was a Libyan oil sector organized differently from the oil industries elsewhere in the Middle East.

Instead of offering the oil rights for the entire country to a single consortium, as Saudi Arabia had to ARAMCO and Iraq had to the IPC, Libya opted to divide its territory into a multitude of exploration zones and then invite companies to bid on specific zones. Any company willing to invest in a zone and meet the minimum expenditure requirements was qualified to participate. Consortia of companies could also bid on specific zones, but they could not monopolize the country's oil industry.

The foreign economic policy enshrined in the 1955 Petroleum Law had some additional wrinkles. Winners of concessions were required to begin work within a specified amount of time and invest a specified amount of money on the concession. If oil was found in the concessionaire's zone, then the amount of required expenditure would increase to a higher minimal level. The law also included surrender provisions under which the concessionaire was required to return a quarter of the area to the Libyan government within five years, half the area within eight years, and an additional part by the tenth year (Gilbert 1967, 35–36; Waddams 1980, 57–62). Areas returned to the Libyan government could simply be put up for bid again, inviting other companies to come and look for oil. Thus an oil company which would have preferred to limit production from Libya, found itself with incentives to return the worst, least promising areas to its competitors, while it rapidly attempted to increase production in the more promising areas before the surrender provisions turned part of that area into a competitor's oil field.

This policy ultimately succeeded in skillfully exploiting a seam in the global structure of control of oil. Had the giant companies—Exxon, Mobil, Texaco, Shell, BP, SOCAL, Gulf, and CFP—been the only oil companies capable of producing Middle Eastern oil economically, the structure of oil production would have been tighter. The seam in the structure was the large number of other oil companies that were eager for access to Middle Eastern oil. Libya exploited that seam by opening its territory to any and all interested companies, including the giant companies that had previously monopolized oil in the Middle East. Numerous companies sought access to Libyan oil and received concessions, including many of the multinational controllers of the Middle East's oil structure as well as other important oil firms such as Agip, Standard Oil of Indiana, Standard Oil of Ohio, and Occidental. And as oil was discovered in Libya, production followed and Libya began to reap income from oil sales.

The main effect of this policy was to move Libya into the ranks of large oil producers much faster than the companies that controlled the production of Middle Eastern oil wished. Although the giant oil companies would have preferred to avoid additional production in the Middle East, by the latter half of the 1960s Libya had become the third largest oil exporter in the world. While this policy did not create oil, it did manage a rearrangement of the politics that had defined the concept of "commercially feasible" in the oil production structure of the Middle East. In an unfavorable international environment where a glut rather than a shortage of oil existed, Libyan foreign economic policy gave a markedly small state leverage over the exploitation of its key raw material. It also enabled a small state to achieve economic goals that the prevailing global oil structure had appeared well placed to prevent.

This policy was a tremendous success for Libya, and it generated sizeable quantities of income. With that income King Idris in the latter years of his monarchy pursued a very open foreign economic policy. Libya welcomed participation at its annual trade fairs by Eastern Bloc nations such as Rumania, Bulgaria, and Poland; it imported from places like the People's Republic of China and Australia; and it signed contracts for infrastructure projects during the 1960s with companies from Britain, Poland, Yugoslavia, Italy, and numerous other states. Citizens from many countries came to work in Libya, consumers had a myriad of items to choose from in the shops, and there appeared to be few constraints on the willingness of Libya to use its hard currency to diversify its sources of imported goods and labor. In contrast to the U.S.-British focus of its foreign security policy, Libyan foreign economic policy seemed designed to avoid dependence.

The Idris Era of Libyan Foreign Policy Change

Beginning with a very predictable policy and circumstances of great weakness, the Idris government developed an innovative economic policy a few years after independence. While it maintained a conventional and predictable security policy, the new foreign economic policy was a change in the context of Middle Eastern states' policies toward oil companies. It was also a change from Libya's earlier deference to existing global structures.

Thus by the end of his rule, the conservative and pro-British King Idris had a foreign security policy and a foreign economic policy that in spirit were quite different. The King's security/political policy was supportive of the U.S.-British structure and very close to what an international structural prediction would expect. In contrast, the foreign economic policy was innovative, did not focus exclusively upon U.S. companies, and thrived because it took advantage of a major seam in the prevailing power structure of the international oil market. The income was spent on goods and contracts from a variety of countries, ensuring that Libya would avoid dependency on any one industrial power. It was a policy that an international structural perspective would not expect.

Two caveats are important at this juncture. First, the combination of an innovative foreign economic policy and a staid, conservative foreign security policy was shrewd. It enabled Libya to glean advantages from its oil wealth without creating security concerns in Washington and London. It avoided the concerns raised during the oil nationalization in Iran when that state appeared to threaten the West with both a takeover of its oil industry and a neutralist security policy that would weaken Western containment of the Soviet Union. Libya, after all, still needed Western technology and markets; the problem was to circumvent the control structure that opposed any additional oil production in the Middle East. Thus a pivotal policy change in the economic realm of Libya's foreign policy may well have been facilitated by lack of change in the security realm. Second, this foreign economic policy set up certain parameters for subsequent actions during the Qadhdhafi era to an extent that is usually overlooked. The Libyan wealth-producing activities that Qadhdhafi later used were an Idris achievement. So was the divide and rule mechanism that enabled Libya to play foreign oil companies against one another. While King Idris did not use this mechanism to challenge company pricing policy, his 1955 Petroleum Law left Libya in a better position to do so than any other oil producing state in the Middle East. Indeed, Qadhdhafi's attempt to raise oil prices was, in fact, an incremental change in the innovative policy developed under Idris.

Structural Arguments and the Qadhdhafi Years

The Qadhdhafi era began in September 1969 and initially produced some apparently dramatic changes in Libyan relationships with the external world of oil companies and nation-states. From the perspective of international structural ideas, one might have expected Qadhdhafi to face the following circumstances. Economically, demand for Libyan oil was strong. Oil consumption was increasing in Western Europe, Japan, and the United States; the 1967 closure of the Suez Canal increased the cost of oil shipments from Asian oil producers to the European industrial world; and oil production in sub-Saharan Africa was low because of the civil war in Nigeria. The result might well be an attractive set of options for Libya, ranging from increasing its oil exports to attempting to obtain more income per barrel of oil. And, of course, the hard currency Libya was earning from its role as the third largest exporter of oil ensured a capacity to buy consumer goods from any part of the world market.

In regard to political/military issues, Libya in 1969 confronted a range of choices wider than that of the 1950s. The aftermath of the 1967 Arab-Israeli War had polarized the Arab world into one group of states that maintained links with Britain and the United States and another group of states that broke diplomatic relationships with the West and dealt instead with the Soviet Union. Libya could tilt in either direction or use its financial resources to seek a middle course. Yet despite this wealth, one would also expect that Libya's marginal military clout and security-related endeavors would work together to weaken Libya's importance to the politics of the region. A significant military force would be difficult to build because Libya's population was small, so it appeared more likely to act as arms supplier to the more powerful states of the Arab Middle East. In fact, Libya did adopt a policy direction outside of the likely structural possibilities. The genuine surprise of the Qadhdhafi era would be its innovative foreign policy change in the military/political category, not its apparently dramatic initial foreign policy change in the economic category.

Qadhdhafi Foreign Economic Policies: An Incremental Step, then a Curious Normalcy

Until the 1970s, the multinational oil companies set the price of oil. Known as the "posted price," this practice had kept the price of a barrel of crude oil practically constant during the 1960s. Within Middle East oil exporting countries many officials suspected that the oil companies were holding the posted price and the producing state's share of the oil revenue at a low level in order to claim huge profits in their refining and marketing activities. Qadhdhafi began to pressure the foreign oil companies operating in Libya to pay a larger percentage of the posted price to Libya. Other Middle Eastern oil producing nations advanced similar demands, but Libya had far more success than other countries in the region in carrying out its demands.

Since all of this happened shortly after Qadhdhafi took control, the policy is understandably claimed by Qadhdhafi and attributed to him. His first cabinet included Libyans with U.S. graduate degrees who had worked for U.S. oil companies, had been imprisoned by the Idris regime for anti-oil company activity, and had developed specific ideas about what they wanted to do and how they would proceed. Yet, the legacy of the monarch's innovative policies, rather than any idiosyncratic qualities of Qadhdhafi, enabled the regime to move effectively and successfully. The king's regime had bequeathed to Qadhdhafi a Libyan oil industry in which it was possible to pressure a single company without jeopardizing all oil production in the country. No other state in the region could do this because their oil production was controlled by a single consortium. The Saudis, for example, could not pressure ARAMCO without risking a shutdown of a very large portion of their oil production and consequentially losing that revenue. Iraq had glimpsed that fate when it sought to change the terms of its contract with the IPC consortium to which it had given its oil rights prior to World War II. IPC simply cut Iraqi oil production in retaliation. Since each major oil company that belonged to the IPC consortium also belonged to at least one other consortium in the Middle East, a decrease of Iraqi oil production did not really hurt most IPC members. Exxon and Mobil, for example, could take less from Iraq and increase their oil production in Saudi Arabia and Iran. The Libyan system King Idris created under the 1955 law uniquely avoided such risks by attracting companies that were not organized into a strong consortium or active elsewhere in the region and thus did not want to reduce their share of production in the low-cost, high quality oil fields of the Middle East.

The Qadhdhafi regime accordingly decided to target its demand for higher revenues on Occidental, Libya's main producer and a company that was vulnerable because all its low-cost, Middle Eastern oil came from Libya (Schuler 1976, 125; Sampson 1975, 211–12). Occidental was told to pay larger royalties to the Libyan government or reduce its production. Occidental conceded after it failed to receive the cooperation it needed from other oil companies, such as Exxon, to resist this demand. Using divide and rule tactics, the Libyan government then proceeded to demand higher prices from other companies with the same successful results. While this exploitation of the seams of the Middle East's oil control structure was more widely publicized than Idris's effort fifteen years earlier, it was, in fact, a set of incremental moves made feasible by the King Idris regime's 1955 Libyan Petroleum Law.

Qadhdhafi soon had the oil companies paying Libya more revenue per barrel of oil than other countries were receiving. Libya's success encouraged leaders of other Middle Eastern oil states to demand an increase in the royalties the monopoly consortia paid to them—to which the companies eventually agreed. Libya would then pressure the companies for even higher prices, would receive them, and then the other oil states of the Middle East would renew their quest for higher royalties. In a very real sense the 1970 to 1972 maneuvering in the Middle East among oil companies and oil exporting states over higher royalty payments was made possible by the independent oil policy that the Libyan monarchy had left to Qadhdhafi. What appeared to be an aggressive and innovative foreign policy change by the Qadhdhafi regime was in fact grounded in the policy of Qadhdhafi's predecessor; he had only extended the exploitation of the structural seams that was initiated by King Idris.

Libya, however, was in the middle of the turmoil in the international oil market in the 1970s. Libya was a full fledged participant in the oil policy developments following the 1973 war, and it aligned itself in the mid-1970s with the "hawks," such as Iraq and Algeria, who sought higher oil prices but were unable to command them against the massive market power of Saudi Arabia, which wanted lower prices. In Libya, as elsewhere in the Middle East after the 1973 war, nationalization of foreign oil concessions spread rapidly, with the Middle Eastern governments acquiring more and more of their oil fields and then arranging contracts with the foreign oil companies—usually the oil companies already there—to do the work. Middle Eastern countries also gained control of pricing and production decisions and helped to orchestrate a quadrupling of the price of a barrel of crude oil in 1973 to 1974. Yet in these post–1973 years there would be no major Libyan innovations akin to the achievements of the Idris regime. American oil companies such Occidental, Amerada Hess, Continental, and Marathon continued to operate in Libya (*Euromoney* 1984, 11), despite eventual requests from the Reagan White House that Americans leave Libya.

The foreign economic policy of the allegedly maverick Qadhdhafi era displayed important continuities with the Idris era, especially in regard to expenditure of the enlarged quantity of oil money for nonmilitary purposes. Despite economic pressures against Italians who had continued to reside in Libya after 1951 and the anti-American tone of Qadhdhafi's rhetoric, Libyan foreign economic policy continued the overall pattern evident in the latter years of the Idris regime. The following data in tables 5.1 and 5.2 are instructive in this regard.

The same point is evident from reports of contracts awarded for development projects. A massive project to build a pipeline bringing two million cubic meters of water a day from the Kufrah oasis in southeast Libya to agricultural areas in the northeast and northwest parts of the country was granted to a South Korean company for $3.3 billion (*Middle East Economic Digest,* 1983). With Libyan

Table 5.1.   Libyan Exports: Percentages of Total

	1972	1975	1978	1981
European Community	73.0	60.4	54.3	60.7
United States	7.7	21.9	40.7	27.4
Soviet Union	1.7	—	—	—
Asia w/o Russia	0.4	5.2	2.7	8.3
(Italy)	19.9	21.9	40.7	27.4

Source: U.N. 1982 Yearbook of International Trade Statistics

Table 5.2.   Libyan Imports: Percentages of Total

	1972	1975	1978	1981
European Community	58.4	60.5	59.8	61.8
United States	6.3	4.0	6.3	6.3
Soviet Union	0.9	0.6	0.6	0.4
Asia w/o Russia	16.9	16.2	13.6	13.6
(Italy)	25.7	25.9	24.1	30.2

Source: U.N. 1982 Yearbook of International Trade Statistics

permission, that company then arranged for subcontracts with, among others, the U.S.-based Hoist and Derrick which was to provide approximately $15 million worth of heavy construction equipment for the project. Asked why the main contract went to a company that had no prior experience in the allegedly anti-American, anti-Saudi, and anti-British Libya of Qadhdhafi, the Libyan project manager stated that "we chose Dong Ah because they have an excellent record of work in the Middle East, with wide experience of projects in Saudi Arabia. It did not matter that they had never worked in Libya before. We also have great confidence in our management consultants, Brown and Root, with whom we of course have worked before on heavy industrial projects and on the oil sector" (*Euromoney,* April 1984, 20). This project was the largest contract that the Libyan government had awarded in years according to the *Middle East Economic Digest.* A review of lesser contracts indicates that most of those went to West European companies and many of the others to Japanese, South Korean, Turkish, or Indian companies.

In regard to oil sales, Libya sold oil to the United States until the Reagan administration broke diplomatic and commercial relations with Libya in 1982. By Spring 1982 the U.S. oil market was supposedly closed to Libyan oil but, according to *Euromoney* (April 1984, 11) "the Libyans have been able to find new markets without any difficulty; in any event it is rumored that despite the ban Libyan crude still reaches the United States through spotmarket deals (because) the U.S. authorities cannot check if petroleum products arriving at their borders are of Libyan origin." According to *Euromoney,* in the first quarter of 1983 Libya was the second most important supplier of oil to Western Europe; trailing only Saudi Arabia, Libya was supplying 13 percent of Western Europe's oil requirements.

Libya's foreign economic policy respected the Arab boycott of Israel, but overall it would seem to be a policy that sought to deal with whatever economic entities had the items that Libyans wanted to purchase. In the parlance of Qadhdhafi's *Green Book* manifesto, which advocates a "Third Way," this economic pattern invents no innovative, third way course of action, nor can it be described as bristling with anti-imperialist or anti-infidel motifs. In Wright's (1982, 169) judgment, "political disfavor rarely interfered with continuing commercial relations based upon sound economic judgments," or as Zartman and Kluge (1984, 185) put it, "Rhetoric aside, Libya has fairly stable commercial relations with the West . . . with the notable exception of military purchases, the pattern of Libyan imports has changed little from before the 1969 revolution to the present."

If King Idris's security policy could be characterized as tiresomely conservative and derivative of the prevailing international structure of the early 1950s, a similar observation could be made about the Qadhdhafi foreign economic policy after the oil shocks of the early 1970s had passed. Libya's economic activities involved numerous nations that Qadhdhafi opposed on other grounds. It should be noted that the income from these activities was crucial to both Qadhdhafi's domestic policy and to the much more innovative foreign policy activities that he would pursue in other areas. There is little here to confound the expectations about Libyan foreign policy that might derive from an international structural perspective.

Qadhdhafi's Foreign Security Policy: Arms Purchases and Efforts to Reconfigure the Political Map

The Qadhdhafi regime canceled existing defense arrangements with the United States and Great Britain and reoriented state defense policy. A sizeable deal was made with France for Mirage aircraft; the magnitude of that purchase, which at the time was a record foreign arms sale by France, caused surprise and generated speculation that Qadhdhafi was actually buying the aircraft for the Egyptian military. In 1974 Libya shifted to the Soviet Union as its primary arms supplier, purchasing fighter aircraft, tanks, and other equipment with the hard currency earned from the sale of oil. The Qadhdhafi security policy in regard to arms supply became the reverse of the Idris policy, swapping one pole of the global bipolar structure for the other pole. There may have been dismay in Washington, but the strategy was conventional and workable because of Libya's abundant hard currency, which increased after the quadrupling of oil prices in 1973–74. Following a path already taken by Syria, Iraq, and Egypt, Libya's policy change posed no innovative challenge to an existing international structure.

The more colorful aspect of change in the first fifteen years of Qadhdhafi's foreign policy was his quest to change the political map. An endeavor that a realist would understand as an aspect of security policy, this arena was a sharp departure from King Idris's tacit acceptance of most existing governments and boundaries. It would be an arena in which Qadhdhafi would achieve a notoriety far beyond what one would expect from a Libyan power base, challenging existing power structures in his own region and in various parts of the world. These Libyan moves ranged from attempts to unify the Arab world to support for Islamic political entities which sought to threaten British and/or American interests in order to reduce the influence of Western imperialism. An underlying theme here pertained to alliances with actors that otherwise might have had less prominence. This policy would give Libya prominence of a kind drastically different from the aspirations of the Idris regime.

In the third edition of his *Arab Cold War,* a study of maneuvering among Egypt, Syria, and Iraq around the issue of Arab unity, Malcolm Kerr (1971, 156) commented that the demise of Egyptian President Nasser left open the possibility that the myth of Arab unity "would persist in the form of a popular belief in the survival of his role, faithful to his memory but henceforth in search of a new hero." Zartman and Kluge commented many years later that Qadhdhafi's stubborn determination to fill such a role coincided with a loss of optimism in much of the Arab world about either the practicality or the importance of Arab unity. The result is that Qadhdhafi has at times seemed to be in "the embarrassing position of playing to an audience that is not paying attention" (1984, 192). This observation conforms to the expectations of the international structure perspective.

In spite of this situation, Qadhdhafi pursued numerous efforts to bring Arab unification. In the Benghazi Agreement of 1971 Libya agreed with Syria and Egypt to form a single Arab state. In the summer of 1972 Libya committed itself to a merger with Egypt. In late 1974 Libya committed itself to a merger with Tunisia. In 1980 Libya reached agreement with Syria on a merger. Qadhdhafi failed to effect unification with any other nation and none of these enterprises produced a change in the boundaries of any Middle Eastern state. Nor was the 1975 attempt to establish a unified military command with Syria, Iraq, and the Palestine Liberation Organization (PLO) successful. What did persist was Libyan involvement in the cross-currents and issues of the Arab world, moving from strong support for Egypt at the end of the Nasser era and the beginning of the Sadat era to strong opposition to Egypt as a result of Sadat's diplomacy and eventual peace treaty with Israel. In the view of Deeb and Deeb (1982, 137), three themes are evident in these activities toward the states of the Arab world: avoid having hostile relationships with all Arab states at once, avoid simultaneous conflicts with all states that neighbor Libya, and oppose the conservative, pro-West states of the region, such as Saudi Arabia.

Libyan foreign policy moved in two circles: one Middle Eastern (Arab) and the other African (Saharan). The Sahara circle overlapped the Arab area in two important respects. The interest in the dispute over what used to be Spanish Sahara affected the Arab states of Algeria, Morocco, and Mauritania. The interest in Chad and the Darfur area involved another Arab state—the Sudan. In a policy strangely akin to that of the original Senussis whose more placid descendent he overthrew in 1969, Qadhdhafi sought Libyan control over parts of the Sahara that were governed by Chad. He declared an annexation of part of Chad and subsequently became deeply involved in its leadership struggles. There were other efforts in regard to Africa, and also various efforts in regard to the Mediterranean area, including arrangements with Malta and a proclamation that Libya's territorial waters extended well into the East-West shipping lanes of the Mediterranean. Yet these do not capture the flair and innovation of Qadhdhafi's policies.

In a very important observation Haley (1984, 12) commented that it is "hard to imagine a (foreign) policy that would press on more neuralgic spots for North America, Europe, and Japan." Although neither Chad nor the Western Sahara were in this category, this comment touches upon a change from the Idris years that can be characterized as genuinely surprising. How is it that a military power, which from the conventional views of military strength may be little more than a procurement office, could gain such visibility in the governing halls of the wealthy capitalist countries? What was remarkable about and central to the Qadhdhafi foreign policy was Libyan support for oppositions and movements of all kinds in many parts of the world. This included support for uprisings in the 1980s in Gabon, Ghana, and Upper Volta in Africa (Zartman and Kluge 1984, 187), as well as support for a variety of Palestinian factions, certain groups in the civil war in Lebanon, the Irish Republican Army (IRA), opposition groups in the Philippines, numerous Islamic groups in areas not governed according to Islamic norms, and terrorist organizations that sought out dissident Libyans.

The reasons why a policy of supporting opposition groups should worry nations like the United States and France are varied and included concerns that friendly leaderships with weak power bases could be overthrown. Libyan efforts against leaders such as Bourguiba in Tunisia and Numeiry in Sudan were viewed with concern in Washington. The Reagan administration advised the Sudan that it would help if there was an attack from Libya and told the Tunisian prime minister that the United States would protect Tunisia from attack. (Subsequently the United States would cut aid to Sudan, contributing to Numeiry's overthrow, and President Reagan would endorse an Israeli attack on Tunisia.) Moreover, the threat of assassination squads to eliminate certain Middle Eastern leaders, to become involved in European politics, or to commit violent acts in the United States were taken seriously by the U.S. government.

It was this category of activity that netted Qadhdhafi the enmity of the Reagan administration, an enmity that was politically convenient for the Reagan White House. Certainly it was here that Qadhdhafi made his worldwide reputation as "the most dangerous man in the world," or "insane," or "the beleaguered but unbowed champion of oppressed and exploited peoples" (Anderson 1985, 197). People paid the most attention to Qadhdhafi's actions in this area because it was here that Libya was perceived as able to influence international affairs despite its small size.

It must be stressed that Qadhdhafi did not need to be successful in order to gain international attention. Anderson's view that the Qadhdhafi policy is strikingly devoid of successes is apt; indeed, certain initiatives of the Qadhdhafi policies failed unequivocally. Nations such as Egypt and Syria were able to resist Libyan unity initiatives and then proceed to other endeavors, such as the October 1973 War, without involving Libya. The details of Qadhdhafi's support for opposition groups have not always turned out as he may have intended, either. For example, Qadhdhafi's support for the Shi'ites' objectives in the Lebanese civil war resulted in a visit to Libya by Lebanese Shi'ite leader al

Sadr, who mysteriously disappeared during that trip, costing Qadhdhafi support of many people in the Shi'ite movement in Lebanon. His efforts to assassinate Sadat of Egypt also backfired in at least one instance. According to Haber, Schiff, and Yaari (1979, 3), Israeli intelligence discovered a Libyan plot to assassinate Sadat. Prime Minister Begin decided to relay that information directly to Sadat, whose people found plotters and supplies where the Israelis said they would be. This Libyan adventure may thus inadvertently have had the result of enhancing the unfolding peace process between Egypt and Israel rather than obstructing it as Qadhdhafi had hoped.

One of Qadhdhafi's major concerns was his support of Islamic oppositions. Daniel Pipes observed that Libya, along with Saudi Arabia, was an important source of support for such groups. While the Saudi tactics "stood above disputes between Arabs, . . . [Qadhdhafi] funded extremist Islamic movements, trained saboteurs, kidnapped enemies, and sponsored terrorism . . . [Saudi] Arabia propped up friends of Islam, Libya brought down its enemies. Between the Saudi anvil and the Libyan hammer many Muslim communities moved perceptibly toward Islam" (Pipes 1983, 301). Pipes concludes that the combination of the Saudi and Libyan approaches played a significant role in global Islamic politics. Yet Pipes also acknowledges that Qadhdhafi's reputation often out-soared his actual activities. "The case of Libya presents especially great problems for Qadhdhafi's activities won him such great notoriety, he may have been sometimes falsely ascribed responsibility" (Pipes 1983, 307).

In the category of trying to redraw the political map, Qadhdhafi's activities in regard to Arab unity, the Sahara, the Mediterranean, Islamic groups, and efforts to undermine Western governments unquestionably attracted more attention and generated more concern than one would have expected for a country of Libya's resources or than can be attributed to actual successes of these policies. The explanation for this notoriety has to do with weaknesses in the seams of international control structures that Qadhdhafi challenged. Perhaps Qadhdhafi was simply underscoring the vulnerability of twentieth-century governments to terrorism and oppositions. Terrorism is a very difficult tactic for nation-states to monopolize or prevent with complete effectiveness. It demands little centralization, requires little logistical support, has too many targets, and benefits from too many arguments about maintaining freedoms in societies. Opposition groups are also difficult for nation-states to eliminate, especially if there are outside parties that are willing to provide funding and other kinds of support. In those contexts Qadhdhafi has devoted extensive resources and attention to weaken the seams in the international structure.

To recapitulate, the foreign economic policy of the Qadhdhafi regime continued the overall pattern of extensive contacts with the West in regard to trade, contracts with companies for development purposes, and oil sales. The foreign security policy of Libya under Qadhdhafi experienced considerable change. Libya shifted from an importer of arms from the West to an importer of Soviet arms. Other security policies reflected idealistic commitments of many kinds, and tactically they ranged from public, formal agreements with established nation-states to terroristic efforts to undercut established governments. In regard to effectiveness, the foreign economic policies enabled Libya to earn substantial amounts of hard currency and to pursue a foreign policy that was not inexpensive. The arms policy has garnered Libya vast quantities of weapons. Where Libya attempted to foist grandiose pan-Arab schemes on stronger nations, such as Egypt, it failed; where it attempted to strengthen opposition groups or weaken the influence of the West, at very least it continued to be taken seriously by states more powerful than Libya.

Conclusions

This chapter has juxtaposed two eras of foreign policy change in Libya, that of the King Idris regime from 1951 to 1969 and that of the Colonel Qadhdhafi era from 1969 into the 1980s. It has also juxtaposed two realms of foreign policy: foreign economic policy and foreign security policy. It has found in each temporal era a combination of policies, in one realm conventional policy that coincides with global structures, and in the other realm an innovative policy that challenges existing structures of control external to Libya. The two eras, moreover, have the quality of mirror images. The Idris regime was innovative in the realm of foreign economic policy while it operated a staid, structurally-derivative foreign security policy. The Qadhdhafi regime continued the foreign economic policy, retaining Libya's role and influence in the world oil control structure. While it made incremental changes in this policy as it pressured companies for higher prices, the Qadhdhafi regime maintained a continuity in its customers and suppliers that is strikingly contrary to the anti-West rhetoric of its leader. In the realm of foreign security policy the Qadhdhafi regime made changes, tilting toward the Soviet pole of the prevailing global security structure and committing itself to reconfiguring the political map, ending the Idris policy of cooperating with the prevailing security structure. While the mixture of change and continuity differs between the two eras, both succeeded in making Libya much more important internationally than an international structure perspective would have anticipated.

The concern of this concluding section is to investigate the extent to which the Libyan case provokes generalizations and insights about foreign policy change and stability that pertain to other cases. Three areas are briefly highlighted to better understand the relationship between international structure and foreign policy change.

Holsti's Earlier Study

In some respects the Libya case meshes with Holsti's classic, *Why Nations Realign*. Small countries are not devoid of foreign policy options, even ones as apparently hopeless as Libya in its early years of independence. A pattern that Holsti found in his case studies echoes in this study: foreign policy changed as the two Libyan regimes looked for ways to "cope with nonmilitary threats"

(Holsti 1982, 202). The Holsti volume indicates that often "economic vulnerability, the social consequences of modernization, dependence, ideological
disputes between factions" and the like are more pertinent as apparent triggers
of foreign policy change than military and strategic vulnerability (Holsti 1982,
3), and that observation is consistent with Libyan foreign policy change
between 1951 and the 1980s.

King Idris's policy innovation was designed to elicit interest in the oil
potential of Libya from major multinational oil companies opposed to any
additional Middle Eastern production and to threats to their control of the
Middle East's oil. In this case, not only was there choice and opportunity for a
weak actor, but also a degree of innovation that would eventually produce the
success whereby Libya became a major oil exporter a decade earlier than the
major companies would have preferred. Qadhdhafi's shift in the realm of foreign
security policy partakes of this success, protecting it through the pursuit of a
conventional and nonideological foreign economic policy. By this era, Libya is
in quite fortunate economic circumstances by the standards of its continent or
region. For this era too, the apparent motivations are congruent with the Holsti
generalization about the nature of challenges that trigger foreign policy change.
Although outside the scope of the present discussion, it can be argued that the
Qadhdhafi policy changes in the noneconomic realm evoke concerns about
autonomy and cultural independence similar to those to which Holsti points in
his volume. Further, it can be asserted that the policy concerns of the
Qadhdhafi era may be closely tied to the magnitude of foreign influence and the
degree and speed of modernization that accompanied the development of
Libya's oil resources during the Idris regime.

Timing, Sequence, and Congruence of Issue Areas

In thinking about foreign policy restructuring as change that occurs in a
number of issue areas, one might wonder whether there should be a time limit
or time frame within which that change must occur in order to qualify it as
foreign policy restructuring as Holsti and others have used that term. Is it
foreign policy restructuring if the changes require ten years to affect a number
of issue areas, or by definition is foreign policy restructuring a more concise
process? The implication of this case study is that the question addresses some
quite important aspects of foreign policy change.

If one contrasts Libyan policy in 1954 with Libyan policy in 1975 or 1980,
there are marked differences that constitute foreign policy restructuring or
realignment in the sense that there were foreign policy changes in a number of
foreign policy categories. Yet it takes many years for the scope of the change
to spread across these categories, affecting both economic and political/secur-
ity issues as it did by the 1970s. Innovation and sustainable change in one realm
consistently seemed to draw upon convention and stability in other policy
realms. The innovative policy of King Idris toward oil companies benefitted
from his support for the conventional British and American security structures.

Qadhdhafi's maverick political policy benefitted from a conventional foreign economic policy that, by the 1980s, looked as conventional as the king's foreign security policy.

Thus, asking whether there is rapid, pervasive foreign policy change in Libya risks missing important features of these cases. Processes of change and challenge to external structures involves the utilization and reinforcement of other structures. The case underscores the centrality of certain kinds of stability and continuity in relation to successful policy change and innovation. The case also illuminates a sequence of change. The 1955 law set up the early 1960s development of oil production, the success of which, in turn, set the stage for a new Libyan regime that would change Libya's security/political policies, align itself with "progressive" trends in the Arab world, and begin the maverick policies supporting various oppositions.

In examining these two Libyan eras one becomes cautious about precise, temporal definitions of foreign policy restructuring. The restructuring process spread across three decades in Libya; it needs to be understood in terms of those dynamics.

Structural Arguments About Foreign Policy Change

What does the Libyan case indicate about international structural arguments concerning foreign policy change? Given that structural arguments would not have anticipated that Libya would be a factor—either in the 1950s to the 1960s oil market or during the 1970s to the 1980s as a threat to more powerful governments—there may be some useful insights here about international structural understandings of foreign policy change.

The problem is that these cases seem to confound ideas about small states. What was a weak entity from the perspective of structural understandings of international politics turns out instead to have been incompletely encapsulated by the prevailing structures. In an era of oil glut, the pious, pro-British King Idris managed to undermine some important parts of the oil control structures in the Middle East. With an unimpressive military, the bellicose Qadhdhafi attracted the concern of a large number of regimes, inside and outside the Middle East, with his policies of support for various oppositions. Under two different regimes Libya's foreign policy change has made it important out of all proportion to what would have been expected from structural predictions of Libya's foreign policy.

From this perspective, these two Libyan cases echo aspects of what interested the Sprouts in their classic *Ecological Perspective on Human Affairs* and their formulation of an *operational milieu* and a *psychological milieu*. The psychological milieu is what decision-makers think can happen. The operational milieu is what can happen. What is seen, preferred, or chosen in the psychological milieu is distinct in some respects from what is feasible vis-à-vis external realities of the operational milieu—be they geographic or less tangible structures of influence. The operational milieu is rarely tightly deterministic;

instead, it presents possibilities for action, meaningful in how they are filtered by the psychological milieu, or as barriers to infeasible policies given the psychological milieu. An implication of the Libyan cases of foreign policy change is that the operational milieu is less clearly delineated by the international structure than one would casually expect. In Libyan foreign policy change the mesh between psychological and operational milieux produces an originality that further prompts one to wonder how the operational milieu can be better understood. Similarly, the cases prompt questions about the nature of the psychological milieu, including the origin of innovative and maverick policy ideas.

The quest of such concerns is to limit myriads of hypothetical possibilities into a narrower set of plausible options for foreign policy change. The quest is, of course, not exclusively academic. Decision-makers also have incentives to understand the plausibilities. Decision-makers, like academics, presumably prefer not to be surprised by counterintuitive events that are attributable to defects in their perception of the stuctures and systems in which they operate. For the analyst, the phenomenon of incomplete structure, of actors that do not conform or of actors who find ways of using one part of the structure to undermine or circumvent other parts of the structure, confounds the devising of tractable, relatively simple understandings of what can happen.

What then has been missed in attempting to understand the failure of structural arguments to anticipate the trajectory of Libyan foreign policy? What accounts for the surprise in the reaction to what Libya achieved? And are there commonalities in the tactics of the Idris regime and the Qadhdhafi regime that contributed to the success of each in accomplishing a foreign policy change that made Libya much more significant than the leaders of existing power structures had expected?

An excursion into the language of rational choice is helpful here, especially if one forgets about static 2 x 2 games and focuses instead on the layers of complexity that rational choice terminology can quickly catalogue. Actor objectives and actor capabilities relative to other actors are basic to rational choice models. Maps of such things often display numerous options. If one thinks about multiple objectives or combinations of objectives, the array of possibilities grows. Adding to those the possibility of coalitions of actors and alternatives of timing, to mention only two considerations, enormously complicates the possibilities and often defies the mapmaking exercise, requiring simplifications which lose much of the detail of the situation.

A crucial point here is that the fewer the number of meaningful actors (alone or in coalitions), the easier it may be to cope with the complexity and predict what is possible in a given structure. To an academic, very complicated structures with nooks and crannies of possibility are often analytically displeasing. To the government decision-maker, very complicated structures may emphasize uncertainty, rather than providing clear information about a few options that the decision-maker can ponder. Thus, a typical explanatory tactic in both academia and the policy world is to reduce the number of meaningful actors, getting away from problems of multiplicity of alternatives and frustrating indeterminacy. What this suggests is not that the international structural arguments that have this property are unimportant or completely wrong; it is that they characteristically presume a more simplistic and complete structuring than exists. And that point alerts the analyst to the possibility that an enterprising actor might significantly complicate a situation by energizing a few other actors that the explanatory schema had overlooked.

Libya's success in this regard lessens the utility of an international structural explanation in determining Libya's foreign policy choices. A structural argument stresses a system of strong and weak states, but fails to adequately address the opportunities in the nooks and crannies of the system and the possibilities of fruitful linkages among marginalized actors. When a foreign policy change takes such a course and results in a foreign policy success in some respect, the analyst is surprised, but clearly options exist in the seams as well as in more conventional directions.

What overarching generalities can be made concerning the kinds of strategies or tactics that the Idris and the Qadhdhafi regimes used to achieve foreign policy changes that confound the expectations of the international structural perspectives? The tactical secret in the successes of both Idris and Qadhdhafi resides in precisely these points about nooks and crannies of structures and the increase in actors combining to produce a more complex matrix of possibilities. In both eras, the Libyan leaders complicated the situation by unexpectedly energizing small actors and using them in ways that the leadership of the structures had to take seriously. What each Libyan leader was able to find, inadvertently or not, was an area within the relevant structure where there were actors who were not benefitting from that structure, whose aspirations were not taken seriously by the powerful at the top of the structure, and who were presumed not to be meaningful participants in the game. For the King Idris regime, those actors were the smaller independent oil companies that had been excluded from lucrative Middle Eastern oil. For the Qadhdhafi regime, those actors were an array of opposition movements—Islamic, Palestinian, and otherwise. In discovering and involving these actors, each Libyan regime identified a seam in the existing structures. The over-arching commonality between the Idris and the Qadhdhafi policies is their success in exploiting those seams.

The Libyan case is also a reminder that simultaneously working with a structure and challenging a structure can be a feasible, internally consistent strategy for producing foreign policy change. To be sure, each Libyan regime made extensive use of certain aspects of the existing structures, as structural approaches would predict. Oil is not so useful to Libya without foreign markets and foreign technical expertise. Opposition movements, Islamic or otherwise, would be less useful without the targets they oppose. In a different sense, King Idris relied upon an existing, Western dominated international security/political system for defense against Egypt as he proceeded in a different realm to undermine a structure of oil control that had been a facet of the larger Western-dominated international economic system. Likewise, Qadhdhafi relied upon the smooth workings of foreign trade and finance structures as he changed Libyan policy to nurture a political security agenda of a very different kind.

In the West the name Qadhdhafi has become associated with numerous adjectives, some pertaining to such notions as maverick, surprising, or unpredictable. This chapter suggests caution in that the entire story is not rooted in his personality or policy preferences. Besides the colorful Qadhdhafi personality, there is also a separate expectation that the world operates within certain kinds of structures. The shortcoming in those structure-based depictions of the system is evident in the surprises and anomalies that confront the researcher in the Libyan case. It is ironic that it was King Idris, the other ruler of modern Libya, who prevailed in an endeavor to challenge a significant structure, transformed the economic circumstances of his country, and in large measure set the stage for the advent of Qadhdhafi and the kinds of change he would make in Libyan foreign policy.

Chapter 6

Bureaucratic Incrementalism, Crisis, and Change in U.S. Foreign Policy Toward Africa

Peter J. Schraeder

Peter Schraeder offers a theoretical framework which demonstrates how the nature of events—ranging from routine to crisis and extended crisis situations— affects the policymaking process and its implications for change in the context of U.S. foreign policy toward Africa. Under routine situations foreign policy is guided at the bureaucratic level where foreign policy continuity and incrementalism tend to prevail. When a crisis situation develops the president and his circle of advisors are more likely to assert control over policymaking thus increasing the likelihood of foreign policy change and restructuring. During an extended crisis situation domestic politics tend to become a vital part of the policymaking process in which Congress, acting either independently or as a result of public pressure, removes the initiative from the executive branch and takes the lead in formulating potentially new policies. The power of Schraeder's conceptual framework is that each of the three policymaking patterns is based on both external and internal sources of foreign policy with different implications for stability and change. Although developed in the context of U.S. interventionism in Africa, the conceptual framework can improve an understanding of foreign policy restructuring in other countries as well.

Peter Schraeder is assistant professor of political science at Loyola University of Chicago. He received a Ph.D. in international studies from the University of South Carolina in 1990 and a B.A. in international studies and French from Bradley University in 1982, as well as a Diplôme Annuel from the Sorbonne in 1982. His research interests center on international relations theories and comparative foreign policy analysis, especially as both fields apply to Africa. He is the author of United States Foreign Policy Toward Africa: Incrementalism, Crisis, and Change, *and editor of* Intervention into the 1990s: U.S. Foreign Policy in the Third World. *His work has also appeared in* African Affairs, African Studies Review, Journal of Modern African Studies, Middle East Journal, Northeast African Studies, Third World Quarterly, *and* TransAfrica Forum. *He has lectured and carried out research throughout Africa, and is currently writing a book on the comparative politics of Africa.*

The purpose of this study is to offer a theoretical framework for understanding foreign policy continuity and change by focusing on U.S. policies toward Africa during the post–World War II period. In order to achieve such an understanding, one must build bridges between the fields of international relations and foreign policy. Specifically, this chapter demonstrates that the nature of events on the African continent historically has affected the operation of the U.S. policymaking process, and therefore the substance of U.S. African policies. Bilateral relationships with various regimes have not remained static, but instead have evolved, as different portions of the foreign policy establishment have asserted their influence within the policymaking process at different points in time. Thus, by focusing on the interplay between the nature of events on the African continent and the U.S. policymaking process, one can gain a clearer understanding of the nature of foreign policy stability and dynamism.[1]

Continuing confusion over the nature of constancy and innovation in U.S. foreign policy toward Africa is at least partially the result of three trends within the scholarly literature focusing on this topic (see Schraeder 1993 for a more extensive analysis of this theme). First, the vast majority of works constitute substantive overviews lacking a clear theoretical basis (see, e.g., Bowles 1956; Emerson 1967; Arkhurst 1975; Jackson 1984; Rotberg 1988; Clough 1992). Although certainly valuable for documenting the substance of policy, the lack of theoretical rigor and conceptualization within these works inhibits the ability to generalize about patterns and regularities. Most important, these types of studies often lend themselves to contradictory conclusions which tend to cloud rather than clarify the continuities and shifts in U.S. foreign policy. A second trend is the tendency of scholars to center on one time period (see, e.g., Kalb 1982), one case study (see, e.g., Lake 1976), or one administration (see, e.g., Mahoney 1983) in attempting to explain U.S. African policies. Despite the valuable contributions of studies such as these, their limited scope hinders the generalizability of their conclusions to other time periods, case studies, and presidential administrations.

A final, and perhaps most important, trend is the tendency of scholars to center on one particular theory which they feel is most useful in explaining stability and change, subsequently creating isolated "islands of theory" which neglect other possible approaches (see, e.g., Arsenault 1972; Marcum 1972; Rodney 1982; Ogene 1983; Love 1985; Wallerstein 1986; Jordan 1987; Kolko 1988; Lefebvre 1991; Gibbs 1991). The primary problem associated with this type of theoretical approach is that the origins, formulations, implementations, and outcomes of U.S. foreign policy toward Africa are extremely complex and do not lend themselves to monocausal explanations. In short, there is a lack of synthesis of theory and a need for multicausal models incorporating the dynamic interplay between various factors of theoretical relevance. This lack of building bridges between disparate islands of theory has impeded the rigorous and systematic portrayal of the dynamics of change, or factors and processes that influence continuity and restructuring in U.S. foreign policy over time.

This chapter offers a conceptual framework for explaining stability and dynamism in U.S. foreign policy toward Africa. A critical aspect of this framework is that the United States is not a monolithic actor that "speaks with one voice." Rather, Washington's foreign policy landscape is comprised of numerous centers of power which have the ability to simultaneously pull U.S. foreign policy in many directions. Therefore, a comprehensive understanding of U.S. foreign policy regarding Africa requires an approach that focuses on three policymaking patterns centered around the national security bureaucracies, presidents and their closest advisors, and the larger arena of domestic politics.

The nature of the situation confronting U.S. policymakers is particularly important in considering whether bureaucratic politics, presidential politics, or domestic politics is likely to predominate. Furthermore, each of the three policymaking patterns has differing implications for the likelihood of foreign policy continuity and change. First, more routine (i.e., noncrisis) situations lead to a policymaking process marked by bureaucratic politics and foreign policy continuity. When the situation shifts from routine to crisis, however, policy often captures the attention of presidents and their immediate circle of foreign policy advisors, providing a possibility for foreign policy reevaluation and change. Finally, under a situation of extended crisis, domestic politics become a factor as Congress asserts itself within the policymaking process and offers the possibility of overturning even staunchly defended executive branch policies. Together, the dynamic movement between each of these three policymaking patterns accounts for constancy and innovation in U.S. African policies. Greater comprehension of these patterns in the U.S. foreign policy process should allow for a broader understanding of foreign policy continuity and dynamism in general.

The remainder of the chapter is divided into four sections. The first three sections describe the three policymaking patterns—bureaucratic politics, presidential politics, and domestic politics—that have characterized the evolution of U.S. foreign policy toward Africa. The final section offers a summary, placing these three policymaking patterns in perspective for better understanding stability and change in foreign policy.

Routine Situations and Bureaucratic Politics

In routine situations marked by the absence of crisis, the tendency has been for the president to relegate the day-to-day responsibility for overseeing U.S.-African relations to the national security bureaucracies which comprise the executive branch. These bureaucracies, which primarily focus on the politico-military aspects of foreign policy relationships, include the State Department, the Defense Department, and the Central Intelligence Agency (CIA), as well as their specialized agencies devoted specifically to Africa.

Bureaucratic Influence Within the Policymaking Process

Three factors contribute to bureaucratic influence[2] within the policymaking process: the low level of attention typically paid to African issues by the president; the executive's traditional assumption that, due to their historical colonial heritage, the European allies should assume primary responsibility for Western interests in Africa; and, at least prior to the end of the cold war, the East-West dimension of a particular situation.

Low Level of Attention Paid to African Issues. "The President," John F. Kennedy noted, "is rightly described as a man of extraordinary powers" (Sorenson 1963). Standing at the apex of an immense bureaucratic machinery, the president as commander-in-chief, head-of-state, chief diplomat, and chief administrator embodies substantial powers allowing the White House to set the agenda for others within the foreign policy establishment. "Yet it is also true," Kennedy continued, "that he must wield those powers under extraordinary limitations" (Sorenson 1963). Among these are the impracticality of one person monitoring relations with over 150 countries (including over fifty in Africa) and the time constraints imposed by the elected term of office (four to eight years). In addition, the president must contend with a Congress that has a separate and often different foreign policy agenda, an uncooperative bureaucracy, and lagging levels of general public support. Newly elected presidents therefore must balance the urge to completely reorient the goals, priorities, and substance of foreign policy with a recognition of the time constraints involved. In a process that inevitably has led to neglect of Africa, presidents have been forced by necessity to select those countries, geographical regions, and functional issues which receive priority attention by their administrations. Indeed, although contacts between the United States and Africa have expanded in both quantity and quality during the post–World War II period, presidents from Harry S Truman to George Bush traditionally have been less interested in, and subsequently devoted less attention to, Africa relative to other regions of the world.[3] It is highly likely that this trend will continue under the Clinton administration, most notably due to President Clinton's desire to downplay the importance of foreign policy and instead focus primarily on U.S. economic concerns.

Assumption of European Responsibility. Africa's enduring relationship with Europe is a second element that reinforces the president's tendency to allow U.S. policies toward Africa to be heavily influenced by the national security bureaucracies. All presidents (although in varying degrees) traditionally have looked upon Africa as a special area under the influence and responsibility of the former European colonial powers. Therefore, they generally have deferred to European sensitivities and maintained a low profile during routine periods when one of these countries has taken the lead on a particular foreign policy issue. This European component was best summarized in 1968 by George Ball, under secretary of state under Kennedy. Ball (1968, 240) noted that the United States recognized Africa as a "special European responsibility" just as European nations recognized "our particular responsibility in Latin America." Although these spheres of influence increasingly have been broached by both sides from the 1970s to the beginning of the 1990s, there is no disputing the fact that the White House continues to look to its European allies—especially France, Britain, and, to a lesser degree, Italy, Belgium, and Portugal—to take the lead in their former colonial territories.

East-West Dimension of the Situation.   The East-West dimension is the final, and perhaps most important, element that historically has influenced presidential attention to African issues. Since 1947 when George F. Kennan formulated the doctrine of containment and the Soviet Union and communism became the central concerns of U.S. strategic thinking, policymakers have tended to view Africa from an East-West perspective. Although there were variations in the assessment of the Soviet threat and the utility of containment as originally conceived, all presidents from Truman to Bush (at least prior to the decline of communism and the fragmentation of the Soviet Union in 1991) have sought to limit Soviet influence on the African continent (Ohaegbulam 1988). The result was increased presidential attention to African issues when the former Soviet Union and its allies became significantly involved on the continent. Yet when the East-West element was lacking, there existed a high probability that the president would remain distant and uninvolved in African issues. The day-to-day responsibility of overseeing policy was left in the hands of the national security bureaucracies. As it became readily apparent in 1991 that the cold war had come to an end, African scholars and policymakers increasingly began to worry that this state of affairs would result in the decline of already low levels of presidential interest in the African continent (and thus reinforce the influence of the national security bureaucracies in the policymaking process). For example, citing the traditional Swahili proverb, "When the elephants [superpowers] fight, the grass [Africa] suffers," one Africanist noted that, "When the elephants make love, the grass suffers just as much."[4]

Bureaucracies and Organizational Missions in Africa

The net result of bureaucratic influence within the policymaking process is that U.S. African policies become fragmented, interpreted differently according to the established organizational missions of each bureaucracy (Halperin 1974). Each bureaucracy historically was created to deal with a particular aspect of the foreign policy relationship. Subsequently, each fosters an institutional culture that both supports its mission and socializes individuals into working toward the attainment of its particular goals. Although other important sources of bureaucratic behavior, such as the substantive views and personal ambitions of individual bureaucrats, can influence bureaucratic positions, the critical theme of this section is that members of a bureaucracy often become the advocates of their agencies and tend to interpret national security according to their agency's role and mission in the foreign policy establishment.

The State Department was the first national security bureaucracy within the executive branch to recognize the importance of Africa through the creation in 1958 of a separate Bureau of African Affairs.[5] Generally recognized as the lead agency as concerns U.S. African policies, the African Bureau is headed by an assistant secretary of state for African Affairs who, in turn, is supported by a senior deputy assistant secretary, three deputy assistant secretaries, as well as a host of regional offices staffed by country directors and desk officers who monitor day-to-day developments within sub-Saharan Africa.[6] The primary mission of the African Bureau is the maintenance of smooth and stable political relationships with all African governments. The emphasis is on quiet diplomacy and negotiated resolution of any conflicts that may arise. Career Foreign Service Officers (FSOs) within the bureau are usually more willing than other members of the executive branch to develop U.S. policies that are in alignment with African aspirations. Consequently, they are also more sensitive to the importance that African leaders attach to regional political associations, such as the Organization of African Unity (OAU). These same officers, when addressing the nature of conflict within a particular African country, also tend to balance the traditional impulse to attach blame to external powers—whether a communist Soviet Union during the cold war era or a "radical" Islamic fundamentalist Iran of the 1990s—with a well-grounded understanding of the conflict's internal cultural, economic, historical, and political roots.[7]

The CIA was the second among the national security bureaucracies to recognize the importance of Africa through the creation in 1960 of a separate African Division within the Deputy Directorate of Operations (DDO).[8] The DDO represents the "operations" side of the CIA responsible for mounting covert actions throughout the globe.[9] Even though it was created during roughly the same period as the State Department's African Bureau, the African Division's official mission and outlook from the 1960s to the beginning of the 1990s was radically different: to carry the ideological battle against the Soviet Union and communism to the African continent, in efforts that ranged from the cultivation of local agents to the mounting of covert operations. Subsequently, African aspirations and the internal causes of conflict on the continent historically have been downplayed by DDO officers. These officers usually have had the greatest tendency within the executive branch to view Africa as a strategic battleground and attribute instability in a particular African country to externally motivated aggression. Openly contemptuous of self-proclaimed Marxist regimes, "leftist" leaders and liberation movements, and, more recently, "radical" activists (such as Libya's Muammar Qadhdhafi) and religious movements (such as Islamic fundamentalism), the CIA prefers close liaison with the security services of the European allies and friendly African regimes.

The Defense Department—most notably its policy office of International Security Affairs (ISA)—has been the relative latecomer among the national security bureaucracies in recognizing the importance of Africa (see, e.g., Volman 1984). The ISA waited until 1982 before appointing a deputy assistant secretary of defense to head the newly created Office of African Affairs.[10] Leaning toward the globalist vision of the CIA, the Office for African Affairs tends to downplay local African concerns in favor of the continent's strategic position within the international military balance, focusing on paramount U.S. interests in Europe, the Middle East, and the former Soviet Union. Moreover, the domestic nature of an African regime is not perceived as an impediment to military cooperation as long as that regime is pro-Western in nature. The primary mission of the Office of African Affairs is the coordination and facilitation of two major military objectives on the African continent: maintaining stable, pro-Western governments through the transfer of military equipment and the training of local forces in its usage; and ensuring continued access to training facilities and strategically located bases for responding to local crises and, most important, military contingencies in Europe or the Middle East. Subsequently, military objectives are carried out by the three major military services—the Navy, Air Force, and Army—each of which has its own particular bureaucratic mission on the African continent.[11]

Other portions of the bureaucracy, of course, deal with the nonpolitico-military aspects of U.S. African policies. The U.S. Agency for International Development (AID) seeks economic development in select African countries through a variety of projects and programs.[12] The Departments of Commerce and Treasury, with their emphasis on strengthening and expanding the U.S. economy, perceive their roles as creating inroads for U.S. trade and investment on the continent. Finally, the U.S. Information Agency (USIA) promotes greater U.S.-African cultural understanding through such activities as exchange programs and goodwill missions.[13] Although each of these bureaucracies obviously plays an important role in U.S. policies toward Africa, the emphasis in this chapter is on the politico-military or "national security" aspects of African policies, and thus focuses primarily on the previously described national security bureaucracies.

The U.S. response to ethnic strife in Burundi in 1972 provides an excellent example illustrating how bureaucratic influence within the policymaking process often yields a foreign policy outcome resulting from established organizational missions.[14] Through the spring and summer of 1972, nearly 250,000 members of Burundi's Hutu ethnic group were killed by the ruling minority Tutsi regime of Colonel Michel Micombero. For reasons to be explained below, President Richard M. Nixon and National Security Adviser Henry A. Kissinger remained largely uninvolved in this issue, allowing policy to be formulated and implemented by the State Department's African Bureau. The two officials recognized as responsible for the policy were Assistant Secretary of State for African Affairs David D. Newsom and Country Director for Central African Affairs Herman J. Cohen (who later served as assistant secretary of state for African Affairs under the Bush administration).

The U.S. response to the internal crisis is revealing both for what the African Bureau did and did not do. In accordance with standard operating procedures, quiet diplomatic efforts were initiated to enlist the support of Burundi's regional neighbors and the OAU to press the Micombero regime to stop the killings. However, it soon became apparent to the African Bureau that the vast majority of African countries—themselves beset by the delicate political problem of how to deal with their respective minority populations—were opposed to this policy. Moreover, it was feared that further actions would run the risk of damaging relations with Burundi and other countries on the continent. Thus, policymakers chose a course of inaction. Indeed, despite the fact that the United States imported nearly 75 percent of Burundi's primary export of coffee, potentially viable options, such as economic sanctions, were dismissed. The African Bureau even suggested that Washington refrain from publicly denouncing the Micombero regime, although such inaction clearly would have been in direct opposition to both international human rights conventions and the frequently invoked U.S. commitment to human rights. The reason behind the decision, according to a group of specialists inclusive of former State Department personnel, was simple: "For a bureaucracy which conceived its day-to-day job as the maintenance of untroubled relations with African governments, an independent American response to the Burundi killings threatened that mission." Noted an official of the African Bureau in the aftermath of the killings, "If we'd involved ourselves in this, we'd be creamed by every country in Africa for butting into an African state's internal affairs. We don't have an interest in Burundi that justified taking that kind of flack" (Brown, Freeman, and Miller 1972, 12).

Bureaucracies and Maintenance of the Status Quo

The African Bureau's tendency to rely on established ways of thinking in formulating policy toward Burundi underscores an important aspect of bureaucratic cultures. This tendency—a fundamental resistance to change or predilection toward maintenance of an established status quo—long has been recognized by both policy analysts and practitioners alike. Among the most important factors contributing to bureaucratic conservatism are the security in following established standard operating procedures, as well as the realization that undue risk-taking may permanently damage one's career by effectively blocking any upward mobility through the ranks (see Allison 1971; Steinbruner 1974; Oneal 1982). The net result, according to Halperin (1974, 99), a respected scholar on bureaucratic politics and foreign policy, is that the "majority of bureaucrats prefer to maintain the status quo, and only a small group is, at any one time, advocating change." Subsequently, members of a bureaucracy—especially its head—will often put up a fierce fight rather than submit to changes that they perceive as infringing on their turf or threatening the integrity of their organization's bureaucratic mission (see Smith 1988).

The importance of entrenched bureaucratic missions in contributing to the maintenance of status quo policies is demonstrated by the fierce bureaucratic struggle waged during the first two years of the Kennedy administration over how to respond to Portugal's colonial policies in Africa, most notably Angola. Prior to 1961, the U.S. government consistently supported Portugal's assertion that the administration of its colonies was an internal affair, subsequently voting against (or at least abstaining) when the issue of self-determination was brought before the United Nations. Speaking with one voice, the various bureaucracies placed Portugal's membership in the North Atlantic Treaty Organization (NATO) alliance and the 1951 joint U.S.-Portugal defense treaty, allowing U.S. access to highly valued military facilities on the Azores Islands, above the demands of African nationalists. However, in the aftermath of Kennedy's inauguration in 1961, this policy changed. Appealing to Kennedy's personal commitment to support the independence aims of African nationalist movements, two political appointees, Assistant Secretary of State for African Affairs G. Mennan Williams and U.S. Ambassador to the United Nations Adlai A. Stevenson, outmaneuvered the Europeanist elements within the bureaucracy and succeeded in altering the once cozy U.S.-Portuguese ties. Restrictions were placed on Portugal's practice of diverting U.S. supplied NATO weaponry to counterinsurgency efforts in Africa; the CIA and other portions of the government were directed to open up contacts with nationalist elements in Angola; and, perhaps most significant, the United States for the first time cast a vote at the United Nations in favor of a resolution calling upon Portugal to make progress toward independence for Angola (see Mahoney 1983, 189–90, 195–97, 204–6).

This shift in policy, although denounced by proponents of the former status quo, did not galvanize opposition within the executive branch until significant bureaucratic missions were threatened or called into question. In a statement which caused particular concern in the Defense Department, Portuguese President Antonio de Oliveira Salazar threatened to refuse renewal of the 1951 agreement allowing U.S. access to the Azores military base—due to expire at the end of 1962—unless interference in Portugal's African policies was terminated. The Defense Department, led by the Joint Chiefs of Staff (JCS), strongly argued that the Azores base was indispensable to security concerns in Europe and the Middle East, and therefore should not be compromised in the pursuit of currying favor with African nationalists. These military rationales were reinforced by political arguments underscoring the importance of maintaining the integrity of the Atlantic Alliance. For example, Dean Acheson (1969, 187), the vocal secretary of state under Truman, argued that continued U.S. interference not only risked access to the Azores base, but inevitably would lead to greater instability in Portuguese Africa and even revolution in Portugal itself. The pro-Portuguese sentiments of both the military and political groups ultimately were supported by Secretary of State Dean Rusk and National Security Adviser McGeorge Bundy. The net result of this debate was a gradual return in late 1962 to the policy favoring Portuguese interests, and thus a reversal of Stevenson's and Williams' shortlived policy of closer alignment with African nationalist concerns (Schlesinger 1967, 536–37).

Bureaucratic Incrementalism

The inherently conservative nature of bureaucracies prompts their members to resist change. In turn, the self-interested nature of these organizations propels their members to attempt to expand their organization's realm of influence within the policymaking establishment. Since, as was noted earlier, members of a bureaucracy tend to identify national security in terms of their agency's mission in the foreign policy establishment, it follows that these same members will seek to widen their organization's role. The primary means of achieving a greater role is through greater amounts of economic and military aid and the expansion of activities within the host country. Efforts to achieve a greater organizational role through closer ties are also evident in the African Bureau's pursuit of White House visits for African heads-of-state, the Defense Department's interest in joint military maneuvers with African militaries, and the CIA's willingness to share intelligence findings with friendly African leaders. Regardless of the particular strategy pursued in strengthening ties with a particular African country, the term "incrementalism" best captures the resulting process of change: once a foreign policy relationship is established with an African country, the self-interested nature of bureaucracies often contributes to the gradual enhancement of relations with that country.

The process of incrementalism helps explain why significant shifts in the majority of U.S. African policies are rare even when a new administration with seemingly different beliefs than its predecessor takes power. As noted earlier, the time constraints of a four-year term of office, coupled with the traditionally low level of attention paid to African issues by the president, favors bureaucratic influence, and therefore generally supports status quo policies. Perhaps the most significant barrier to change, however, is that the numerous activities of the bureaucracy simply do not fall under the realm of presidential action. As Rusk commented during the transition from the Johnson to the Nixon administrations, "A transition is not so earth-shaking. Of the thousand or so cables that go out of here every day, I see only five or six and the President only one or two. Those who send out the other 994 cables will still be here." Adopting a train metaphor to clarify his thoughts, Rusk noted that a transition "is a little bit like changing engineers on a train going steadily down the track. The new engineer has some switches he can make choices about—but 4,500 intergovernmental agreements don't change" (Halperin 1974, 292). Although somewhat exaggerating the importance of bureaucracies during presidential transitions, Rusk's train metaphor is correct in one key respect. It suggests that established bureaucratic missions greatly increase the possibility that U.S. African policies will continue to chug along established tracks until some event (such as a crisis or an extended crisis situation) attracts the attention of the White House or other domestic actors and provides the basis for a reassessment. In the absence of crisis, White House attention usually is focused elsewhere, as established policies continue to be maintained and strengthened by the bureaucratic freight train.

Crisis Situations and the High Politics of White House Involvement

The president plays a potentially pivotal role in reorienting U.S. policies toward Africa regardless of the nature of events on the African continent. If a bureaucratic rift during a routine or noncrisis period cannot be decided at the level of the secretary of state or the secretary of defense, for example, the issue may be pushed to the level of the White House for resolution by the president. Similarly, general policy reviews, especially at the beginning of a new administration, as well as the internal processes that lead to the drafting and subsequent interpretation of presidential speeches, also offer unique opportunities for the president to take a more active stance. However, although presidents periodically become involved in policy regardless of the nature of events on the African continent, Africa's low standing relative to other regions of the world ensures that such involvement is very rare and episodic. Rather, the likelihood of presidential involvement only significantly increases during so-called periods of "crisis" on the African continent. Specifically, when the context of the situation confronting policymakers changes from routine to crisis, what may have been a formerly obscure African country often becomes the focus of the president and White House staff (see Rosati 1981). If an African issue is perceived to be of importance by the White House, the African affairs bureaucracies are likely to lose control of policy as the president asserts executive control over the policymaking process.

Crisis and Presidential Attention to U.S. African Policies

The unfolding of a crisis situation—defined as an intense politico-military conflict either within or between one or more African countries—usually serves as the triggering mechanism for sustained presidential attention to African issues.[15] It is the foreign dimension of an African conflict, however, which constitutes the critical aspect of whether that conflict becomes a crisis in the eyes of the president. Specifically, crisis situations, at least prior to the end of the cold war in the early 1990s, generally evolved due to White House perceptions of the involvement of two key sets of foreign actors: Washington's European allies and the former Soviet Union and other "radical powers," particularly Cuba and East Germany.

Crisis and the Role of European Powers

United States' presidents generally have recognized European spheres of influence within their former African colonies, in essence relying upon these allies to maintain Western interests on a day-to-day basis. Similarly, U.S. involvement in crisis situations in Africa is generally peripheral when a European power is embroiled. Specifically, if it is perceived that a European power can handle the crisis situation, the tendency has been for the White House to defer to European intervention, essentially producing little if any change in policy.

The initial U.S. response to the 1967 to 1970 Nigerian civil war provides an excellent illustration of White House sensitivity to European preferences in a crisis situation (see Stremlau 1977; Ogene 1983). After a year of spiraling ethnic violence, the Ibo-dominated province of Eastern Nigeria seceded from Nigeria and proclaimed itself the Republic of Biafra on 30 May 1967. Nearly two months later, the Nigerian federal government launched a military attack to end the secession by force, signaling the start of a bloody civil war. While Britain, the Soviet Union, and the majority of African countries supported the Nigerian federal government, France, Portugal, South Africa, and four other African countries provided economic and military support to Biafra. Despite Nigeria's significance in the Western camp as Africa's most populous country, a major producer of oil, and one of the continent's most avid supporters of a capitalist path of development, the United States embargoed the sale of arms to both sides in the conflict and maintained a low profile. Characteristic White House sensitivity to British policy preferences was one of the major reasons for remaining peripheral to the conflict. The United States kept out of the conflict despite pro-federal sympathies in the Johnson administration (and later pro-Biafran sympathies in the Nixon administration), as well as repeated requests by the Nigerian government to purchase armaments. "It had been suggested by the British government that Britain should supply all the arms needed by Nigeria since Nigeria was a British sphere of influence," notes F. Chidozie Ogene (1983, 84), a former member of the Nigerian Diplomatic Service. "The U.S., according to the British proposal, should not supply arms [but] was required to give full support for the British position in Nigeria."

In sharp contrast, when there is a politico-military power "vacuum" on the continent—historically due to the inability or refusal of a weakened and withdrawing colonial power to maintain order—the tendency has been for the White House to take a much more active role in the situation, sometimes transforming U.S. foreign policy toward the African country in question. For example, prior to 1974, Angola remained a low priority for the White House, with presidents from Truman to Nixon ultimately deferring to Portugal's efforts to maintain colonial rule over its colonies in Africa (Marcum 1972). U.S. policy continued to be dominated by traditional political and military arguments over the need to maintain access to military bases in the Portuguese-controlled Azores Islands. Yet a military coup d'état on 25 April 1974, overthrowing the Portuguese regime of Marcello Caetano, set off warning bells in Washington (Danaher 1985, 109). The coup was carried out by a group of young military officers determined to end failing, and increasingly costly, counterinsurgency efforts in Africa by granting independence to Portugal's colonies—all of which were confronted by guerrilla insurgencies supported by the Soviet bloc. The power vacuum and the potential for instability created by the voluntary withdrawal of Portuguese colonial rule ensured that Central Africa, and particularly Angola, would become top priorities of the White House.

Crisis and the Role of the Former Soviet Union and Other "Radical" Powers

The former Soviet Union's involvement in a crisis situation on the African continent constituted perhaps the most important factor in determining the level of presidential involvement in the policymaking process concerning U.S.

policies toward Africa during the cold war era. In those crisis situations in which an East-West dimension was lacking or somehow neutralized, the White House would generally avoid involvement in the conflict, resulting in foreign policy continuity so that incrementalism prevailed. Returning to the example of ethnic strife in Burundi in 1972, it has been documented that the Nixon White House, although aware of the situation, left the formulation and implementation of the U.S. policy response to the African specialists in the State Department's African Bureau, almost certainly because the massacres in a region of little strategic concern lacked any hint of communist involvement (see Brown, Freeman, and Miller 1972).

White House inaction in Burundi starkly contrasts with the marked degree of attention focused on Angola after the 1974 Portuguese coup d'état. One of the primary differences between the two cases was that the Soviet Union and Cuba were the major backers of Agostinho Neto's Popular Movement for the Liberation of Angola (MPLA)—the other two guerrilla groups vying for power were Holden Roberto's National Front for the Liberation of Angola (FNLA), backed by the People's Republic of China (PRC) and Zaire, and Jonas Savimbi's National Union for the Total Independence of Angola (UNITA), backed by the PRC and South Africa. Ignoring the advice of those in several State Department bureaus who argued against assisting any of the guerrilla factions seeking control, Ford, at the urging of Kissinger and the CIA, decided to covertly intervene on the side of the FNLA.[16] According to John Stockwell (1978, 41), the CIA chief of the Angola Task Force who managed the covert operation to assist the FNLA, Soviet involvement on the side of the MPLA was the primary factor guiding White House policy: "Kissinger saw the Angolan conflict solely in terms of global politics and was determined that the Soviets should not be permitted to make a move in any remote part of the world without being confronted militarily by the United States." In short, the crucial element driving U.S. involvement in the civil war was not identification with the aims of a particular guerrilla group or even an interest in Angola. Rather, the fact that the Soviet Union aligned itself with one of the guerrilla factions was the deciding factor in turning the Angolan conflict into a crisis, and therefore providing the impetus for U.S. support for the FNLA and UNITA.

The decline of the cold war, however, does not mean that African conflicts will cease to attract the attention of the White House. Indeed, although the end of the cold war offers tremendous opportunities—particularly the possibility of replacing superpower confrontation with a greater sensitivity to a host of development problems in Africa—it has also ushered in an altered international system replete with familiar problems such as rising ethno-religious conflict and economic nationalism. Additionally, there are also a variety of more recent but equally threatening problems: nuclear proliferation, chemical weapons production, and the spread of international drug cartels. Most important, there appears to be a growing perception at the highest levels of the U.S. policymaking establishment that Islamic fundamentalism is a threat to U.S. interests on the African continent.[17] Many officials privately note, for example, that the decline of the Soviet Union and communism have created a power vacuum on the African continent that could easily be filled by "radical forms" of Islamic fundamentalism, particularly the Shi'a variety espoused by Iran.[18] In a statement indicative of the growing concern throughout the policymaking establishment, a senior-level Bush administration official noted that the "march of Islamic fundamentalism" was "the single most worrisome trend for policymakers."[19] In a sense, the anticommunist logic of the cold war era may be in the process of being replaced by an anti-Islamic variant focused specifically on preventing the establishment of fundamentalist regimes in the Middle East and North Africa. In this regard, conflicts perceived as being manipulated by agents of Islamic fundamentalism may possibly become the triggers of sustained presidential attention in the emerging post–cold war international system.

Crisis and the Impact of Administration Worldviews

The process of bureaucratic incrementalism suggests that, in the absence of crisis, many of the African policies of a previous administration are likely to continue even though they may differ from a new administration's "worldview." An administration's worldview, simply put, constitutes the perceptions of the nature of the world held by the president and the president's closest foreign policy advisors (usually the secretary of state and the national security advisor) which subsequently form the basis of their foreign policy initiatives (see Rosati 1987). The reason behind this discrepancy between beliefs and behavior is the traditionally low level of interest accorded to African issues by the White House. Thus, despite the inauguration of an administration with widely varying beliefs than its predecessor, policies often continue along established lines.

Indeed, Africa's lower priority relative to other regions of the world perhaps makes U.S. policies toward it more susceptible to the influence of domestic political considerations in White House policymaking which can also result in policy deviating from strongly held administration beliefs. For example, as already noted, despite Kennedy's strong anticolonial beliefs, his administration largely failed to move beyond rhetoric in the case of Portuguese-ruled Africa. Although it was argued that established bureaucratic missions played the major role in ultimately ensuring policy continuity, domestic political considerations also influenced Kennedy's decision in favor of the pro-Portuguese forces within the administration. Kennedy allegedly feared that a rift in the NATO alliance (threatened by Portuguese leaders if the United States continued to interfere in its colonial affairs) would alienate security-minded Republicans in the Senate, and thus doom any chances of Senate ratification of a much desired U.S.-Soviet test ban treaty (Marcum 1972, 10). According to Arthur M. Schlesinger (1967, 536–37), Kennedy also was looking ahead to the 1964 presidential elections, and "had to take into account the possibility that the loss of the Azores, on top of a test ban, might open the way to a Republican attack on the administration for alleged neglect of vital national interests."

Yet bureaucratic factors and domestic influences are considerably less of a factor when crisis situations prompt the White House to critically examine and review—often for the first time—the nature and goals of U.S. policy toward a particular African country. In addition, crisis situations also serve as natural opportunities for the president to shape public opinion, and to make the parochial policies of individual bureaucracies more consistent with each other, as well as with that administration's worldview (see Oneal 1982, 42). During the cold war, the most important element of any administration's worldview—from which all other assumptions were derived—was the collective perception of the Soviet Union and its ability to create instability in the Third World.

A notable example of the importance of an administration's worldview in contributing to a particular policy outcome during a crisis situation is the illustration of U.S. intervention in the 1975 Angolan civil war. In March 1975 policymakers faced a crucial turning point in Angola when the FNLA attacked the MPLA and a latent power struggle erupted into an escalating civil war among the three competing guerrilla factions. The politico-military vacuum created by Portugal's abrupt withdrawal from the region, as well as Washington's perception of the Soviet Union's willingness to profit from the situation (it sent nearly one hundred tons of arms to the MPLA from March to July), prompted the White House to pursue greater involvement in the crisis. Although receiving final approval from President Ford, Kissinger is recognized as the key architect of the interventionist response.

Conflict had arisen among the national security bureaucracies, primarily between the CIA, which pushed for increases in aid to the FNLA (as well as for the initiation of aid to UNITA), and the State Department, especially the African Bureau, which argued against aiding any of the guerrilla factions. Although secretary of state at the time, Kissinger dismissed the opinions of the State Department and leaned instead toward the CIA's policy of providing greater amounts of covert aid to the FNLA (and, shortly thereafter, to UNITA). An important element of defeating the MPLA on the battlefield was U.S. reliance on funneling significant amounts of aid through both South Africa and Zaire, as well as tacit support for these two countries to introduce their regular forces onto the Angolan battlefield. The net result was a significant change in policy as the White House became heavily involved in the civil war.

The critical aspect of this case is that the dramatic change in policy was the result of Kissinger's worldview as shared by Ford. The primary component of this worldview was a perception of the Soviet Union as a traditional great power with which the United States could negotiate. "We have sought—and with some successes—to build more constructive relations with the USSR," Kissinger (1976, 311–33) noted in testimony before the Senate Subcommittee on Africa, "to reduce tensions in areas where our vital interests impinge on one another; to avoid destabilizing confrontations in peripheral areas of the globe—such as Angola." However, constructive relations depended on Kissinger's perception of the need to maintain and regulate the existing balance of power between the two superpowers in Africa. According to Kissinger (1976,

174–82), this was upset by the arrival of Soviet-backed Cuban troops to assist the MPLA regime: "Let there be no mistake about it—the culprits in the tragedy that is now unfolding in Angola are the Soviet Union and its client state Cuba." Kissinger's concern, however, was not for Angola, which was described as of "modest direct strategic interest," but rather was tied to greater East-West issues of global stability and U.S. credibility. "If the United States is seen to emasculate itself in the face of massive, unprecedented Soviet and Cuban intervention," explained Kissinger (1976, 174–82), "what will be the perception of leaders around the world as they make decisions concerning their future security?" Most important, by denigrating the internal aspects of the conflict in favor of its East-West dimension, U.S. intervention became justified, if not necessary, to contain perceived Soviet expansionism. In accordance with the Nixon Doctrine and the constraints imposed by the Vietnam War on direct military involvement in the Third World, the proper means of intervention was indirect military support of regional proxies (such as the FNLA in Angola) as aided by local client states (such as South Africa and Zaire).

Extended Crisis Situations and Domestic Politics

The longer an African crisis continues, the greater is the likelihood that more factions outside the executive branch will become involved in the formulation of policy as debate eventually spills over into the public domain. This often leads to a situation in which domestic politics, generally played out within a congressional context, increases in importance as a determinant of policy. Although public opinion and the activities of interest groups theoretically can directly influence the deliberations of the president, the most common pattern is one in which Congress, either acting independently or as the result of public opinion and organized interests, takes the initiative away from the executive branch and asserts its influence within the policymaking process.

Congressional Involvement in the Policymaking Process

Congress historically has played a limited role in the realm of foreign policy, particularly with respect to Africa (Rosati 1984). Reelection pressures and time constraints imposed by elected terms of office (two years for representatives and six years for senators) force members of Congress to select and prioritize those domestic and international issues which will receive their attention. Since the primary objective of most members is to be reelected, and since most citizens (read "voting constituents") know or care very little about the African continent, conventional wisdom suggests that it is politically smart to avoid potentially alienating their constituencies by pursuing unpopular issues (Danaher 1985, 49). The rationale for such a perspective, as presented in its most cynical form: "If my constituents don't care about Africa, why should I?"[20]

The desire for career advancement also contributes to the benign neglect of Africa. For example, due to their limited financial and staff resources, the

African subcommittees of both the House and the Senate usually are the least valued posts among those aspiring to the foreign relations committees of either house of Congress. Thus, even those members who are appointed to the African subcommittees generally attempt to use their post as a "launching pad" for more prestigious appointments, such as those relating to Europe or Japan. Charles C. Diggs (Democrat from Michigan), former chairperson of the House Subcommittee on Africa, placed this state of affairs in perspective: "As soon as somebody on the Foreign Relations Committee becomes eligible for a subcommittee, that person is usually given Africa." Yet, "as soon as they can get off of the Africa Subcommittee," Diggs continued, "they do get off of it and move on to something else."[21]

The twin concerns of political survival and career advancement have fostered congressional apathy about Africa, which is ultimately reinforced by the already limited constitutional role of Congress in framing U.S. foreign policies in general. This limited congressional influence on U.S. policies toward Africa during noncrisis periods occurs in four realms.

First is the confirmation of presidential appointees. In one of its most basic but important legislative roles, Congress confirms numerous presidential appointees who will carry out executive branch policies in Africa. Among these appointments are the assistant secretary of state for African Affairs and designated ambassadors for individual African countries. Although congressional approval for Africa-related presidential appointees rarely has been denied, this power has occasionally been used by individual senators on the Senate Foreign Relations Committee to temporarily frustrate executive branch policy.[22]

A second realm of congressional involvement includes the conducting of hearings, the sponsorship of trips and fact-finding missions to the African continent, and the convening of meetings with visiting African dignitaries and heads-of-state. The conducting of hearings on African issues, which increased dramatically in the late 1970s and early 1980s, is especially important. Able to request testimony by those within the administration responsible for U.S. African policies, hearings serve to broaden congressional awareness and understanding of executive branch policies, as well as provide the basis for policy debate.

A third significant component of congressional power is its constitutionally mandated roles to authorize and appropriate all military and economic aid requested by the executive branch (Lancaster 1984, 1988). Traditionally, Congress and the executive branch usually are less willing to do battle with each other over aid priorities in Africa as opposed to other regions of greater concern. In addition, the combination of executive branch priorities and the traditional congressional reflex to cut foreign assistance levels consistently has led to Africa receiving the least amount of aid relative to the other regions of the world.[23] Indeed, due to Africa's low status in the eyes of most policymakers, aid levels to the continent are especially hard hit during times of tight budgetary restrictions, such as in the aftermath of congressional passage of the 1986 Gramm-Rudman-Hollings deficit reduction act.

Finally, Congress can also affect U.S. African policies by passing legislation on issues of particular importance. Although legislative efforts theoretically offer an almost unlimited avenue for Congress to assert its influence within the policymaking process, in order to be successful, these efforts must transcend the innumerable partisan and ideological splits both within and between the two houses of Congress. Historically, these differences have limited the ability of Congress during noncrisis periods to pass legislation either independent of, or counter to, established executive branch policies toward Africa. As Stephen R. Weissman, former staff director of the House Subcommittee on Africa, is quick to point out, the executive branch enjoys several "natural advantages" in the realm of foreign policy. Among these are its veto power, superior organizational capacity, and political clout with congress members and interest groups, especially those affiliated with the White House (Weissman and Carson 1981, 134). The executive branch's natural advantage is further enhanced by the large degree of apathy among the majority of congresspersons concerning Africa.

Interest Groups and the Public

Domestic influence in the policymaking process comes from both interest groups and the general public. Traditionally, interest groups have attempted to articulate their constituents' points of view through elected representatives in Congress. The potential for influencing congressional behavior is especially great in that Congress as a body is largely reactive to events in Africa and, most important, the majority of members exhibit a low level of interest in issues relating to the continent. In this regard, an apathetic Congress is potentially highly responsive to organized and articulate interest groups. Even more important, this responsiveness increases when those interests are shared by constituents in an elected official's congressional district.

As Congress increasingly has involved itself in matters of foreign policy from the mid-1970s onward, the potential for interest groups to make their voices heard in the formulation of policy has also grown (Ornstein 1984). Among the numerous types of African affairs interest groups which have sought to influence the substance of U.S. African policies are academic organizations, such as the African Studies Association; nonprofit organizations, such as the New York-based Rainbow Lobby (a citizen's group dedicated to civil and human rights); relief organizations, such as the Mennonite Central Committee; foreign lobbyists, such as Fenton Communications, a Washington-based company which has served as an agent of the Angolan government; private institutions, such as the Carnegie, Rockefeller, and Ford Foundations, each of which actively has been involved in funding a variety of African-related programs; private corporations, such as Foote Mineral and its active lobbying in pursuit of the repeal of sanctions against Southern Rhodesia in 1972; and, finally, human rights organizations, such as the London-based Africa Watch organization.

An equally important aspect of domestic politics is the nature of public opinion. In general, the public remains largely unaware and disinterested in U.S. African policies, embodying what is best described as a "National Geographic" image of the African continent. Rather than being aware of the intricacies of African domestic and international policies, the public instead holds stereotypical images of lush jungles, exotic animals, and drought and famine. These images are reinforced by a popular press which highlights the negative and sensationalist aspects of African politics, as well as the "safari tradition" of U.S. journalism: sending generalists to Africa on short-term assignments as opposed to those willing to make a long-term commitment to becoming authorities on Africa (Roberts 1971; Segal 1976; Harrison and Palmer 1986; Fitzgerald 1989; Kitchen 1990).

Although there are many interest groups and portions of the general public along the political spectrum which have attempted to influence U.S. African policies, one of particular importance is the thirty million African Americans who comprise roughly 12 percent of the electorate. Yet although practitioners from all points of the ideological spectrum agree that, as a group, African Americans are a logical lobby for African interests (see Lake 1976, 285; Crocker 1981, 155–56), their voice historically has been very weak and noninfluential, especially when compared to the influence purportedly wielded by other ethnic groups in support of their homelands (such as Jewish Americans regarding U.S. foreign policy toward Israel). One of the primary reasons for this lack of influence has been the absence of an organized policy constituency capable of effectively working within the U.S. policymaking establishment (see Challenor 1981; Walters 1987).[24]

The creation and evolution during the 1970s and 1980s of two political organizations—the Congressional Black Caucus (CBC) and TransAfrica—are indicative of efforts among African-American elites to increase the leverage of their racial group within the foreign policy establishment. The CBC was formed in 1971 by thirteen African-American members of the House of Representatives who were determined to make the issue of the domestic plight of African Americans and U.S. African policies a greater concern within Congress as a whole. Yet at the time, most members were lacking in seniority (and, therefore, power) in the House and, perhaps of greater significance, were willing to leave issues concerning Africa largely in the hands of CBC Chairperson Diggs (who was also the chairperson of the House Subcommittee on Africa). Only after Diggs left the Congress in the late 1970s did more members assume greater responsibility for African issues.[25] Most important, by the beginning of 1993 the membership of the CBC had tripled in number to thirty-nine members, and its membership throughout the 1980s and the 1990s had steadily risen in seniority and power. Not only did Democratic Caucus Chairperson William H. Gray III (Democrat from Pennsylvania) assume the office of Majority Whip (one of the most powerful positions in the House) in 1989, and Ronald V.

Dellums (Democrat from California) acquire the prestigious position of chairperson of the House Armed Services Committee in 1993, but as of 1993 two other full House committees and thirteen subcommittees were also chaired by CBC members. As Bob Brauer, special council to Dellums, once proudly noted: "The power of the CBC is disproportionate to its numbers. We now have a significant constituency in the House."[26] Despite such glowing reports, CBC members are quick to note that their primary responsibility will continue to be the *domestic* plight of African Americans.

Whereas the CBC is constantly organizing support within the House of Representatives, the strategy of TransAfrica—a political lobby for a broad range of issues concerning Africa and the Caribbean—is to organize and mobilize the African-American electorate. This strategy specifically focuses on those congressional districts where African Americans are found in great numbers. "There must be as many as 100 congressional districts across the country in which we can make a significant difference in the voting patterns of congressional members," notes Randall Robinson, executive director of TransAfrica. "Our efforts are focused on those people in those districts" (Hughes 1980, 9). The commitment to forge this political lobby emerged from a Black Leadership Conference convened by CBC members Diggs and Andrew Young in September 1976 in opposition to the Ford administration's policies in southern Africa. Incorporated as a political lobby in July 1977, TransAfrica boasts over fifteen thousand members located in fifteen chapters throughout the country as of 1993.

Although the CBC and TransAfrica constitute a powerful lobbying apparatus potentially able to mobilize a growing African-American electoral voice, the fact remains that they rarely have the power to significantly alter U.S. policies toward Africa during routine periods. Like both the House and Senate subcommittees on Africa, members of the CBC and TransAfrica face an uphill battle in any attempt to persuade the largely uninterested majority of congresspersons that changes are in order. Part of a "critical mass" of individuals that coalesced during the late 1970s, these two groups are nonetheless regularly concerned about Africa and can be counted on to make their voices heard in Congress.[27] For example, when conservative elements in Congress attempted to repeal sanctions against Southern Rhodesia in 1979 (after the Carter administration had been successful in convincing Congress to reinstate them in 1977), the CBC and TransAfrica, along with other liberal elements within the House of Representatives, were successful in defeating the pro-repeal forces (Weissman and Carson 1981). In this sense, the CBC and TransAfrica have an important "watchdog" role to play in defending established policies which they perceive as beneficial to U.S. interests in Africa.

Extended Crisis and Domestic Politics

The combination of congressional and popular neglect of African issues relative to the more extensive and consistent involvement of the executive branch, and particularly the national security bureaucracies, has two conclusive results. First, a relatively disinterested Congress, in the absence of crisis, generally will not support the efforts of small groups within that body, or among the general public, to significantly alter existing U.S. African policies. Second, even during short-term crises when an issue may attract the attention of a significant number of congresspersons, as well as the involvement of a variety of interest groups and portions of the general public, control of the policymaking process naturally flows to the president and the bureaucracies of the executive branch. A typical aspect of such situations is that presidents generally are able to rally public and congressional support for their administrations' foreign policy objective (Holloway 1985, 90).

The longer a crisis continues, however, the greater is the possibility that the extent of U.S. involvement in a particular African country will become the concern of ever increasing numbers of congresspersons, and of other interested individuals outside of the executive branch. This is especially true if an issue becomes the focus of popular opinion. When executive branch policy veers too sharply away from mainstream congressional opinion—which tends to mirror that generally held by the public—the combination of extended crisis and popular pressure may result in congressional attempts to alter administration policy. In this regard, the media often plays a crucial role in determining whether a previously ignored aspect of U.S. African policies is transformed into a mainstream domestic political issue. Specifically, the mobilization of sympathetic public support for a more activist role by Congress is generally fed by extensive media coverage of a particular event—a phenomenon which, in turn, is fueled by extended crisis situations and the ability of crises to sell newspapers and commercial time.

The potentially significant role that domestic politics can play in affecting U.S. intervention in the African continent during extended crisis situations is clearly portrayed by congressional passage of the Comprehensive Anti-Apartheid Act of 1986 (see Baker 1989). In the face of the extended crisis in South Africa and the refusal of the Reagan administration to act, TransAfrica, as part of a larger antiapartheid movement, spearheaded a protest drive beginning in 1984 that eventually mobilized such popular domestic pressure for change that Congress two years later adopted sanctions over the veto of President Reagan. On 29 September 1986 the House voted 317–83 to override the president's veto. Four days later, the Senate followed suit by a margin of 78–21, providing the Reagan administration with one of its greatest foreign policy defeats. The reasons for this dramatic setback in administration policy were basically fourfold. First, the rising electoral strength of African Americans was translated into increasingly effective political organizations—such as TransAfrica and the CBC—capable of bringing pressure to bear on Congress (Baker 1989). In the South, for example, the numbers of African-American registered voters had doubled from less than two million in 1968 to nearly four million in 1988. Similarly, the numbers of African Americans holding key political offices at the federal, state, and local levels had quadrupled from roughly 1,500 in 1970 to over 6,000 in 1985.

Second, some Republican leaders were becoming increasingly concerned with the issue of race in U.S. foreign policy, a factor which contributed to divisiveness within the Republican Party in 1986 so crucial to the passage of sanctions legislation in the Republican-controlled Senate (Baker 1989). In 1984, for example, thirty-five Republicans sent a letter to Bernadus G. Fourie, the South African Ambassador to the United States, warning that they would support sanctions against South Africa unless meaningful steps were taken to begin the dismantling of apartheid. The authors of this letter belonged to the Conservative Opportunity Society (COS), a group of young Republicans who recognized the growing political influence of African Americans and wanted to channel that influence into support for the Republican Party. Since the issue of sanctions against South Africa by 1986 had become a litmus test of where members of Congress stood on the issues of racial equality and civil rights, a vote for sanctions was the most visible way to dramatically signal the new commitment of the COS.

A third reason was the steady growth of grass roots antiapartheid organizations (see Love 1985). National leadership for hundreds of such groups was provided by the American Committee on Africa (ACOA) and its Washington counterpart, the Washington Committee on Africa (WCOA); the Interfaith Center on Corporate Responsibility (ICCR); and the American Friends Service Committee (AFSC). "Since the 1970s, these groups had made slow but steady gains," explains Pauline H. Baker (1989, 31), a senior associate at the Carnegie Endowment for International Peace and a noted specialist on U.S. foreign policy toward South Africa. "However, their impact increased significantly after 1984 as the public became more aware of the issue through extensive media coverage of the South African crisis." For example, by mid-1985, twenty state governments and twenty-three cities had either passed or were considering various forms of divestment legislation. Indeed, by 1986, nineteen state governments, sixty-eight cities and counties, and 131 colleges and universities had adopted various types of restrictions that affected nearly $220 billion of institutional assets related to pension and endowment funds. In addition to seeking divestment and disinvestment at the local and state levels, these groups provided invaluable organizational support when the sanctions movement became a national phenomenon in 1986. Specifically, these groups became part of a national network that was able to cooperate with liberal allies within Congress, particularly the House Subcommittee on Africa, to seek passage of antiapartheid legislation. The efforts of these groups ranged from the collection of data crucial to congressional hearings to the provision of expert witnesses and the coordination of massive letter-writing campaigns to wavering congresspersons.

The most important factor contributing to passage of the 1986 sanctions legislation was the unfolding of what became perceived among the U.S. public as an extended crisis situation in South Africa. In the early stages of the crisis, Reagan was able to hold the line on initial sanctions legislation in 1985 by issuing an executive order. The short-lived success of this tactical move—the defeat of the 1985 legislation—demonstrated how, even during short-term crises when an issue attracted the attention of a significant number of congresspersons, initial control of the policymaking process naturally flowed to the president and the bureaucracies of the executive branch. However, as the violence in South Africa continued to intensify night after night on all the major television networks, U.S.-South African relations increasingly became more and more a domestic political issue for an electorate increasingly prone to equate protests in South Africa with the U.S. civil rights movement of the 1960s. Specifically, rising popular demands for the U.S. government to "do something" to stop the unfolding tragedy in South Africa galvanized the antiapartheid activities of African-American lobbying groups, Republican splinter groups, and grass-roots antiapartheid organizations. These groups, in turn, placed increasing pressure on vote-conscious congresspersons who recognized the popular political backlash that would accompany defeat of some sort of sanctions package. In hearings devoted to the question of sanctions against South Africa, Wolpe dramatized the crucial relationship between events in South Africa and the policymaking process. "Why are we so concerned with the passage [of sanctions legislation] at this point?" rhetorically demanded Wolpe. "The reason, very simply, because of the dramatic—very dramatic, I want to underscore that—deterioration of developments in South Africa" (U.S. House 1986, 246). The fact that these developments obviously were linked to the politicization of the issue of apartheid within U.S. domestic politics was underscored by Republican leader Robert Dole. "Let's face it," explained Dole in 1986, "there's a lot of politics involved . . . this has now become a civil rights issue" (Baker 1986).

Patterns and Process in Perspective

In order to fully understand continuity and change in U.S. intervention in Africa during the post–World War II period and, more specifically, why the United States has strengthened or weakened security relationships with individual African regimes over time, the nature of events on the African continent should be understood. It is this nature which, historically, has affected the operation of the policymaking process, and therefore the substance of U.S. interventionism in Africa. Although the often "messy" politics of foreign policy formulation and implementation are inherently fuzzy and blurred, the evolution of U.S. relations with a particular African regime can be traced according to the three major patterns (see table 6.1).

1. Routine Situations and Bureaucratic Influence Within the Policymaking Process. Due to the historic neglect of African issues by both the White House and Congress, U.S. African policies—perhaps more so than those directed toward any other region of the world—are best explained by focusing on the level of the bureaucracies and the evolution of bureaucratic politics. Specifically, policies during routine periods tend to be driven by the established organizational missions of the national security bureaucracies comprising the executive

Table 6.1.   Pattern and Process in U.S. Intervention in Africa

External Environment		Domestic Environment		Continuity and Change	
Local Situation	External Involvement Soviet Union/ Europe	Policy Process	Policy Determinants	Outcome	Chance for Change
Extended Crisis	High/Low	Domestic Politics	Societal Interests	Uncertainty	High
Crisis	High/Low	Presidential Politics	Administration Worldview	Uncertainty	High
Routine	Low/High	Bureaucratic Politics	Organizational Missions	Incremen-talism	Low

branch, including the State Department, the Defense Department, and the CIA, as well as their specialized offices devoted to Africa. The net result of bureaucratic preeminence within the policymaking process is an incrementalist foreign policy outcome in which the potential for change in interventionist practices is extremely limited. In fact, the best predictor for future policy is current policy.

2. Crisis Situations and Presidential Influence Within the Policymaking Process.   When the situation on the African continent changes from routine to crisis, the likelihood increases that the African affairs bureaucracies will lose control of policy as presidents and their most senior advisors assert their control over the policymaking process. The most important determinants of whether a situation took on a crisis atmosphere—at least prior to the end of the cold war—historically have been the nature of European involvement, as well as that of the former Soviet Union and its allies. Crisis situations not only prompt the White House to critically examine and review—often for the first time—the nature and purposes of policy toward a particular African country, but also serve to make the parochial policies of individual bureaucracies more consistent with each other, as well as with that administration's worldview. The net result of presidential involvement in the policymaking process is an uncertain policy outcome in which the possibility for change in interventionist practices is extremely high.

3. Extended Crisis Situations and Domestic Influence Within the Policymaking Process.   Finally, the longer that a crisis situation continues to confront policymakers, the greater is the possibility that more groups and individuals outside of the executive branch will become involved in the policy process as debate spills over into the public domain. This spill-over effect has the potential of leading to a situation marked by domestic politics in which Congress, acting either independently or as a result of public pressure, takes the initiative away from the executive branch and asserts its influence within the policymaking process.

Although the possibility for change in policy under such situations is significant, congressional ability to influence events dramatically decreases in the absence of crisis as traditional partisan and ideological rivalries stand in the way of unified action by both houses of Congress.

Together these three patterns capture the dynamic nature of the foreign policymaking process and provide one with the framework for analyzing the evolution of U.S. foreign policy in the context of Africa. Indeed, U.S. relations with various African regimes do not remain static over time, but instead evolve as different portions of the foreign policy establishment assert their influence within the policymaking process at different points in time. These three patterns, of course, are not mutually exclusive. Rather, the concept of influence infers that, at any given point in time, one particular portion of the U.S. foreign policy establishment is the primary or "dominant" force within the policymaking process (see Rosati 1981). Such patterns not only prevail for U.S. security policy toward Africa, but can serve as the basis for a general understanding of the politics of foreign policy continuity and change.

One can, therefore, conceive of U.S. intervention as a kind of continuum in which periods of bureaucratic influence are briefly interrupted by episodes of presidential and domestic involvement during crisis and extended crisis situations. Yet even if change and restructuring occur in a given relationship due to presidential or domestic politics, once the crisis situation subsides, policy again usually falls under the realm of the national security bureaucracies and the process of routine and incrementalism again prevails, albeit in an altered form.

Notes

1. This chapter derives from a larger body of research on U.S. foreign policy toward Africa for a forthcoming volume (Schraeder 1994), *United States Foreign Policy Toward Africa: Incrementalism, Crisis and Change*. A more extensive presentation of the initial results of this research can be found in Schraeder (1991).
2. The concept of bureaucratic influence was inspired by the theoretical work of Rosati (1981) which centered on the similar concept of "bureaucratic dominance."
3. Even under President Jimmy Carter—recognized as pursuing one of the most enlightened African policies during the post–World War II period—Africa ranked last in terms of foreign policy attention. Whereas Africa accounted for nearly 11 percent of the Carter administration's foreign policy behavior in 1977, the continent still trailed all other regions of the world and in fact decreased in importance by nearly 50 percent over the next three years. For figures, see Rosati (1987, 123, 130, 139, 147).
4. Statement by Francis Kornegay, Jr., chair of a panel entitled, "Great Power Relations After Perestroika," 31st Annual Meeting of the African Studies Association, McCormick Center Hotel, Chicago, Illinois, 28–31 October 1988.
5. African issues previously were handled by the State Department's Bureau of Near Eastern and African Affairs, which itself was preceded by the Bureau of Near Eastern, South Asian and African Affairs.

6. Events within northern Africa are monitored by the State Department's Bureau of Near Eastern and South Asian Affairs.

7. The African Bureau, however, is but one of many regionally and functionally organized bureaus at the State Department which periodically become involved in African issues. Other bureaus, although generally in agreement over the necessity to pursue diplomatic options, have missions which can conflict with those pursued by the Bureau of African Affairs. For example, the Bureau of European and Canadian Affairs is naturally more concerned with European sensitivities when African issues arise, and thus serves to reinforce the executive branch's tendency to defer to European, as opposed to African, sensitivities.

8. African issues previously were divided between the Agency's European and Middle Eastern Divisions. For a useful critical anthology of CIA activities in Africa, see Ray, Schaap, Van Meter, and Wolf (1979).

9. Not to be confused with the Deputy Directorate of Intelligence (DDI) and its African-related Office of African and Latin American Analysis, or that portion of the CIA committed to providing the Director of Central Intelligence (DCI) and the executive with up-to-date summaries and analyses of gathered intelligence.

10. African issues were handled prior to 1982 by the deputy assistant secretary of defense for the Near East, Africa, and South Asia. For an overview of growing Defense Department interest in Africa, see Volman (1984).

11. The U.S. Marines are also involved in a very minor way on the African continent. Marine Security Detachments (MSDs) of varying (but limited) sizes guard U.S. Embassies.

12. For a critical view of AID's activities in Africa, see Gervasi, Seidman, Wallerstein, and Wiley (1977).

13. For an overview of USIA's role in Africa, see Culverson (1989).

14. Discussion of this case is taken from Brown, Freeman, and Miller (1972), as well as Melady (1974). For discussion of the U.S. response to the more recent outbreak of ethnic violence in Burundi in August 1988, see Lemarchand (1989).

15. For an overview of the concept of crisis, see Brecher, Wilkenfeld, and Moser (1988); Hermann (1969); and James, Brecher, and Hoffman (1988). The definition for this concept was derived from Bender, Coleman, and Sklar (1985).

16. For a succinct analysis of this topic, from which the discussion throughout the remainder of this article is based, see Bender (1981). See also Davis (1978) and Hyland (1987).

17. See Leon T. Hadar, "The 'Green Peril': Creating the Islamic Fundamentalist Threat," *Cato Institute Policy Analysis* 177: 27 August 1992.

18. For a discussion of the spread of fundamentalist movements throughout North Africa, see Abramson (1992).

19. Quoted in Crossette (1992).

20. Confidential interview.

21. Interview with Charles Diggs, 13 June 1989.

22. For example, Senator Helms attempted to derail the Reagan administration's policy of constructive engagement by delaying Crocker's confirmation for a period of six months.

23. In fiscal year 1991, for example, Africa received only roughly 6.5 percent of all U.S. economic and military bilateral aid.

24. "Blacks as blacks may identify with Africa," noted Martin Weil (1974) in a

prescient article in 1974, "but it is only as Americans that they can change U.S. foreign policy in Africa." If African Americans ever "gain leverage," he continued, "it will be those black politicians who are most successful *within* the system who will do so—those who can command the respect of their black constituents and reassure white America at the same time." See also Plummer (1989) and Walters (1987).

25. Interview with Bob Brauer, special counsel to Representative Ronald V. Dellums, 25 May 1989.
26. Ibid.
27. The terminology is that of Stephen R. Weissman, former staff director of the House Subcommittee on Africa. Interview on 17 May 1989.

Chapter 7

Domestic Political Regime Change and Foreign Policy Restructuring
A Framework for Comparative Analysis

Joe D. Hagan

Joe Hagan develops a conceptual framework for assessing the role of domestic political regime changes in the restructuring of foreign policies. Like the Schraeder chapter before, his framework adds an additional perspective illustrating how the domestic political context affects the dynamics of continuity and change in foreign policy. Hagan's theoretical framework seeks to capture more fully the diversity of regime changes and the complex, yet subtle ways such changes influence foreign policy. From this perspective, the key to understanding foreign policy change is a series of tasks designed to examine the relationship between the types of regime change, the orientation of regimes, the extent to which regimes are fragmented, and their effect on several dimensions of foreign policy behavior. Through the concept of political regimes, the conceptual framework integrates the role of both domestic and international sources of foreign policy change. Moreover, the broader significance of the regime change approach to foreign policy is that it highlights the role of domestic political forces not only on foreign policy but also international change. In short, Hagan's conceptual framework provides a valuable perspective for developing cross-national analyses in order to better understand the dynamics of continuity and change in foreign policy.

Joe Hagan is associate professor of political science at West Virginia University and a faculty associate at the Mershon Center at Ohio State University. He received his Ph.D. in political science from the University of

The initial version of this chapter was presented at the annual meeting of the American Political Science Association, Washington, D.C., 3–6 September 1987. Since then I have received valuable comments on this evolving project at the meetings of the Stockholm comparative foreign policy working group in Stockholm (1989), Vancouver (1991), and Helsinki (1991). Comments and critiques from Philip Everts, Kjell Goldmann, Olav Knudson, Ben Soedendorp, and Bengt Sundelius have been especially helpful, as has my ongoing conversation with Jerel Rosati. The Third World component of this research has been aided by Bruce Moon's willingness to share with me his regime change research. Earlier stages of this research were funded by the Division of Basic Research at the University of Wyoming, and the chapter's completion was supported by the Eberly College of Arts and Science at West Virginia University.

Kentucky in 1980, a M.A. in political science from Kentucky in 1977, and a B.A. in political science from Drew University in 1974. His research interests involve the study of U.S. and comparative foreign policy, with a focus on the role of political regimes and domestic oppositions. He is the author of Political Opposition and Foreign Policy in Comparative Perspective *and coeditor (with Charles and Margaret Hermann) of* Leaders, Groups, and Coalitions: How Decision Units Shape Foreign Policy. *His work also has appeared in such journals as* Cooperation and Conflict, International Interactions, International Organization, *and* Journal of Asian and African Studies.

With growing frequency over the past two decades, domestic political regime changes in a wide variety of states have led to foreign policy "restructurings," often with considerable implications for international and regional stability. Shifting "strategies of containment" of Soviet power—ranging from noncontainment to aggressive military containment—have been a dominant feature of American foreign policy in the post-Vietnam era across the Nixon, Ford, Carter, Reagan, and Bush administrations, and concerns about Russian power probably will continue to influence the Clinton administration. Leadership changes in the former Soviet Union also regularly influenced superpower tensions, and the cold war ultimately was ended due to the reorientation of Soviet foreign policies under Gorbachev and Yeltsin away from its long-held anti-status quo posture. Foreign policy changes also have repeatedly affected the cohesiveness of the Western alliance and usually can be traced to the exchange of power between moderate and hardline parties or factions in countries such as France, Britain, Japan, New Zealand, and West Germany. While regime changes and foreign policy shifts in the former socialist bloc were usually quite limited during the cold war, instances of profound foreign policy changes are evident in China's relationship with the superpowers since the late 1950s and in Eastern Europe's realignment following the recent collapse of its pro-Soviet regimes. Equally dramatic have been shifts in the Third World, which include not only the political revolutions and realignments of Chile, Cuba, Egypt, Iran, Iraq, and Nicaragua, but also the more subtle regime changes and foreign policy shifts in Burma, Taiwan, Jamaica, India, the Philippines, Israel, and Syria, and post-revolutionary Egypt.

These cases highlight the degree to which foreign policy restructuring is influenced by *domestic* political regime changes in which a new leadership group, or coalition of groups, comes to power and takes control of the authoritative policymaking bodies of the government. Regime changes are at the nexus of political change across domestic and international systems. On the one hand, the emergence of a new group in power is the ultimate manifestation of political trends and crises within society—which may shape the new regime's orientation to world affairs and persist long after the events that brought the regime to power have dissipated. On the other hand, a political regime's conduct of foreign policy is also partially a function of its current internal political dynamics. Therefore, long after the regime has taken power, political processes within the regime, as well as challenges to it from opposition groups in the wider environment, condition the political willingness and ability of leaders to implement major changes in past policies. All this is not to say that all foreign policy change is domestically driven; clearly it is not. Rather, the rise and fall of political regimes modify the pervasive effects of international change, acting both as a source of politically redefined foreign policy orientations and as a constraint on governments' ability to respond to that change.

This chapter sketches out a conceptual framework for assessing the role of domestic political regime changes in the restructuring of states' foreign policies. This framework is designed to be appropriate for executing broad comparative analyses that capture the diversity of the regime changes and their varied foreign policy effects evident in the countries discussed in the opening of the chapter. The premise of this effort is that empirically based research prematurely has cast the linkage between regime changes and foreign policy in a simplistic and narrow manner. Much of this literature considers only one type of regime change (revolutions), only one property of regimes (political system structures), and only one form of foreign policy restructuring (realignment). However, as suggested by the above occurrences, important cases of domestic political regime change and resultant foreign policy restructuring are by no means limited to domestic revolutions, changes in the political structure of the system, and foreign policy realignments. Thus, a broader perspective is needed in order to account more fully for diverse regime change–foreign policy restructuring phenomena. Existing research needs to be expanded in order to incorporate (1) nonrevolutionary regime changes, (2) shifts in nonstructural properties of regimes such as leaders' core policy beliefs and political constraints, and (3) changes that affect the nature, but not the existence, of alignments in foreign affairs. This chapter's presentation of the framework is organized to address sequentially each of these three tasks, utilizing preliminary data on a common set of regime changes (in the states cited earlier) to illustrate points at each stage of the framework's development.[1]

Research on Political Regime Change and Foreign Policy Restructuring: A Survey and Critique

Despite its small volume, the existing research on the relationship of regime change to foreign policy is quite useful. Political factors are included in the three major theoretical explanations of foreign policy change (Goldmann 1988; Holsti 1982a; Hermann 1990). Goldmann argues that political variables (along with administrative, cognitive, and international ones) influence the ability of a government to maintain a coherent policy. These political "stabilizers" are consensus, issue salience, and the institutionalization of policy (Goldmann 1988, 248); together they combine to determine whether a policy can be insulated from domestic opponents seeking its termination. Holsti incorporates a somewhat different set of variables. Political opposition, or "fractionalization," is one of several pressures affecting foreign policy restructuring. Its effects are, in turn, mediated by various leadership traits—elite attitudes toward external actors, personality factors, policymaking processes, and decision-makers' perceptions and calculations (Holsti 1982a, 14). Political influences on government decisions to "change course" in foreign affairs are interwoven throughout much of Hermann's framework. Domestic political restructuring is one of the four primary agents of change, and political dynamics are involved in the decision-making processes that link other agents of change to foreign policy. Decision-making phases with significant political dimensions include the leaders' initial policy expectations, the recognition of discrepant information, the development of alternatives, and most obviously the building of an authoritative consensus for new options.[2]

These frameworks are valuable because they capture some of the complexity of political opposition and leadership characteristics beyond simply the state's institutions and other political structures. They also illustrate the importance of regime changes which, although not provoking realignments, may affect more subtle dimensions of foreign relations. However, none provides much direct insight into the precise character of the regime changes themselves and their foreign policy effects in a way that would allow cross-national comparison. One must look further for more explicit conceptualizations of regime changes and their foreign policy implications.

Useful in this regard are several cross-national, empirical analyses of regime changes and foreign policy. Andriole and Hopple (1986, 365) examine the impact of changes in "a country's patterns of political authority and political structure" on their patterns of trade with the superpowers. Informed by the structurally-oriented frameworks of Gurr (1974) and the Interstate Behavior Analysis Project (Wilkenfeld, Hopple, Rossa, and Andriole 1980), these political patterns are recruitment, political participation, decision constraints, and military versus civilian control, with a "significant" regime change occurring when two or more of these conditions are fundamentally altered. The findings from their analysis of foreign policy realignments, however, provide little support for the structuralist view of regimes. Andriole and Hopple (1986, 389–90) conclude that "virtually no changes in the levels of imports and exports followed major political changes in the Third World" and further speculate that nonstructural leadership properties might better account for these foreign policy changes.

Studies by Moon (1985) and Midlarsky (1981) stem from their interest in the political economy of Third World dependence and its effects on foreign relations within the capitalist world economy. Each examines in some detail the most dramatic type of regime change—revolutionary transformation—which is largely violent political change where "there occurred at least some transformation of the structure of political authority and perhaps also some change in economic and social spheres above and beyond the illegal change in personnel within the structure of political authority" (Midlarsky 1981, 50). Moon and Midlarsky offer consistent evidence that regime changes (Venezuela, Bolivia,

Guatemala, Cuba, Iraq, and Chile) have provoked major foreign policy realignments, as indicated by changes in the degree to which their voting pattern was consistent with that of the United States in the General Assembly of the United Nations. However, the two studies report contradictory findings about the effects (or noneffects) of major regime changes for Argentina, Columbia, Indonesia, Laos, and Peru. Indeed, a sizeable proportion of the cases of realignments examined in each study arguably resulted from milder, nonrevolutionary regime changes.

A recent study by Maoz (1989) contributes to the growing literature on the "war proneness" of different types of political systems by injecting notions of political change. Instead of focusing simply on the differing conflict propensities of democratic and authoritarian polities, Maoz employs a "political development model" with the argument that war proneness has more to do with the evolution of political structures. Maoz (1989, 226–27) reports statistically robust findings supportive of this kind of argument, specifically that the most war prone political systems are those that recently have experienced a revolutionary change in any one of Gurr's (1974) political system structures. In contrast, "evolutionary" regime changes are found to produce no more conflicts than are those in more established political systems. This lends further support to the argument that revolutionary changes in political structure do lead to major foreign policy shifts, although Maoz acknowledges the high conflict propensities of new revolutionary regimes may be due in part to hostile reactions by established, status-quo powers.

Despite the value of these findings, this empirical research has two overriding limitations. The first is that it has failed to capture the diversity of major regime changes and the complex, yet subtle, ways these changes influence foreign relations. This is true in three ways: (1) it has assumed that only the most dramatic regime changes—violent, revolutionary transformations—produce major foreign policy changes, (2) it has focused only on changes in political structure and state-society relations, and (3) with the exception of the Maoz study, it has sought to explain mainly one dimension of foreign policy change—realignment with the superpowers. In essence, this empirical research has been oriented toward the most dramatic types of regime changes and the most dramatic forms of foreign policy restructuring. Although this focus might be appropriate for political economy research, it is too restrictive for purposes of developing general foreign policy theory. The kinds of political sources of foreign policy change—emphasized in the Goldmann, Hermann, and Holsti theoretical frameworks—are left largely ignored. It also fails to address adequately the diverse cases cited at the opening of this chapter, many of which were nonrevolutionary changes which resulted in significant foreign policy changes, even though they fell far short of realignment.

The second weakness with the empirical research is that it is has examined only Third World countries. With the exception of a recent study by Volgy and Schwarz (1991), no theoretically-informed, comparative study has assessed the foreign policy effects of political regime changes in advanced industrial states.

Perhaps because of the theoretical preoccupation with dependence, revolutions, and cold war realignments, the assumption appears to have been that significant changes in regimes and/or foreign policy are rare among the advanced industrial states. However, especially after the past few years (1989 to 1991), even political revolutions are clearly no longer limited to the Third World.[3] Furthermore, as indicated at the opening of this chapter, regime changes have led to important shifts in American, Soviet, and Western European foreign policies. Even if they did not involve realignments (except for Gaullist France), they did significantly affect the intensity of superpower tensions and the cohesiveness of their blocs. Not only does this reinforce the need to look at less dramatic forms of the regime change–foreign policy restructuring, it also points to the need for a conceptual focus that cuts across polities in both the advanced industrial states and the Third World.

This project, then, seeks to inject some complexity into research on regime change and foreign policy restructuring that would allow for systematic comparisons across the full array of political systems. It responds to the above limitations in empirically based studies by (1) identifying three additional, nonrevolutionary types of regime changes, (2) conceptualizing nonstructural properties of regimes which can be altered with any of these types of regime change (including revolutions), and (3) relating these shifting regime properties to restructuring of a wider array of foreign policy dimensions, including not only alignment but also the level of conflict, independence, and commitment. These three tasks are intended to guide cross-national data collection efforts and subsequent analyses linking regime change to foreign policy restructuring.

Task I: Broadening the Definition of "Significant" Regime Changes

The first research task is to broaden the scope of what is defined to be a "significant" regime change, away from only those involving extreme violence and profound changes in political structure. While not denying the importance of such revolutionary transformations, attention only to changes in political structures leads one to ignore changes involving the "nonrevolutionary" exchange of power between mainstream political groups or factions occurring in accordance with regular, established political procedures.[4] These kinds of regime changes can lead to major foreign policy restructurings, including even full realignments (e.g., post-revolutionary changes in Egypt and China). Therefore, systematic data collection and analysis need to be conducted in terms of the broadest possible definition of regime change.

What constitutes a significant regime change, though, depends upon one's conceptualization of political regime. This author considers it to be the political group, or coalition of groups, who control the authoritative policymaking bodies of the state's governmental institutions. Such groups include revolutionary movements, political parties, military juntas, institutional actors, as well as factional organizations within any of these political groups. It is further assumed that even within an established political system there may be contending political groups with significantly different orientations for foreign policy. A significant regime change may therefore occur when one set of leaders is replaced by another, even though the state's political structures remain fixed and the overall structure of the political system is unaltered. As one gets away from structural notions of political regime change, however, it is equally important to avoid the opposite extreme of theorizing that a change in any individual leader marks an important regime change. Rather, given the group-based conception of political regimes argued here, a change in an individual leader is assumed to be significant only if that new leader is the representative of a different political group or faction (thus a change in head of state or a cabinet shakeup may be of minor importance if the same group or coalition of groups remain in power).

To develop such a comprehensive and flexible conceptualization of a regime change, the focus of this framework is on changes in the political makeup of the ruling group occupying the set of roles that constitute the central political structure of a government. Thus, a regime change is identified when there is a change in one or more of the key actors within the central leadership body. For purposes of broad, cross-national data collection and analyses, it is useful to think in terms of four basic types of regime changes, derived from a consideration of the full range of possible changes in the types of groups who compete for control of a government. Ranging from relatively mild ones to more dramatic ones, there are four types of regime changes.

Type I: A Change in the Predominant Leader.   In this scenario, there is a change in the politically predominant leader, but it does not alter the regime's basic political makeup in terms of its component factions or parties. The change is limited to the replacement of the current leader by an individual from the same faction or party, typically occurring with the resignation of or death of a powerful leader and his or her replacement by the designated successor who *also* becomes a predominant leader.[5] Examples of these are leadership changes in the United States from Kennedy to Johnson, in Taiwan from Chiang Kai-shek to his son Chiang Ching-kuo, one postwar president to another in Mexico's remarkably cohesive Partido Revolucionario Institucional (PRI), and perhaps also in Britain from Margaret Thatcher to John Major.[6]

Type II: A Major Factional or Coalition Shift.   In this scenario, there is a change in the leadership body in terms of its component factions (in the case of fragmented single-party regimes) or in terms of parties or other autonomous political groups (in the case of coalitions). When a regime is divided by permanent factions or parties, leadership changes (often even with the head of state retaining power) may affect the regime's internal political balance with the emergence of a new dominant faction or party, as has occurred in parliamentary democracies such as India, Italy, Israel, and Japan.[7] Factional shifts are especially significant in the restrictive settings of authoritarian systems that are dominated by a fragmented single party or group, as has been the case in China since the late 1950s first under Mao Zedong and now under Deng Xiopeng, in Iran under Khomeini and then the current leadership, and in the

USSR under Gorbachev as illustrated by the failed right wing coup in August 1991 and then in the subsequent power sharing arrangement in Russia with Yeltsin.

Type III: A Regular Exchange of Power Between Contending, Mainstream Parties or Groups. In this scenario, there is a replacement of the entire ruling group or coalition with the change occurring between groups who are part of the established political order and in accordance with regular political norms.[8] These are situations in which there is the complete exchange of power between separate political parties or groups—neither of which has an "antisystem" orientation.[9] The familiar case is the electoral defeat of one party or coalition by another party or coalition—such as the defeats of the India National Congress by the Janata coalition, the Israeli Labour alignment by the Likud coalition, the National Party by the Labour Party in New Zealand, as well the Carter administration by the Republican Party under Reagan in the United States. Cases in closed polities include the rise to power of the Ba'athist parties in Syria and Iraq in the mid-1960s, the overthrow of Indonesia's Sukarno by the military under Suharto, and the revolt against the Marcos family by the Aquino coalition in the Philippines.

Type IV: A Political Revolution Bringing to Power an "Antisystem" Group or Coalition. This is a revolutionary transformation in which a ruling party or group is replaced by an antisystem group that fundamentally restructures the political system. In cases where a previously excluded group takes power by overthrowing the entire political establishment, the political changes are often the most dramatic because the new regime rearranges the entire domestic political order by rewriting political norms, changing basic structural arrangements, and ultimately altering the influence (perhaps even the existence) of formerly dominant socioeconomic elites. Type IV changes result from one of three mechanisms: the overthrow of the political establishment (a) by a mass-based movements (as in the Chinese, Cuban, and Iranian revolutions; the demise of communism in Eastern Europe; and the collapse of right wing regimes in Spain, Portugal, and Greece), (b) by senior military elements in previously nonpraetorian politics (as in the right wing military assaults on institutionalized democracies in Chile and Uruguay), or (c) by antisystem junior elements within a politically active military (as in the 1952 Egyptian, 1958 Iraqi, and 1969 Libyan revolutions).

It is assumed in this framework that any one of these four types of regime change may lead to significant foreign policy restructuring. But, this is not to say that any one of these four types *always* leads to important foreign policy changes; for each type of regime change there are some cases that may lead to foreign policy changes, while there are others that may not. In other words, no *a priori* assumptions can be made about which types of regime changes lead to important foreign policy changes and which ones do not. While not dismissing the theoretical dynamics underlying the progression of political phenomena across the four categories, the typology specified here primarily serves as a device for explicating the range of regime changes to be included in the analysis of regime effects on foreign policy restructuring.[10] Distinguishing major regime changes (those resulting in significant foreign policy restructuring) from minor ones requires further theoretical effort—namely, ascertaining whether the political groups exchanging power are actually different in their policy orientations and whether or not they are politically capable of initiating policy changes.

Task II: Conceptualizing the Shifting Properties of Political Regimes

The task of this second stage is the conceptualization of regime properties that might change with a new leadership and subsequently pursue foreign policy restructuring. To begin with, one must reject the assumption that change based upon the transformation of political structures is the single most important feature of political change underlying foreign policy restructuring. Instead, the focus here is directly on the characteristics of the actors involved in the exchange of power—be they predominant leaders, intra-party factions, mainstream parties, or pro/antisystem parties. Following the Goldmann, Hermann, and Holsti frameworks, as well as comparative foreign policy research on political regimes (Hagan 1993, 1987; Salmore and Salmore 1978), two properties of regimes are useful in isolating the altered political conditions that most directly underlay foreign policy change. They are "regime orientation" and "regime fragmentation."

A regime change is theorized to lead to major foreign policy restructuring only if it meets two criteria: first, it involves political actors with different orientations to foreign affairs and, second, the new regime is politically cohesive enough (i.e., not fragmented internally) to be able to implement new foreign policy initiatives. Because neither regime property is tied to the structure of the political system, each criterion requires consideration when analyzing regime changes in either democratic or authoritarian political systems.[11] Furthermore, the conceptualization of both attributes is open enough to permit the extensive gathering of cross-national data.

Regime Orientation

The orientation of a political regime reflects (1) the ruling group's basic beliefs about international affairs as they relate to their state's domestic and foreign concerns and (2) the coalition of societal, economic, and political interests aligned with the regime. It is, in effect, the "national interest" of the country *as defined* by the group or coalition currently in power. As an agent of foreign policy restructuring, it is assumed here that different political groups may bring to office alternative views regarding the state's international situation and interests. Furthermore, these overall orientations are largely shared by actors within all but the most fragmented regimes and are usually stable and unchanging throughout the life of the regime.

The theoretical premise of this concept is that a particular leadership group or coalition puts its own imprint on the goals the state pursues in foreign affairs and the nature of the state's reaction to international pressures. This idea is certainly not new; the purpose here is to conceptualize it so that it will be appropriate for comparative analysis across successive regimes. It is the core premise for much of the political psychology literature that holds that leader belief systems (and the resultant perceptions) define the broad outlines of foreign policy under different leaders (see Hermann 1988; Holsti 1969; Jervis 1976; Larson 1985; Rosati 1987; Starr 1984). Its impact on U.S. policy is suggested by Gaddis's (1982) analysis of the alternative "strategies of contain-ment" of successive cold war American administrations. An equally important (though less studied) dynamic is that regime leaders act in the interest of the domestic political, economic, and societal groups to which they are aligned. Works by Bruce Moon (1983) on Third World dependence and Jack Snyder (1991) on the sources of expansionist foreign policies show how support groups work through consensus and logrolling in defining the regime's orientation in foreign affairs. It is assumed that such political alignments, as well as percep-tual dynamics, vary across different regimes and contribute to the emergence of the different orientations described below.

Regime orientations vary with respect to, first, the identification and relative ranking of foreign threats and problems and, second, perceptions of the nature, or severity, of those threats and the appropriate strategies by which to counter them. The identification and ranking of foreign threats and problems is the more familiar dimension of regime orientation, particularly the determination of alignment patterns in the bipolar structure of the cold war international system in which most states (or actually their regimes) were either pro-Western/ anti-Soviet, pro-Soviet/anti-Western, or nonaligned. This kind of scheme is undoubtedly useful because it gets directly at the threats and problems that motivate governments to act. However, it also has clear limitations for purposes of regime classification. First, superpower alignments do not capture the complexity of positions taken by various states. Especially in the Third World, many issues are defined in terms of *regional* considerations, and threat percep-tions center around traditional adversaries and regional power balances which often outweighed superpower cold war concerns. Second, and especially in the post–cold war world, the reinforcing issues defined by the system's bipolar structure no longer define foreign policy agendas. Trade and monetary issues, problems of integration within the European Community, and now regional issues such as the Yugoslav civil war cannot be interpreted in terms of cold war alignments. In either case, any attempt to look at regime orientation will have to expand beyond the orientation scheme developed in the cold war if it is to capture the increasingly complex agendas of states across different regions and issues areas.

In addition, and whatever the outcome of these efforts, the identification of foreign threats must be supplemented by a scheme that accounts for the second, more subtle dimension of regime orientation: leadership perceptions of the severity of those foreign threats. This is often important when accounting for the foreign policy effects of regime changes involving political groups, who, though they agree on the identification of foreign threats, disagree fundamentally over how to respond to those threats. In fact, given the complexity of classification problems and the variety of threats across issues and regions, this may well be the only aspect of regime orientation that can be used to classify regimes in a general manner, particularly in a post–cold war world with varying alignments. A leadership's assessment of the severity of a foreign threat underlies the general kind of policy strategy—confrontation or accommodation—used to cope with a perceived threat or problem.

The following scheme is an attempt to classify the orientations that result from differing images of the intensity of foreign threats. With the hope of doing broad cross-national comparisons, this scheme is designed to apply across all types of issues and threats by asking whether the leaders see the international system as a hostile place (without regard to specific issues). Four types of regimes are identified, ranging from ones with very moderate orientations to those with extremely hardline postures. These are derived from several questions concerning leaders' beliefs about the degree of threat in the international system. First, what is the essential character of the adversary; is it a "typical" state, or does it have a domestic system driven by fundamentally different (and presumably aggressive) forces? Second, what is the range and scope of the threat posed by the adversary; are its goals limited and legitimate or are they unlimited in the sense that they could threaten the very existence of one's own state? Third, to what extent must the adversary cope with domestic and foreign constraints; are there internal limits on its power, or does it have a strong power base and exceptional unity of purpose in its use? Ranging from moderate to progressively more hardline orientations, there are four regime types.

Type 1: Moderate Regimes. Leaders in these regimes do not see the international environment as inherently hostile or dramatically threatening to their state's security, well-being, or international status. Conflicts among states are seen as issue-specific or situation-bound in which adversaries have relatively legitimate motives and limited goals. Other states are perceived to be more or less typical actors who are motivated by the same kinds of pressures that guide one's own state, and who recognize significant internal economic, societal, and political constraints on their use of power. Thus moderate leaders tend to be restrained and flexible in their own foreign policy behavior, often emphasizing a wider array of problems as they work to accommodate a variety of international concerns and cooperate with other states toward their resolution. Such was the case in the Carter administration's (attempted) "internationalist" shift away from cold war containment. In its extreme form, this moderation stems from a redirected concern for domestic crises with a need to ease tensions with and even attract aid and investment from adversaries. This kind of domestically-driven acquiescence appears to have been at the root of Gorbachev's acceptance of the retrenchment of Soviet power in Eastern Europe and Asia and also the basis of Egypt's realignment toward the West and peace initiative with Israel under Sadat. In Latin America the rise of moderate regimes replacing anti-American ones often involves new leaders who place little emphasis on foreign threats and are concerned primarily with reestablishing the network of economic ties with the United States, as demonstrated by new regimes in post-Sandinista Nicaragua, post-Noriega Panama, and post-Manley Jamaica under Seaga.

Type II: Pragmatic Regimes.   Leaders of these regimes, as well as their counterparts in the two other relatively hardline regimes below, perceive the international system to be a threatening environment. However preoccupied with such threats, these pragmatic leaders have relatively restrained and complex views of those threats as posed to their state. Adversaries are seen to have limited goals and constrained capabilities such that they do not pose an immediate threat to the state's survival. This makes "room for diplomacy" (Yergin 1977) in which bargaining, compromise, and even some limited forms of cooperation are in each state's interest—indeed, skilled diplomacy enhancing areas of mutual interest is an important means of containing the adversary's behavior. While not precluding confrontation entirely, these regimes show some flexibility and restraint in coping with foreign threats. Beliefs such as these underlay the moderation of superpower tensions during the détente of the early 1970s in both the Nixon/Kissinger and Brezhnev regimes, as well as the West German policy of "Ostpolitik" under the Brandt government. Among Third World states, pragmatic foreign policy shifts are reflected in attempts at increasing foreign diplomatic and economic relations with a recognized adversary, even though ties with any major power may jeopardize the government's autonomy in domestic and foreign affairs. Dramatic cases of openings to the West include China under Deng and Indonesia under Suharto, while pragmatic shifts away from close dependence on the United States have been sought by Aquino in the Philippines and Mubarak in Egypt. A similar pragmatic balancing act is Taiwan's accelerating ties with the People's Republic of China after the passing of the Chiang family dominance in the Nationalist Party regime.

Type III: Militant Regimes.   Leaders in these regimes perceive the international system to be an inherently hostile one in which interaction between adversaries is an essentially zero-sum relationship. The political, economic, and social systems of adversaries are thought to lead them to inherently aggressive foreign policies. Adversaries are viewed as having unlimited goals in that they directly threaten the security, well-being, and international status of the regime's own state and pose a threat across a wide variety of substantive and regional issues. The severity of these threats largely precludes any kind of normal diplomatic accommodation, and necessitates ongoing confrontation using political, economic, and ultimately military pressure in an effort to contain the threat and maintain the credibility of deterrence in one's own state. But, this is not to say that these regimes expect unrestrained confrontation. Two sources of perceived restraint are, first, that adversaries are "rational" (i.e., cold and calculating) and thus capable of being deterred from confrontation and, second, that conflicts occur within the bounds of established international norms. The origins of the cold war in the 1940s reflected the rise of militant orientations in the American and Soviet governments under Truman and Stalin (much the same could be said about the collapse of 1970s détente). While militant regimes were the norm in Western Europe at the height of the cold war (e.g., Germany's Adenauer), later foreign policy restructurings can be traced to the rise of a more militant view of world affairs (e.g., Thatcher's anticommunism in the 1980s and de Gaulle's assertion of French independence in the 1960s). The Middle East conflicts have, over the years, been affected by the emergence of hardline governments—such as the rise to dominance of Israel's Ben-Gurion prior to the 1956 Suez War who replaced the more moderate Sharret, as well as the emergence of the relatively (by Arab standards) less radical Assad regime in Syria.

Type IV: Radical Regimes.   The belief systems of radical leaderships reflect the most extreme beliefs about the nature of international politics as well as the imperatives they pose for the state's foreign policy. Going beyond the militant orientation, a radical orientation to world affairs views foreign adversaries as posing an even more unrelenting and immediate threat to the established international and regional order. Radical leaders consider adversaries to be ''evil'' actors who have a nonrational aggressiveness grounded in an expansionist ideology, unrestrained nationalism, and/or severe domestic crises. Bargaining and restraint is meaningless; only clearly superior military power is an effective means of deterring aggression. Furthermore, there is an important offensive dimension to the radical orientation. Given the ''evil'' character of these adversaries, radical leaders see it as imperative to maintain strong initiative in countering the ever-present threat and, indeed, mobilizing domestic and foreign players behind a sort of moral crusade against the adversary. There is a maximum propensity to perceive all sorts of international (and domestic) issues as being directly connected to the primary adversary's global scheme. As a result, radical regimes are likely to reject the very legitimacy of the current international status quo and, if necessary, are willing to violate international norms and domestic constraints in achieving the moral imperatives of their foreign policy. Frequently, the emergence of radical regimes in the Third World are dramatic events, in particular because these new regimes typically take an extreme anti-Western stance and replace largely compliant, pragmatic, or moderate pro-Western regimes—for instance, the cases of Castro in Cuba, Mao in China, Khomeini in Iran, Sukarno in Indonesia, Nasser in Egypt, and the highly unstable Ba'athist regimes in Syria during the 1960s. Among status quo-oriented Western countries, it is more difficult to identify such radical states, but some of the rhetoric of American administrations under Reagan (and perhaps Eisenhower to the extent Dulles was influential) suggest certain radical tendencies in their view of the Soviet Union, similar to Stalin's image of the United States. The hardline in Israeli foreign policy under the Likud Party also stemmed from a relatively radical image (by Israeli political standards) of the Arab threat necessitating the use of force and the acquisition of more secure boarders.[12]

It is important to emphasize that these categories are ideal types. Although for illustrative purposes relatively familiar regimes have been placed into one category or another, the case of radical orientations indicates that this is not such a simple exercise. Most regimes would seem, instead, to fall between ideal types of regime orientation, although with a tendency to gravitate more closely to one of the two orientations. Note, for example, the relative positions of American administrations since the 1960s, as diagrammed in figure 7.1. The Reagan administration (originally, at least) had a relatively radical image of the Soviet Union and the American strategy of containment, but certainly it was not as radical as, say, Nazi Germany or Fascist Italy. Rather, if anything, it was an essentially militant regime with radical tendencies and therefore falls between the ideal categories of militant and radical. This distinguishes it clearly from other essentially militant regimes that instead leaned in the direction of greater pragmatism (e.g., those of Kennedy and Johnson). Such subtleties are also apparent in the differentiation of the otherwise similarly pro-détente administrations of Nixon/Kissinger and Carter. Both were clearly pragmatic, but if anything Carter leaned in the direction of non-cold war moderation while Nixon and Kissinger showed elements of militancy. Finally, this scheme also captures the apparently subtle shift between the Bush and Clinton administrations—a change from an essentially pragmatic leadership with militant tendencies to one which is similarly pragmatic but with more moderate views of the nature of world politics.

Regime Fragmentation

Although a regime's orientation indicates a great deal about the broad outlines of its foreign policy, one must also determine the extent to which the leadership is politically able to initiate and maintain new policies consistent with that foreign policy orientation. In other words, is the regime politically able to implement its preferences in substantively meaningful ways? Can it achieve a political consensus that permits it to commit the state to a coherent set of policies? Or, will it find itself limited to only vague rhetoric which, though often intensely expressed, in no way alters the basic structure of the state's foreign relationships? Indeed, there even may be broader political

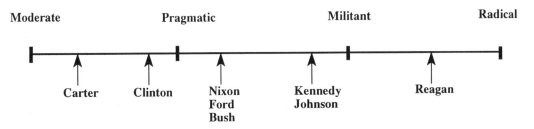

Note. For sake of simplicity, these orientations are for the original posture of each administration. Thus, the shifts later on in the Carter and Reagan administrations are not indicated.

Figure 7.1   American Postwar Regime Orientations, 1960–1994

pressures that actually "push" a new leadership into initiating foreign policy changes not on its agenda.

These questions consider the extent to which domestic politics affect the implementation of the new regime's orientation once it has taken power. As argued elsewhere in detail (Hagan 1993), domestic politics has a pervasive yet complex influence on foreign policy. As new leaders institute change in foreign policy, they must simultaneously cope with two domestic political imperatives: first, within the regime advocates of change must build a coalition of supporters if they are to have the authority (e.g., votes) to initiate new policy (Putnam 1988; Allison 1971) and, second, they must carry out change in a way that does not alienate regime supporters and, if anything, enhances the regime's own legitimacy and that of its policies (George 1980; Trout 1975). Strong political opposition can constrain the new regime's implementation of its proposed foreign policy changes, either because the regime is forced to compromise (or deadlock) or because it fears generating public controversies that could destabilize it. Whereas this dynamic undercuts change in foreign policy, under certain circumstances domestic pressures actually may push new leaders toward aggressive implementation of change, especially when they see foreign policy initiatives as critical to enhancing the legitimacy of their regime and its foreign policy orientation. Either way, and for whatever reason, there are strong theoretical reasons to expect domestic politics to distort the implementation of the policy orientation of the new regime.

The primary regime property affecting leaders' ability to initiate major policy changes is regime fragmentation (Hagan 1993, 1987a; Salmore and Salmore 1978).[13] This concerns the extent to which the central political leadership has persisting internal political divisions in the form of competing personalities, bureaucracies/institutions, factions, parties, or other kinds of autonomous political groups. In this comparative framework, regime fragmentation is treated as the central locus of political constraints for two reasons. First, opposition in this arena (as opposed to that outside the regime) is in the most immediate position to block policy changes. Actors here retain authority essential for the implementation of policy decisions, and substantial factional or party opposition to the initiative can ultimately bring about the collapse of the government. Second, political divisions within the regime are possible in any type of political system, and thus an analysis of regime fragmentation effectively addresses the existence of "significant" oppositions in various types of political systems without reference to the level of democratization or development. For purposes of making cross-national comparisons, at least five types of regimes can be identified with respect to their internal mix of cabinet, legislative, and/or party divisions. These types range from highly cohesive regimes to highly fragmented ones.

Type I: Single Party Regimes Dominated by a Single, Individual Leader. In these cases the ruling party or group is dominated by a single personality who cannot be challenged significantly by any other individuals, cliques, or factions in the regime. This preeminence is not usually institutionally grounded, and depends instead on the leader's own organizational skills within the party and his/her public charisma. Falling in this category are regimes in a number of Third World states, especially in the Middle East (e.g., Iraq's Sadaam Hussein, Syria's Assad, Libya's Qadhdhafi, and Egypt's Nasser and Sadat) and sub-Saharan Africa (e.g., Ghana's Nkrumah, Zaire's Mobuto, and the Ivory Coast's Houphouet-Boigny) where there is a tradition of personal rule and strong leadership. Predominant leaders can also be found in more established political systems where a highly popular individual emerges (at least temporarily) to a politically unassailable position within the regime, such as Reagan in the United States, de Gaulle in France, Thatcher in Britain, Adenauer in Germany, Stalin in the Soviet Union, Tito in Yugoslavia, Ben-Gurion in Israel, and Nehru in India. Clearly, each of these leaders when entering office had exceptional authority to mount major foreign policy initiatives. And, as argued later, there may be additional conditions in the political system that prompt these kinds of leaders to initiate change in foreign policy as a means of sustaining the legitimacy of their policies and personal position.

Type II: Regimes Fragmented Solely by the Existence of Established, Autonomous Political Institutions/Bureaucracies. These are cases of regimes controlled by a single party which are reasonably cohesive and disciplined, as indicated largely by the absence of established factions. Power is not concentrated in the hands of any single predominant individual, but rather is dispersed within a collective leadership and across separate institutions and party structures. Foreign policy initiatives must thus be based on a consensus among relevant players and institutions, although constructing this agreement may be facilitated by the absence of ongoing political competition and/or substantive policy differences which occur in factionalized and coalition regimes. Regimes falling into this category include cohesive single party cabinets in the advanced industrial states (e.g., the post-1971 Brezhnev politburo in the U.S.S.R., Labour and Conservative Party cabinets in Britain, and Labour and National Party cabinets in New Zealand), and cases of presidential democracies when the executive and Congress are controlled by the same (cohesive) party (e.g., the United States under Kennedy, Carter, and Truman). Also in this category are single party leaderships in institutionally complex third world polities, (e.g., Taiwan since Chiang Kai-shek and military regimes in the bureaucratic-authoritarian polities of Chile under Pinochet and Indonesia under Suharto). Although hardly an exhaustive listing, none of these regimes appears to have been strongly precluded from initiating policy changes after winning power.

Type III: Regimes Controlled by a Single Party/Group Which is Itself Internally Divided by Established Political Factions. Although ruled by a single party or group, this party or group is itself so internally fragmented that it is little more than a coalition of entrenched factional organizations. Within the framework of a single party organization and ideology, these factions openly compete for control of major political party positions and often have divergent policy positions. Single party cabinets often are actually tenuous factional coalitions (which are in turn opposed by those party factions excluded from the cabinet), and, once in power, leaders must avoid disrupting these arrangements. These internal divisions also open avenues for considerable influence of bureaucratic and institutional interests. Examples of factionalized regimes are Japan under the long-ruling Liberal Democratic Party, India's National Congress Party, the Soviet Union during the later stages of Khrushchev's tenure, the Chinese Communist Party in the early 1960s as well as throughout the post-Mao era, the loosely organized Aquino leadership in the Philippines, and the divided military in either a consolidating or decaying junta (Argentina under Galtieri is one example). Foreign policymaking in most of these cases is considerably complicated, especially when there is no strong leader to mediate factions. The result has often been that leaders are unable to implement consistent policies in a sustained fashion (e.g., Khrushchev, Aquino, and China since Mao) or unwilling to risk a break from the status quo from the beginning (repeatedly the case with Japan's Liberal Democratic Party).

Type IV: Regimes Ruled by a Coalition of Autonomous Political Groups in Which One Actor Has Clear Predominance. In this case and the one below, power in the regime is dispersed across separate political parties or other such groups, and within this coalition there are likely to be sharper policy differences and more severe competition for power than would occur in a single party. In this case, though, this intense fragmentation is mitigated by the presence of an individual or group who clearly has predominant power relative to the other players. Coalition cabinets in democratic states take this form when one party controls most ministries, as often occurs in West Germany and Israel where alternating dominant parties have shared power with junior partners. Presidential, quasi-presidential, and monarchical regimes take this form when the executive branch and legislature are held by opposing parties—frequently found in the United States, many Latin American democracies, the Middle East (e.g., Lebanon and recently Jordan), France during periods of cohabitation, and Russia under Yeltsin. Among authoritarian regimes, this kind of power sharing occurs during periods of protracted instability with a highly charismatic leader sharing some power with otherwise dependent actors (e.g., Iran under Khomeini, Indonesia under Sukarno, China under Mao during the Cultural Revolution, and the Soviet Union under Gorbachev prior to the failed August 1991 coup). Although often offering intense verbal support for the interests of the dominant actor, the recurring pattern has been an inability to restructure policies completely because of the need to balance the interests and positions of hardline/radical and reformist/moderate elements. Thus, even a Khomeini was unable to impose a solution on the contending factions involved in the hostage crisis, while Gorbachev had to waver continuously between reformist and hardline elements prior to the August coup.

Type V: Regimes Ruled by a Coalition in Which There is No Clear, Single Dominant Actor. Here there is a coalition of two or more groups of equivalent strength, and authority is very fragmented because no single actor is able to assert leadership within the regime. Parliamentary coalitions frequently take this pattern in either the form of a "grand coalition" as with Germany's late-1960s

Christian Democratic-Socialist cabinet and Israel's 1980s Labour-Likud cabinet or a cabinet consisting of three or more equal partners as in the successive cabinets of Fourth Republic France and Italy.[14] All of these are the classic cases of deadlock; none was capable of initiating recognized policy changes, be it the launching of German Ostpolitik, the future relationship of the West Bank to Israel, the French war in Algeria, the Dutch acceptance of NATO missiles, or the extent of Italy's involvement in the European integration. Coalition arrangements are also possible in authoritarian systems and take a variety of forms. In the army-party regimes of Syria and Iraq, at least prior to the consolidation of power by Assad and Sadaam, respectively, there were sharp, ongoing conflicts between each state's military and Ba'athist party players. Consociational arrangements became the basis of power in ethnically fragmented Yugoslavia in the 1980s after the death of Tito.

Reinforcing Political System Conditions

Although fragmentation is the most immediate political constraint, its precise impact on foreign policy is further affected by aspects of the wider political system. These political system conditions are important in at least three ways. First, they pressure even the most cohesive of political regimes. In other words, while not plagued by the fragmentation of the authority within the regime, this is not to say that such cohesive regimes are immune from other kinds of political pressures. Second, political constraints within a regime are intensified if factions and parties closely align with powerful actors and interests outside the regime. Finally, certain political pressures point not only to constraining effects, but also specific conditions which might push leaders to initiate major policy changes. What follows are several political system conditions that are likely to reduce, or enhance, the ability of new leadership to overcome internal political constraints as they try to implement foreign policy changes.

Political Opposition to the Regime.   Even though the political divisions within the regime are assumed here to be the most central form of political constraint, it is also useful to consider political opposition outside the regime likely to influence the leadership within the regime (Hagan 1993; Hermann 1987). Particularly significant is the strength and intensity of organized opposition immediate to the regime—i.e., dissenting actors within the ruling party, the legislature, the military, and regional governments. These are arenas for formal opposition to the regime, and the ability of the regime to retain power over the long term necessitates support of these institutions. Not all opposition, though, is institutional in character. It may be that in "weak states" (Katzenstein 1977; Krasner 1978a) powerful societal interests wield veto power over certain issues, while in less stable systems the main challenge may be from organized protest movements and insurgencies.

Polarization Over Foreign Policy Issues.   This concerns the extent to which actors in a regime (and oppositions outside of it) have substantive differences over foreign policy issues. It asks: is there a consensus among the regime's contending actors on the basic identification of threats and problems facing the state—in other words, agreement on the national interest? Perhaps more relevant in most regimes is whether or not there are differences on the basic strategies for coping with those threats; in other words, whether there are divisions between "moderates" favoring diplomatic accommodation and "hardliners" arguing for increased confrontation (Holsti and Rosenau 1984; Snyder and Deising 1977; Vasquez 1987). Competition for power occurs in all political settings; what is important here is that it is connected to substantive foreign policy issues. Where splits occur, political constraints are further intensified as foreign policy debates become tied up with the political competition for office. If foreign policy issues are not themselves controversial, they can be better insulated from internal political competition, and leaders will then be in a better position to implement new initiatives.

Regime Vulnerability. This concerns the possibility that a regime will be removed from power. Do conditions exist that suggest the leadership believes that opposition can effectively challenge their control of the regime? One indicator of this is the competitiveness of the political system, asking if a single party (and faction within it) has controlled the regime for an extended period of time, or if there have been regular exchanges of power such that opponents inside and outside the regime have a reasonable chance of regaining control. Another is the extent of political uncertainty within the regime. In fragmented regimes, political constraints can be greatly intensified if the regime faces an immediate leadership crisis, in which its factions and coalition members do not fully support it. Research from several projects indicates that highly vulnerable foreign policymakers are especially sensitive to domestic oppositions (Hagan 1993; Lebow 1981; Ostrom and Job 1986).

Political System Structure. Although this chapter originally argued against the primacy of this property, within the scheme presented here structural arrangements do affect how leaders respond to constraints within the regime and oppositions outside of it. This dimension has two intertwined elements. The first is the familiar notion of *accountability* underlying the democratic versus nondemocratic distinction. This concerns the formal structural arrangements governing the relationship of the regime to the wider polity—i.e., the ability of the public to participate and challenge officials and their policies in meaningful ways (Dahl 1971; Hermann 1987). Leaders in open polities must take into account a wider array of actors and possess fewer options for managing dissent (e.g., coercive suppression has little legitimacy). Political system *institutionalization* is the second dimension. Drawing on Huntington (1968), this is the extent to which political norms regulating the interaction between leaders and opponents (both inside and outside the regime) are widely accepted and adhered. The premise here is that democratization matters little unless political actors actually adhere to those rules tolerating oppositions and regulating policymaking; furthermore, even authoritarian leaders operate with structural constraints when within well-institutionalized regimes.[15] Taken together, structural constraints are greatest in established democracies and minimal in noninstitutionalized closed polities, while hybrid cases fall in between.

Although probably not an exhaustive list of conditioning factors, these four are useful in assessing the final impact of regime fragmentation. They could provide some insight into puzzling cases in which highly fragmented regimes seem unrestrained as well as those cases in which cohesive ones appear to be surprisingly deadlocked. Furthermore, certain configurations might form the political basis (or push) for major foreign policy initiatives by a new regime— e.g., situations in which a strong consensus on a foreign policy issue enables a highly vulnerable regime in a noninstitutionalized polity to gain some desperately needed political legitimacy.

Task III: Broadening the Consideration of Foreign Policy Properties Subject to Change Across Regimes

As should be evident from the discussion thus far, a third task for regime change research is to broaden the conceptualization of the dependent variable: the dimensions of foreign policy subject to restructuring. The Midlarsky, Moon, and the Andriole and Hopple studies (with the significant exception of Maoz's war proneness analysis) focus exclusively on foreign policy realignment. Although realignment is a major aspect of foreign policy restructuring, examination of only this dimension would likely lead to a biased assessment of the effects of regime changes. This is because realignments are unlikely to be sensitive to the effects of milder regime changes—i.e., ones involving groups who agree on the identification of foreign threats but differ in their estimation of the severity of those threats and/or face different levels of domestic opposition. Although not leading to major realignments, these types of regime changes lead (as do many revolutions; see Hagan 1989) to important shifts in relations between actors between, and within, established blocs. The systemic implications of these nonrealigning aspects of foreign policy should not be dismissed lightly, because they can significantly affect the intensity of regional and global conflicts, as suggested by the cases cited at the beginning of this chapter. These three dimensions, to be briefly explored here, are accommodation/confrontation, independence/interdependence of action, and level of commitment.

Accommodation/Confrontation

This dimension refers to a regime's propensity to deal with adversaries through diplomatic bargaining as opposed to confrontational strategies involving sanctions such as military force, nationalization or tariffs, or diplomatic pressure to isolate and condemn adversaries. The overall mix of cooperation and accommodation in foreign policy is very much tied to its regime's orientation. The imperative of confrontation (if not expansion) is at the core of the hardline mentalities of militant and revolutionary regimes, while diplomatic accommodation with even adversaries is the hallmark of the flexible and restrained foreign policy postures of moderate and pragmatic regimes. The shifting mix of confrontation and accommodation was the dominant feature of the post-Vietnam U.S. containment policies across the pragmatic Nixon, moderate Carter, and hardline Reagan administrations; similarly, the key feature of Gorbachev's foreign policy was the shift toward greater accommodation, if not acquiescence, toward the West as a status quo power. Much the same can be said of regional conflicts. The intensity of the decades old Arab-Israeli conflict, for example, has been affected by the rise and fall of hardline regimes in Israel (Likud and Labour, respectively), Egypt (Nasser to Sadat to Mubarak), and Syria (the militant Assad regime as opposed to its extremely radical predecessors). Domestic politics also affect the level of confrontation and accommodation in a new regime's foreign policy. The Nixon/Kissinger pragmatism, for example, was dictated by the anti-interventionist mood of the U.S. Congress and public opinion, while the Reagan administration in its early years found it politically beneficial to take a hardline stance toward the Soviet Union and other recognized adversaries. More dramatically, the severe political infighting in post-revolutionary regimes (e.g., Ba'athist Syria and Khomeini's Iran) intensified—if not drove—hostility toward the West and Israel and precluded any pragmatic restraint or flexibility.

Independence/Interdependence of Action

This dimension is the "degree of autonomy a government tries to maintain in its foreign policy actions" (Hermann 1982, 254). High independence is characterized by self-initiated and unilateral behaviors, often reflective of more hardline images of international affairs. Militant and revolutionary regimes have highly independent foreign policies as they confront what they see as a hostile and even nonlegitimate international system. Pragmatic regimes, in contrast, are likely to see more opportunities and possibilities for contacts and multilateral ties with other states, while reactive postures are a key pattern of acquiescence by moderate regimes. Shifting levels of independence have characterized the foreign policies of France (particularly with the rise and fall of de Gaulle), the Peoples' Republic of China with its factionalized Communist Party, and even smaller actors such as New Zealand on matters of U.S. nuclear weapons deployment. The effects of domestic politics are also relevant here. Alliance ties to, say, the United States have long been a controversial issue for the politics of Western European and East Asian allies. For example, asserting independence from the United States was a primary means of legitimizing the new regimes in France under De Gaulle and the Philippines under post-Marcos leaders. At the other extreme, though, are situations in which political constraints preclude independent initiatives. New leaders in Japan and Mexico seem to have been able to do little to overcome the institutional and factional opposition to distancing their countries from the United States, despite occasional protestations to do so.

Level of Commitment

Commitment refers to the degree to which current actions limit future options through the allocation of resources or the generation of expectations in others (Callahan 1982). Indicators of major commitments are the signing or breaking of agreements, deployment of resources abroad (military forces or foreign aid), and budgetary allocations to foreign and military bureaucracies. Lesser commitments center around verbal behaviors, ones ranging from simply commenting on international situations to making specific promises or threats to act. Assuming that regimes of any type of orientation engage in some type of commitment, this foreign policy dimension would seem most linked to regime fragmentation and other forms of domestic politics. Often it is the case that a new regime comes to power, but finds it is simply unable to implement its new preferences. All post-Vietnam U.S. administrations have been unable to implement key aspects of the containment strategies (see Gaddis 1982; Brown 1983); while in Russia, the new Yeltsin regime now finds it difficult to sustain cooperation with the Western interventionist policies in Iraq and the former Yugoslavia. Both reflect a mix of presidential constraints from legislatures as well as the need to conform to shifting public taste for assertiveness or restraint in foreign policy. In more severe episodes, political constraints have plagued a regime that came to power with promises to change existing policies. None of the successive regimes of Fourth Republic France, for example, were able to commit the state to a resolution of the Algerian War; nor, in the 1980s, was a succession of Dutch governments able to choose fully between accepting or rejecting the deployment of NATO cruise missiles. Political constraints were even apparent in post-revolutionary Iran; namely, despite virulent anti-Americanism, the fragmented coalition was unable to resolve the hostage crisis, either by putting the hostages on trial or releasing them. Release of the hostages, as well as the implementation of some of the other policies above, only came about after a further consolidation of power by certain leadership groups within the regime.

Summary

This chapter has sought to respond to a perceived narrowness in the evolving cross-national research on regime change and foreign policy restructuring, in particular its nearly exclusive focus on revolutionary transformations and foreign policy realignment. Drawing upon diverse episodes of important, though less dramatic, regime changes and foreign policy restructuring, this chapter has sketched a conceptual framework that incorporates nonrevolutionary regime changes, considers nonstructural regime properties and dynamics, and posits several important, nonrealigning dimensions of foreign policy restructuring. This framework can be summarized as a three-stage program of research tasks, as diagrammed in figure 7.2. The first task (or independent variable) is the identification of political regime changes according to a four-

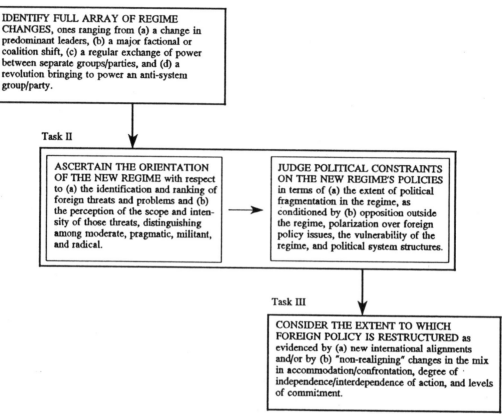

Task I

IDENTIFY FULL ARRAY OF REGIME CHANGES, ones ranging from (a) a change in predominant leaders, (b) a major factional or coalition shift, (c) a regular exchange of power between separate groups/parties, and (d) a revolution bringing to power an anti-system group/party.

Task II

ASCERTAIN THE ORIENTATION OF THE NEW REGIME with respect to (a) the identification and ranking of foreign threats and problems and (b) the perception of the scope and intensity of those threats, distinguishing among moderate, pragmatic, militant, and radical.

JUDGE POLITICAL CONSTRAINTS ON THE NEW REGIME'S POLICIES in terms of (a) the extent of political fragmentation in the regime, as conditioned by (b) opposition outside the regime, polarization over foreign policy issues, the vulnerability of the regime, and political system structures.

Task III

CONSIDER THE EXTENT TO WHICH FOREIGN POLICY IS RESTRUCTURED as evidenced by (a) new international alignments and/or by (b) "non-realigning" changes in the mix in accommodation/confrontation, degree of independence/interdependence of action, and levels of commitment.

Figure 7.2   Sequence of Tasks for Assessing the Impact of Regime Change on Foreign Policy Restructuring

fold classification of leadership changes, that include both revolutions and a range of nonstructural changes in which contending groups exchange power. The second task (or intervening variable) is the conceptualization of the precise regime properties subject to change. Particularly important here is the foreign policy orientation of the new ruling group, and the determination if it differs from its predecessor on the identification of threats, issues, and assessment of the severity of those dangers and concerns. Supplementing this, is the issue of whether the new regime is politically able to implement new foreign policy preferences in substantively meaningful ways. The third task (or dependent variable) is the linking of the dynamics of regime change to several foreign policy dimensions, which include realignment as well as nonrealigning behaviors such as accommodation/confrontation, independence/interdependence of action, and level of commitment. This framework is, admittedly, very general in some respects, but the hope is that it illustrates the kinds of basic concepts and underlying theoretical logic that might be useful in developing more comprehensive comparative analyses of regime change and foreign policy restructuring.

Although concerned mainly with explicating tasks for comparative research on regime change and foreign policy restructuring, the framework developed here has wider implications for the understanding of the sources of international system transformation. At a minimum, a regime perspective adds to other chapters in this volume illustrating how domestic factors affect government responses to international change. Elements of regime orientation shape leaders' sensitivity to (or alarm with) evolving threats and emerging global problems, and regime fragmentation and political system conditions set internal parameters on the range of choice that leaders have in adapting to those external pressures. However, the broader significance of the regime change-foreign policy restructuring linkage is that domestic political factors can also act as a driving force behind international system change. A new political regime in a major power may ultimately reshape basic patterns of regional and global conflict. The rise to power of a militant regime likely intensifies ongoing conflicts, and, even more dramatically, the appearance of a radical regime with expansionist ambitions (e.g., Napoleonic France or Nazi Germany) may itself alter basic international patterns by creating new threats and alignments. In sum, dynamic political processes within the nation-state, as manifested by the character of their regimes, do not simply mediate responses to international change; in their more extreme forms, they are primary agents of that change in ways that are deeply embedded in complex processes of political decay and consolidation within—not outside—the nation-state.

Notes

1. Judgments on the identification of regime changes are based on accounts by area specialists as reported in political handbooks and national histories, annual journal reports, and specialized books and articles, as explained in Hagan (1989a, 1989b). The following sources are the primary materials used to classify the regime orientations and oppositions involved in these regime changes. Advanced industrial democracies are: the United States (Gaddis 1982; Brown 1983; Garthoff 1985); Britain (Handreider and Auton 1980); France (Andrews 1962; Handreider and Auton 1980; LePrestre 1984; Macridis 1989; Rioux 1988); Germany (Goldmann 1988; Handreider 1970; Handreider and Auton 1980; Joffe 1989); Netherlands (Everts 1985); Italy (Kogan 1983; Vanicelli 1974; Willis 1971); Sweden (Faurby 1982; Sundelius 1989); Japan (Akaha 1991; Destler, Clapp, Sato, and Fukui 1976; Fukui 1970; Ori 1976); and New Zealand (Alves 1989). Communist regimes included are: the Soviet Union (Dallin 1981; Gelman 1984; Linden 1976; Schwartz 1975); Yugoslavia (Rusinow 1977; Zimmerman 1987); and the People's Republic of China (Bachman 1989; Fingar 1980; Harding 1980; Hinton 1972; Lieberthal 1984; Robinson 1982; Sutter 1978; Thornton 1982; Whiting 1983). Middle East countries are: Egypt (Ajami 1981; Dekmejian 1971; Dessouki 1984; Ismael and Ismael 1986; Kerr 1971; Taylor 1982); Israel (Aronson 1982–83; Brecher 1972; Dowty 1984; Perlmutter 1978, 1982; Safran 1978; Shalim 1983); Syria (Bar-Siman-Tov 1983; Hinnebusch 1984; Ismael and Ismael 1986; Kerr 1971; Rabinovich 1972; Seale 1965, 1988; Taylor 1982); Saudi Arabia (Korany 1984;

Quandt 1981); and Iran (Cottam 1989; Ramazani 1989; Stempel 1981). Other Third World nations are: Burma (Holsti 1982b); Chile (Zylberberg and Monterichanrd 1982); Cuba (Dominguez 1989); Ghana (Pellow and Chazan 1986; Thompson 1969); India (Appadorai 1981; Kochanek 1968); Indonesia (Weinstein 1976); Jamaica (Biddle and Stephens 1989); and the Philippines (Bresnan 1986).

2. Hermann's framework is a situationally-oriented model centered around decision-making phenomenon. Although it points to political dynamics essential of foreign policy change, the regime-centered framework developed in this chapter does not deal directly with much of Hermann's decision-making dynamics. This is attempted elsewhere (Hagan, forthcoming) where, following Hermann's scheme, the focus is on political pressures that lead to foreign policy changes even when the regime itself *does not* change.

3. This is not to say, however, that political revolutions were ever limited solely to the Third World; recall that Portugal, Spain, and Greece experienced these kinds of political changes in the 1970s, and almost equally dramatic was the replacement of France's Fourth Republic by the Fifth Republic.

4. In unstable political systems, "regular" procedures for leadership change can include military coups and other prevailing nondemocratic procedures.

5. The criteria of political predominance of both the preceding and succeeding incumbent is critical here. First, if either the predecessor or the successor—but not both—qualify as a politically predominant leader, then the regime change is more indicative of the rise/fall of a powerful group actor in the regime and thus falls in the Type II category. Second, there are many changes in the incumbent head of state involving simply the exchange of power between individuals, both of whom share power extensively with their cabinet, politburo, or junta colleagues. Thus leadership changes (including even the prime minister) would be excluded if they simply reflected "ministerial merry-go-rounds" of unstable parliamentary systems or cabinet shakeups in authoritarian systems when a prime minister is dismissed by the predominant leader.

6. For discussions of the decision-making role of predominant leaders, see relevant theoretical materials by M. Hermann and case studies in Hagan, Hermann, and Hermann (forthcoming).

7. This may include the complete removal of junior players in the party or factional coalition and their replacement by other new junior players, but the major or dominant actor(s) must persist in power. Also included here are cases in which a single group consolidates control by evicting other members of the coalition, as for example in Israel when the right-wing Likud coalition replaced the Likud-Labour coalition.

8. This category collapses a scale used in an earlier analysis of Third World regime changes (Hagan 1989a). In that scale, exchanges of power between separate groups were differentiated depending on whether the groups or parties involved were from the same or opposite ends of the political spectrum. While this distinction is important, ideological distance is captured separately with the conditioning property of political polarization used below.

9. This does not exclude the possibility of junior parties from the previous regime continuing in office in the new regime, but there must have been a clear change in the sense that a formally excluded group (or set of actors) is now dominant within the regime.

10. The progression of regime changes across the four categories encompass a progressively broader range of political phenomenon—e.g., Type I changes are limited to the personal traits of a single powerful individual, Type II changes incorporate shifting political constraints within the regime, Type III changes encompass entirely separate parties and groups operating within an unchanged political environment, and Type IV changes extend to alterations in political structures as well as socioeconomic elites. An interesting preliminary theoretical question is whether the range of purely domestic political phenomena involved determine the magnitude of foreign policy restructuring. For some clear evidence that this is the case for Third World countries, see Hagan (1989a).

11. All this is not to imply that political revolutions are not important, and the focus developed here suggests that their significance lies in their transferring of power to groups with completely different orientations toward foreign affairs and their restructuring of the domestic political environment.

12. Of course, the emergence of radical regimes has had a clear imprint on earlier periods of world affairs—sixteenth-century Spanish foreign policy under the Habsburgs (Charles V and Philip II), Revolutionary and Napoleonic France, Nazi Germany, and Japan's military-driven regimes of the 1930s.

13. The centrality of politics within the regime is argued in comparative foreign policy research by Hagan (1993, 1987a) and Salmore and Salmore (1978). This theme is now emerging in some of the research on democracy and war proneness (Morgan and Campbell 1991; Risse-Krippen 1991).

14. Regimes with a predominant political actor are included in this level of fragmentation, if that party/group is itself internally fragmented by structural factions (on the assumption that this internal competition negates its otherwise predominant position). This has long been the typical cabinet situation of the Christian Democratic Party in Italian coalitions, and in recent years has often emerged in the Dutch Christian Democratic Party on certain foreign policy issues.

15. Two studies indicate that institutionalization is a much more potent influence than democratization. Maoz (1989) finds that new revolutionary regimes (either authoritarian or democratic ones) are more conflict prone than are either new nonrevolutionary regimes or long established regimes. These findings are far clearer than those in his or other assessments of the relative conflict proneness of democratic and authoritarian states. Similarly, Hagan (1993) finds that institutionalization has strong mediating effects on correlations between oppositions and foreign policy behavior, while the corresponding effects of accountability are far weaker.

Chapter 8

Democratization and Foreign Policy Change in the East Asian NICs

Tong Whan Park, Dae-Won Ko, and Kyu-Ryoon Kim

Tong Whan Park, Dae-Won Ko, and Kyu-Ryoon Kim emphasize the impor-tance of the process of democratization on foreign policy restructuring. Like Volgy, Schraeder, and others, Park, Ko, and Kim draw on both domestic and international sources of foreign policy change. Like Hagan, however, they highlight the importance of the domestic context on democratization and its impact on foreign policy change. Park, Ko, and Kim present a framework for understanding the foreign policy changes of countries in transition from authoritarian rule to democracy. Specifically, they explain the foreign policy changes of South Korea and Taiwan in terms of each nation's ideology, state-society relationship, political structure, and political interest. Alterations in each of these factors result in changes in each country's foreign policy goals, capacity to act, and policymaking process, which necessarily lead to changes in foreign policy behavior. In explaining foreign policy developments in South Korea and Taiwan, especially their rapprochement with socialist countries, they also touch on the significant role of economic development and interna-tional change. In stressing the importance of the democratization of domestic political structures, the authors add an important dimension to the understand-ing of foreign policy restructuring.

Tong Whan Park is associate professor of political science at Northwestern University. He received a Ph.D. in political science from the University of Hawaii in 1969 and an Ll.B in law from Seoul National University in 1964. His research interests center on international relations and Northeast Asian poli-tics. His work has appeared in such journals as Asian Survey, Comparative Political Studies, Journal of East Asian Affairs, *and* Journal of East and West Studies. *Dae-Won Ko received a Ph.D. in political science from Northwestern University in 1993. His research interests center on international relations and the political economy of East Asian countries. Kyu-Ryoon Kim is an associate research fellow in the Political Studies Department at the Research Institute for National Unification in Seoul, Korea. He received a Ph.D. in political science from Northwestern University in 1989 after earning a B.A. in political science from Sogang University in Seoul, Korea in 1981. His research interests include international political economy and Pacific Basin area studies.*

The newly industrializing countries (NICs) in East Asia are experiencing a new wave of revolutionary changes. While their economic success is being emulated in the developing world as a model for industrialization, they face a fresh challenge on the political front. The movements toward democratization in Korea and Taiwan are eloquent testimony to this process of socio-political change. For some time, it has been anticipated that citizens of these NICs would sooner or later demand a political system commensurate with their high level of industrial growth, so it is not surprising that this long-suppressed energy for political participation has finally "boiled over." As seen in the recent turmoil within the NICs, this process of political transition will continue to be complex and dynamic, defying any simple theoretical explanation. Given the complexity of the topic, it is not the aim of this study to cover the entire spectrum of the NICs' political changes. Instead, this chapter focuses on one dimension of this development, mainly the impact of democratization on foreign policy change. From a comparison of the process of democratization in Korea and Taiwan, a synthetic theoretical framework is developed that may be applicable to other cases of democratization and foreign policy restructuring.

Since the transition to democracy began in the late 1980s, foreign policy changes made by Seoul and Taipei have been indeed Copernican, with the most pronounced changes taking place in their relationship with the socialist bloc countries. Having successfully hosted the largest-ever Olympic games in 1988, Korea's popularly elected government felt confident enough to launch a series of bold overtures toward its northern neighbors. Designed to win political favor with economic incentives, Seoul's Nordpolitik signifies the widening of its sphere of foreign relations which has hitherto been limited largely to its Western allies. In retrospect, it is a historical irony that Seoul is now in a position to reach out to the Eastern Bloc nations. At the beginning, the military regime started the process of industrialization in order to justify its authoritarian control. Eventually, Korea's successful economic development made Korea a leader among the NICs and produced an increase in wealth which ignited popular demand for an end to the long succession of authoritarian regimes and the establishment of a democratic political system. It was ironic that the economic growth which had acted as an essential pillar justifying authoritarian rule, also helped bring an end to that rule in 1988. At that time, Korea entered the initial phase of political democratization and began to undertake major shifts in its foreign policy behavior. With sustained popular support resulting from increased democratization, the new government has continued to pursue a foreign policy which deviates from that of earlier regimes. That Seoul is assuming a more self-reliant and pragmatic posture toward Washington and Tokyo while cultivating relations with socialist countries is clear evidence of this trend.

As far as the demise of authoritarianism is concerned, Taiwan's experience is not much different from that of Korea. Despite its expulsion from the United Nations in 1972, Taiwan continued its economic growth and survived the shock of international isolation, including the severance of diplomatic ties with the United States and Japan. It is widely known that the Chiang family sought the twin goals of industrialization and authoritarian control by combining paternalism and laissez-faire—leave politics to the government and people will be free to pursue their well-being. As the increasing lag between high economic development and low political modernization bred popular discontent, the late President Chiang Ching-kuo responded by ordering a sweeping political reform in 1986. The thirty-eight-year-old martial law was replaced in 1987 by a national security law, thus paving the way for competitive political activities. The ruling Kuomintang Party also lifted its ban on travel to mainland China to allow the reunion of families separated by the civil war. This "political reform from above" did not lose momentum with the death of Chiang Ching-kuo in 1988. He was succeeded by Lee Teng-hui, a Taiwanese technocrat turned politician, who has continued to push forward democratization. On the top of Lee's agenda has been the question of how to respond to rising demands for democratization while consolidating Taiwan's position in the international system, especially its relations with mainland China and the former Soviet Union. As democracy takes root in Taiwan, its new leaders are expected to launch a more autonomous foreign policy driven less by dogmatic ideology and more by practical considerations. Thus it is no accident that the Taipei government has substantially upgraded its relationship with socialist countries during the last few years.

With the anticipation that Korea and Taiwan will continue their political-economic modernization and assume more important roles in the international system, the purpose of this chapter is to provide a broad sketch and explanation of foreign policy restructuring in these two East Asian NICs with special emphasis on their rapprochement with socialist countries. To begin with, a synthetic analytical framework to explain the foreign policy shifts caused by political democratization is described. The framework then is applied in order to understand changes and recent developments in the foreign policy of Korea and Taiwan.

Democratization and Foreign Policymaking

Frequent references to the relationship between domestic politics and foreign policy notwithstanding, the impact of democratization upon foreign policy behavior has not yet received much scholarly attention. In the field of comparative foreign policy, democratization has been treated, at best, as one type of regime change when accompanied by a change in leadership (Hagan 1989a, 1989b, 1987a, 1987b; Hermann 1990; Boyd and Hopple 1987; Holsti 1982; Goldmann 1988; Andriole and Hopple 1986; Midlarsky 1981). By analyzing the impact of regime change on foreign policy behavior, these studies attempted to link the specific types of regimes and their changes to different kinds of foreign policy shifts. In addition, the major thrust of this body of literature was to categorize the regime change according to its magnitude and pace rather than its content. Consequently, it was often difficult to delineate the substantive direction and intensity of the causal relationship between regime and foreign policy changes. Through comparative and cross-national analyses, however, these studies have laid the groundwork from which in-depth longitudinal research can be launched. This study's approach is an outgrowth of the comparative foreign policy tradition and utilizes many of its concepts and findings. At the same time, this study analyzes the dynamics of regime and foreign policy change by investigating the evolution of the unique relationship between democratization and restructuring in foreign policy. Before presenting the analytical framework, it is necessary to clarify the two key concepts of this study—democratization and foreign policymaking—in the context of recent developments in Korea and Taiwan.

Democratization in Korea and Taiwan

It is evident that democratization resulted from the breakdown of authoritarian regimes in the East Asian NICs. The Korean and Taiwanese political systems between the late 1960s and late 1980s could be labeled bureaucratic-authoritarian (B-A) regimes (O'Donnell 1973), though the economic determinist models alone cannot fully explain the atypical preconditions, ingredients, and formation of the political systems in Korea and Taiwan.[1] Besides the structural changes in the dependent capitalist economies and their interaction with the international system, other factors should also be added to explain the formation of B-A regimes in these two countries. They include the centralized and authoritarian political culture (Henderson 1968) derived from the Confucian tradition (Pye 1985); the strong state inherited from the colonial powers (Alavi 1972; Saul 1974; Leys 1976); and the legacy of modern history of the two countries, especially the civil war experiences and perpetual state of conflict which has led to a militarization of the societies (Han 1986).

The main traits of the B-A systems in Korea and Taiwan included the exclusion of the popular sector from the political process, the suppression of workers' rights, the imposition of a disciplined and centralized executive structure, the adoption of an outward-oriented development strategy, the utilization of the military as the power base, the depoliticization of social issues in exchange for technical rationality, and the use of "security, stability, and economic growth" as the legitimizing ideology. In particular, there are three specific areas where the Korean and Taiwanese B-A systems differ from the Latin American cases: national security has been a more important factor legitimizing the regime than economic growth or political stability, the alliance between the state and the international capitalist system has been relatively weak, and the societies were built on the paternalistic structure of power.

Given these characteristics of the Korean and Taiwanese B-A systems, what is the proper way to analyze their disintegration? Though not originally formulated for either the Korean or Taiwanese case, several analytical frameworks offer a point of departure. For example, four factors were identified by Przeworski (1986) as contributing to the breakdown of an authoritarian regime: the weakening of functional needs provided by the B-A regime, especially gradual disillusionment with the claims of security, stability, and economic growth; the resultant loss of legitimacy and, more importantly, the strengthening of a democratic alternative; conflicts within the ruling bloc; and the decision by some ruling factions to appeal to outside groups for support. Undoubtedly, all these factors have some relevance to Korea and Taiwan. Stepan (1986) also presented a model of the breakdown of B-A regimes, part of which appears quite applicable to recent experiences of Korea and Taiwan. Specifically, developments in these states can be seen as a combination of a "society-led regime termination" movement, activities by organized opposition groups, and "democratization initiated from within the regime."

All three of Stepan's elements were present in Korea and Taiwan. Beginning in 1986, Korean students and dissidents led sporadic but nationwide protests against the authoritarian rule that resulted in massive arrests. As the reports of police brutality increased, popular sentiment began to turn against the Seoul government. In the meantime, opposition groups led by the two Kims (Kim Dae-jung and Kim Young-sam) made steady gains in their power struggle against the governing party. Domestic unrest peaked in the spring of 1987 when it was disclosed that the police tried to cover up the torture death of a student activist. To defuse the crisis, Roh Tae-woo, president of the ruling Democratic Justice Party (DJP), made a bold gesture toward democratization. Named the "Special Declaration for National Harmony and Progress Toward a Great Nation," Roh's 29 June declaration not only accepted the direct election of president as demanded by the opposition groups, but also offered a set of sweeping reforms designed to bring about a genuine liberal democracy. Following the declaration, more than one thousand political prisoners were released and more than two thousand received amnesty, while the press became more independent and college campuses more autonomous. Boosted by these reform measures and the opposition's failure to produce a coalition candidate, Roh won the presidency with a sizable margin in the 16 December election, though he gained only 36.6 percent of the votes cast. In the subsequent parliamentary election of 1988, no single party won the majority in the National Assembly, the result of which was an extremely unstable relationship among the four political parties. In 1990 an unlikely coalition was forged among the ruling DJP and two of the three opposition parties, leaving Kim Dae-jung's Party for Peace and Democracy as the only opposition group. This new coalition, named the Democratic Liberal Party (DLP), has since controlled more than half the seats in the National Assembly, and the DLP makes no secret of its intention to follow the footsteps of Japan's Liberal Democratic Party (LDP) which enjoyed a one-party dominance for almost forty years.

The process of democratization in Taiwan, as was evident in the Korean case, also contained these three elements from Stepan's model. Compared to Korea, however, the Taiwanese experience has shown a much greater degree of "democratization initiated from within the regime." It has also been a slower and less violent process. Although in 1985 there was a crisis of confidence resulting from a political scandal, Taiwan has not experienced any revolutionary upheaval or massive protests. The process of political reform began on 9 April 1986 when the late President Chiang Ching-kuo appointed a special subcommittee to study the implementation of the political reform resolution passed by the Third Plenum of the Central Committee. Thus, Taiwan falls into the category of "democratization from above" (Teng 1988). Simply put, the Taiwanese leadership accommodated the popular demand for democratization arising from the changing socioeconomic environment, while suppressing resistance from its bureaucracy. Consequently, political reforms initiated by the political elites since martial law was lifted in 1987 have greatly stimulated popular political participation in Taiwan.

The process of democratization in Korea and Taiwan will likely be far from smooth in the future. Although popular demands for a pluralist democracy are too strong to be suppressed, there still exist in both Korea and Taiwan powerful groups that have benefitted under the previous B-A regimes. Moreover, it should be noted that there remain two critical factors which have contributed to the birth and maintenance of the B-A regimes in these countries: their territorial division and the legacy of paternalistic authoritarianism. These will continue to have a dampening effect on the progress toward a pluralist democracy.

Foreign Policymaking in Korea and Taiwan

Turning to the process and practice of foreign policy in Korea and Taiwan, it is evident that before the beginning of democratization, foreign policy in each of the two countries had been determined, controlled, and manipulated by the authoritarian regimes and their leadership. As such, foreign policymaking in these countries exhibited a number of attributes common to many B-A systems.[2] The first characteristic was the depoliticization of the foreign policy process which virtually excluded any influence from the popular sector. Such exclusion was justified by the government on grounds of efficiency and unwavering determinism (Koo and Han 1985, 44). Second, the decision-making process became highly personalized and dominated by the president. Information and ideas concerning foreign policy would flow only vertically (Ko 1984, 115–21). Usually, only a handful of institutions with access to the president would play a significant role. These institutions included the intelligence agencies and top personnel in the presidential secretariat. Even the ministries of foreign affairs lacked the power to formulate important foreign policies. Instead, their role was often downgraded to that of doing the paper work for the decisions made in the presidential offices. Political parties and the legislative bodies also had very limited influence in setting foreign policy, as the interpellation was rather ritualistic.

Third, national security was given the top policy priority, for it was utilized as the most important basis for maintaining authoritarian rule. Consequently, highly inflexible and dogmatic policies were formulated to deal with both of their immediate adversaries (i.e., North Korea and the People's Republic of China) as well as other socialist countries. Finally, Korea's and Taiwan's foreign policies have been severely constrained by the high sensitivity to their relations with the United States, Japan, and other friendly powers. The source of this constraint was not limited to military and economic dependence on those countries. In the case of Korea, the B-A regimes suffered from what has often been referred to as an "insecurity complex about the regime's legitimacy" and thus needed recognition by the allies. Likewise, the advent of China as a major international actor since the early 1970s and the relative decline of Taiwan's position in the world community made Taipei extremely concerned about the decline in its diplomatic recognition—formal or de facto— by other states. These weaknesses frequently undermined the efficiency and consistency of foreign policymaking in the Korean and Taiwanese B-A systems.

There is no doubt that these characteristics of foreign policymaking under the B-A regimes are being altered in the ongoing process of democratization in Korea and Taiwan. Yet, as there exists no theoretical model readily applicable to the East Asian NICs, an analytical framework formulated to help better understand the impact of democratization on foreign policy change and restructuring will now be outlined.

The Impact of Democratization on Foreign Policy: A Framework

The framework presented below is not an entirely new one. Rather, many ideas, concepts, and propositions are borrowed from the existing literature on comparative foreign policy (see Hagan 1987a, 1987b; Salmore and Salmore 1978; and East 1978a).[3] Nevertheless, this analytical structure has distinctive objectives and characteristics. First, although its primary focus is the impact of a specific type of political change, the framework's applicability is not necessarily limited to democratization. This structure would work as well in analyzing a wide spectrum of political changes ranging from the gradual to the revolutionary. Second, while most previous studies on the influence of domestic sources on foreign policy behavior have emphasized the importance of socio-political structures and their changes, this framework goes further by analyzing the change in value systems and political ideologies. In some cases, the change in value systems and ideologies may be reflected in structural changes, while in other cases there may be considerable time lag between the two. Third, efforts are made to overcome the intrinsic limitations of the statist rational actor model in developing the analytical framework. Though much attention has been paid to the bureaucratic-organizational processes and various domestic political constraints on foreign policymaking, the implicit acceptance of rationality in terms of national interest is still common.[4] But the interaction between the perceived national interest and the regime's domestic political interest needs to be investigated in depth. While it is assumed that every regime would try to protect its political position, B-A regimes have often put parochial political interests ahead of the larger national interests. Thus, the regime's political interest is treated in this framework as one of the most critical variables in relating the domestic political process to foreign policy behavior.

The analytical structure is presented in figure 8.1 as a schematic diagram. There are two stages in the causal link leading to foreign policy change. In the first stage, democratization brings about changes in the nation's ideology and value systems, the state-society relationship, the political structure and process, and the regime's political interest. These developments, in turn, affect the foreign policy goals, capacity, and decision-making, ultimately producing specific changes in foreign policy behavior in the second stage.

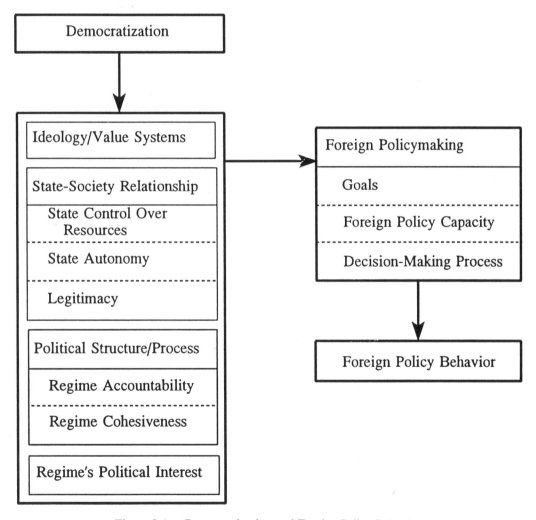

Figure 8.1   Democratization and Foreign Policy Behavior

To begin with, changes in the ideologies and value systems of the society come with the breakdown of an authoritarian regime and its subsequent democratization. Authoritarian regimes are known to employ certain ideologies for legitimation—most commonly nationalism and the dogmatic principles of national security, economic development, and social stability. Often, disintegration of authoritarian regimes begins with the public's disillusionment with such ideologies and the corresponding rise in the popularity of democratic ideals. Social changes resulting from economic growth also include the decline of the authoritarian and paternalistic cultural patterns in the East Asian NICs (Pye 1985). The changing ideologies and value systems affect the state-society relationship as well as the political structures and processes. At the same time, they have direct impact on the choice of foreign policy goals and objectives, such as in the reexamination of national security as a legitimizing ideology. Such a reexamination has often led to critical changes in foreign policy toward both allies and enemies. The transition from authoritarian to democratic value systems in a society is also likely to influence the foreign policy decision-making structures and processes. The exclusion of the popular sector and the depoliticization of foreign policy development as well as the personalized decision-making dominated by the president are likely to diminish with these changes.

Second, major political change, including democratization, necessitates the rearrangement of the state-society relationship. In general, the transition from authoritarianism to democracy results in reduced state autonomy vis-à-vis the public and increased state autonomy vis-à-vis social elites. This transition also weakens state control over foreign policy resources but enhances state legitimacy. Each of these changes seriously affects a regime's foreign policy goals and capacity. Before examining the impact of each, it should be noted that specifying relationships among the various factors is a complicated task unless the specifics of the context are known. Indeed, the actual effects of changes may vary or even contradict each other according to the particular conditions of a given situation.

The degree of state control over foreign policy resources is defined as the scope of state control over all resources that may be mobilized in conducting foreign policy (Salmore and Salmore 1978, 111; East 1978, 134). Democratization would have both positive and negative influence on state control over foreign policy resources. As democratization proceeds, the scope and efficiency of state control over such resources as manpower, economic activities, and the mass media become more limited. This in turn produces a decrease in the state's foreign policy capacity. On the other hand, the shift in the nature of resource control from "coercive" to "collaborative" (Crone 1988, 257), resulting in part from the increasing legitimacy of the regime, is expected to strengthen the government's ability to utilize foreign policy resources.

Democratization also may cause fundamental changes in the autonomy of the state in relation to the society as a whole. Although Hagan (1987a) and Salmore and Salmore (1978) view the "regime representation of society" and the "existence of powerful societal actors" as political constraints in the making of foreign policy, these are not sufficient to explain the linkage between the state-society relationship and foreign policy behavior. As suggested by Crone (1988), state autonomy consists of two aspects: autonomy from social elites and from the masses. One of the common features of authoritarian regimes is the existence of strong state autonomy from popular influence and a weak autonomy from elite influence, especially that of military and business groups. Democratization, however, alters the relationships by lowering state autonomy from the public. This enhances the regime's capacity to mobilize popular support. At the same time, the impact of democratization on state autonomy from social elites becomes more complex. Dominant elites in the previous authoritarian regimes will certainly lose their political influence, while a relatively large number of social groups (e.g., labor unions, political parties, interest groups, and the mass media) will emerge as new pressure groups. Despite the widely accepted proposition that increased state autonomy from social elites would generally boost a nation's overall policy performance, its impact upon foreign policy capacity is not so straightforward. For instance, because new elites have much broader power bases in the society than those that existed for elites under the authoritarian regimes, a reciprocal relationship between the state and these new social elites may have a more positive impact upon the nation's foreign policy capacity.

The lack of legitimacy and dependence on coercive forces for political control are other shortcomings of authoritarian regimes. While the level of legitimacy may be relatively high in the early stage of authoritarianism, the regime's breakdown usually begins with the loss of legitimacy. Many authoritarian regimes also tend to waste foreign policy resources to ensure recognition from other countries, especially superpowers, because of their "insecurity complex." All in all, enhanced legitimacy is expected to increase a regime's foreign policy capacity and to strongly influence its foreign policy goals.

Third, democratization produces important changes in the political structure and process, which have been well-documented in the literature (Hagan 1987a, 1987b; Goldmann 1982; Holsti 1982; Salmore and Salmore 1978). Among the changes in the political structure and process, two variables can be considered most relevant: regime accountability and regime cohesiveness. Regime accountability finds its origins in the "political rules of the game, especially those relating to de facto and de jure procedures for implementing policy and retaining political office" (Salmore and Salmore 1978, 12). In an authoritarian government, regime accountability is often very low because the procedures for power transfer are not institutionalized. The continuity of a regime does not depend upon the legislative process, elections, judicial decisions, nor even the regime's performance. Thus, accountability does not impose a severe limitation on authoritarian regimes in their foreign policymaking. In contrast, democratization increases regime accountability and, therefore restricts the regime's latitude of decision-making in foreign affairs.

Turning to regime cohesiveness, it is defined as the lack of "persisting internal political divisions in the form of competing personalities, institutions/ bureaucracies, factions, or competing parties or other such political groups'' (Hagan 1987b, 344). Although factions may exist within the power elite or relatively strong opposition political parties, the cohesiveness of an authoritarian regime tends to be high and allow for great freedom of action. Democratization breeds a division of power among various political actors and institutions. A democratic regime is inevitably confronted with many political constraints arising from lower regime cohesiveness. It can hence be hypothesized that the lower the regime cohesiveness, the lower the regime's foreign policy capacity, the net result of which is the increasing importance of the organizational and bureaucratic factors in the foreign policymaking process.

The final sphere of change associated with democratization is the regime's political interest. A regime's political interest—more accurately its identification of interest—is determined by a combination of the factors explained above, where regime accountability and legitimacy are of particular importance. As was evident in Korea during Roh Tae-woo's presidency, it can be expected that a high level of regime accountability, when combined with insufficient legitimacy, would make the regime extremely sensitive to the question of its survival. In such a case, there arises the potential for conflict between the regime's immediate political interest and the long-term national interest. Consequently, the substantive content of a regime's political interest in the context of specific issues needs to be examined before their impact on foreign policy behavior can be determined.

Economic Development and International Change

What has been discussed so far concerns how democratization would bring about change and restructuring in foreign policy. However, there are two additional sets of factors relevant to foreign policy change in Korea and Taiwan. They are the role of economic development and international systemic change. These two factors interact with the process of democratization and, therefore, the compounding effects among the three need to be discussed. Although these additional factors have not been incorporated in the analytical framework, portrayed in figure 8.1, a brief sketch is provided of their influence on foreign policy change.

In understanding the role of economic development, two factors are most relevant: the nature of the relationship between a nation's economy and the international political economy and the impact of international systemic change. The phenomenal economic growth of Korea and Taiwan has strengthened their relative positions in the international political economy—even their entry to the Organization of Economic Cooperation and Development (OECD) is being discussed by its members. Their successful industrialization and the ensuing accumulation of wealth increases their foreign policy capacity and enables them to pursue a more independent line of foreign policy. At the same time, however, their export-led growth policies have changed the nature of the relationship between these national economies and the international political economy. One important result is their increasing vulnerability to international economic changes. The developed economies, in particular, have already begun to demand that the NICs assume a fair share of burden in the liberal international economic order. Korea and Taiwan both face increased protectionist pressures from the United States and the European Community and can no longer rely upon their goodwill. External economic policies of Korea and Taiwan will necessarily reflect the changed reality which was in part a result of their growth. Long accustomed to a policy of growth maximization, they will find it difficult to harmonize their own economic interests with those of others, but their entry into the club of advanced industrial economies will only be possible when this is achieved.

International systemic changes also affect a nation's foreign policy goals and capacities. Although Korea and Taiwan do not make strong cases for the argument that, for smaller and weaker nations, international systemic factors are much more important in explaining their foreign policy behavior than national or societal ones, the importance of these external factors should not be underestimated in explaining foreign policy changes in these East Asian NICs. More importantly, the changes in the international environment have been occurring simultaneously with domestic democratization and have thus produced significant interaction effects. Recent improvements in East-West relations, for example, have made the Koreans and Taiwanese feel further disillusioned with the emphasis on national security as a source of ideological legitimacy for the state. In addition, the rising protectionist pressure from the developed countries has prompted various interest groups, especially both nation's farmers, to loudly voice their opinion in the making of foreign trade policy. Because the two countries are located at the cross-section of the EastWest and North-South confrontation, they tend to be influenced heavily by changes in the world's politics and economy. In particular, East-West relations, intra-bloc interactions, and international trade and finance regimes are crucial in explaining foreign policy changes in Korea and Taiwan. Most important among those external changes are: the improvement in East-West relations, the relative decline of American hegemonic power, the changing nature of the liberal international economic order, the domestic reforms and open door policies of the Eastern Bloc countries, and the improvement in Sino-Soviet relations. Except for the problems with the liberal international economic order, these changes are likely to enable Korea and Taiwan to maneuver more freely in their external relations.

Nordpolitik Initiatives of Korea and Taiwan

It is only natural that many foreign policy changes should emerge in South Korea and Taiwan from the ongoing democratization. The process of foreign policymaking has become more politicized with increased input from the popular sector, while the bureaucracy is regaining its status as the chief architect of foreign policy. Not only is domestic pressure mounting in Korea and Taiwan to revise their "patron-client" relationships with the United States and Japan, but also their governments are raising their capacity to make independent foreign policies. The most dramatic foreign policy restructuring to date by Seoul and Taipei has come in the rapprochement with socialist countries including their respective archrivals, North Korea and China. What follows is an illustrative application of this analytical framework to the development commonly known as "Nordpolitik."

Korea's Search for a Self-Reliant External Posture

The B-A regimes in Korea and Taiwan had long been handicapped in their management of East-West relations. There was no choice for both countries but to take an extremely rigid anticommunist stance. Seoul and Taipei's standing conflicts with Pyongyang and Beijing, respectively, had combined with their dependence on the American security umbrella to produce an environment that was not conducive to cooperative interactions with socialist countries. Another contributing factor to their inflexible foreign policy posture toward socialist countries was the presence of authoritarian regimes which depended heavily on national security as a legitimizing ideology. The resulting situation constrained the flexibility of the B-A regimes of Korea and Taiwan in dealing with the Eastern Bloc nations.

As Korea's authoritarian regime was replaced in 1988 by a more democratic one, Seoul's leaders felt confident enough to change direction in their relations with "northern neighbors." Specifically, Seoul's Nordpolitik initiative can be seen to have originated from the following aspects of democratization: disillusionment with the ideologies of economic growth and national security employed by the authoritarian regimes to justify their existence; growing nationalistic aspiration and the pursuit of democratic ideals as the alternative ideology; increasing regime accountability requiring the government to respond to public sentiment; increasing popular legitimacy of the new government that reduces the necessity of using security as a legitimizer and boosts its international bargaining power; and the government's interest in northward diplomacy as a tool to garner domestic political support. Therefore, as the democratization proceeds, the government in Seoul is likely to pursue Nordpolitik even further.

Nordpolitik has become a viable policy option because of Seoul's altered political and economic interests. First, Korea has strong economic incentives in improving its relationships with its major neighbors, especially China and the former Soviet Union. Access to natural resources and inexpensive labor from North Korea, China, and the former Soviet Union; large potential export markets in China and the former Soviet Union; and opportunities for direct investment in the infrastructure of the Eastern Bloc countries are all possible economic benefits from South Korea's new policy. Second, Seoul's increasing economic friction with OECD countries along with the global trends toward protectionism and economic bloc formation are forcing Korea to develop new trade strategies. By expanding economic ties with socialist countries, Korea will be able to reduce trade dependence on OECD countries and energy dependence on OPEC nations. All this is reinforced by the likelihood that the international economic environment will become less and less favorable to Korea and other NICs in terms of treatment received from the advanced industrialized countries (Wariavalla 1988, 268). Although Korea's strategic military value to the United States has allowed it to retain a favorable economic position, Washington appears likely to seek a more balanced economic relationship with Seoul in the future.

It is important to emphasize that the division of the Korean peninsula and the state of perpetual conflict between the two Koreas have continued to hinder Seoul's pursuit of independence and status in the international community. Even a slight easing of the tension between the two Koreas, let alone unification, would greatly enhance Seoul's capacity to conduct its external relations. Now that Seoul has finally established formal diplomatic relations with Beijing and Moscow, the environment on the Korean peninsula has become quite favorable to inter-Korean talks.

The South Korean government has given a top priority to northward diplomacy, and invested significant political and economic resources to make it successful. Though the previous authoritarian regimes had pursued a quiet diplomacy toward the Soviet Union and China, mainly through commercial transactions, their policy was different in nature from the Nordpolitik begun in the late 1980s. Until the mid-1980s, Korea's efforts to improve relations with Beijing and Moscow had been consistent with the Western idea of "containment" as well as the eastern dictum of "making friends with distant states to attack the enemy nearby." Nordpolitik of the past was part of a larger plan to isolate or neutralize North Korea. Domestically, it was intended to allay some of the popular discontent with the harsh anticommunist ideology, without undermining its foundation.

Unlike its predecessors, Roh's Sixth Republic adopted a flexible attitude toward North Korea. Beginning in 1988, it called for an end to the unnecessary diplomatic competition with Pyongyang. President Roh was quoted as saying, "The time has already passed for us to end this war of attrition with North Korea" (*The Korea Times* (Seoul), 12 March 1988). And the government took further steps to improve relations with Pyongyang including the declaration of 7 July 1988. In what is known as the "7.7 declaration," the Korean government proposed:

1. Inter-Korean human exchanges and free visits by overseas Korean residents to South and North Korea;
2. Exchange of mail and mutual visits between dispersed family members;
3. Trade between the two Koreas as domestic transactions;
4. Permission of trade in nonmilitary goods between Pyongyang and Seoul's allies;

5. Termination of counterproductive and competitive diplomacy; and
6. Cooperation in Pyongyang's moves to improve relations with the United States and Japan.

The catalyst for Korea's diplomatic gestures to the North was the successful completion of the 24th Olympiad in the summer of 1988. To protect the Olympic games from a possible disruption instigated by the Pyongyang regime, the Seoul government sought assurances from Pyongyang's patrons that no such hostile acts would occur. As part of this attempt, Seoul made it clear that its Nordpolitik was no longer intended to isolate North Korea, but to bring it into the community of nations. With the success of the Olympics, it became easier for the former Soviet Union, China, and other Eastern European countries to formalize their commercial and diplomatic relations with South Korea.

Korea's Nordpolitik has already produced many visible results vis-à-vis its former adversaries. Most importantly, Korea and the former Soviet Union established formal diplomatic relations in September 1990 and soon held three summit meetings. As part of the agreement to establish these ties, Seoul provided a loan package of $3 billion to Moscow. Both nations also rapidly increased bilateral trade and made marked progress in Korean firms' negotiations to participate in the Soviet Far East free enterprise zone projects and the development of Siberia.

With regard to China, Korea upgraded its economic exchanges from 1988 and saw their bilateral trade grow to $5.7 billion in 1991. In October 1990, just one month after the Seoul-Moscow normalization of relations, Korea and China came to an agreement to open trade offices in each other's capital. Though Pyongyang expressed concern and irritation about the rapid improvement in the Seoul-Beijing relationship, it failed to deter the establishment of full diplomatic relations between the two in August 1992. It should be noted that, besides China and the former Soviet Union, Korea was able to set up diplomatic relations with virtually all of the Eastern Bloc countries including Hungary, Poland, Romania, Czechoslovakia, Bulgaria, Yugoslavia, and Mongolia.

Inter-Korean relations have also improved since the start of Seoul's new Nordpolitik. Bilateral talks at various levels have been held including a number of visits exchanged by the prime ministers of each Korea. Especially in sports, the two Koreas have greatly increased bilateral exchanges and cooperation. A good example is the formation in 1991 of a single "Korean" team to compete in international ping-pong and soccer matches. Direct inter-Korean trade still remains at a low level as seen in the total volume of exports and imports by Seoul from October 1988 to May 1992 which was only $10 million and $170 million, respectively. With several joint venture projects under negotiation, however, economic cooperation between Seoul and Pyongyang is expected to quicken.

Perhaps the most crucial turning point in inter-Korean relations was Pyongyang's declaration in May 1991 that it would accept the separate entry of North and South Korea into the United Nations. The Pyongyang regime had long objected to this on the grounds that it would perpetuate the "two Koreas" on the peninsula. It appears that three factors have prompted Pyongyang's change of mind. First, South Korea has threatened to apply for separate U.N. admission, should North Korea decline Seoul's proposal for simultaneous entry. Second, China and the former Soviet Union let it be known that they were in no position to exercise a veto against South Korea's solo entry to the United Nations. Third, it became evident that Pyongyang desperately needed to improve relations with Tokyo and Washington. From Japan, it sought economic assistance including the possible payment of reparations for Japan's colonial occupation. From the United States, North Korea wanted political recognition in order to enhance its status in the international community. Pyongyang opened government-level talks with Tokyo in 1991 as a prelude to normalization and increased its official and unofficial contacts with Washington.

One critical stumbling block to Pyongyang's rapprochement with Tokyo and Washington is the issue of nuclear weapons development in the Yongbyon area.[5] By delaying the on-site inspection of its nuclear facilities by the International Atomic Energy Agency (IAEA), North Korea played such a dangerous game of nuclear politics that Japan and the United States have made Pyongyang's acceptance of the full IAEA safeguards a precondition for improved relations. Apparently bowing to international pressure, the Pyongyang government signed the IAEA's safeguard accords on 30 January 1992 and allowed it to stage a number of inspections. While the acceptance of the IAEA's inspection regime is significant, Pyongyang must still honor all of IAEA demands including the special inspection of undeclared sites, close its plutonium reprocessing facilities, and accept a bilateral inspection regime with Seoul, which would include short-notice challenge inspections, to end the controversy. The amount of political and economic mileage Pyongyang will be able to exact before surrendering its nuclear weapons program is uncertain.

How the South Korean government can utilize its increased foreign policy capacity to respond to North Korean nuclear diplomacy is also unclear. For Seoul's leaders, it will be a litmus test of their ability to translate their democratic mandate into foreign policy behavior. The test is especially critical due to a lack of progress in the inter-Korean dialogue since the signing of two historic documents in December 1991. The Basic Agreement on Reconciliation, Nonaggression, and Exchanges and Cooperation between the South and the North, the first comprehensive agreement between the authorities of the two Koreas since the division, was designed to lay the foundation for their peaceful coexistence. The Joint Declaration on the Denuclearization of the Korean Peninsula banned even the construction of facilities for uranium enrichment and plutonium reprocessing. The resolution of the nuclear issue has indeed become a critical challenge for Seoul's new bilateral and multilateral foreign policy.

The Seoul government seems to take pride in its Nordpolitik and will try to further upgrade its relations with northern neighbors. For South Korea, the

Nordpolitik initiative may not only bear tangible fruits in economic exchanges, but may also tremendously enhance its political leverage toward friends and foes alike. Moreover, it has not yet caused any serious strain on its relations with the United States and Japan. For the time being, however, the processes of democratization and Nordpolitik in Korea have not shown a linear relationship. As democratization proceeds, Seoul's Nordpolitik initiative, especially its policy towards North Korea, has often met serious challenges from domestic opposition groups staging mass protests against the government.

After President Roh's declaration of 7 July 1988, some opposition groups' dissatisfaction with the slow pace and the substance of Nordpolitik and with the Sixth Republic led to unauthorized visits to Pyongyang by a student and a prominent opposition leader. Sensing that their demand for democratization was finally bringing changes, ultranationalistic groups began to shift their attention to the issue of national unification. The Seoul government could only regard these dissidents as a threat to its viability and its prerogative in dealing with North Korea. Thus, the Roh administration found itself in a dilemma between democratization and Nordpolitik, and was forced to employ somewhat "reactionary" measures against both democratization and Nordpolitik. When Roh was replaced by Kim Young-sam in February 1993, the first civilian government since 1961 began to push ahead toward democratization while not making any radical shift in northward diplomacy. If anything, the Kim administration is recalibrating the pace of Nordpolitik to reflect its autonomous posture in foreign policymaking.

Taiwan's Return to the International Arena

The causal linkage between democratization and foreign policy change in Taiwan parallels that of Korea. First, the weakening of governmental control over the mass media in 1988 allowed the press to report, discuss, and criticize the government's foreign policy stance. Second, the appearance of de facto political parties following the democratic reforms in the same year enabled people to articulate their interests and opinions on foreign policy issues more effectively. As a result of these developments, the Taipei government was severely criticized for the rigidity in its mainland China policy which had produced a wide gap in foreign policy orientation between the public and the decision-makers. What the mass media and the concerned public demanded was a fundamental shift in Taiwan's foreign policy direction in order to accommodate the changes that have taken place in inter-Chinese relations over the past forty years. However, there exists an important difference between Korea and Taiwan arising from Taipei's long experience of diplomatic isolation since the early 1970s. In part, Taipei's democratizing reforms were aimed at soothing the cumulated diplomatic frustration of the Taiwanese people. At the same time, the Taiwanese government has made many foreign policy changes to distract attention from the slow pace of political development. Now this strategy of procrastination appears to have lost its potency and Taipei's leadership has come to realize that they cannot break out of international isolation unless they improve their relations with the mainlanders and accept pragmatism as a guiding principle of foreign policy.

Two issues have emerged to test Taiwan's ability and willingness to change course in foreign policy. These were the questions of rejoining international organizations, especially membership in the Asian Development Bank (ADB), and of improving its relations with the Eastern Bloc countries. Though the two issues are closely interrelated, the latter was easier to handle than the former, largely because it consisted of bilateral relations. In March 1988 the Taipei government adopted measures permitting direct trade with East Germany, Poland, Hungary, Romania, Bulgaria, Czechoslovakia, and Yugoslavia while allowing indirect trade with the Soviet Union and Albania. In August 1989 Moscow and Taipei agreed to open a joint venture corporation in Thailand to facilitate their direct trading. Apparently, the two nations no longer saw the need to use the Japanese firms as an intermediary.

As to inter-Chinese trade, the mainland has become Taiwan's fifth largest trading partner despite Taipei's official ban on direct bilateral trading. From 1979 to 1988, trade across the Taiwan Straits increased twenty-four fold. The total volume of exports and imports between the two reached a record high of over $2.7 billion in 1988—a 79.5 percent increase over 1987. Given the huge volume of Taiwan's trade, however, its dealings with the mainland constitute merely 2.4 percent of its total international trade—3.7 percent of its exports and 0.9 percent of its imports. Nevertheless, Taipei's leaders have already begun to worry about the so-called "mainland fever." Such a concern becomes understandable as inter-Chinese trade has since grown exponentially—$8.8 billion in 1989 and $10.98 billion in 1990, while Taiwan's accumulated investment in the mainland reached $1.24 billion in 1990. Although too high a dependence on the mainland market may have negative implications for Taiwan's viability as a state, recent policy changes made by the Lee government suggest, however, that it recognizes the reality of expanding economic and cultural exchanges.

The ADB issue was more delicate than the resumption of trade with Taiwan's northern neighbors. According to an observation made by a Taiwanese specialist,

> The issue concerning Taiwan's membership in ADB can be traced back to February 20, 1986 when the Bank's Board of Executive Directors decided to accept the People's Republic of China (mainland) and to change the official name of the Republic of China (Taiwan) to "Taipei, China." In a memorandum, the ADB recognized that there was only one China, and the PRC was the only legal representative of China making "Taipei, China" a local government. Since this move by the ADB put the ROC in an inferior and disadvantageous position, the Taipei government took a three-no policy of "no acceptance, no withdrawal, and no attendance." The ADB's

> decision put the ROC in a dilemma: while the ROC government would prefer to stay in the Bank avoiding isolation from the international society, it remains reluctant to accept the local government status. . . . Heated debate ensued in the government, and it was the technocrats who finally won the argument of "interest vs. face." (Teng 1988, 12)

The Taiwanese delegation's attendance at the 22nd annual meeting of the Asian Development Bank held in Beijing in May 1989 represents a historical milestone in Taiwan's foreign policy far beyond the immediate event itself. Despite the administration's urging that its presence in the Beijing meeting will in no way affect its anticommunist policy, the move was a signal to the rest of the world that the new democratic government in Taipei would no longer be bound by the rigid ideological doctrine of its authoritarian predecessors. In fact, there seems to be a consensus in Taiwan that it is desirable to return to the United Nations even under the title of "Taipei, China." According to a statement made by the Taiwanese foreign minister in a closed meeting of the Legislative Yuan, the government intends to participate actively in all international organizations, and to seek reentry into the United Nations for "Taiwan is entitled to membership in that global institution" (*United Daily News* (Taipei), 8 April 1989).

Developments like these have paved way for the recent breakthroughs in Taiwan's domestic political structure and foreign policy posture. President Lee Teng-hui promised sweeping political reform measures for democratization and declared on 20 May 1990 the renouncement of its broad "Three-No Policy" (no contact, no negotiation, and no compromise) against mainland China. He also championed the early abolition of emergency measures instituted in 1947 which had allowed continued one-party control in Taiwan. Known as "the Temporary Measures for the Period of National Mobilization for Suppression of the Communist Rebellion," this act also placed inter-Chinese relations in a state of war. It was indeed a pivotal move for Lee to abrogate this act on 1 May 1991 and hence to acknowledge the existence of the communist regime on the mainland. With its abolition, the Taipei government at long last gave up the slogan of "restoring the mainland" and subsequently established the Mainland Committee under the control of the Executive Yuan for direct communication and negotiation with China. And on 29 April 1993 delegates from China and Taiwan concluded the first high level meeting held since 1949 by signing four agreements which called for increased exchanges across the Taiwan Strait. These changes, incidentally, were made by the Taipei gevernment in part to counteract the growing movement for independence of Taiwan led by the opposition parties that feel less bound by the legacy of a unified China. As a further gesture of reconciliation, the government repealed a law that stipulated capital punishment for people who claim Taiwanese independence in May 1991.

Taiwan's Nordpolitik is part of the larger trend in its foreign policy. The government acknowledges its accountability to the Taiwanese people and is likely, therefore, to pursue foreign policy goals that maximize their collective interest. The legacy of the previous regime's dogmatic ideologies is giving way to a realistic assessment of Taiwan's international position and the policies it needs in order to survive as an independent political entity.

The Continuing Process of Democratization

Democratization has brought foreign policy restructuring to Korea and Taiwan, of which the most important aspect has been rapprochement with their northern neighbors. With the Nordpolitik initiative, the governments of these two countries were able to become proactive, rather than reactive, in the making of foreign policy for the first time in their modern history. Using Nordpolitik as a lever, they have been able to increase their capacity to influence the external environment for the maximization of their respective national interests. As Korea and Taiwan become more assertive in their foreign policy posture and their Nordpolitik begins to bear fruit, it is likely that their actions will not only prompt changes in the responses of the countries they interact with, but also make lasting imprints on the regional and international political economy. The changes in the international system wrought by Korea and Taiwan will, in turn, further influence their domestic politics and foreign policymaking.

The analytical framework presented above provides an understanding of how the process of democratization has contributed to changes and restructuring in the foreign policies of South Korea and Taiwan. Democratization is an ongoing process that will continue to affect the politics of many countries in a post–cold war international environment. In this respect, not only does it provide a framework for understanding the recent developments and changes of the foreign policies of South Korea and Taiwan, it may also serve as a useful template for explaining the process of democratization and foreign policy change wherever it occurs.

Notes

1. For the discussions on the preconditions, ingredients, and formation of authoritarian regimes, see O'Donnell (1973, 1979); Pye (1985); Alavi (1972); Leys (1976). For the Korean case, see Im (1987) and Han (1986). Recent studies on the causes, patterns, and potential paths of the breakdown of bureaucratic-authoritarian regimes include: O'Donnell, et. al. (1986); Foxley, et. al. (1986); Dix (1982). For Asian countries, see Gigot (1987); Holbrooke (1986); Stanley (1986); Park, Kim, and Ko (1988); Teng (1988); Sutter (1988); Copper (1988).
2. The characteristics of foreign policy making and behavior of the B-A regimes, especially in the Korean case, is discussed in Ko (1984); Koo and Han (1985); Park, Kim, and Ko (1988).
3. The frameworks of Salmore and Salmore (1978) and East (1978a) deserve special scrutiny, though they do not focus upon "changes" in the domestic environment and foreign policy behavior. Salmore and Salmore identified three clusters of

important political variables: resource availability, political constraints, and the regime's disposition to use resources. With these independent variables, they developed a number of propositions on foreign policy behavior regarding the amount of policy activity, levels of commitment, and levels of independence. On the other hand, East employed two mediating concepts to explain the relations of national attributes to foreign policy behavior. One is the "capacity to act" determined by the amount of resources (size) and the ability to use resources (social organization), both of which, in turn, result from national attributes. The other is the "choice of foreign policy" which is to be determined by the regime's predisposition to act along with such factors as regime constraints and decision structures.

Building on these studies, Hagan argues that the mistakes of many previous scholarly works include an over-emphasis on the structural approach and on dramatic types of regime and policy changes. "To capture the diversity of major Third World regime changes and the complex, yet subtle ways" (Hagan 1987a, 4) they affect foreign policy behavior, he maintains that the following sequence of tasks should be followed: (1) identify the type of regime change; (2) ascertain the difference in foreign policy orientation of the new leadership and the political capability to implement new policies, given the degree of regime fragmentation and vulnerability as well as the existence of dissenting, powerful and societal actors, and/or a predominant leader; and (3) examine the range of foreign policy restructuring in terms of foreign policy alignment, scope of involvement, conflict proneness, independence of action, and/or the level of commitment. Though it represents an improvement over previous studies, Hagan's framework appears to require further refinement for a comprehensive analysis of the relationship between the regime and foreign policy change. See chapter 7 in this volume.

4. Hagan (1987a, 1987b) and Salmore and Salmore (1978) are exceptions to this norm.
5. Nuclear facilities in Yongbyon include one research reactor, one 5 megawatt reactor, one 200 megawatt reactor, a uranium enrichment plant, and a partially finished plutonium reprocessing plant. Of these, the research reactor was built in the 1960s with Soviet technology and the 5 megawatt reactor has been in operation since 1986. With the completion of the 200 megawatt reactor and the reprocessing plant, North Korea may be able to mass produce nuclear bombs (of note is the absence of facilities normally found in a nuclear-powered electric plant). See *Wolgan-Chosun* (Seoul), March 1991, 118–35; *Chosun-Ilbo*-Chicago Ed., 1 June 1991.

Chapter 9

Explaining Foreign Policy Continuity and Change
U.S. Dyadic Relations with the Soviet Union, 1948–1988

William J. Dixon and Stephen M. Gaarder

William Dixon and Stephen Gaarder attempt to account for patterns of continuity and change in U.S. foreign policy toward the Soviet Union during the post–World War II era. They begin by providing a review of three theoretical approaches to the study of foreign policy: political realism, decision-making, and the study of elites. On the one hand, Dixon and Gaarder find that the literature on political realism and decision-making emphasize the existence of formidable constraints on policymakers and the likelihood that foreign policy incrementalism and continuity are likely to prevail. On the other hand, the study of elites indicates that leadership turnover and regime change are likely to result in foreign policy change and restructuring. Applied in the context of U.S. foreign policy toward the Soviet Union, Dixon and Gaarder predict that given the nature of presidential leadership and American regimes over time, continuity in foreign policy is likely to predominate. The proposition is empirically tested through the development of action-reaction equations to examine U.S.-Soviet relations across administrations from 1948 to 1988. As suggested by the theoretical literature, Dixon and Gaarder find that U.S. foreign policy may be better understood in terms of persistence and continuity, than in terms of flux and change. Such a conceptual and empirical study of the persistence of foreign policy continuity provides insights into the likelihood and occurrence of foreign policy change and restructuring. As Dixon and Gaarder conclude, their research serves as a first step toward the examination of additional dyadic relationships in order to build an understanding of continuity and change in foreign policy.

William Dixon is associate professor of political science at the University of Arizona. He received a Ph.D. in political science from Ohio State University in 1981. His principal research interests are in the areas of international political economy, foreign policy, and international interactions. His research has appeared in American Journal of Political Science, International Interactions, International Organization, International Studies Quarterly, Journal of

Conflict Resolution, Social Sciences Quarterly, *and* World Politics. *Stephen Gaarder is a doctoral candidate in political science at the University of Arizona. His dissertation research focuses on the role of the presidency in American foreign policy toward Latin America in the post–World War II era. He has published a study of presidential succession and U.S.-Soviet relations with William Dixon in the* Journal of Politics.

Nowhere are the foreign policy differences between postwar presidencies more sharply drawn than between Jimmy Carter and Ronald Reagan. These two administrations exemplify just how broadly policy styles and priorities can diverge from one president to another. For purposes of illustration, consider the matter of nuclear testing, an issue thrust upon the agenda of both administrations by the Soviet Union. In the fall of 1977, Soviet Premier Leonid Brezhnev proposed that the superpowers adopt a bilateral ban on nuclear testing. The Carter administration responded favorably with Secretary of State Cyrus Vance characterizing the Soviet action as "a major step forward toward a comprehensive test ban" (*New York Times*, 3 November 1977). Nine years later the Soviet Union initiated a unilateral moratorium on nuclear testing, once again hoping to draw the United States into a comprehensive test ban. When the Soviets invited the United States to join the moratorium, the Reagan administration dismissed the Soviet proposal as merely a "propaganda gesture" (*New York Times*, 22 March 1986) and promptly detonated a test device in the Nevada desert as previously planned. Not surprisingly, the Soviets soon abandoned their testing moratorium.

Despite the obvious similarities between the Soviet initiatives of 1977 and 1986, the reactions by Presidents Carter and Reagan were markedly different. Of course, identifying specific policy differences in anecdotal fashion cannot move very far toward a more fundamental understanding of change and persistence in United States foreign policy. This chapter considers whether there is a broader pattern of variation in postwar American diplomacy corresponding to changes in leadership, or rather if continuity is the more predominant theme.

The aim of this study is to systematically examine the effects of changing presidencies on selected patterns of American foreign policy behavior. The empirical test case consists of what was arguably the paramount foreign policy preoccupation of the last eight presidencies—diplomatic relations with the Soviet Union. This inquiry begins in the next section with a brief tour of the theoretical literature in search of some general principles which can guide expectations regarding change and persistence in the pattern of superpower diplomacy. Then a partial theory of dynamic foreign policy interaction which serves as a kind of theoretical template through which the potentially varying effects of successive presidential administrations can be given precise empirical interpretation is specified. Once this interpretative framework is in place, attention turns to the details of analysis design and measurement. The final section presents the results of the analysis and discusses their implications for future foreign policy research.

Persistence and Change in Foreign Policy

Lacking a specific theory of foreign policy restructuring, a rather wide conceptual net is cast in search of theories and theory fragments that could be of value in understanding change and persistence. It will be convenient to divide this theoretical work into three loosely structured approaches or genres each encompassing an assortment of models and frameworks. The distinctions between these approaches are seen more as matter of degree than of kind. The three approaches are political realism, decision-making, and elite change. Each of these theoretical groupings takes an identifiably different approach to the issue of foreign policy change. These categories and the works they subsume are more cursory than comprehensive in coverage and are intended as only a sampling of a large and diverse literature.

Political Realism

As far back as Thucydides, observers have maintained that states are fundamentally motivated by the pursuit of power and that to understand the nature of politics between states one must take into account this craving for power. Variously known as power theory, Realpolitik, and political realism, this approach remains the single most widely used analytical perspective on world politics. It would be incorrect to conceive of realism as a single cohesive theoretical system. It is rather a broadly structured perspective that emphasizes power as the central motivating force in world politics. Realist approaches also share a common image of nation-states as unitary rational actors. Thus the hallmark of political realism is a view of world politics as a kind of contest among states where each actor seeks to advance its own interests (i.e., its power) through calculated rational action. From this highly simplified charac- terization it is easy to see why realists have traditionally focused on the state rather than the state system as a whole or subnational units such as bureau- cratic organizations or individual leaders. Realist literature is large and diverse, but for this chapter it will suffice to examine two items that represent significant advances to contemporary realist thinking. This chapter begins with the struc- tural realist approach articulated by Kenneth Waltz (1979), and then considers the expected utility formulation developed by Bruce Bueno de Mesquita (1981, 1983, 1985).

Of the recent revisions to realist thinking, perhaps the most influential is the structural realism articulated by Waltz (1979). Although Waltz shares with other realists an emphasis on state power, he denies that states are entirely autonomous actors and that they are necessarily rational in pursuit of their interests. But what most clearly distinguishes Waltz from other realists is his strong emphasis on the structure of the international system—hence the label, structural realism. For Waltz, this structure is not only the central feature of the international system but also the key to understanding state behavior.

Waltz identifies three structural characteristics of the international system that require attention: the anarchic nature of the system, the absence of functional differentiation, and the variable distribution of capabilities in the system. Waltz differentiates political systems according to their distribution of authority, with domestic systems as primarily hierarchical and international systems as anarchic. On this point some similarity to traditional realism is seen since it too conceives of international relations within an anarchic environment. Waltz's second point is also based upon a distinction between domestic and international political systems. In the domestic system there exists some functional differentiation among a state's constituent units, while there is no such differentiation at the international level. All states must perform similar tasks to survive—making and enforcing laws, raising revenue, and defending themselves. The only significant variable characteristic of the international system is its distribution of capabilities. That is, the distribution of resources and capabilities varies across different types of international systems and across time, and involves the distribution of power.

For Waltz and other structural realists (e.g., Gilpin 1981), the distribution of capabilities in the system is thus the principal determinant of international outcomes. This structure favors some actors and constrains others through a variety of processes such as socialization and competition. Indeed, Waltz is fond of using the market analogy in relation to international systems by pointing out that just as the economic market constrains the behavior of firms and individuals, the international system constrains the behavior of nation-states. Nation-states are clearly subordinated to the invisible hand of the international system. Nations and individual decision-makers within the nation-state are not fully autonomous agents whose actions are wholly separate from other actors, but rather they are system dependent. Structural realism thus leads one to expect highly stable foreign policy behavior with little evidence of any discontinuities corresponding to changes in political leadership. This approach subordinates the roles played by political leaders and the nations they lead to larger processes involving the structure of the international system and the pursuit and maintenance of power within that system.

A rather different interpretation of realism underlies the formal expected utility models of conflict behavior developed by Bueno de Mesquita (1981, 1983, 1985). Although the structure of these models is fairly complex, and they have evolved significantly since their introduction a decade ago, their basic elements can be easily summarized. The aim of these models is to elucidate necessary conditions for war involvement based on a rational decision calculus that incorporates expectations of gains and losses together with probability estimates of winning and losing. The realist view of states as unitary rational actors, an assumption of obvious importance to this approach, is explicitly integrated into the models in their assumption that war-related decisions are dominated by single strong leaders who are assumed to be utility maximizers.

Power also plays a central role since it is the relative strength of states or coalitions of states that determines the likelihood of winning or losing, and this likelihood in turn defines the expected outcome as a net gain or loss. For war involvement it is thus necessary (though not sufficient) for this calculus to yield an expected gain.

The expected utility calculus requires leaders to make judgments about their own power relative to others. In the strictly bilateral case this is difficult enough, but the presence of defense agreements of various kinds raises additional questions about commitments to one's own state as well as those of one's potential opponents. There is thus considerable uncertainty about which states will enter a war and even about whose side they will join. Recognizing that different leaders cope with uncertainty in different ways, Bueno de Mesquita assumed that some leaders would be more risk averse than others. In the context of war, involvement risk aversion implies a skepticism regarding the resolve of one's own allies to fulfill commitments. The inclusion of risk-taking behavior in these models is particularly interesting because it explicitly introduces leadership variation into an otherwise thoroughly realist framework. To be sure, the accommodation of risk-taking dispositions does not alter the driving force of the basic model—leaders maximize gains and minimize losses based on their relative power. Furthermore, risk-taking becomes relevant only under uncertainty, a condition that itself is related to national power. Still, when uncertainty is high the utility calculus can be significantly affected by individual differences toward risk-taking.

Although having only skimmed the surface of a vast realist literature, it is nevertheless clear that power is situated at the core of this approach. For Waltz, national behavior is constrained by a system structure defined by the distribution of power. For Bueno de Mesquita, power figures as a key element in expected utility calculations determining potential gains or losses in war. This emphasis on power relegates political leadership to a secondary role in charting the course of foreign policy behavior. Nevertheless, Bueno de Mesquita's treatment of risk-taking demonstrates that realism can make room for individual differences in decision-making under conditions of uncertainty.

Decision-Making

It is certainly reasonable to assume, as Bueno de Mesquita does, that great decisions of war and peace must often be made with only partial or ambiguous information. However, even routine day-to-day foreign policy decisions may involve substantial uncertainty. Large organizations such as foreign policy bureaucracies cope with uncertainty by relying on established routine and by making decisions incrementally. These two strategies figure prominently in the organizational decision-making models of Charles Lindblom (1959), John Steinbruner (1974), Graham Allison (1971), and others.

Lindblom (1959) was one of the first to articulate a theory of incremental decision-making to challenge what he called "rational-comprehensive" decision-making. The rational-comprehensive model assumes that decision-makers clearly picture their goals and objectives, that they engage in some sort of cost-benefit analysis of how to achieve the goals and objectives and, perhaps most importantly, that they have near or complete information. Lindblom and others have pointed out that such a view of foreign policy decision-making is both overly optimistic and simplistic. In its place he proposed a model of incremental decision-making suggesting that decision-makers approach decisions one at a time, that today's decisions are usually only marginally different from those made yesterday, and that the long-run effects of day-to-day actions usually escape notice.

Steinbruner (1974) too was dissatisfied with the rational model of decision-making, arguing that it failed to capture the complexity of the decision-making environment. The "cybernetic model," as it is labelled by Steinbruner, is designed to deal with the uncertainty, ambiguity, and complexity of the decision-making environment. This model suggests that the individual decision-maker is not "engaged in the pursuit of an explicitly designed result," but rather is engaged "primarily and necessarily . . . in buffering himself against the overwhelming variety which inheres in his world" (Steinbruner 1974, 66).

Both of these approaches suggest that the decision-making environment is fraught with uncertainty and ambiguity, and that decision-makers respond by looking for the familiar and predictable as guides for their present and future decisions. In other words, decision-makers look to previous experiences and decisions to aid them in the present. Another means for coping with uncertainty that also emphasizes past behavior involves the use of established operational routines. This was referred to as "organizational process" by Allison (1971) but it can be understood in much the same way as the incremental and cybernetic approaches developed by Lindblom and Steinbruner. It rests on the assumption that foreign policy institutions, at least those of major powers like the United States, are highly bureaucratized organizations that, like all such organizations, tend to adopt and rigidly follow standardized procedures and to resist change of established routine (Kissinger 1966; Allison 1971).

The models of decision-making examined thus far focus on the problem of novelty, variety, and uncertainty in the external environment. They resolve this problem in similar ways by strongly emphasizing continuity while having little to say about changes in leadership. But foreign policy decision-making is more than coping with uncertainty, for there is also the problem of coping with competing interests within the policymaking bureaucracy. Yet another approach to explaining this complex process emphasizes bureaucratic politics, that is, the power seeking behavior of bureaucrats and bureaucratic agencies (Allison 1971). Whether it be domestic or foreign policy, this approach assumes that policy is often merely a "political resultant," meaning that policy may be the outcome of extended bargaining and compromise among the interested bureaucratic participants. Like the incremental, cybernetic, and organizational process models discussed above, the bargaining and compromise of bureaucratic politics is unlikely to produce more than marginal changes in foreign policy over time.

To summarize, realist and decision-making theories of incrementalism and bureaucratic politics all point to the existence of formidable constraints on decision-makers, constraints which make change unlikely. However, foreign policy changes do occur. Over the last decade or so, there has been restructuring in the foreign policies of Nicaragua and Iran, and the beginnings of significant foreign policy changes in Eastern Europe. These foreign policy restructurings have resulted when significant changes in the ideology of the leadership have occurred. The next section examines elite change to account for such restructuring.

Elite Change

There is a sizable amount of research literature focusing directly on the impact of political leaders and their advisors on governmental foreign policy. Much of this literature is fixed at the individual level of analysis (see, e.g., Herrmann 1986; M. Hermann 1980; Hopple 1979; and Walker 1977). All of these efforts posit that it is the psychological or idiosyncratic attributes of individual leaders and advisors which contribute most significantly to shaping foreign policy. Margaret Hermann (1980, 8) asserts that personal characteristics of chief executives have a significant impact upon the "content as well as the means of making political decisions." That is, a political leader's beliefs, motives, decision style, and interpersonal style largely determine a nation's external behavior. Similarly, Richard Herrmann (1986) contends that the perceptions held by political leaders influence policy, arguing that American leaders' perceptions, or "schemata" of the Soviets, go a long way in accounting for U.S. policy abroad.

Evidence from empirical comparative research also suggests that foreign policies are not immune to discontinuities inherent to leadership change. For example, Manus Midlarsky's (1981) investigation of fourteen developing nations experiencing political revolutions between 1945 and 1975 found systematic foreign policy changes emerging in subsequent United Nations voting patterns. Midlarsky found that regime change resulted in changes in voting behavior that tended to shift support away from the United States and closer to the Soviet Union, a pattern attributed to the influence of Marxist-Leninist ideology and fear of U.S. power. And Joe Hagan's (1989) comparative study of domestic political regimes across a much larger sample of Third World nations confirmed that even less dramatic changes in leadership can carry significant diplomatic consequences. Hagan examined regime change along a continuum ranging from relatively minor shuffling of officials to revolutionary transformation of the political system in eighty-seven less developed nations. He found that regime change did have an impact on U.N. voting alignments in about half of the sample of nations.

These findings are consistent with James Rosenau's (1966) early conjecture that individual leadership characteristics would have a relatively potent impact on foreign policy in small, less developed societies. But, what about states having a more highly developed foreign policy establishment? Philip Roeder's (1984) investigation of the Soviet Union establishes that even superpowers may be affected by changes in leadership. He theorized that foreign policy behavior in the Soviet case is likely to be shaped by patterns of decision-making, particularly the concentration of authority and political competitiveness within the elite. By tracking U.S.-Soviet relations over the 1953 to 1977 period, he was able to demonstrate that changes in these patterns do indeed regularly coincide with variations in observable foreign behavior.

All of these approaches, whether they concentrate upon characteristics of individual leaders and their advisors or upon the occurrence of elite turnover and regime change, suggest that changes in leadership may well result in changes in foreign policy behavior. Although dramatic wholesale change in foreign policy—what Kal Holsti (1982) has called "restructuring"—usually coincides with fundamental ideological shifts, even marginal alterations in regimes can sometimes produce discernable change in external relations. The differences between American presidential administrations appear to fall into the latter category.

Although the theoretical approaches reviewed in this section exhibit variation on the question of leadership change and foreign policy, on balance this literature points more clearly toward an expectation of stability and continuity than of appreciable change, at least in the context of U.S. foreign relations. But the question cannot be settled by theory alone. The diverse theoretical and empirical works considered here do not all speak directly to the question of leadership change and foreign policy. Furthermore, the literature on leadership change—the area most directly applicable to the query—does raise at least a possibility of foreign policy discontinuities across American presidencies. It therefore seems prudent to regard the question as open to empirical adjudication. The next section, using the test case of U.S. relations with the Soviet Union from 1948 to 1988, moves toward just such an empirical analysis to determine if leadership changes in the American system do significantly affect U.S. foreign policy behavior.

A Partial Theory of Foreign Policy Interaction

The model of foreign policy interaction proposed here is comprised of two interrelated propositions that describe in a stylized way the principal sources of the behavior one nation directs toward another over time. As developed here, the model highlights the behavior of a single nation toward a specific target, a representation designated the "directed dyad" in Kegley and Skinner's (1976) terminology. Note, however, that the propositions quite naturally extend to both parties of a dyad in a manner analogous to the familiar pairing of Richardson equations.

The first proposition maintains that a nation (that is, its foreign policy officials) will devise and attempt to implement behaviors toward a particular target nation based in some measure on behaviors recently received from that nation. This proposition can be formally represented as:

$$Y^*_t = \alpha_0 + \alpha_1 X_t + \epsilon_t. \tag{9.1}$$

Although equation 9.1 will be immediately understood as describing nation Y's responsiveness to nation X, several specific points warrant elaboration. First, it is important to notice that the focus is on Y's desired response at time t rather than the actual behavior that eventually filters through the foreign policy process. Foreign policy behavior is conceived as purposeful action deriving from political level decisions to influence the attitudes or actions of others (Hermann 1982). This conceptualization is symbolized by the asterisk appended to the conventional notation for Y's behavior. The Y^*_tM term in equation 9.1 thus represents an attempt to recognize and take account of the intentional component of foreign policy behavior. In addition, the α_0 and α_1 terms also carry substantive meaning. The α_0 component signifies the presence of a historical disposition to act, absent the influence of any other factor, whereas the α_1 term indicates the intended degree of responsiveness to behavior received from nation X.

The proposition formalized in equation 9.1 states merely that Y's intended response is contingent on behavior received from X and that on average this contingency is described by parameter α_1. It does not imply that Y will seek to respond in a particular way on any given occasion, such as matching X's behavior in tit for tat fashion ($\alpha_1 = 1$) or overreacting in the heat of international crisis ($\alpha_1 > 1$). While these are plausible responses, so are many others. Accordingly, no *a priori* assumptions are made about the magnitude or sign of the α_1 coefficient. The proposition is thus probabilistic (also indicated by the error term ϵt) in the sense that it models the average disposition to respond over an extended period of diplomatic exchange.

Naturally, portrayal of Y's intended response as a function of X's behavior and some long-term disposition must be regarded as an over-simplification that ignores numerous other elements generally thought to influence the foreign policy process (see, e.g., East, Salmore, and Hermann 1978). This omission is the principal reason to concur with Ward (1982) and others in regarding this formulation as no more than a partial theory. Yet previous research reveals the effects of others' behavior to be of such overwhelming significance when compared to other potential influences that any additional explanatory patterns are rendered virtually inconsequential (Wilkenfeld, Hopple, Rossa, and Andriole 1980). Although such findings raise some unsettling theoretical issues, they nevertheless afford some credibility to the specification in equation 9.1.

Finally, the intended time frame of equation 9.1 should be clarified. Even though both sides of this equation are keyed to identical time points by inclusion of a subscripted t, this does not suggest instantaneous causality in the formulation of Y's intended response to X. If one were to explicitly recognize the time lag that must surely intervene, the right side of the equation would be indexed by $t-n$, where the value of n would depend on the particular time units under consideration. As the length of the relevant time units increases—say, from days to weeks to months—expected values of n will decrease, eventually approaching zero. The indexing of time used in equation 9.1 thus reflects the relatively lengthy time units appearing in the empirical portion of this study and not some notion of instantaneous response.

The first leg of this model is purely a conceptual device highlighting only Y's intended response to X; as presently formulated it says nothing about Y's actual behavior. An intended response is conceived as a short term goal or target that will typically require some change from past behavior to be achieved. This element of change provides the critical link between the target behavior specified in equation 9.1 and Y's actual response. In particular, the actual change in nation Y's behavior from one time period to the next will be constrained to some fixed positive fraction of the desired level of change. Stated in formal terms, this second proposition appears as:

$$Y_t - Y_{t-1} = \delta(Y^*_t - Y_{t-1}) + u_t,$$
where $0 < \delta \le 1.$ [9.2]

Large organizations are frequently characterized as repetitive, routine, or incremental, and this is precisely the idea conveyed by equation 9.2. As noted earlier, foreign policy institutions, at least those of major powers like the United States, are highly bureaucratized organizations and like all such organizations tend to adopt and rigidly follow standardized procedures and resist change of established routine (Kissinger 1966; Allison 1971). Equation 9.2 thus incorporates a bureaucratic inertia component into the partial theory.

Two additional features of this equation deserve substantive interpretation. First, as in equation 9.1, a disturbance term, u_t, is included in recognition of the varying circumstances that can influence the effects of bureaucratic inertia. Put differently, the adjustment process represented in equation 9.2 is conceptualized as an average effect occurring over a great many policy issues and coalescing over an extended period of time. In some issues bureaucratic resistance may be extremely potent while in others it may be virtually imperceptible; the u_t error term is used to represent this variation of bureaucratic influences around an average adjustment factor symbolized by δ.

Second, unlike equation 9.1 where the key constant was completely free from constraining assumptions, the δ coefficient of equation 9.2 is located within a narrow band of possible values. This proposed constraint carries certain substantive implications that can be understood in terms of the probabilistic nature of the bureaucratic component. The upper bound of unity is meant to formalize the belief that, on average, bureaucratic inertia is a force resistant to change, while the lower bound permits the bureaucratic effect to retard desired policy changes and perhaps to halt them entirely, but not to systematically reverse the intended direction of change. In particular, equation 9.2 should not be construed to mean that policymakers do not sometimes overreact or even that bureaucratic routine might not occasionally impose an even more extreme reaction than was originally intended. The point here is that on average—that is, over an extended sequence of policy episodes—bureaucratic influences are presumed to discourage change. In any case, the proposed constraint is actually open to empirical investigation, as will be demonstrated below.

The essential features of the partial interaction theory are now in hand. The two equations form interlocking pieces of a familiar whole that reduces dyadic foreign policy behavior to a response function operating on behavior received from another actor, and a bureaucratic inertia function serving as a kind of governor on proposed policy changes. As expressed in equations 1 and 2, the model can capture theoretical ideas but it cannot extend to the level of empirical analysis. This is because the linchpin of this model, the Y^*_t, term representing intentions, is an essentially unobservable element of the policy process. Certainly there are public clues to what a nation's intentions might be, and both analysts and practitioners routinely attribute intentions to other nations as a matter of course, but the prospect of systematically and reliably ascertaining the intentions of government policymakers is well beyond the capabilities of even the most astute observer (Hermann 1978; Milburn, Stewart, and Hermann 1982).

It turns out that the problem of foreign policy intentions may not be as debilitating as it first appears. The solution requires that one substitute for Y^*_t in equation 9.2, its equivalent form from the right side of equation 9.1:

$$Y_t - Y_{t-1} = \delta(\alpha_0 + \alpha_1 X_t + \epsilon_t) - \delta Y_{t-1} + U_t \qquad [9.3]$$

Collecting terms in this reduced form specification reveals a standard autoregressive model that directly connects the actual (rather than intended) behavior of nation Y to nation X:

$$Y_t = \alpha_0 \delta + \alpha_1 \delta X_t + (1 - \delta) Y_{t-1} + (\delta\epsilon_t + U_t) \qquad [9.4]$$

Several interesting results emerge from this derivation. First, the specification in equation 9.4 excludes all references to Y's intended response, Y^*_t, leaving an equation that is empirically estimable entirely in observed behavior variables. In addition, it is evident that the reactivity of one nation to another is indicated by a positive product of two theoretical parameters signifying the intended magnitude of change (α_1) and the effects of bureaucratic inertia (δ). When behaviors are perfectly matched to one another this product will take on a value of unity, although the more common pattern is one in which observed reactivity falls below unity, and this is exactly what one would predict from the partial theory under the assumption that bureaucratic inertia discounts intended change by some positive fraction. The effects of bureaucratic inertia extend in parallel fashion to the other components of the model. The historical disposition to respond (α_0) is also discounted by the inertia term to reveal a long-term behavioral (rather than dispositional) tendency. This compound term is sometimes designated long-term memory to distinguish it from the short-term memory $(1 - \delta)$ of Y's immediately previous actions (Ward 1982).

Design and Measurement

Specification of the partial theory permits the identification of three broad patterns of foreign policy behavior that may be presumed to lie within the general control of top level political leadership. The three patterns of interest are long-term behavioral memory, reactivity, and short-term memory, all operationally defined by the estimable components of equation 9.4. As presently formulated, these foreign policy patterns are presumed to be constant over the long-term, untouched by periodic changes of presidential leadership. This original specification will serve as a restricted model against which to test an alternative version that is modified to allow these patterns to vary across successive administrations. The alternative model, which is based on standard covariance assumptions, is the key to this analysis design.

The distinctive feature of the alternative model is the assumption that the behavior patterns indicated by the parameters of equation 9.4 are not fixed. More specifically, these parameters are presumed to vary depending on the individuals and policies associated with the incumbent president. This proposition is introduced into the model in equations 5, 6, and 7, by formally defining each parameter to be a function of successive presidential administrations.

$$\alpha_0 \delta = \beta_0 + \Sigma \beta_{0i} P_i \qquad [9.5]$$
$$\alpha_1 \delta = \beta_1 + \Sigma \beta_{1i} P_i \qquad [9.6]$$
$$1 - \delta = \beta_2 + \Sigma \beta_{2i} P_i \qquad [9.7]$$

All three equations assume the same linear form with a baseline value (β_0, β_1, and β_2) supplemented by a series of i terms representing the distinctive contribution of each administration. Each of the P_i terms is set to 1 for time points during which president i holds office and 0 otherwise. The equations thus comprise a set of working hypotheses about presidential foreign policy effects. Evaluation of the hypotheses proceeds by estimating values of the presidential adjustment weights (β_{0i}, β_{1i}, and β_{2i}) to assess what improvement, if any, they bring to the explanatory power of the basic action-reaction model.

As specified above, these three equations are not empirically estimable, but by combining them with equation 9.4 they can be rendered estimable. This involves substituting for each parameter of equation 9.4 the appropriate elements from the right side of equations 9.5, 9.6, and 9.7 to produce a reduced form version.

$$Y_t = (\beta_0 + \Sigma \beta_{0i} P_i) + (\beta_1 + \Sigma \beta_{1i} P_i) X_t + (\beta_2 + \Sigma \beta_{2i} P_i) Y_{t-1} + (\delta \epsilon_t + U_t) \quad [9.8]$$

Collecting terms in equation 9.8 shows that this reduced form specification is actually a covariance model constructed from the P_i presidential indicators and their multiplicative interactions.

$$Y_t = \beta_0 + \Sigma \beta_{0i} P_i + \beta_1 X_t + \Sigma \beta_{1i} (P_i \cdot X_t) + \beta_2 Y_{t-1} + $$
$$\Sigma \beta_{2i} (P_i \cdot Y_{t-1}) + (\delta \epsilon_t + U_t) \quad [9.9]$$

This approach to the analysis of presidential effects thus employs a straightforward extension of the model in equation 9.4. This expanded model will be compared to the restricted version in the usual way by testing the joint significance of each set of elements in which P_i terms permit presidential variation.

To carry out these tests systematic measures of U.S. and Soviet bilateral behavior spanning the cold war period are required. For this purpose, the Conflict and Peace Data Bank (COPDAB) event file for the years 1948 to 1978 (Azar 1980) supplemented by the Rajmaira and Ward (1990) World Event Interaction Survey (WEIS) extension for 1979 to 1988 are utilized.[1] The COPDAB observation and coding scheme was developed to operationalize the properties of cooperation and conflict in the foreign behavior of national governments. Discrete behaviors directed toward specific external targets—typically other governments—have been abstracted from journalistic sources and situated on a fifteen-point scale reflecting the degree of cooperation or conflict expressed by the action. The extension covering the years 1979 to 1988 are WEIS event descriptions coded into the 15-point COPDAB scale by Rajmaira and Ward (1990).

Two distinct measures of superpower relations derived from the joined events series—*affective balance and attentiveness*—are examined. The measure of affect registers the average monthly level of hostility or friendliness in directed U.S.-Soviet behavior. In order to take into account the vast differences in the severity or impact of the COPDAB behavior categories, Azar and Havener's (1976) judgmental weights to the observed events have been applied. Conflictual behaviors were scored with negative weights ranging from -6 to -102, cooperative events range from 6 to 92, and neutral behaviors—those neither conflictual nor cooperative—are weighted zero. The theoretical rationale for this measurement procedure is fully developed elsewhere (Dixon 1983). The second measure, attentiveness, is recorded as a simple count of discrete U.S-Soviet events cumulated monthly, irrespective of their affective content. Attentiveness is thus a pure measure of the volume of behavior purged of affect, while affect measures the quality of behavior purged of volume.

In light of the correspondence problems exposed by Howell (1983) and Vincent (1983), splicing these two event sets together may appear to threaten the validity of the U.S.-Soviet behavior series. There are, however, several reasons for confidence in this procedure, at least for the present inquiry. First, as noted above, the Rajmaira and Ward (1990) extension is not merely a reorganization of precoded event categories but a fresh coding of the original WEIS textual descriptions. Second, simple visual inspection of the behavior series over time does not reveal any pronounced deviation at the splice point beginning in 1979. Third, and most importantly, precautions have been taken in the analyses to insure that the conclusions are not affected by the decision to join these series together. These precautions follow the same covariance logic used in the detection of presidential effects, though here the purpose is to guard against unwarranted inferences. This procedure introduces additional adjustments to both the restricted and unrestricted models in order to absorb any variance in the series that could be attributed to the WEIS extension. Three adjustment terms are necessary: an indicator variable coded 1 after the shift to the WEIS extension in 1979, the product of this indicator and measures of past U.S. behavior, and the product of the indicator and concurrent Soviet behavior.[2]

Results

Implementation of this analytic strategy begins by empirically estimating the full and restricted models specified above for each of the two measures of U.S.-Soviet relations. The restricted model depicts foreign policy behavior toward the Soviet Union as a function of prior U.S. behavior (short-term memory), behavior received from the Soviets (reactivity), and long-term institutional memory (measured by the constant). The restricted model is estimated first, and then the restrictions (of no presidency effects) are relaxed in successive estimations by incorporating sets of independent variables carrying differential presidency effects. All estimations also incorporate the WEIS extension adjustments to insure that any observed presidency effects are not simply an artifact of the shift in behavior series. For each estimation in the hierarchical sequence, incremental F statistics are reported to assess the increase in explanatory power associated with the additional regressors. Table 9.1 presents summary results from this series of regressions for U.S. affective behavior. Here, and in the following table, the number of cases is fixed at 491 monthly observations.

The first entry in table 9.1 summarizes the fit of the restricted affect model and serves as a baseline against which to compare the incremental contribution of presidency effect terms. Next added to the basic equation is the set of seven

Table 9.1.   Hierarchical Regression Tests for Differential Presidency Effects
on U.S. Affective Behavior to the Soviet Union, 1948–1988

Terms in Model	Cumulative R-squared	Standard Error	Incremental F	Degrees of Freedom
Restricted Model (no presidency effects)	.403	5.46		
Restricted Model plus presidency effects	.486	5.12	11.09*	7,478
Restricted Model plus presidency effects plus memory adjustments	.497	5.10	1.43	7,471
Restricted Model plus presidency effects plus reactivity adjustments	.500	5.09	1.82	7,471

*p ≤ .01, two-tailed test

indicator variables ($\Sigma\beta_{0i}P_i$ from equation 9.9) representing adjustments to long-term memory for each presidential administration from Eisenhower through Reagan (with Truman the omitted baseline category). The relatively robust F statistic from this estimation reveals that the indicator variables *as a set* do offer a substantial improvement over the basic action-reaction model. The remaining two entries in table 9.1 retain these simple presidency effects and introduce additional adjustments modifying short-term memory [$\Sigma\beta_{2i}(P_i \cdot Y_{t-1})$] and reactivity [$\Sigma\beta_{1i}(P_i \cdot X_t)$], respectively.[3] These sets of adjustments are constructed in parallel fashion as multiplicative interactions of presidency indicator variables and the U.S. and Soviet affect measures. In neither case, however, do the resulting F statistics bear any evidence of a need to accommodate differential presidency effects.[4]

Results from this first analysis suggest that for the past four decades America's affective behavior toward its chief cold war rival has remained remarkably unaffected by the personalities and policies associated with succeeding presidential administrations. Periodic shifts in long-term behavioral tendencies toward friendlier or more hostile relations (the regression constant) do appear to regularly coincide with changes in administration, but there is no evidence of systematic presidency effects on either reactivity or short-term memory. In retrospect, it is not too surprising that this analysis has identified significant variations in long-term memory. The tenor of U.S.-Soviet diplomatic relations has drifted in and out of periods of détente over the years, and this is exactly what has been captured by the long-term memory adjustment factors.

The analysis is now repeated with the measure of U.S. attentiveness to the Soviet Union. Results are displayed in table 9.2 in the same format as before. The restricted attentiveness model, summarized in the first table entry, reveals a somewhat closer fit than for the affect model. Introduction of the seven

Table 9.2.   Hierarchical Regression Tests for Differential Presidency Effects on U.S. Attentiveness to the Soviet Union, 1948–1988

Terms in Model	Cumulative R-squared	Standard Error	Incremental F	Degrees of Freedom
Restricted Model (no presidency effects)	.681	5.74		
Restricted Model plus presidency effects	.692	5.67	2.60*	7,478
Restricted Model plus presidency effects plus memory adjustments	.694	5.70	.27	7,471
Restricted Model plus presidency effects plus reactivity adjustments	.696	5.68	.71	7,471

*p ≤ .05, two-tailed test

presidential administration indicator variables once again establishes the need for adjustments to long-term memory, though the margin of improvement is substantially below that observed for affect. The next two entries in the table again retain simple presidency effects in testing adjustments to short-term memory and reactivity by introduction of multiplicative interaction terms. As in the previous analysis, neither set of adjustments offers any noticeable improvement over the model restricting short-term memory and reactivity from varying across presidential administrations.

These results generally provide support for the proposition that U.S. foreign policy has been characterized by a high degree of persistence and continuity, at least when viewed through the lens of action-reaction dynamics. Because the addition of the reactivity and memory adjustment terms failed to contribute any appreciable explanatory power to the model, it appears that changes in the presidency have not marked systematic changes in superpower interaction. These results would seem also to be supported by descriptive evidence of U.S.-Soviet relations during the postwar period. One could turn to a number of foreign policy issues or themes which lend historical support to these findings. For example, there is considerable evidence of persistence and continuity in the area of diplomatic expulsions. This evidence indicates that U.S. administrations from Truman through Reagan have all engaged in regularized tit for tat behavior with the Soviet Union when it comes to expelling each other's diplomatic personnel (Wilson 1991). Of course the record of superpower military spending also provides plentiful evidence of U.S. foreign policy continuity toward the Soviets. This suggests that the historical record is replete with both anecdotal and systematic examples of superpower interaction characteristic of persistence and continuity.

Conclusion

These results suggest that U.S. foreign policy behavior may be better understood in terms of persistence and continuity, rather than in terms of flux and change. Presidential administrations do appear to be associated with periodic shifts in long-term behavioral tendencies toward friendlier or more hostile relations, but there is no evidence of presidency effects on either reactivity or short-term memory. Clearly evaluating the implications of these findings, despite the enormous differences between the presidencies of Eisenhower and Johnson, or between Truman and Nixon, there are no appreciable differences in the way these administrations built on their own past behavior or in the way they responded to Soviet actions. Despite such changeable factors as presidential character, personality, leadership style, policy commitments, bureaucratic and White House structure, advisory personnel, and so forth, postwar presidencies from Truman to Reagan reveal a remarkable degree of consistency in the properties of reactivity and short-term memory. These findings thus support Kegley and Wittkopf's (1987) conclusion that U.S. foreign policy behavior is characterized more by constancy than inconstancy.

These findings are also supported by the theoretical expectations of the international literature focusing upon the international system and decision-making structures. If one acknowledges the utility of these theoretical expectations, the empirical findings reported here should not be surprising. As suggested earlier, minor leadership changes, such as changes between U.S. presidents, are not apt to impart substantial alterations in the sort of foreign policy behavior examined here. Rather, one is likely to see a fundamental redirection in foreign policy in association with fundamental changes in leadership, particularly those involving radical ideological shifts. It is exactly these kinds of transitions that appear to be occurring in Eastern and Central Europe.

To qualify these results note that this analysis is restricted to the U.S.-Soviet Union dyad during the cold war years of 1948 through 1988. It is unfortunate that limited data availability precluded extending this examination through the momentous years of the Bush presidency. Extrapolating the above findings to a study limited to exclusively the leadership changes in the U.S. side of the superpower dyad would anticipate a fairly high degree of continuity associated with the transition from Reagan to Bush. Obviously, the profound changes on the Soviet side would not have been accounted for—changes not only in the prevailing leadership ideology, but also in the very identity and composition of the state itself. There is little doubt that the end of the cold war and the dissolution of the Soviet state represent an acute discontinuity in America's foremost foreign policy relationship since World War II. Yet how these changes might affect the more subtle elements of responsiveness and short-term memory are questions that must await future inquiry.

It is also important to bear in mind that precisely because American-Soviet relations have, for these past forty odd years, been entrenched in superpower rivalry, these relations may have exhibited peculiar behavioral patterns. This situation may in fact have severely constrained each nation's behavior toward the other. Thus to test the generality of these findings, it would seem especially useful to examine other, less institutionalized, dyadic relationships. One might expect U.S. foreign policy behavior in less regularized relationships to exhibit more variation across regimes; the logic being that presidents have comparatively more latitude to exercise individual prerogatives in less familiar relationships. In this vein, a useful next step in this research program would be the examination of additional dyads in order to build on one's understanding of continuity and change in foreign policy.

Notes

1. We are indebted to the late Edward Azar (1948–1978 COPDAB) as well as Sheen Rajmaira and Michael Ward (1979–1988 extension) for kindly making these data available to us. Naturally, these individuals should not be held accountable for the use and interpretation of data in the present study. Note that the WEIS extension is available only through 1988, so we are unable to include consideration of the Bush presidency in this analysis.

2. We can illustrate this procedure with the following equation using W to symbolize the WEIS extension indicator variable.

$$Y_t = \beta_0 + \beta_1 W + \beta_2 X_t + \beta_3 (W \cdot X_t) + \beta_4 Y_{t-1} + \beta_5 (W \cdot Y_{t-1}) + (\delta \epsilon_t + U_t)$$

It is evident that this strategy permits adjustments on each action-reaction parameter to accommodate variation in the series attributable to the WEIS extension. These adjustments are used for both the affect and attentiveness analyses, though they are likely to be more important for the latter since raw numbers of events have been observed to differ between the two sets (Howell 1983).

3. We retain the simple indicator variables not only because the previous estimation revealed their importance, but also because their variance must be partialed out prior to the introduction of multiplicative terms in order to detect the presence of interactions (Jaccard, Turrisi, and Wan 1990).

4. Analyses on just the 1948–1978 original COPDAB series produce comparable results. Inclusion of the presidency effect variables alone yields an F of 10.7 (6,362); the memory adjustment F is 1.4 (6,356); and the reactivity F is 1.6 (6,356). Thus, there is little reason to believe that conclusions from this first stage of analysis are in any way affected by the splicing together of the two events sets. These results are also robust against changes in the weighting of events. Although our reported results for affect rely on Azar and Havener's (1976) weights, we replicated the analyses with a simpler scheme distinguishing only cooperative from conflictual events.

Chapter 10

Foreign Policy Stabilization
and the Camp David Accords
Opportunities and Obstacles to the
Institutionalization of Peace

Steven F. Greffenius

Steven Greffenius seeks to advance an understanding of foreign policy restructuring and the institutionalization of peace from a situation of war. Like Dixon and Schwarz, he integrates the role of both domestic and international sources of foreign policy. Building on the work of Kjell Goldmann, Greffenius develops an argument about foreign policy stabilization that illuminates processes of foreign policy change. The framework depicts a foreign policy process in tension between pressures for change and factors that promote stability where policymakers are able to influence international and domestic "stabilizers" in an attempt to achieve a desired foreign policy outcome. He applies this framework of foreign policy stabilization to explain the Camp David peace process between Egypt, Israel, and the United States. Greffenius also suggests that restructuring is a process subject to constraints that are open to influence by policymakers rather than merely limitations that hinder a policymaker's ability to effect foreign policy restructuring. The difference is subtle, but crucial in highlighting yet another important aspect of foreign policy restructuring.

Steven Greffenius is codirector of the Olin Center for International Study in Boston, Massachusetts, and associate professor of political science at Carthage College in Kenosha, Wisconsin. He has taught international politics at the University of Wisconsin in Madison and at the Hopkins-Nanjing Center for Chinese and American Studies in Nanjing, China. He received his Ph.D. in political science from the University of Iowa in 1987 and a B.A. in history from Reed College in 1976. His research interests include international relations, Middle East politics, and political thought and philosophy. He is the author of The Logic of Conflict: Making War and Peace in the Middle East. *His work has also appeared in such journals as* Journal of Peace Research *and* International Interactions.

At least two schools of thought about the nature of foreign policymaking have arisen. The first emphasizes the rigidity of the process and argues that precedent exercises an inordinate influence over the formation of policy in complex organizations. The second stresses the fluidity of the process and contends that a pluralist, competitive mode of decision-making is too anarchic to permit rational policymaking.[1] This chapter asserts that conceptual advances in the analysis of foreign policy restructuring make it possible to build upon the insights and theoretical implications of both of these perspectives. These advances center on the concept of foreign policy stabilizers and the role they play in adapting foreign policies to a necessarily fluid and stressful environment. They suggest that theories of foreign policy change which take the process of stabilization into account can explain how and why changed policies become institutionalized while others remain vulnerable to external stress. The question is particularly apt in the context of the Arab-Israeli relationship.

The study thus aims to advance theories of foreign policy stabilization and change. It draws on detailed accounts of Middle East peace negotiations from January 1977 to March 1979 for evidence relating to foreign policy stability and change during a significant period of transition in the Middle East and in the world. The study discusses the peace talks among Egypt, Israel, and the United States in the critical months surrounding the Camp David accords, and relates key features of the negotiations to problems in foreign policy innovation. Enough time has passed, and enough materials are now available, to make an analytical assessment of the Egyptian-Israeli negotiations possible. Added to studies of foreign policy change and stability in other contexts, this study and others like it can contribute to knowledge concerning the ability of a range of variables to stabilize (or destabilize) peaceful relations.

The research contributes to knowledge of foreign policy change in several ways. First, it explores the issue of how the policymaking environment influenced Egyptian-Israeli interaction in the two years preceding their historic peace treaty. Second, it evaluates why Israel responded as it did to Egypt's overture. Lastly, it considers the degree to which foreign policy change depends on policymakers' deliberations and the degree to which it depends on environmental and structural factors beyond their control. All of these research foci promise to increase analysts' understanding of the relationship between foreign policy change and the systemic factors that affect the policymaking process.

The study's argument develops in three major sections. The first presents a framework of continuity and change by introducing the concept of foreign policy stabilization and six policy stabilizers relevant to this analysis. The next section gives an overview of the negotiations leading to the Egyptian-Israeli peace treaty, and discusses some of the significant features of the peacemaking process in light of this analytical framework. The last section explains how peace in the Middle East was only partially institutionalized due to the obstacles encountered in the stabilization process. A brief conclusion completes the argument.

A Framework of Foreign Policy Stability and Change

Goldmann (1988) argues that relationships among states undergo disturbances or destabilizing influences unique to their circumstances and history.[2]
Foreign policy stabilizers, by contrast, seem to be common to many relationships, so it may be more feasible to construct a theory about foreign policy
stability. If the process of stabilization is tied conceptually to the process of
institutionalizing changes in foreign policy, then analysts have a powerful
theory for explaining change as well. Goldmann's analysis of foreign policy
stabilization helps to explain how the process of institutionalizing change can
succeed and how it can fail. In doing so it identifies obstacles to change as well
as ingredients necessary for its successful institutionalization.

The Process of Foreign Policy Stabilization

According to Goldmann, three general factors influence the likelihood of
change: policymakers' sensitivity to the environment, the availability of alternatives to current policy, and the costs of change. Foreign policy stabilizers
are those factors which reduce sensitivity to the environment, limit the number
of alternatives, and increase the costs of changing the current policy. Foreign
policy stabilizers defined in this way may affect the policy process at several
points. For instance, a perceptual bias may lead policymakers to overlook
critical changes in the international environment, so that what might have
become a source of change remains ineffectual. Alternatively, policymakers
may be very much aware of a need to respond to altered circumstances, but
face a domestic political environment that drastically limits the range of
acceptable options. Lastly, the need for change may be keenly felt and options
may be available, but constraints originating in the state system make it too
costly. Hence it is possible for stabilizers to operate (1) early in the policy
process, so that the process of change does not actually get underway, (2) on
the policy process itself, so that they influence organizational choice, or (3)
quite late in the process, so that the willingness or ability to implement change
is limited.

Policymakers may consciously use stabilizers to achieve their own aims
rather than simply let constraining influences operate on them. Two analogies
help to make this point. Conservationists can take measures to reduce wind
and water erosion even if these forces cannot themselves be contained. Archi-
tects can minimize the danger of structural collapse even if they cannot prevent
or even predict earthquakes. In both cases, their aim is to reduce the effects of
inevitable stresses, whether these stresses are continuous or sudden. Similarly,
statesmen cannot prevent the tensions and even catastrophes that will afflict
normal relations between independent states, but they can construct a peace in
which these stresses will not lead to collapse. A peace thus institutionalized
can withstand crises and severe conflicts of interest, even if their source or the

timing of their occurrence cannot be predicted. Goldmann points to the factors that operate to institutionalize peaceful relations in this way.

In summary, tension and balance exist between pressures for change and the factors that promote stability in a foreign policy. Figure 10.1 illustrates this tension and places it in the context of the sources and outcomes of foreign policy change. One can expect change to occur when disturbances or stresses are particularly strong, such as in a crisis or a war, or when stabilizers are weak. Because they do not appear as unanticipated shocks, the evaluation of the strength or weakness of policy stabilizers can help predict the likelihood of change. For instance, to estimate the likelihood that a given policy will remain in place, analysts can determine what factors, if any, stabilize the policy and assess their strength. Further, knowledge of the manner and degree of policy stabilization enables the prediction of how it could be undermined and the direction policy change should occur (Goldmann 1988, 77).

Foreign Policy Stabilizers and the Institutionalization of Peace

Imagine that international relationships are a kind of social institution. Social institutions are established in large part by the network of laws, customs, and practices that define and regulate them. The notion that the institutionalization of peace should be viewed as a process in foreign policymaking implies a similarly complex interaction among the treaties, customs, and practices embodied in international law. The outcomes of this process of interaction which manifest themselves in both international and domestic affairs are summarized in the points below. The foreign policy stabilizer itself is in italics, and the

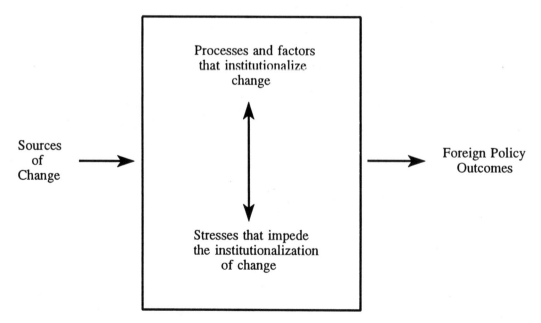

Figure 10.1   The Process of Foreign Policy Stabilization

explanatory material sets forth the conditions that should exist when peace between adversaries has been fully stabilized. One would not expect to find all of these conditions in a particular relationship, since perfect stability is highly unlikely. The stabilizers are listed together below to specify more clearly the notion of institutionalization as a process.[3]

International Stabilizers:

Normative regulation. Binding treaties prescribe the conditions of peace in a precise and noncontradictory fashion, and international norms create expectations that states will abide by these agreements.

Third parties. Common friends and common enemies reinforce the peace, and the motivation to collude with third parties to the detriment of peace is at a minimum.

Psychopolitical and Administrative Stabilizers:

Salience. The issue of peace is critical in the domestic politics of both parties, so that substantive changes in the government's position regarding peace would affect the pattern of coalitions and cleavages in the domestic political arena.

Centrality. Both parties believe that the pursuit of peace is a prerequisite for the successful pursuit of other aims, and that the ideas and policies supporting peace are strongly linked to other important ideas and policies.

Support. Domestic opinion strongly supports peace, and opposition to it, if it exists at all, is weak.

Decision structure. Decisions about whether and how to modify peace policies cannot be made quickly and decisively and instead are delegated to the bureaucracy rather than to centralized decisionmakers at high levels of the government.

These six stabilizers may be applied to the Middle East peace negotiations that occurred from January 1977 to March 1979. They highlight the tension between foreign policy stability and change during an important period of transition in the region.

The Egyptian-Israeli Peace Treaty

Anwar Sadat's visit to Jerusalem in November 1977 permanently altered the nature of relations between Egypt and Israel, which had been characterized by extraordinarily durable enmity. Yet the factors that made the Egyptian-Israeli conflict so lasting—the Palestinian question, in particular—did not disappear and thus the peace that Sadat wanted remained vulnerable. In the Camp David accords, President Carter, in collaboration with Sadat and Menachem Begin, sought to make the peace less fragile—that is, to institutionalize it. The peace settlement that emerged brought an end to their war, a relaxation of tensions, and a commitment to the peaceful resolution of differences. More particularly, the parties to the negotiations managed to achieve the following aims:

1. They ended the state of belligerency between the two states according to the formula, recognition for withdrawal, or, as it became known in the context of U.N. Resolution 242, territory for peace.
2. They controlled and limited the deployment and use of arms, renounced war as an instrument of national policy in their mutual relations, and created a demilitarized zone in Sinai.
3. They increased cooperation, contacts, and communication: e.g., tourism, open borders, and the like.[4]

From the perspective of the dynamic illustrated in figure 10.1, Sadat's visit can be viewed as a source of change and the Egyptian-Israeli peace treaty as the outcome of the resulting processes of change. The new status quo Sadat created would be seen as a set of policies that were exposed to pressures for change from a variety sources, protected to some extent by foreign policy stabilizers, and modified to a certain degree as the tension between the pressures for change and the stabilizers was resolved during the peace negotiations (Goldmann 1988, 81–82). The present study traces this process during its critical early stages.

The primary source materials for this research were the memoirs of principal figures in the Israeli-Egyptian peace negotiations. Several people closely involved in the negotiations left a record of their experiences, including President Anwar Sadat, Foreign Minister Moshe Dayan, President Jimmy Carter, Secretary of State Cyrus Vance, National Security Advisor Zbigniew Brzezinski, and presidential advisor William Quandt. These recollections and analyses reveal much about the way the foreign policy apparatus of the three states functioned, how the chiefs of state and their closest advisors made choices about the diplomatic and military problems facing their countries, the aims that guided policymaking in all three states, the effectiveness of these leaders in enforcing or implementing their choices, and the factors that enhanced foreign policy stability and those that promoted change in a trilateral bargaining process.

Negotiating Peace

President Carter placed a high priority on reaching a settlement in the Middle East when he took office in January 1977—just a little over three years after the first oil shock, the 1973 Arab-Israeli war, and the superpower confrontation it engendered. An early breakthrough in the Middle East would ease anxieties about another conflict and sustain Carter's popularity among the voters. About this time, two other events occurred that lent a degree of urgency to the problem of starting negotiations in the Middle East. First, the Israeli government decided to have elections in May rather than toward the end of the year. Thus a government with enough strength to enter serious negotiations would be in place sooner than expected. Second, food riots erupted in Cairo after sudden price increases. Sadat's government was weaker than first appearances had suggested, and Carter's advisors worried that its standing might decline even further if Sadat failed to reach an agreement with Israel (Quandt 1986, 35–36). A brief synopsis of Middle Eastern diplomacy from this juncture to the signing of the peace treaty helps explain how negotiations and ultimately peace developed from these roots.[5]

During the first nine months of the Carter administration, the president and his advisors directed all of their peacemaking efforts toward convening a conference in Geneva. As designed, all of the parties to the conflict in the Middle East would attend in an attempt to achieve a comprehensive settlement. In line with this goal, the National Security Council met in February to outline a policy for achieving an agreement between Israel and all of its adversaries. During subsequent months, Carter met key leaders from the region, including President Anwar Sadat, Israeli Prime Minister Yitzhak Rabin and, later, the new Israeli prime minister elected that May, Menachem Begin. By fall Carter's team began to see that a comprehensive treaty was unrealistic, but they lacked a strategy for initiating bilateral negotiations between the principal antagonists, Egypt and Israel.

The watershed event that shaped all subsequent diplomacy and provided the needed diplomatic opening occurred when President Sadat travelled to Jerusalem in November 1977 and expressed his desire for peace between Israel and Egypt in an address to the Knesset. To use Goldmann's language, Sadat's visit was a highly destabilizing act (and was recognized as such at the time). As Sadat himself put it, he wanted to bring down the "huge wall of suspicion, fear, hate, and misunderstanding" that divided Israel and the Arabs: to create shock waves—positive ones—that would completely change the atmosphere of conflict in the Middle East (Sadat 1978, 303).[6] In this he succeeded. The problem for negotiators then became one of transforming the shock waves into permanent changes in the structure of relations in the Middle East.

Begin did not reciprocate Sadat's dramatic gesture with one of his own, and talks between the two countries stalled. In January 1978 the United States resumed its role as mediator, since it appeared clear that the two parties did not trust each other enough to achieve a peace settlement on their own. Carter met with Sadat in February 1978 and fashioned a joint strategy for bringing peace in the Middle East.[7] A congressional debate on a Middle East arms package interrupted peacemaking efforts, however, and in the end the Carter-Sadat plan of action was ineffectual. By July the peace talks had still not achieved measurable progress, so President Carter took a somewhat unorthodox step and invited the principals to meet at Camp David. By accepting, Begin and Sadat knew they had committed themselves to reaching some sort of agreement, for failure to achieve this goal would severely damage their credibility and prestige.

The Camp David summit lasted from 5 September to 19 September. For two weeks the negotiators discussed the issues dividing them in an unusually informal setting and atmosphere. Disappointingly, the informality at Camp David did not lead to a rapid resolution of differences, and the negotiators nearly went home with no agreement. Carter's persistence bore fruit, however, with the signing of the Camp David Accords, which became the high point of his Presidency. They outlined the essential elements of a comprehensive peace in terms vague enough to accommodate (and to obscure) the parties' irreconcilable differences, and set forth the steps to a bilateral peace in terms specific enough that remaining differences over the Sinai could be readily addressed. It appeared that the parties might have reached a workable and durable peace in the Middle East.

Despite high hopes, snags developed in the implementation of the Camp David accords almost immediately. Consequently, Carter again committed the prestige of his office to redeem the negotiations from a futile cycle of offers and refusals. In March 1979 Carter staked everything on a personal diplomatic effort and travelled to Jerusalem. Again he almost failed to achieve his aim—Moshe Dayan mediated between the president and Begin when matters looked their bleakest—but he succeeded at last in reconciling outstanding differences. Egypt's president accepted the agreement Carter brought with him to Cairo, and President Carter announced the main ingredients of the settlement there. Begin and Sadat signed the peace treaty in Washington on 26 March 1979.

Analysis of the Camp David Process

To put the best face on their achievement, the parties that went to Camp David stressed that the accords and the treaty were but the first steps toward a comprehensive peace. Yet each recognized that Israel would have little incentive to address the national aspirations of the Palestinians once peace with Egypt had been concluded. Although this point was not explicitly stated during the negotiations, each side understood that the combined pressure that Syria, Jordan, and the Palestinians could exert on Israel would be insufficient to bring about a favorable comprehensive peace agreement if Egypt was sidelined, and thus the negotiations stalled many times. Quandt summarized the problem when he wrote, "Camp David would reduce the chances of ever achieving a comprehensive Middle East peace settlement. With Egypt at peace, Israel would have little incentive to make further territorial concessions. Without return of territory, other Arab leaders would have no incentive to make peace with Israel" (Quandt 1986, 330).

The United States gave up the idea of a multilateral conference in Geneva in favor of bilateral talks between Egypt and Israel after Sadat's visit, but the objective of a comprehensive peace survived. Carter wanted to settle the whole problem—not just part of it—and only later acknowledged that a bilateral peace accord was probably the only realistic agreement. The Egyptians, for their part, did not want to open themselves to charges from the other Arab states that they had concluded a separate peace, which implied negotiating an advantageous settlement with the Israelis and leaving the Palestinians—not to mention Syria and Jordan—to fend for themselves. While Egypt felt it essential for the Palestinians to reap at least a few tangible benefits from the newly-concluded peace, the Israelis resisted creating even the appearance of concessions. They knew that doing so would create expectations they could not meet, and the resulting disappointment on the part of the Palestinians would only postpone a final settlement. Moreover, they wanted to avoid charges of bad faith from the United States and Egypt.[8]

The effort to link the Egyptian-Israeli peace to the Palestinian question placed the process of institutionalization under great stress during the early stages of peacemaking. Begin maintained consistently that the status of the West Bank and Gaza should be kept separate from the Egyptian-Israeli agreement under discussion. He steadfastly refused to concede control over the occupied territories as the price of peace with Egypt. Carter was equally determined to extract from Begin a concession that would tie the Egyptian-Israeli peace to the ultimate resolution of the Palestinian question. Similarly, Sadat wanted to use the prospect of normalized bilateral relations first to induce, then to pressure the Israelis into accepting a comprehensive settlement. The Israelis strongly resisted such pressure, arguing that the only means of addressing Palestinian concerns lay in negotiations with Jordan and the Palestinian inhabitants of the West Bank. As noted above, the Americans sided with the Egyptians in their belief that a comprehensive peace would be very difficult to achieve if a separate peace between Egypt and Israel were concluded first. This ultimately proved correct, but Israel had the staying power during the negotiations to resist the inclusion of the Palestinian problem in any substantial way in the final Egyptian-Israeli agreement.

Obstacles to Stabilization of Peace

It may be helpful at this point to recapitulate briefly the argument made in the introductory section. The analysis of obstacles to stabilization in this section rests on several of the points made there and highlights several important connections between the policymaking environment and the dynamics of trilateral bargaining. As argued earlier, grasping the role of foreign policy stabilizers in the bargaining process yields insight into the factors that induce lasting change in foreign policies and those that inhibit it. Comparison of the findings in this study with those of others should improve not only accounts of the process by which foreign policymaking organizations respond to their environments, but also explanations of foreign policy change in general. If analysts know why foreign policy change occurs in some instances but not in others, their ability to assess the likelihood of change in particular circumstances is enhanced. Thus the ultimate purpose of this analysis is not only to reconstruct the origins of a historically important treaty, but to contribute to theories of stability and change more general in their application.

International Stabilizers

International stabilizers operate earliest in the process of institutionalizing change. They originate in the international system itself rather than in the culture, politics, or governmental apparatus of individual states. Because they operate at so fundamental a level, they may be seen as factors which are necessary but insufficient to bring about the full stabilization of peace. That is certainly true of normative regulation, the first of the international stabilizers considered here. Third-party stabilization is more problematic, and may be neither necessary nor sufficient in other contexts. In the case of the Egyptian-Israeli peace, however, it is clear that third-party mediation was essential to success.

Normative Regulation.   In international as in domestic politics, laws and customs institutionalize norms. When the Israelis pleaded for the normalization of relations, they asked for a relationship regulated by the international norms that govern relations among any group of states seeking to live together in peace. In this light, U.N. Resolution 242 acted as a kind of constitutive declaration for the region since its provisions evoked and reinforced these norms. Additionally, the resolution set out in very general terms the territory-for-peace formula that inspired the Egyptian-Israeli peace treaty. Hence Israel strove for diplomatic recognition, an exchange of ambassadors, borders open to trade, tourism and other travel, and an end to the formal state of war that had existed between the two states since the first Arab-Israeli War in 1948. In return, Israel agreed to return the Sinai to Egypt.

If international law was the first sphere of normative regulation in the peacemaking process, the issue of human rights was the second. As seen before, the central human rights issue in the Arab-Israeli conflict—Palestinian autonomy—complicated efforts to reach a settlement on the territorial and military spheres. When extricated from the complexities of Middle Eastern politics, the Palestinian question reduces to a claim of national self-determination. On a variety of grounds—primarily those of national security and ancient biblical rights—Israel strove to keep the West Bank districts of Judea and Samaria, and implicitly sought to gain American acquiescence in this aim. Carter pressed Begin to soften his stand on this issue, but Begin held firm on virtually every point and conceded ground only after months of painstaking negotiations. Israel was willing to make concessions on territorial and military issues with Egypt only if it was given freedom to deal with the Palestinian question as it saw necessary. Sadat and Carter, however, expected Israeli concessions in the West Bank and Gaza as well as in the Sinai; consequently Israel's rigid adherence to the principle of bilateral negotiations for solely bilateral issues frustrated both leaders. Carter and Sadat, each for his own reasons, were unwilling to abandon the opportunity for a comprehensive peace, and Begin's recalcitrance proved to be a source of great stress on the institutionalization process.

In short, Sadat found Begin willing to negotiate on bilateral issues, and extremely resistant to any change in the status quo on the central human rights issue: a Palestinian homeland. Moreover, Begin negotiated in a spirit of suspicion and legalism rather than generosity on the territorial and military problems in the Sinai that had to be resolved. He wanted to write the norms and principles that would govern Egyptian-Israeli relations into a detailed treaty that would have the status of international law. Sadat, who also recognized the necessity of a treaty, remained impatient with a legalistic approach, believing instead that mutual trust and goodwill should suffice. To an extent, both leaders were right. Sadat argued correctly that the spirit of cooperation quickened by his visit should lead to an expeditious resolution of outstanding conflicts. Yet Begin foresaw that the structure of peace they built must be founded on more than their immediate personal relationship and goodwill, and thus sought to define the peace in a detailed document to which the parties had publicly committed themselves.

To sum up, international norms strongly influenced the goals and behavior of all three parties to the negotiations. They governed Israel's conception of the kind of relationship it wanted to have with its neighbors. They influenced the American position in terms of Carter's commitment to a just peace and to human rights, which made him fight hard for the Palestinians even though he was certainly sympathetic to the existence of a Jewish state. Finally, they governed Egypt's views in that Sadat, like Carter, wanted to see progress on the Palestinian question as well as retain normal relations with other Arab nations. The problem was that the rejectionist Arab states subscribed to a set of norms different from those implicit in his visit to Jerusalem. When Sadat was forced to choose between the two, he chose peace with Israel and accepted isolation and a loss of prestige among his Arab neighbors who supported continued conflict with Israel.

Of all the actors in the drama, Egypt faced the most acute dilemma due to conflicting international norms. Sadat's commitment to the norms of peace sparked negotiations, but his inability to link the human rights issues inherent in the Palestinian question to the resolution of Egypt's conflict with Israel ensured that the peace remained fragile. It brought a formal commitment not to go to war rather than the establishment of genuinely friendly relations. It became clear as time passed that the peace would not become institutionalized in the political culture of the two states until the Palestinian question was resolved. As it stood, it was institutionalized only in international law. This was no small achievement, but fell short of the hopes of all the participants.

Third-Party Stabilization. One assumption of alliance and balance-of-power theory is that relations between two states can be affected by their respective relations with a third. This assumption suggests that third-party influences can be a factor in the stabilization of peace. The process of third-party stabilization, according to this reasoning, comprises three steps:

1. When tension between two states subsides, the relations others have with each of the two parties tend to change accordingly.
2. These changes tend to go in the direction of structural balance as common enemies and common friends bind the first two parties more closely together.
3. When a balanced structure emerges, it tends to be stable, including the newly established peaceful relationship between the two former adversaries.[9]

The condition of structural balance in trilateral relationships holds when all three parties are on good terms, or when the friendship of a pair effectively isolates a third. Egypt's foreign relations during the peace negotiations illustrate how decreasing tensions with Israel transformed its other relationships. Former friends, such as Syria and Iraq, became enemies, and former adversaries, such as the United States, became better friends. Egypt's difficulties with the other Arab states, however, hampered its efforts to stabilize its relationship with Israel, and the friend it held in common with Israel. Meanwhile, Egypt's friendship with the United States, which Israel shared, acted more as a buffer between the two states than as a binding influence which pulled them closer. These conditions depart from what might be expected under the theory of structural balance, and suggest that the theory in its simple form cannot be applied readily to the Camp David process. Still, it is worth emphasizing that third parties influenced the negotiations in important ways, whether as constraining factors (the other Arab states) or as a principal mediator (the United States).

A second assumption posited by international relations theorists is that collusion can disturb relations in a three-party system. Spanier (1987, 148) summarizes the strategic principles that guide states as they deal with this problem:

1. The possibility of collusion between any two members of a triad to the detriment of the third always exists. Bad relations between two members increase the likelihood that one of the antagonists will collude with the third.
2. Each of the three members aims to reduce collusion between the others to a minimum.
3. It is in the interest of each to bluff or blackmail its chief adversary by threatening collusion with the other.
4. The surest way for any of the three to provoke the other two into collusion is to display undue aggressiveness.

These principles are useful in analyzing how the possibility (and occurrence) of collusion influenced the talks among the United States, Egypt, and Israel. The threat of collusion made its appearance quite early in the talks. During one of the Carter administration's planning sessions early in 1978, William Quandt proposed a strategy whereby the United States and Egypt would purposely give Israel the impression that they had jointly formulated a negotiating position in order to undermine Israel's will to resist. Their hope was that Israel would make concessions if it believed that its intransigence had driven the United States into collusion with Egypt. Quandt believed this strategy to be manipulative and somewhat risky—it could easily make Israel more, not less, intransigent—but he wanted to try it nonetheless. Begin seemed impervious to such maneuvering one way or the other, but other members of his cabinet (Moshe Dayan in particular) seem to have been keenly aware of Israel's isolation as a result of Carter's obvious preference for dealing with Sadat.

Zbigniew Brzezinski interpreted Quandt's strategy somewhat differently, giving it an even more Machiavellian twist. Sadat should make an unyielding proposal which he knew contained provisions unacceptable to Israel. The United States and Egypt would agree on these provisions in advance. After the proposal was on the table, the United States would "compel" Egypt to make "concessions," and thereby induce Israel to accept the more reasonable position. Like Quandt's proposal, this idea relied on collusion to manipulate Israel into a desired position. Its defect was its transparency: experience suggested that it was a mistake to underestimate the canniness of Israel's policymakers. In the end, neither strategy was tried because these plans were overtaken by the various other lines of action that Carter and Sadat pursued.

At Camp David and throughout the negotiations, the role of the United States as the third party was critical to the restructuring of Egyptian-Israeli relations. President Carter, in particular, became impatient with Begin because he bargained so hard. He thought Israel's behavior was too aggressive in light of what it stood to gain from a durable peace, and made that clear during his talks with Begin. The outcome of Israel's tenaciousness was predictable enough: it drove the United States into virtual collusion with Egypt. Even though Israel complained about the situation on more than one occasion, Egypt did not after a time see its cooperative relationship with the United States as collusion. What appeared to the Israelis as collusion seemed to the Egyptians to be American pressure for Egyptian concessions, since Israel remained intransigent after years of warfare with the Arabs. Egypt felt its good relationship with the United States gained it nothing, but that it was expected to concede when an impasse emerged. In the end, Israel was willing to push the United States toward Egypt if that was the price to be paid for adherence to their primary principle: bilateral negotiations for bilateral issues, with minimum linkage of the Egyptian-Israeli peace to the issue of Palestinian self-determination.

The idea of third-party stabilization implies that a common friend or common adversary can stabilize a relationship at critical points. It is clear, for example, that the U.S. mediating role was essential to the stabilization of the Egyptian-Israeli relationship. The two sides would not or could not talk to each other without a mediator, and Carter's willingness to play that difficult role proved to be absolutely necessary to the final settlement. But the history of the negotiations also suggests that trilateral relationships are likely to undergo periods of stress and uncertainty if one of the parties is willing and able to resist the combined action of the other two against it. In this case, Israel successfully resisted American pressure on behalf of Egypt for concessions on the Palestinian issue. This set of circumstances greatly complicated the parties' progress toward peace and indicates how stressful triadic relationships can be.

Psychopolitical and Administrative Stabilizers

This section discusses the importance of psychopolitical and administrative stabilizers to the process of foreign policy change and the institutionalization of peace. These two impediments to wholesale change were relevant to the negotiation of the Camp David accords, but their full effects were not evident in Egyptian-Israeli relations until after the initial moves toward peace. Hence this section selects a few salient issues, largely from Israeli politics, to illustrate how these two types of stabilizers operated during the process of peacemaking.

Salience, Centrality, and Support. Three psychopolitical stabilizers figured prominently in the domestic competition for control over the shape of the Egyptian-Israeli peace in each of the three countries. The salience of peace in terms of its ability to induce consensus or division, its centrality in the belief systems of the participants, and its degree of public support all influence the link between domestic political competition and the stabilization of peace (Goldmann 1988, 39). These three variables serve as a point of departure for the analysis that follows. The discussion focuses on the system of attitudes and beliefs held by many Israelis at the time, and the significance of the change in regime that occurred when Menachem Begin came to power.

Kegley's (1987) work on decision regimes echoes Goldmann's argument that foreign policy stabilizers can be a powerful predictive tool. He writes that "the emergence of a set of widely and intensely held beliefs about Israel's foreign policy made only a narrow range of foreign policy outcomes possible" (Kegley 1987, 267).[10] Brecher (1972) calls this set of beliefs a security complex. This complex of attitudes and beliefs became especially strong after the 1967 war, so that security considerations pervaded all foreign policy decisions of importance even when they were marginal or irrelevant to the issue (Brecher 1972, 564).[11] The rationale behind this way of thinking was a conviction that the price of defeat was national extinction. This fear is reflected in the words of Abba Eban in a speech delivered after the 1967 war: "If the war had ended as those who launched it had planned, there would be no discussion now of territories, populations, negotiations, agreements, occupied areas or boundary settlements. There would be a ghastly sequel, leaving nothing to be discussed—an ending with no renewal and no consolation" (Brecher 1972, 93).

At the time of Sadat's visit, memories of two wars with Egypt were still fresh and the Palestine Liberation Organization was still an active enemy. As a result, Israel was very particular about security matters in the negotiating process. The important point is that the forces that might have moderated these beliefs were extraordinarily weak despite Sadat's overture, and could only have their effect over time. Despite the strong desire for peace in Israel, many attitudinal factors worked almost wholly against its institutionalization. Consequently the peace process was problematic and the peace settlement remained a partial one.

Begin's accession to power helped Israel's public overcome at least partially its suspicion of Egypt during the peace negotiations. The regime change appears to confirm the conventional assumption that hardline leaders can more readily make peace with long-time adversaries.[12] Begin had spent his public life in opposition to Israel's Labor governments, warning against the Arab threat. Thus the Israeli public knew he would do nothing to compromise Israel's security interests. From the American and Egyptian perspectives, it was advantageous for the United States and Egypt to have a conservative in power because they could be more sure of the backing of the Israeli opposition (see Brzezinski 1983). A Labor government would have had much more difficulty making peace because of the vehement opposition to its efforts from the right. As it was, even Begin faced stiff opposition to his efforts from the hardline members of his own coalition. Most of the resistance to Begin's policies came from Ariel Sharon and other outspoken defenders of Greater Israel in the cabinet. In the last analysis, Begin took his stand as leader of all the Israelis—hawks and doves alike—and moderated his position somewhat during the negotiations. Consequently several of the members of his cabinet worried about his intentions and made matters difficult for him at several points.

Decision Structure. Administrative stabilizers impede and constrain the smooth operation of decision-making processes in large organizations, and may be conceived as organizational friction or bureaucratic inertia. Their effect is to reduce the responsiveness of organizations to changes in their environment. Freed from the constraining effects of administrative stabilizers, foreign policymakers and their assistants would be more likely to discover changes in the environment relevant to their policy, to have alternatives to the current policy already prepared, to arrive at a decision to change the policy in question, and to implement their decision without delay (Goldmann 1988, 54–55). Naturally bureaucratic organizations do not and indeed cannot operate according to this ideal, since they are subject to a certain degree of internal friction and inertia. A study of administrative stabilizers, then, focuses on the characteristics of foreign policymaking organizations that make change more difficult.

The decision structure in Israel was democratic and even volatile in nature, so it is not surprising that it made the achievement of peace problematic. The most significant point is that Begin had less autonomy than Sadat. Sadat as chief executive could afford to ignore the advice of his senior ministers—at least he did so often without the danger of being forced from office. Begin, as leader of his party in a parliamentary system, was conscious of his status as first among equals in his cabinet. He could not afford to ignore the reactions of the rest of his ministers: if he could not persuade them to accept a negotiating position he had taken, he had to retreat from it or risk being ejected from his post. Vance writes that several times "misunderstandings" arose between

Carter and Begin when the prime minister had to modify a commitment he had made without leave of his cabinet. For instance, Carter consistently pressed Begin to declare a freeze on further settlement activity in the occupied territories. On occasion Begin conceded the point in a limited way, only to find the concession vehemently rejected by the cabinet upon his return to Jerusalem. Begin's only alternative when Carter inquired about Israel's failure to cease settlement activity was to claim that there must have been a misunderstanding. Vance found these episodes irritating, but recognized that little could be done about them given the situation in Israel (Vance 1983, chaps. 9–11).[13]

Thus the contentiousness of democratic politics in Israel made the consummation of peace with Egypt arduous. It is significant that even though the psychopolitical and administrative stabilizers worked largely against the establishment of peace, Sadat's overture resulted in a lasting treaty nevertheless. It demonstrates the important role of political leadership, which could overcome the obstacles that political culture and decision-making processes placed in its way. The durability of the peace despite these obstacles also suggests that the force of international norms in the stabilization of peace between former adversaries cannot be discounted. In light of the history of the Arab-Israeli conflict since 1979, it appears that normative stabilizers have been the principal force sustaining the peace that Sadat and Begin concluded. In other words, domestic political factors did not prevail over international ones to produce renewed conflict after the configuration of influences at the international level created the breakthrough necessary for peace.

Conclusion

The settlement that developed out of the negotiations between Egypt and Israel constituted a radical change in their bilateral relationship, but represented only partial change from a regional perspective. The two parties established a lasting, if somewhat lukewarm, peace in their own relations, but failed to achieve progress in building a larger framework for peace. In the end, the Egyptians accepted a separate peace because removing Israel from the Sinai was more important to them than removing Israel from the West Bank and Gaza, and because they lacked the means to retake the contested territories even though they had the will. The concept of foreign policy stabilization can help to explain this partial outcome, indicating how permanent foreign policy restructuring occurred in the bilateral relationship, even though no substantive progress took place on any other front.

This case study sought to apply the concept of foreign policy stabilization to an important instance of peacemaking. One aim of this application has been to improve explanations of policy change using new analytical tools; a second aim has been to refine and improve Goldmann's analytical framework in light of the evidence in this case. In general, bringing the analytical tools to bear on the evidence has sharpened the definitions and conceptual relationships in Goldmann's analysis. Only one weakness in the original framework needs to be pointed out. As Goldmann himself concedes, the theoretical grasp of third-party stabilization requires improvement. The simple postulates of structural balance theory do not appear to be adequate to explain the complex relationships in at least some trilateral bargaining situations. This study points out how analyses of third-party stabilization might profit from extending structural balance theory to incorporate the problem of collusion, but more needs to be done in this area. Currently, only this stabilizer can be and often is known to be important, but one needs to know more about how and why it is significant.

A study of Egyptian and Israeli foreign policies toward each other, and especially toward third parties in the ten years following Camp David, would give a more extended view of the stabilization process. A comprehensive and theoretic understanding of how the initial moves toward peace affected stability in the region as a whole would contribute to the understanding of the dynamics of foreign policy change. Inquiry along these lines implies analyzing foreign policies comparatively, where the probability of substantial foreign policy change by one or more parties in a given bargaining situation is the variable of interest. The determinants of this change, within this framework, are the constraining effects of strong stabilizers or the permissive effects of weak ones, as they interact with stresses or forces of change which are themselves strong or weak.

As this chapter has argued, tension exists between the factors that cause stress in a peace and those that stabilize it. Goldmann (1988, 218) refers to this tension when he writes that "the stabilization of a relationship of amity among enemies is a race between the incidence of disturbances and the progressive growth of stabilizers." The memoirs consulted for this study detail the often painstaking efforts of policymakers in Egypt, Israel, and the United States to put foreign policy stabilizers in place during the first phase of the peacemaking process. The obstacles they faced as well as the successes they achieved can teach their successors much about how to restructure foreign policy and build enduring institutions of peace in the future.

Notes

1. Henry Kissinger (1967) is a leading theorist of the first school; Roger Hilsman (1964) is often associated with the second. These two theories—which after all claim to describe the same thing—serve to highlight the virtues and defects of the foreign policymaking process in the United States. Sometimes the process is rigid when it should be flexible, but other times stability is a much-needed virtue. Sometimes incipient anarchy seems to threaten the efficacy of the entire foreign policy apparatus, but normally a competitive mode of policymaking is applauded for its democratic character. See also Allison (1971).

2. The unpredictability of foreign policy destabilization does not imply that anything can happen to any policy. It does suggest that the study of foreign policy stabilization may yield theoretical purchase on the circumstances favoring foreign policy change.

3. The list is based on Goldmann (1988, 26–69, 187–90). It is adapted to the present case, where the focus is on the very early stages of institutionalization.
4. Based on Goldmann (1988, 82).
5. This account is based on Brzezinski (1983, 82, 194–95) and Quandt (1986).
6. See also Sadat (1978, 301–13) and Sadat (1984, 97–107).
7. See Sadat (1983, 19–20) for a discussion of this strategy.
8. Ironically, both parties suffered the consequences of the peace that they most feared. Egypt was ostracized by the entire Arab world and Israel faced a Palestinian population united by its disappointment and anger over Israel's perceived failure to honor its commitments to them.
9. See Goldmann (1988, 111).
10. Kegley continues: "To the extent that such confining 'decision regimes' can be discovered for other states, we may be able to obtain unprecedented predictive leverage of foreign policy outputs by reference to them" (1987, 267).
11. See also Greffenius (1986, 1987).
12. For further analysis of the effects of regime change on the substance of foreign policy, see Hagan (1987a, 1989a, 1989b).
13. To make matters still more difficult, Begin was beholden not only to the cabinet, but for major issues to Israel's legislative body as well. At Camp David, Begin agreed under great pressure to withdraw Israel's settlements from Sinai, but only on condition of a favorable vote in the Knesset. The parliament eventually approved the measure.

Chapter 11

Cycles in Foreign Policy Restructuring
The Politics of Continuity and Change in U.S. Foreign Policy

Jerel A. Rosati

Jerel Rosati takes a broad theoretical perspective in developing a model of foreign policy change. Like many of the chapters above, his model is based on a synthesis of both domestic and international sources for understanding the dynamics of continuity and change in foreign policy. The theoretical model posits that governmental foreign policy evolves dialectically as a state goes through different cycles or phases over time: from a period of stability, where foreign policy continuity is the norm, to a period of transition, in which change in foreign policy is most probable, before returning to a new period of stability and foreign policy continuity in an ongoing process. The key to understanding the dynamics of foreign policy is the interaction of the state, the society, and the environment which produces a political process that usually reinforces governmental resistance to change and the maintenance of foreign policy continuity; sometimes, however, it produces contradictions to the status quo that contribute to foreign policy change. The cyclical model is used to illustrate and explain continuity and change through an in-depth study of U.S. foreign policy since the interwar years. Although applied to the case of the United States, the cyclical model provides a generalized understanding of the dynamics of foreign policy continuity and change. By synthesizing much of the literature discussed in earlier chapters, it also serves as a fitting close to this section on theoretical perspectives in foreign policy restructuring.

Jerel Rosati is associate professor of political science in the Department of Government and International Studies at the University of South Carolina. He received his Ph.D. in international studies from American University in 1982, a M.A. in political science from Arizona State University in 1978, and a B.A. in political science from the University of California, Los Angeles in 1975. His

This project has been in development for a number of years and has been fortunate to receive feedback from numerous individuals who I would like to thank: Mark Amen, Moss Blachmann, John Burton, William Clark, Roger Coate, Mark DeLancey, Joe Hagan, Rich Heauber, Charles Hermann, Steve Hildreth, David Hurt, Charles Kegley, Bill Kreml, Janeen Klinger, Bruce Moon, Roger Moore, Robert Phillips, Don Puchala, James Rosenau, Martin Sampson, Peter Schraeder, David Skidmore, Art Van den Houten, Dan Sabia, Darin Van Tassall, Steve Walker, Brian Whitmore, and Ekhart Zimmerman.

research interests include the theory and practice of foreign policy, with an emphasis on the study of the U.S. foreign policymaking process. He is the author of The Carter Administration's Quest for Global Community: Beliefs and Their Impact on Behavior *and coeditor of* The Power of Human Needs in World Society. *His work also has appeared in such journals as* International Journal, Journal of Political and Military Sociology, Political Psychology, World Development, *and* World Politics. *He has recently finished a book titled* The Politics of United States Foreign Policy.

Much has been learned in the general study of foreign policy over the last few decades. Yet, as the field of foreign policy has matured and progressed, scholars of foreign policy have not given adequate attention and thought to foreign policy change. There is little understanding of the long-term dynamics of foreign policy that encompass the processes of continuity and change. In this chapter, a theoretical approach is offered so as to better comprehend foreign policy continuity and change in general and the evolution of U.S. foreign policy in particular.

The dynamics of foreign policy can be best understood as a cyclical process where foreign policy tends to be relatively continuous over time, periodically interrupted by times of change. It is a cyclical process in the sense that governmental foreign policy tends to experience continuity which is eventually interrupted by change, followed by another period of continuity that eventually again will be interrupted by change. The cyclical nature of the process develops from the interaction of the state, the society, and the environment which generally acts to produce a political process that reinforces continuity, but which also eventually produces contradictions to the status quo that contribute to change. The result is that governmental foreign policy tends to experience both continuity and change over time. These dynamics are consistent with earlier work on foreign policy change, such as Rosenau's (1981) treatment of a state as an adaptive entity, Goldmann's (1988) finding that foreign policy stabilization tends to be the norm over time, and Holsti's (1982) discussion of restructuring as abrupt and nonincremental change. This often results in a cyclical process because, as Hermann (1990) and most of the authors in this volume have pointed out, it is very difficult to overcome the politics of the status quo and continuity in foreign policy—hence producing step-level change when policy shifts.

In order to better understand the dynamics of foreign policy change presented in this chapter, an overview of the model of foreign policy restructuring is presented in the next section. The model includes a close inspection of the cyclical process in the politics of foreign policy, the causes of continuity and change, and the likely outcome for foreign policy change. The model is then applied through an in-depth case study to explain the continuities and changes that have transpired in U.S. foreign policy since the interwar years. The chapter concludes with a brief discussion of the general implications for the understanding of foreign policy change and restructuring presented by such a cyclical approach.

A Model of Foreign Policy Restructuring

In this section a model is presented for identifying and explaining the dominant patterns of continuity, which change in governmental foreign policy over time. The model posits that the interaction of the state, the society, and the global environment produces a dialectical process where governmental foreign policy evolves through different cycles or phases over time: from a period of stability (or equilibrium) in which continuity in policy tends to prevail to a period of transition (or disequilibrium) in which change in policy is most likely. Governmental foreign policy normally tends to resist change but is interrupted occasionally by political crises which stimulate change. Should changes in foreign policy occur, a new pattern of foreign policy eventually will become established and entrenched in the government, bringing a new period of stability (and equilibrium) in which continuity in policy again prevails. Therefore, an ongoing cyclical process tends to occur where continuity in governmental foreign policy is periodically interrupted by change.

Before describing the model in greater depth, a few general points of clarification are appropriate. First, the notion of change as a cyclical process has become an increasingly common way to explain change in a variety of fields and has served, to some extent, as inspiration and reaffirmation in the development of this particular model of foreign policy restructuring. Cyclical notions of global change once again have become popular in international relations (for an overview, see Goldstein 1988). Strategic hegemonic theory involving the rise and decline of hegemonic power, for example, is explained by Robert Gilpin (1981) as a function of cyclical change. The "great transformation" in Western civilization between the nineteenth and twentieth centuries is accounted for by Karl Polanyi (1944) in terms of a disequilibrium process. Social change throughout Western history is interpreted by Robert Nisbet (1969) as being discontinuous and abrupt rather than incremental and gradual, while Chalmers Johnson (1966) theorizes that social systems, in general, experience steady states which are periodically interrupted by upheaval and revitalization. In the field of epistemology, likewise, Thomas Kuhn (1962) explains paradigm shifts as a discontinuous process due to the rise of anomalies that the prevailing theoretical orientation is unable to explain. Stephen Gould and Niles Eldredge (1977) describe the process of evolutionary biology in terms of "punctuated equilibrium," while Ilya Prigogine and Isabelle Stengers (1984) demonstrate how the static and deterministic notion of Newtonian mechanics in physics has been superseded by an evolutionary process of "nonlinear dynamics." Therefore, viewing the evolution of foreign policy as a cyclical process is consistent with a larger interdisciplinary intellectual tradition that has contributed to an understanding of the phenomena of change.[1]

Second, the cyclical model of foreign policy restructuring is specifically developed with U.S. foreign policy in mind, although it is generalizable beyond the United States. Clearly, while political systems do proceed down different historical paths, it is evident that particular cyclical patterns of continuity and change tend to prevail in American politics and U.S. foreign policy (see, e.g., Broesamle 1990; Fraser and Gerstle 1989; Huntington 1981; Roskin 1974; Resnick and Thomas 1990; Schlesinger 1986; Sundquist 1968).[2] Nevertheless, since the case of the United States is not unique across time and space, it also serves as a general model of continuity and change in foreign policy. As Skidmore (chap. 3) suggests in his discussion of sporadic change, this model is particularly appropriate for an enhanced understanding of foreign policy re- structuring in larger countries with complex societies that are highly developed, institutionalized, and bureaucratized (see also Morse 1973). At the same time, it should have relevance for other types of states as well. Obviously, the foreign policy phenomena to be examined determines the relevance of the model and the necessity for appropriate modifications, as the situation dictates.

Third, a cyclical model of foreign policy change is offered because it appears to fit empirical reality as an especially useful metaphor for understanding broad patterns of continuity and change in foreign policy over time.[3] It is *cyclical* because the politics of different societies tend to move back and forth between a period of stability (and equilibrium) and a period of transition (and disequilib- rium). However, it is a complex cyclical pattern that lacks regular periodicity and, although it resembles a pendulum swing, it does not move to precisely the same point twice (see Broesamle 1990, chap. 3). The cyclical process also is dialectical in that transition and change result from the contradictions (or disequilibrium) that develop during a time of stability and foreign policy continuity, which gradually lay the foundation for major challenges to the status quo.[4] Such a cyclical process captures the dynamics of foreign policy continuity and change over time.

Finally, this model of foreign policy change incorporates the essence of politics and its dynamics due to the interplay of three forces—the state, society, and the environment (see Ikenberry 1988; Lake 1988).[5] Although there is little agreement concerning definitions, in this model *state* is a legal concept which refers to the governmental institutions through which policymakers act in the name of the people of a given territory; *society* refers to the social collectivity and to the specific institutions, beliefs, and relationships that have developed among a population; and *environment* refers to the resources of a state as well as the opportunities and constraints it faces in a global context. The cyclical model is premised on the necessity to synthesize and integrate explanations from each perspective to produce an understanding of the dynamics of foreign policy (see Carlsnaes 1992; Dessler 1991; Rosati 1987).[6] Governmental foreign policy reflects the beliefs and actions of policymakers in state bureaucratic institutions who are influenced, in varying degrees and in varying ways, by the society and the environment in which they operate. This interaction results in a politics of foreign policy where either one of two patterns prevail: a period of stability, equilibrium and continuity in governmental foreign policy or a period of instability and disequilibrium where foreign policy change is most likely.

What follows is a sketch of the cyclical model of foreign policy change. In this work *foreign policy* refers to the scope and collection of goals, strategies, and instruments that are selected by governmental policymakers to respond abroad to the present and future environment. The concept of *change* refers to foreign policy phenomena that experience broad alteration, ranging from more modest shifts to major foreign policy restructuring (see Holsti 1977; Rosati, Sampson, and Hagan, chap. 1); *continuity* refers to broad patterns in foreign policy that tend to persist over time, encompassing more micro and incremental changes (since nothing is totally constant; see Sorokin 1957, chap. 38).[7] Continuity and change "are thus conceived to be opposite sides of the same coin," as James Rosenau (1990, 19) notes. The cyclical model of foreign policy change described represents a general and initial formulation. In this respect it is important to keep in mind what Albert Somit and Steven Peterson (1992) discovered in *The Dynamics of Evolution: The Punctuated Equilibrium Debate in the Natural and Social Sciences:* after twenty years there is still little agreement concerning the concepts and contentions behind the punctuated equilibrium model of biological change.[8]

Cycles of Stability and Transition

The interaction of the state with society and the environment provides the sources of stability and transition resulting in the politics of continuity and change in foreign policy. "The fact is that any society as it exists at a given moment of time," Kenneth Boulding (1970, 129) observes, "is a complex aggregation of elements some of them reinforcing each other and some of them contradictory." How these competing forces play out determines the dynamics of politics and the propensities for policy change.

Usually, the state, society, and the environment interact to produce and reinforce a *period of stability* where the politics of the status quo prevails to produce foreign policy continuity. Foreign policy during such a period tends to be highly resistant to change. This is usually the case because the beliefs and actions of key individuals and groups supporting the status quo have become institutionalized throughout society and the state. In other words, the patterns of stratification that exist in the structures and beliefs throughout society and the state tend to favor the status quo and continuity over the political forces in support of change. Under these conditions, interests advocating the status quo are able to oppose challenges to their positions and policies within government and society. According to V. O. Key, Jr. (1964, 70), in *Politics, Parties, and Pressure Groups:*

> The system—the established way of doing things—constitutes a powerful brake on political change. Those who agitate for a new order invariably encounter the resistance of the old order which

exists, in considerable degree at least, in the revered values more or less firmly anchored in group life. These patterns of behavior, traditional modes of action, group norms, or social equilibria—the concept employed in their description may not matter—possess a powerful capacity for their own perpetuation and resist movements that would disturb them.

Such a period of stability is a time when the *politics of the status quo* prevails.

With time, however, changes in the society and the environment interact with the state to create contradictions in the prevailing status quo that produce a *period of transition* and increase the likelihood of foreign policy change. This eventually occurs because of the growing gap that develops between the incrementalist policies of the government and the inevitable change experienced throughout the environment and society. As the politics of the status quo continues to prevail and governmental policies fail to adjust to new developments in the international and domestic environment, the contradictions grow, increasing the likelihood of policy failure abroad and the growth of internal opposition at home. Should these contradictory developments continue and intensify with time, governmental policy becomes increasingly maladaptive. Eventually, this may lead to major political crises at home that politicize members of society to challenge the legitimacy of the policies and the beliefs held by the individuals and groups that dominate society and the state. Such a period of transition, in other words, is a time of political instability and disequilibrium where the *politics of adjustment* prevails. Therefore, changes throughout society and the environment are the key sources triggering a period of transition where policies of the status quo are vulnerable to change.

Hence states go through different cycles—a period of stability producing foreign policy continuity is eventually superseded by a period of transition where change in foreign policy may occur (see figure 11.1 for the basic structure of the model).[9] According to Samuel Huntington (1981, 89) in *American Politics: The Politics of Disharmony,* "There are thus two American politics: the politics of movements and causes, of creedal passion and reform, and the politics of interests and groups, of pragmatic bargaining and compromise."[10] Since resistance to change is the norm, foreign policy change tends to be, not continuous or evolutionary, but abrupt, discontinuous, and step-level. Such a depiction of cyclical change is consistent with the observation made by Robert Nisbet in *Social Change and History:* "Despite the testimony of conventional wisdom in social theory, despite the first and abiding premise of the theory of social development, it is not change but persistence that is the 'natural' or 'normal' condition of any given form of social behavior. . . . Change in any degree of notable significance is intermittent rather than continuous, mutational, even explosive, rather than the simple accumulation of internal variations" (1969, 274, 281).

The changes in foreign policy that do occur soon result in a new period where stability is restored and continuity in policy is again the norm. As

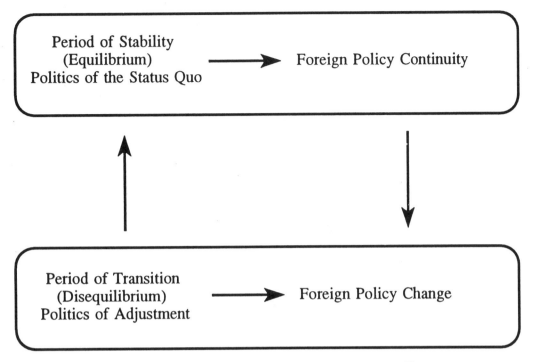

Figure 11.1   The Cycle of Foreign Policy Continuity and Change

described by David Truman (1951, 44) in *The Governmental Process,* "The moving pattern of a complex society such as the one in which we live is one of changes and disturbances in the habitual subpatterns of interaction, followed by a return to the previous state of equilibrium or, if the disturbances are intense or prolonged, by the emergence of new groups" which establish "a new balance, a new adjustment in the habitual interactions of individuals."[11] This produces another period of equilibrium as the challenges to the old status quo wither or become legitimized and successfully included in the established structures and beliefs of society and the state. The result, as Key (1964, 30) found, is governmental policy which gains "if not immortality, an enormous capacity to resist attempts to modify it." Or, as stated by Huntington (1981, 119), "The reforms of one generation often produce the vested interests of the next."

   The model is actually much more complex in delineating the dynamics of change than the simple cyclical process portrayed suggests. For example, changes throughout the state, society, and environment not only lead to changes in foreign policy, but changes in foreign policy also affect the state, society, and environment—it is a complex interactive process.[12] Similarly, movement from a period of stability to transition and then to a new period of stability does not always occur in a straightforward fashion. Different periods of continuity and change tend to overlap—for example, contradictions which build within the politics of the status quo eventually give impetus to the politics of change. According to Huntington (1981, 166), "The high points of historical eras are usually clearly visible. . . . The starting and ending points of eras, however, are often lost in the complexity, ambiguity, and incrementalism of history."[13] Furthermore, even though a period of transition tends to occur abruptly and for a short period of time, it may nonetheless last for months and years (figure 11.2 reflects this greater complexity).

There is a rich literature from various disciplines in the social sciences which provides the basis for this cyclical model of foreign policy restructuring. As David Resnick and Norman Thomas (1990, 7) recommend in their review of cyclical theories of American politics, "If we are to have faith in the validity of cycles and set aside the nagging suspicion that their existence is simply an instance of a clever observer imposing a pattern on the past or else the result of essentially random variation, we need to ground our observations in more well-established social science theory." Briefly, some of the significant work on the state, society, and environment for explaining why the politics of foreign policy continuity is the norm and why the politics of foreign policy change is the occasional, but inevitable, exception to the rule is highlighted below.

Sources of Stability and Foreign Policy Continuity

Students of international relations who take a rational actor approach to explain state behavior assume that governments readily change their foreign policy in response to changes in the global environment (see, e.g., Skidmore Chap. 3).[14] Rational actors adapt their foreign policies to reflect the changes in

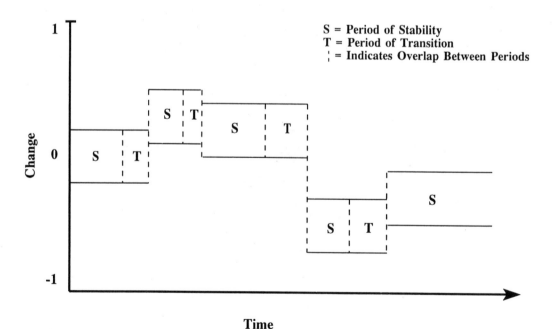

Figure 11.2   The Complex Cyclical Process Over Time

the opportunities and constraints in their environment so as to maximize their interests. There may, in fact, be times when policymakers do recognize changes throughout the international system and do take swift and appropriate action to change and restructure their foreign policies to promote their national interests. But, for the most part, this ignores an extensive theoretical and empirical literature on governmental decision-making and the state, the role of domestic politics and society, and the larger environment which interact to produce a politics that leads, not to swift adaptation, but to governmental resistance to foreign policy change (see, e.g., Goldmann 1988; Hermann 1990; Volgy and Schwarz, chap. 2). As Joseph Schumpeter (1949, 84) once was fond of stating, "All knowledge and habit once acquired becomes as firmly rooted in ourselves as a railway embankment in the earth."

For any country much of the conduct of foreign policy is a function of bureaucracy which tends to act as a major source of continuity over time. The literature on governmental decision-making in political science, public administration, and business administration demonstrates that once bureaucracies are formed, policy incrementalism is the order of the day (Allison 1971; Steinbruner 1974; Wilson 1989). This is because members of governmental institutions tend to resist changes in organizational structures, subcultures, and policy routines which have been established over time. Therefore, according to Morton Halperin (1974, 308, 399) in *Bureaucratic Politics and Foreign Policy,* "One of the truisms of bureaucracy is that it resists change. . . . The bureaucratic system is basically inert; it moves only when pushed hard and persistently. The majority of bureaucrats prefer to maintain the status quo, and only a small group is, at any one time, advocating change."

Foreign policy is not solely bureaucratic in nature, but is also responsive to government leaders. The psychological literature indicates, however, that high-level policymakers are resistant to changing their beliefs once they are formed (Holsti 1967; Jervis 1976; Rosati 1987). Strong domineering leaders, in fact, often produce a policymaking process that approximates "groupthink" (Janis 1982). Furthermore, bureaucratic politics often prevails among policymakers who make decisions based on coalition building, political viability, and compromise rather than optimal solutions, which rarely produces more than minor deviations from past policy (Allison 1971; Halperin 1974; Rosati 1981). Under such conditions, governmental decision-making usually results in individuals, organizations, and policymaking which resist change and restructuring, producing instead foreign policy continuity and incrementalism over time (see Schraeder, chap. 7).

Resistance to change in policy, once it has been formed and implemented, also occurs because of the conservative nature of the dominant structures and beliefs that exist throughout society. As the political sociological literature makes clear, all political systems—whether pluralist, class, or elitist in nature—tend to resist change, although with varying degrees of rigidity and success (see, e.g., Alford 1975; Katzenstein 1978). Pluralists argue that governmental policy tends to reflect the existence of competing societal elites, producing a politics of compromise and small incremental changes in policy over time (Dahl 1967; Nisbet 1953; Rose 1967). Hyperpluralists emphasize the close networks that develop between private groups and the government around particular issues, producing powerful vested interests which resist changes to the status quo (Lowi 1969; McConnell 1966; Olson 1982). Marxists tend to see an authoritative system in which the state is an instrument of the capitalist class or is constrained by the structures and demands of capitalist society, either of which allows the ruling elite to resist changes to their policies (Domhoff 1978; Miliband 1982). Finally, elitists see democracy only for a few because of the interlocking relationships between private and public institutional elites (Dye 1976; Mills 1956; Prewitt and Stone 1973). Although each approach may provide separate insights into state-societal relations, each helps to explain why the politics of the status quo tends to prevail.[15]

Continuity in policy prevails, in other words, because *established* groups and institutions throughout government and society engage in politics to promote their interests and protect the status quo from *challenging* groups and ideas, often with the support of the mass public. Although predominantly apolitical, most members of the public usually passively support the mainstream institutions and beliefs to which they have grown accustomed, ultimately providing the political system with its legitimacy and political stability (Key 1961; Neuman 1986; Risse-Kappen 1991).[16] The prevalence of such a politics of the status quo throughout society is reinforced by the work within history and political psychology which emphasizes the rigidity and stability of culture and ideology over time (Dower 1986; Eckstein 1988; Inglehart 1977; Sampson 1987).

The resistance to change and the support for the politics of the status quo that develops at the state and societal level are further reinforced by the structures and constraints which exist throughout the larger environment (Gourevitch 1978; Morse 1973). Students of international relations, for example, have long recognized that the government is not a purely autonomous and independent international actor (Bull 1977; Waltz 1959). States often react to external events, issues, and other actors involving patterns where previous behavior and relationships constrain the freedom of action available to any country in an increasingly interdependent world. Governmental foreign policies are influenced by past alliance agreements, political commitments, and long-standing commercial relationships. Such behavior usually reflects the regional and global roles that states occupy throughout the international political economy. Furthermore, governmental foreign policy must operate in a world constrained by the existence of international laws, norms, and regimes which have come increasingly to define and influence the policies of states (Keohane and Nye 1977). Thus, international patterns and constraints limit government independence and often act to reinforce state and societal causes of foreign policy continuity.

Sources of Transition and Foreign Policy Change

The interaction of those elements within the state, society, and environment that promote the status quo are in tension with those elements of the state, society, and environment that act as the sources of change. The sources of stability and continuity often prevail, but eventually the tensions between the sources of continuity and the sources of change grow over time, especially when governmental policies fail to adapt to changes that occur throughout society and the environment. The politics of adjustment is most likely to prevail over the politics of the status quo during times of crisis and political instability, when the legitimacy of the political system is more likely to be questioned and challenged throughout society and within government. During such times, greater numbers of people are likely to challenge and criticize the status quo, new and larger numbers of issues are placed on the political agenda, challenging groups and ideas gain strength, the dominant groups and beliefs throughout society and government have less success dominating politics, and public policies once considered successful are now increasingly seen as failures and counterproductive. Therefore, periods of crises and political instability are often accompanied by change in politics and foreign policy. In the language of Huntington (1981, 105),

> Interest-group politics accounts for most of American politics most of the time, but it does not describe all of American politics all of the time. . . . Interest-group politics is thus at times supplemented, and even supplanted, by creedal politics. In contrast to interest-group politics, creedal politics tends to be intermittent rather than continuous, passionate rather than pragmatic, idealistic rather than materialistic, reform-minded rather than status-quo oriented, and formulated in terms of right and wrong rather than more or less.

In this section, the sources and politics of change are examined more closely. Although much of the social science literature allows one to conclude that stability and continuity is the norm, it also sheds light on the politics of adjustment. Typically, over time bureaucratic behavior tends to become dysfunctional, societal structures and institutions become unresponsive, and the prevalent beliefs throughout society and the state become increasingly anachronistic to alterations in the domestic and international environment. This prompts challenges to the status quo leading to a period of transition in which foreign policy change is most likely to occur. Hence, "no political system is proof against decay and dissolution. Regardless of the flexibility of the structure, within any society changes of great severity and extent may occur that will rupture the established governmental process." Yet, as Truman (1951, 524–25) continued, "at the same time governments vary in the ease with which they can adjust to changes, in the adequacy with which their procedures reflect the widespread unorganized interests in the society, and in the speed with which they can arrive at acceptable solutions for the problems which confront them.''

Challenges to the status quo and change do occur within the government. Bureaucracy, normally resistant to change, sometimes is vulnerable to change. As Graham Allison (1971, 85) notes, "Dramatic change occurs usually in response to major disasters. Confronted with an undeniable failure of procedures and repertoires, authorities outside the organization demand change, existing personnel are less resistant to change, and key members of the organization are replaced by individuals committed to change'' (see also Bendor and Hammond 1992). Likewise, changes may also occur in policymaking processes and the beliefs of political leaders (Rosati 1987; Steinbruner 1974), as well as in the nature of the leadership and regime during the period of transition (Bunce 1981; Hagan 1989a).

Maladaptive policies and political instability clearly can lead to changes in leadership, regime, institutions, and beliefs within the state and society for they politicize issues and give rise to individuals, groups, and social movements which challenge the status quo. During more stable periods, established groups in support of the status quo tend to dominate. Challenging groups exist, but they are often few in number, small in size and support, and limited in impact. However, times of greater political instability produce considerable social movement activity and interest group expansion. During these periods, major political challenges to the status quo occur in which efforts are made to change the policy agendas, ideological beliefs, and institutions that dominate society and the government (Berry 1989; Burton 1979; Dalton and Kuechler 1990; Gamson 1975; Lowi 1971; McFarland 1991; Mendelson 1993; Truman 1971; Schattschneider 1975; Wilson 1973).[17] Hence, in the words of Key (1964, 20), "The political equilibrium among social groups is from time to time disturbed. One class or group becomes discontented with existing conditions, and the processes of politics go into operation to create a new equilibrium.''

As James MacGregor Burns (1989, 656) has observed near the end of his three-volume history of America:

> Like their counterparts in other countries, American social protest movements were unruly, untidy, and unpredictable in effect, but they displayed continuities and similarities in their very dynamics. The pattern was clear, even dramatic: these movements emerged out of economic stress and social tension and erupted in conflict, often violent. After a time they dominated political debate, overshadowed more traditional issues, cut across existing lines of party cleavage, polarized groups and parties. The immediate test of success was whether the movement could force one major party or both of them to embrace in its cause. The test of long-run success was whether the movement left the whole party system altered and, even more, left the political landscape transformed.

The forces in support of the status quo usually have a great advantage in resisting challenging groups, for the status quo tends to have considerable support throughout the government and much of society. Nevertheless, it is during times of political instability that changes, including foreign policy change, have the greatest potential and possibility of occurring.

Changes in the larger environment are the prime determinant as to why policies of the past are likely to be anachronistic and lead to challenges to the status quo. Environmental changes, for example, affect the sensitivity and vulnerability of states and their foreign policies (Keohane and Nye 1977). Harold and Margaret Sprout (1965, 1969), for example, have theorized that the relationship between the policymakers' *psychological milieu* and *operational milieu* determines a government's ability to accomplish its aims. In their view, actual state capacity depends on its correspondence to changes in the environment. If policymakers fail to perceive the increasing contradictions between the continuity of governmental policies and the constraints and opportunities in a dynamic environment, foreign policy tends to become maladaptive and unsuccessful with time (see also Choucri and North 1975). In the words of Morse (1976, 179), "Foreign policy today, whether it is conducted by a great or lesser power, in a highly industrialized or relatively non-industrialized society, tends to reflect an almost inevitable gap between perceptions of what the world is and the actual structures of international relationships. Reality changes so quickly that the reflexes for action typical of governments tend always to lag behind." For Edward Carr (1964), Robert Gilpin (1981), and Paul Kennedy (1987), the development of these contradictions explain the rise and decline of great powers. Eventually, maladaptive policies produce negative events that politicize individuals and groups to challenge the dominant institutions, beliefs, and policies that emanate from society and the state.

The growing contradictions between policy continuity and environmental changes accounts for the major role crises play in the evolution of foreign policy and international relations. According to Gilpin (1981, 103), "Unfortunately, as a society ages it becomes decreasingly able to learn from others and to adapt itself to changing circumstances. Tradition and vested interests inhibit further reordering and reform of the society." This is consistent with Mancur Olson's thesis in *The Rise and Decline of Nations* (1982) that the longer a society enjoys political stability, the more likely it is to develop powerful special interests and social rigidities that reinforce the politics of the status quo.

Events and crises, therefore, act as catalysts for overcoming the sources that promote the status quo and resist change. As Stephen Krasner (1976, 341) puts it, "Once policies have been adopted, they are pursued until a new crisis demonstrates that they are no longer feasible." Events and crises act as the immediate cause of change, reflecting the underlying relationship and contradictions which exist between the sources of continuity and the sources of change emanating from the interaction of the state, society, and environment.[18] As described by Nisbet (1969, 282), "The very tendency of social behavior to persist, to hold fast to values and convenience, makes a degree of crisis inevitable in all but the most minor of changes. A given way of behaving tends to persist as long as circumstances permit. Then . . . the way of behaving ceases to be possible, as the result of some intrusion, some difficulty which is the consequence of event or impact, and a period of crisis ensues.''

To be more specific, two general types of events affect the possibility of foreign policy change: spectacular events and cumulative events (Deutsch and Merritt 1965; see also Zimmerman 1979). Domestic and international crises, for example, may politicize issues that impact on the society, the state, and, therefore, foreign policy. Revolutions and wars, in particular, are major agents of change for they are events which are both spectacular and cumulative for the members of society and the state involved (Goldstone 1980; Lebow 1981; Stein and Russett 1980). As described by Robert Jervis (1976, 262), ''since events with major consequences for a nation absorb so much of the citizen's time and attention, they both socialize the previously unconcerned and change the perceptual predispositions of many people with established views.'' However, much depends on how individuals interpret these events—a function of the politics of the times and, increasingly, media coverage—for they ''are largely creations of the language used to describe them'' (Edelman 1964, 65; see also Baumgartner 1989). Events and crises with a negative impact on people are likely to lead to greater change; positive events tend to reinforce beliefs, political stability, and foreign policy continuity.

The key to policy change, therefore, is increasingly maladaptive policies that come to be perceived as inappropriate and counterproductive. For although ''political systems may exist in a stable, even static, form over long periods,'' argued Key (1964, 40), ''the equilibrium—the balance, the ordered course of affairs, the established pattern—is disturbed from time to time by some change that generates discontent.'' As Charles Hermann (1990, 12–13) found from his review of the theoretical literature and its implications for foreign policy change:

> All the material examined seems explicitly or implicitly to assume that change is driven by failure. The inadequacy of an existing schemata to account for some critical experience forces the individual into a learning mode that may lead to a restructuring of his or her mental model. Information that existing policy is not performing properly motivates advocates of change in a government and serves as ammunition in their struggle with the bureaucracy. Realignment of the domestic system often results from large-scale discontent with the existing government or the failure of the system to meet the demands of present or newly powerful constituents.

In other words, as long as the policies of the states are perceived to be successful by members of government and society, political stability and policy continuity are reinforced. When policies, however, are no longer perceived as being appropriate and successful throughout society, more and more participants within society and government become willing to challenge the established institutions and beliefs of the state and society that formed the basis of the policies, thus opening up the possibility for change (Baumgartner and Jones 1991; Hagan 1987, chap. 8).

Maladaptive policy and crises may trigger political instability and disequilibrium for society and the state—a period of transition—which produces a politics of adjustment and possible foreign policy change. It is during such times that the legitimacy of the status quo becomes questioned and challenged. The importance of policy outcomes to the legitimacy of any regime is clarified by Karl Deutsch (1974, 17), "Most governments are obeyed most of the time by their subjects, and a great deal has to happen before an established government will lose its legitimacy in the eyes of its people. What will count most heavily in the long run are results—what difference, if any, the actions or omissions of the government will seem to make in the lives of those who count in politics, and eventually in the lives of the mass of the population." The necessity of crises for triggering challenges to the legitimacy of the status quo and overcoming resistance to change accounts for the tendency of social change to be cyclical and, when it does occur, abrupt, sporadic, and step-level (Krasner 1984).

The Transitional Outcome: Foreign Policy Change and Continuity

Foreign policy change, in sum, tends to reflect changes that take place in the structures, beliefs, and politics of society and the state within a dynamic environmental context. A period of political instability and transition may produce such changes, but the outcome is not preordained, for the scope, intensity, and direction of change in society, government, and foreign policy do not follow predictable patterns. This is because of the unique nature and timing of events and crises in triggering change and the uncertainty of their outcomes in the politics of foreign policy. As James Broesamle (1990, 460) found in his study of American political reform and reaction, "crisis underlies all reform eras, and one cannot predict with much certainty just when crises will erupt or what form they will take."

Some critical events, such as war, may politicize issues across the board and, consequently, have a wide impact on the institutions, beliefs, and politics of society, the state, and, thus, foreign policy in general. Other events may only politicize a few general issues, affecting only facets of society, the state, and foreign policy. As stated by Burns (1989, 614), for example, "the more nearly total the war, the faster and broader the flow of change tends to be." During such times of political instability and flux, "fortune" also affects the dynamics of politics and foreign policy change.[19] Ultimately, the outcome will depend on the nature of the critical events and their political impact on the interaction of the state, society, and environment in terms of its affect on the strength of the sources of the status quo in comparison to the sources of change

(Mansbach and Vasquez 1981; Vasquez 1985). As described by Huntington (1981, 108), "In creedal passion periods, politics tends to become polarized between those who are in favor of reform and change and those who are willing to accept existing institutions as they are. . . . The latter always exist; the former are more evanescent, and the intensity of the conflict varies with their rise and fall."

In examining the range of likely foreign policy patterns resulting from a period of transition, four outcomes are possible:

1. *Intensification:* No or little change—the scope, goals, and strategy of foreign policy are reinforced.
2. *Refinement:* Minor changes in the scope, goals, and strategy of foreign policy.
3. *Reform:* Moderate changes in the scope, goals, and strategy of foreign policy.
4. *Restructuring:* Major changes in the scope, goals, and strategy of foreign policy.

In this cyclical model, no political or ideological orientation is assumed to prevail with any degree of certainty or regularity. Rather, transitional outcomes are a function of politics and history.[20]

To clarify, politics during a time of instability and transition may produce a range of foreign policy outcomes from little change at all (where foreign policy continuity prevails) to foreign policy restructuring (most visible and intense following revolution and war). Intensification occurs when the political forces of the status quo overwhelm the political forces of change, such as through the use of repression. Restructuring involves the reverse process in which the sources of change have a profound impact on the society and the state, thus altering foreign policy. Refinement and reform represent more mixed patterns, where society, the state, and foreign policy experience both continuity and change (see Hagan 1989a).

Given the existence of continuity in policy over a prolonged period of time, based on the power of established social networks and the presence of vested interests throughout society and the state, the likelihood that some policy continuity will survive a period of transition is quite high. Major challenges to the status quo throughout society and the state are rare and often unsuccessful, thus restructuring is infrequent. This explains the importance of catastrophic events as catalysts for foreign policy change and restructuring. Therefore, when foreign policy change does occur, it is likely to be relatively abrupt but accompanied by some continuity in foreign policy from the past. As James Rosenau (1990, 19) notes, change and continuity "both are likely to be present, and each will account for a proportion of the outcome." Or in the words of the late sociologist Pitirim Sorokin (1957, 674) from his classic work *Social and Cultural Dynamics,* "thus history ever repeats itself and never repeats itself; both seemingly contradictory statements are true and are not contradictory at all, when properly understood." Whatever the policy outcome, the net result is a new period of foreign policy continuity where political stability eventually is restored until instability increases and a period of transition ensues once again. Hence, according to this model, the general pattern of social evolution is a cyclical process of stability and transition over time resulting in the ebb and flow of foreign policy continuity and change (see figure 11.3 for a schematic overview of the dynamics of foreign policy change).

Continuity and Change in U.S. Foreign Policy Since the Interwar Years

"One way to assure that metatheoretical discussions do not drift too far above the plane of empirical research is to ground them in efforts to construct causal models." Hence, states David Dessler (1991, 352), "these efforts will demand detailed case studies . . . since only careful and intensive examination of individual cases can reveal the generative structures and processes that causal theory aims to describe." Thus this section analyzes in some depth the continuity and change in the general *foreign policy orientation*—that is the scope, goals, and basic strategy—of the United States since World War I to illustrate the power of the cyclical model of foreign policy change described above.[21]

Most people who study U.S. foreign policy argue that World War II represented a watershed which fundamentally shifted policy from isolationism to internationalism, and maintain that the dominant pattern during the postwar era has been one of foreign policy continuity. In other words, the general foreign policy orientation of the United States underwent restructuring as a result of World War II and the postwar experience. This orthodox interpretation has emphasized that the goal of U.S. internationalism since World War II has

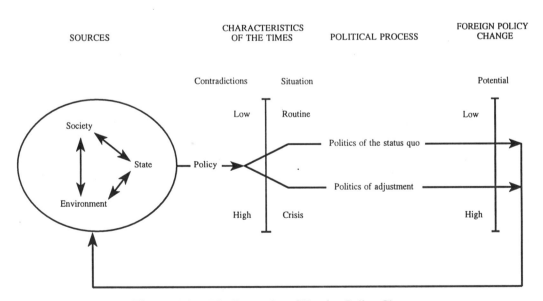

Figure 11.3   The Dynamics of Foreign Policy Change

been to prevent the global spread of Soviet communism through a strategy of containment reliant on the threat and use of force (Brown 1983; Gaddis 1982; Kegley and Wittkopf 1987; Spanier 1988). While some scholars within this interpretation acknowledge that different administrations have emphasized different policy instruments over time, especially since Vietnam, they nevertheless stress that the U.S. global policy of communist containment has consistently been the foundation of its foreign policy since the end of World War II.[22]

Although the orthodox interpretation has been the most popular, a revisionist literature has developed on U.S. foreign policy (see, e.g., Walker 1981; Melanson 1983). The most popular revisionist interpretation, influenced in part by the Marxist tradition, emphasizes the flip side of the coin in comparison to the orthodox interpretation. Revisionists tend to ignore what the United States was trying to prevent—Soviet and communist expansion—and emphasize, instead, what the United States was attempting to promote—a liberal world order under American leadership. They recognize that World War II produced greater American activism throughout the globe, but contend that its new policies were designed to support the goal of a capitalist international political economy and the promotion of American private investment and trade abroad. Therefore, unlike the orthodox interpretation, revisionists see much greater continuity in U.S. foreign policy before and after 1941 (Berkowitz, Bock, and Fuccillo 1977; Parenti 1989).

A close look at the empirical literature suggests that each interpretation captures an important part of U.S. foreign policy, but that each is simplistic in its overall portrayal. The orthodox interpretation tends to emphasize national security policy while the revisionist interpretation highlights foreign economic policy. Furthermore, where the orthodox interpretation argues discontinuity in U.S. foreign policy with World War II and continuity thereafter, the revisionist interpretation emphasizes overall continuity over time. Unfortunately, a comprehensive understanding of continuity and change in U.S. foreign policy since the interwar years is not simply a matter of stapling together the two interpretations.

Clearly, national security and foreign economic policy are the two basic elements that makeup U.S. foreign policy. However, the history of U.S. foreign policy has experienced a more complex pattern of continuity and change over time than offered by either of the two competing interpretations. In addition to the impact of World War II, an increasing number of scholars and analysts have come to the conclusion that the consequences of the Vietnam War resulted in significant changes in U.S. foreign policy (see, e.g., Destler, Gelb, and Lake 1976; Melanson 1973; Oye, Lieber, and Rothchild 1987; Rosati 1993; Roskin 1974).[23] The evolution of the dominant patterns in U.S. foreign policy described below is derived from a synthesis of the scholarly literature.

Since the interwar years, U.S. foreign policy has undergone two restructurings. The first and more significant restructuring occurred throughout the 1940s in response to World War II. The second restructuring occurred during the late 1960s and early 1970s in response to Vietnam and the end of the Bretton Woods system.[24] United States' foreign policy, therefore, has experienced two periods of transition and two periods of continuity since the interwar years:

1. World War II, transition, and foreign policy change,
2. The cold war years of stability and foreign policy continuity,
3. The Vietnam War, transition, and foreign policy change,
4. The post-Vietnam War years of stability and foreign policy continuity.

The result of this cyclical process has been considerable change as well as continuity in the evolution of U.S. foreign policy. World War II produced a restructuring of U.S. foreign policy from the interwar years, although certain continuities remained into the cold war years. Likewise, although U.S. foreign policy during the post-Vietnam years had much in common with the cold war years, Vietnam did trigger some significant changes as well. And with the end of the cold war, the politics of U.S. foreign policy may have entered a new period of transition and possible foreign policy change, although much of past policy will continue into the future. These patterns of continuity and change in U.S. foreign policy are a consequence of the dynamics of the state's interaction with its society and the environment over time. These patterns in U.S. foreign policy are discussed in greater depth below and are informed by the model of foreign policy restructuring presented above.

Models, Reality, and U.S. Foreign Policy

Before proceeding it should be understood that, although the purpose of developing a model is to better capture the dynamics of reality, a model necessarily simplifies reality in the process. Historical reality rarely evolves in the cut and dried fashion described in a model. The complex and messy politics of U.S. foreign policy involve the influence of numerous structures and actors throughout the state, society, and environment. A model cannot capture all of this complexity nor will the cyclical nature of change embodied in this model, as laid out above, be neatly found in the history of U.S. foreign policy. For example, as James Rosenau (1990, 75) has noted, "Only the analyst's sense of tidiness is served by efforts to construct compartments that neatly delineate where continuity ends and change begins."

Although the model of foreign policy restructuring cannot fully capture the dynamics of historical reality, it is able to provide the theoretical perspective for highlighting and explaining the dominant patterns of continuity and change in the foreign policy orientations of the United States over time. As a result, the general depiction of U.S. foreign policy below is presented in a more coherent fashion than its complex reality—involving a loose collection of policies pursued by different bureaucratic organizations and policymakers—warrants. With this in mind, an overview of the cycles and political dynamics of U.S. foreign policy since the interwar years follows (a more in-depth discussion appears in Rosati's *The Politics of United States Foreign Policy*, 1993).

World War II, Transition, and Foreign Policy Change

Three items are discussed in this section on World War II and foreign policy change. First, a brief overview of the American policy of regionalism that prevailed during the interwar years is explored. Second, the impact of World War II in changing U.S. foreign policy is briefly discussed. Finally, the possibility and failure of America's first globalist foreign policy for the postwar era during the Roosevelt administration is analyzed. Together, this should provide an overview for understanding the role that World War II played in restructuring U.S. foreign policy from a regional orientation to a global orientation.

American Regionalism During the Interwar Years.   Although the 1920s and 1930s are popularly thought of as the height of isolationism in U.S. foreign policy, from World War I to World War II U.S. foreign policy could best be characterized as regionalist in scope and orientation (Bolt 1981; Cohen 1987). United States' foreign policy actively promoted political stability and economic expansion abroad, principally in Latin American and Asia where it had long been active. The U.S. government and American business, in fact, dramatically increased their presence and influence in these regions, especially throughout Central America and the Caribbean. During this time, the United States also was active in other parts of the world, such as in its commercial relations with Europe, but U.S. foreign policy outside of Latin America and Asia lacked coherence and consistent involvement. The United States during this period became the leading industrial power of its time, yet U.S. foreign policy reflected a regionalist orientation because of the limited capacity of the executive branch within the government to act abroad; the prevalence of isolationist, or anti-imperialist, sentiment that prevailed throughout American society during this time; and the continued prominence of European great powers on the global scene.

The Impact of World War II.   World War II gave rise to a period of transition and a restructuring of U.S. foreign policy that lasted throughout the cold war years. The Japanese attack on Pearl Harbor on 7 December 1941 abruptly ended the regional era in U.S. foreign policy. The next four years saw the beginning of a new era of global involvement in which the United States—along with the Soviets, British, Chinese, French, and other allies—fought the Axis powers of Germany and Japan around the globe. With World War II, the United States became a complete global power and pursued a globalist foreign policy.

World War II demonstrated that the United States could no longer afford to play the regional role it had preferred in the past because of crucial changes in the global environment. In this respect, World War II symbolized the shift of global power away from Great Britain and France toward Germany, Japan, the Soviet Union, and, in particular, the United States. These global changes intensified during the war and, with the defeat of the Axis powers, resulted in the rise of the Soviet Union as a Eurasian power and the United States as the preeminent global power of its time. World War II, likewise, produced numerous changes in the beliefs and institutions of American society and government which led to a restructuring of its foreign policy in a globalist direction as evident in the rise of presidential power, the expansion of the national security bureaucracy, and broad public support for American interventionism to pursue the war effort.

America's Initial Postwar Globalist Policy Under Roosevelt. These changes in the state, society, and environment were the basis from which the Roosevelt administration made the first major post–World War II effort to pursue a globalist foreign policy following the war, based on the two key issues of economics and national security. The first goal involved the need to restore economic stability and prosperity in the United States, as well as in Western Europe and throughout the world—deemed essential because the U.S. economy had suffered from depression and was heavily intertwined with the larger global capitalist economy, particularly the Western European economies. The original strategy, arrived at in Bretton Woods, New Hampshire in 1944, was to promote multilateral efforts with American allies to restore and manage the global market economy based on a new system of fixed exchange rates and free trade with the support of newly created international governmental organizations (such as the International Bank for Reconstruction and Development, the International Monetary Fund, and the General Agreement on Trade and Tariffs). The second goal involved U.S. attempts to construct a new international political order that was stable and promoted the national security of the United States and its wartime allies, thus preventing the outbreak of further wars. With the collapse of Europe, President Roosevelt relied on a strategy of multilateral cooperation based on a spheres-of-influence approach and the creation of the United Nations. Success on both the economic and national security fronts after the war was thought to be· crucial for insuring peace and minimizing new threats to national security, as occurred when the great depression led to the rise of Adolf Hitler (Dallek 1979; Gaddis 1972; Stoler 1981; Yergin 1977).[25]

Although America's initial globalist orientation was attempted during the Roosevelt administration, U.S. foreign policy designed to restore economic prosperity and national security quickly unraveled as President Roosevelt died and was succeeded by President Harry Truman. The European economies were unable to recover following the war, and, most importantly, distrust, fear, and conflict between the Soviet Union and the United States escalated. In other words, changes in the state, society, and environment contributed both to Roosevelt's global postwar initiatives and their failure. This demonstrates the difficulty of changing course in foreign policy and institutionalizing policy changes during times of transition and instability. Ultimately, the collapse of Roosevelt's grand strategy turned foreign policy into a major domestic issue which became instrumental in determining the content of American globalist policy that prevailed throughout the cold war.

The Cold War Years of Stability and Foreign Policy Continuity

For roughly twenty years, from the administrations of President Truman through President Johnson, the globalist orientation of U.S. foreign policy experienced considerable continuity. It was based upon, first, achieving security and stability throughout the globe from the threat of Soviet communist expansionism through the strategy of containment and, second, the promotion of a stable and prosperous international market economy under American leadership based on the principles of free trade and fixed exchange rates. The United States ultimately adopted these policies to address the twin goals of national security and economic prosperity that had remained unresolved following World War II. America's globalist policy during the cold war years is described more fully below, followed by a discussion of the international and domestic sources of this foreign policy restructuring.

The Policy of Global Containment and a Liberal Economic Order. Following World War II, Americans began to perceive a major external threat to their national security for the first time since independence: the advance of Soviet communism. Because the fear of Soviet communism became the key international problem in the minds of most Americans, national security concerns drove U.S. foreign policy during the cold war. The threat was perceived to be global in nature and American leaders believed that, with the collapse of the British and French empires, only the United States had the power to respond. Therefore, under American leadership a strategy of containment was developed which aimed to deter the spread of Soviet communism through the threat and use of coercion, first in Europe, then Asia, and eventually throughout the world.[26]

The U.S. global strategy that emerged was designed to surround the Soviet Union and its allies in Eastern Europe and mainland Asia with American allies, alliances, and military forces in order to deter the Soviet Union from initiating aggression that could trigger World War III. Containment of the Soviet Union and the People's Republic of China throughout the Eurasian continent was to be accomplished through the threat of nuclear war and reliance on conventional military forces. In the Third World, where the U.S.-Soviet confrontation tended to be fought more indirectly over the "hearts and minds" of local elites and peoples, the United States relied on its foreign assistance, counterinsurgency, and use of covert paramilitary operations to promote friendly regimes. Containment of the Soviet Union was also pursued through the use of broad economic sanctions by the United States. Diplomacy and other non-coercive instruments of policy were superseded by the threat and use of coercion in responding to what American leaders saw as major challenges to American national security commitments and national interests.[27]

Although national security policy became high policy during the cold war years, the low policy of foreign economics remained a vital element in U.S. foreign policy. The roots of U.S. foreign economic policy resided with the Bretton Woods strategy to restore a capitalist international political economy based on fixed exchange rates and free trade under American leadership and multilateralism. Given the inability of Western European economies to recover from depression and war, the United States took the lead to promote a stable and prosperous international market economy. The revival of the European economies was to be accomplished by providing massive capital outlays in the form of American assistance (such as the Marshall Plan), encouraging private investment and loans abroad by U.S. multinational corporations, and promoting trade through opening the U.S. domestic market to foreign imports. Therefore, the Bretton Woods international economic system became dependent on the United States acting as the world's banker. Although primarily European-oriented, and later also Japanese-oriented, U.S. foreign economic policy was also active in promoting a market system in the third world through its support for private investment and development abroad.

In sum, a major restructuring of U.S. foreign policy occurred between the 1930s and the 1950s. The scope of U.S. foreign policy changed from a regionalist to a globalist orientation. The United States no longer acted as a "free rider" or a supporter of other great powers, but took an active role as hegemonic leader in world affairs (Lake 1976). Beginning with President Truman, U.S. foreign policy goals became global in nature: defender and promoter of a liberal world order threatened by Soviet communism.[28] Although this represented a restructuring of U.S. foreign policy from before World War II, a certain amount of continuity, nonetheless, accompanied these changes. The United States had long been preoccupied with promoting stability and a liberal economic order abroad, but the focus had been predominantly at a regional level. For example, American military intervention and economic expansion had a long history in China and, in particular, throughout Central America and the Caribbean. Furthermore, American fear of communism also had long historical roots as exemplified by the U.S. policy of antibolshevism during World War I and the domestic Red Scares following the war.[29] Therefore, it must be reemphasized that the restructuring of U.S. foreign policy reflected both discontinuity as well as continuity with the past.

International and Domestic Sources of Cold War Policies.   This movement from regionalism to globalism and the cold war policies that subsequently prevailed took place throughout the 1940s and were institutionalized during the 1950s as a result of five key developments throughout the state, society, and environment:

1. The rise of Soviet power in Eurasia and American hegemony throughout the world,
2. The rise of an anticommunist consensus throughout the state and society,
3. The rise of presidential power and the foreign policy bureaucracy,

4. The rise of the foreign policy establishment—the informal network linking societal and governmental elites and institutions, and
5. The development of a national security infrastructure throughout society. These five developments paralleled and reinforced each other, producing continuity in America's cold war policies until the mid-1960s.

First, the most important initial development was the rise of the Soviet Union and American hegemony in global affairs (Barraclough 1964; Gaddis 1978; Gilpin 1981; Kennedy 1987). The global economic depression and World War II eclipsed European power, leaving the Soviet Union and the United States as the only great powers. Clearly, the United States had replaced Great Britain as the most powerful country in the world—the hegemon of its time. Unless the United States was able and willing to return to its isolationist shell and pursue a regionalist foreign policy, as it did following World War I, U.S. foreign policy had to change, for it was not commensurate with new global realities.

While the characteristics of the global system are consequential in defining the parameters of possible behavior—that is, the opportunities and constraints a country will face—the global environment does not dictate the path U.S. foreign policy will take. According to David Lake (1976, 539–40), systemic-centered approaches lack "a conception of process, or an explanation of how the constraints or interests derived from the international economic structure are transformed into decisions or political strategies within particular countries." For example, there may have been a degree of inevitability that an adversarial relationship would develop between the United States and the Soviet Union in response to the vacuum in political power left by the defeat of the Axis powers, but there was no inevitability in the actual type of cold war relationship that soon emerged. In order to understand why U.S. foreign policy pursued this particular globalist path, one must examine the four major changes which occurred throughout American society and the state.

Second, the 1940s and 1950s resulted in the crucial development of the rise of domestic anticommunism, which became the foundation for the U.S. global policy of containment. The dominant orientation before the war—isolationism—was discredited with the Japanese bombing of Pearl Harbor and U.S. entry into the conflict. Where American interventionism was premised on the need to defeat the threat of fascism posed by the Axis powers, Americans following the end of the war became increasingly preoccupied with a different enemy—the Soviet Union and communism. This development did not occur overnight, it evolved out of a great debate among American leaders and intellectuals about the nature of the world, the Soviet Union, and the proper postwar policy of the United States. Events, however, such as the dispute over Poland and a divided Germany, the communist coup in Czechoslovakia, the Berlin blockade, the "fall" of China, and, most importantly, the Korean War, convinced most members of the Truman administration, and most citizens throughout American society, that the Soviet Union was a revolutionary, communist state attempting to achieve world domination. Therefore, it increasingly was argued that the United States had no choice but to assume the role of leader of the "free world" to stop communist aggression. Such sentiment was reinforced by an underlying anticommunist sentiment in American society that resurfaced with the rise of McCarthyism.

McCarthyism was unsuccessful in forcing either the Truman or Eisenhower administrations to redirect their foreign policies in an even more interventionist direction beyond containment. However, this challenge to the status quo policy had two lasting effects. First, it reinforced conservative perceptions held by American policymakers and the public that communism was a monolithic and ever present threat, controlled by the Soviet Union. Second, liberals and those of the political left who were critical of containment and argued for more cooperative policies lost all credibility and legitimacy during the cold war years that followed. In short, by the 1950s a consensus had developed within American government and society that the world was divided into two hostile forces: communist forces led by the Soviet Union and forces of freedom led by the United States (Almond 1965; Gelb and Betts 1979; Goldman 1961; Hodgson 1976). Despite disagreements over tactics (e.g., how much force and where), most Americans and organized interests in society agreed upon the nature of the threat—communism—and the justifiable use of force to fight it.

This consensus fostered the development of certain U.S. institutions to fight communism, lending increasing power to the president and the foreign policy bureaucracy—the third major development. Before World War II, few institutions within the government were oriented toward foreign affairs and national security. The policymaking elite was extremely small and centered within the State Department. World War II changed this dramatically. Overnight, the U.S. government was redirected to devote itself to fighting a global war: the military expanded enormously and civilian agencies grew to assist the president in fighting the war. The governmental war effort, in turn, put the economy and society on a war-footing to provide the necessary personnel, equipment, and services to achieve U.S. victory. However, unlike previous wars in American history, the United States demobilized only for a short time following victory. With the rise of anticommunism, the United States quickly remobilized and expanded its resources in order to fight a global cold war. The power of the presidency and the foreign policy bureaucracy, thus, continued to grow during the cold war years, becoming a permanent part of the American landscape (Hodgson 1976; Wilson 1989; Yergin 1977).

The president became the predominant actor in the making of foreign policy. The 1950s and 1960s were perceived to be a time when the security of the United States was directly threatened by communism. During such times of perceived national emergency, the president was able to exert considerable powers as commander-in-chief, head-of-state, chief diplomat, and chief administrator, with Congress increasingly acquiescent to presidential initiatives (Pious 1979; Schlesinger 1973). In fact, by the mid-1950s a bipartisan consensus developed between Democrats and Republicans in support of the president and U.S. foreign policy. Congressional passage of the National Security Act of 1947 also resulted in the rise of the foreign policy bureaucracy. The Act created the National Security Council (NSC), reorganized the military into the Department of Defense (DOD), and developed an intelligence community under the Central Intelligence Agency (CIA). These and other bureaucratic agencies grew dramatically in size and scope during the cold war, giving the U.S. government the capacity to implement, as well as to institutionalize, its national security and foreign economic policies abroad (Halperin 1974; Ikenberry 1988).

The cold war years also saw the rise of a foreign policy establishment, the fourth major development. The foreign policy establishment represented an informal network of prominent individuals who shared the assumptions of the anticommunist consensus and exerted a great influence on the making of U.S. foreign policy. People like Dean Acheson, McGeorge Bundy, and Dean Rusk have been referred to as the "establishment" (Hodgson 1973), the "best and the brightest" (Halberstam 1969), "national security managers" (Barnet 1971), and the "wise men" (Isaacson and Thomas 1986). As described by Godfrey Hodgson (1973, 10–11), their aspiration was to follow the footsteps of the British and exercise the "moral and political leadership of the world" in the belief that it was a time of the "American century." Such a group of individuals began to exercise influence during World War II when the government recruited personnel throughout American society to staff the ever-expanding foreign policy bureaucracy: especially scientists, academics, lawyers, and businessmen. Individuals in the foreign policy establishment were usually appointed by the president to policymaking positions within the foreign policy bureaucracy. The most prominent constantly moved back and forth between government and the private world, interacting informally and through membership in prominent foreign policy groups, most notably the Council on Foreign Relations. The development of the foreign policy establishment played a significant role in the foreign policy continuity of the cold war years for it provided a critical bridge between the president, the foreign policy bureaucracy, and the key groups and institutions throughout American society.

The final development was the rise of a national security infrastructure throughout society in support of U.S. foreign policy. Before World War II, few institutions throughout American society were oriented toward foreign affairs and national security. World War II changed this situation dramatically and permanently when the economy and the society were placed on a war footing to provide the necessary personnel, equipment, and services to achieve allied victory. Many of America's largest companies—such as General Motors, Chrysler, McDonnell Douglas, and Boeing—retooled their assembly lines to produce not cars and commercial airplanes, but tanks and bombers. With the rise of the cold war, these same companies continued to work for the government, especially DOD—thus was born the permanent cold war economy. Furthermore, as America became the world's policeman and banker, most companies were able to benefit economically from America's favorable position. Thus, corporate America and organized as well as unorganized labor became bulwarks of the anticommunist crusade. Activity by business and labor was further reinforced by behavior in the scientific, educational, journalistic, and even religious and intellectual communities which supported the cold war effort. Thus, mainstream groups and institutions were mobilized throughout society, becoming part of the consensus politics in support of U.S. cold war policy (Barnet 1971; Hodgson 1976).

Hence, the 1940s and 1950s witnessed the rise of the Soviet Union and American power and a domestic anticommunism that led to the development of a powerful president and foreign policy bureaucracy, the foreign policy establishment, and a national security infrastructure. All developed alongside each other and reinforced each other, contributing to the restructuring of U.S. foreign policy toward a policy of global communist containment. At the same time, they provided the foundation for a period of foreign policy stability with greater U.S. involvement and interventionism throughout the globe in order to contain communism and promote a liberal economic order under American leadership. Eventually, such a cold war foreign policy led directly to America's ill-fated involvement in the Vietnam War.

The Vietnam War, Transition, and Foreign Policy Change

Throughout the 1950s and early 1960s, America's quest for global security from communism and a liberal world order through containment and economic expansion was perceived as being relatively successful. The dominant structures and beliefs of society and the state were thus reinforced, resulting in the politics of the status quo and continuity in America's foreign policy for roughly twenty years following World War II. America's involvement in Vietnam, however, began a series of events which caused a large segment of society to question and eventually challenge America's foreign policy. This, reinforced by the ending of the Bretton Woods system in 1971, resulted in political instability and disequilibrium where the politics of change challenged the cold war policies of the past and affected the parameters of likely U.S. foreign policy for the future. To better understand the change and continuity produced by this period of transition, the impact of global change and the Vietnam War on American politics is examined.

The Impact of Global Change and Vietnam. By the middle and late 1960s, America's capabilities had altered as the world grew in complexity with the rise of pluralism and interdependence. Although the United States continued to grow more powerful on an absolute scale, changes occurring throughout the globe were resulting in a relative decline of American power by the 1960s (Brown 1988; Kennedy 1987; Mead 1987; Nye 1990). This was inevitable, for American hegemony could not be maintained forever in a dynamic environment. A number of actors and issues grew in importance during the 1950s and 1960s. In the national security sphere, the United States faced the rise of Third World nationalism and a Soviet Union which was becoming more powerful militarily. Foreign economic policy was threatening once again to become high policy as Japan and the Western Europe recovered and became increasingly competitive with the United States. Therefore, contradictions were growing between the globalist cold war policies of the United States and its ability to successfully carry them out. Such changes notwithstanding, societal and state institutions and beliefs persevered and American foreign policy resisted change. The clearest example of this perseverance of the containment policy in an environment nonconducive to its successful application was evident in the United States' policy on Vietnam. As the conditions in South Vietnam deteriorated throughout the 1960s the war was increasingly Americanized without an end in sight.

The Vietnam War represented the first major political-military failure in America's history. Simply put, after investing as much as $30 billion and over five hundred thousand troops per year during the height of American involvement in a war which lasted at least fifteen years, America was unsuccessful in its strategy of containment and nation-building in Vietnam. This spectacular and cumulative set of events, reinforced by the turmoil over civil rights and Watergate, triggered increasing dissatisfaction among the public. Thus, Vietnam politicized a variety of issues which resulted in the development of massive social movements within society. According to Holsti and Rosenau (1984, 249), "the war in Vietnam represented a major landmark in American history, comparable to what students of domestic politics call 'watershed' elections." The net consequence was a period of transition in the late 1960s and early 1970s in which large segments of American society underwent an agonizing reappraisal of American foreign policy. These developments were reinforced in 1971 when President Nixon discarded the convertability of the U.S. dollar based on gold and placed a 10 percent surcharge on Japanese imports, symbolizing the continuing decline of the American economy and the end of the Bretton Woods postwar economic strategy.

Change and Continuity in the Politics of U.S. Foreign Policy. These environmental changes and events triggered significant developments in the politics of U.S. foreign policy. The result was change and continuity in the dominant structures and beliefs of society and the state in four areas that were the basis of America's cold war policies:

1. The domestic anticommunist consensus collapsed, producing greater ideological and intellectual diversity regarding foreign policy,
2. The foreign policy establishment collapsed and fragmented,
3. Presidential power declined as domestic politics became more pluralistic, and
4. The foreign policy bureaucracy and national security infrastructure continued to operate as in the past, but in a less politically supportive domestic environment.

In other words, the events of the 1960s surrounding America's failure in Vietnam deeply affected the politics of U.S. foreign policy and consequently resulted in a new political status quo of greater flexibility as well as constraints for post-Vietnam administrations.

The first major political development was the collapse of the anticommunist consensus among the mass and elite public. Throughout the 1950s and 1960s, the American public—both the elites and the mass public—supported increasing U.S. involvement in Southeast Asia. If the president stated that Vietnam was being threatened by communism and that the dominoes would fall if the threat was not contained, the American people stood behind him. It took U.S. involvement in the Vietnam quagmire to get people to question the nature of the world and the proper U.S. foreign policy response. What made Vietnam so traumatic for many Americans and so significant for American society was that it was the first war that the United States had lost in its history. Americans were used to winning; they expected to succeed. Yet, how could the most powerful country in the history of the world lose to a small Asian army? Why were over fifty-five thousand Americans dying for a lost cause? Popular reaction resulted in the rise of a massive antiwar movement and led people to question the purpose and viability of a foreign policy based on the global containment of monolithic communism which brought the collapse of the anticommunist consensus (Vasquez 1976).

As studies by Holsti and Rosenau (1984) and William Schneider (1984) have demonstrated, in the wake of Vietnam three general foreign policy orientations competed for ascendancy within American society: conservative internationalism, liberal internationalism, and noninternationalism. Some people, especially those on the political right, continued to believe that the major global threat to the United States was communism directed by the Soviet Union. This conservative internationalist position argued that American foreign policy needed to contain, if not rollback, Soviet communism, unilaterally if necessary. The events of the 1960s also resulted in the rise of liberalism and the political left which emphasized a much more complex and interdependent world. The liberal internationalist position argued that in a complex global environment, the United States needed to de-emphasize the role of force and act multilaterally in addressing East-West issues (e.g., the U.S.-Soviet conflict), West-West issues (e.g., U.S.-Japanese trade), and North-South issues (e.g., Third World debt). The third most popular position in the political spectrum, especially among the mass public, also recognized the increasing complexity of the world and the difficulty the United States had in affecting it. However, in contrast to liberal internationalists, they argued that the United States needed to focus on the home front and minimize its international involvement, concentrating on a few areas where it has truly vital interests—especially Western Europe and Japan. This noninternationalist view, unlike the two above, was also prone to take a more protectionist position on international economic matters. In other words, where one globalist orientation—conservative internationalism—dominated U.S. foreign policy during the cold war era, with Vietnam two globalist orientations and one orientation against globalism competed for ascendancy in American politics.[30]

The second major domestic development was the collapse and fragmentation of the foreign policy establishment. The key to the American foreign policy establishment's past ability to serve as the bridge between the different elements in governmental and private institutions was the existence of an informal network of like-minded individuals. However, once the Vietnam War shattered this consensus, members of the establishment differed over the Vietnam War and proper U.S. foreign policy. Where once such foreign policy elites saw eye-to-eye concerning the need to contain communism and exercise American leadership throughout the world, the collapse of consensus resulted in divisions along the lines of the three different schools of thought discussed above. So, as public beliefs fragmented, the consensus that held the foreign policy establishment together also fragmented—even more intensely, given the level of individual interest and involvement in foreign policy (Destler, Gelb, and Lake 1984; Hodgson 1973; Isaacson and Thomas 1986). Therefore, no longer would the development of foreign policy reside in the hands of an exclusive network of individuals operating mainly through the presidency.

The breakdown of the consensus and the collapse of the foreign policy establishment resulted in a more pluralistic domestic environment where the power of the president declined in the making of U.S. foreign policy (Destler, Gelb, and Lake 1984; Hodgson 1980; Mann 1990; Smith 1988). The Vietnam War and Watergate shattered trust in the power of the presidency. Three areas in particular were affected: the role of Congress, the media, and group politics. Congress, unwilling to play an acquiescent role to an unresponsive and unaccountable "Imperial Presidency," reasserted much of its constitutional authority through its power over appropriations, investigations, and legislation. Journalists and the media, who during the cold war years played a major role in communicating the "perils of communism," were more likely to be critical of the government and foreign policy after Vietnam and Watergate. Finally, where America's industry, labor, academia, and intellectual community formerly had stood united behind a global, interventionist U.S. foreign policy, new interest groups representing a variety of different ideological perspectives proliferated and became involved in questions of foreign policy. Therefore, where once the president was near-supreme in the making of U.S. foreign policy during the cold war years of consensus, after Vietnam he was increasingly challenged in a more pluralistic environment by a more assertive Congress, a more critical media, and a diverse array of societal groups.

The final domestic development, of great importance, was the continued existence of the foreign policy bureaucracy and the military-industrial-scientific infrastructure that developed during the cold war years, both oriented around a strong defense posture and the threat of force as the basis of U.S. foreign policy (Coates and Kilian 1985; Kotz 1988; Tyler 1986). The NSC, DOD, intelligence community, industrial defense contractors, and defense-oriented research community, as well as the individual networks that tie them together, continued to exist and even prosper in the 1980s. The foreign policy bureaucracy and the national security infrastructure, along with those who reflected a conservative internationalist orientation, acted as a powerful source of continuity with the cold war past. They operated, however, in a domestic environment which was much less supportive than during the consensus years. Therefore, the politics of U.S. foreign policy during the post-Vietnam years experienced both continuity and change with the past.

The Post-Vietnam Years of Stability and Foreign Policy Continuity

During the cold war era, changes in administration, party, or personnel had little affect on foreign policy because of the shared conservative internationalist beliefs within society and throughout the state. However, as a result of America's failure in Vietnam, the policy of global containment of Soviet communism which had prevailed since World War II was challenged by competing foreign policy perspectives and could no longer predominate. United States' foreign economic policy also changed in 1971 when President Nixon violated the principles of fixed exchange rates and free trade, demonstrating the Bretton Woods strategy was no longer sustainable. As described above, this resulted in a more pluralistic international and domestic environment which broadened the parameters of likely administration foreign policy within a liberal or conservative internationalist orientation. This section discusses these dominant patterns of U.S. foreign policy that have prevailed in the post-Vietnam era and the resulting crisis of leadership and governance they produced in the making of U.S. foreign policy.

Post-Vietnam Patterns in U.S. Foreign Policy. The failure in Vietnam and the breakdown of the Bretton Woods system represented international and domestic changes that have resulted in two new patterns in U.S. foreign policy during the post-Vietnam years. First, foreign economic policy became "high" policy again and since 1970 all administrations have had to give this area considerable attention. Second, the "parameters" of U.S. foreign policy have broadened considerably beyond the cold war years giving administrations more flexibility, as well as constraints, in pursuing their foreign policies. As the policy debate widened, two policy orientations, in particular, gained legitimacy and influenced the policymaking process and U.S. foreign policy: conservative internationalism and liberal internationalism (noninternationalism had little appeal among the elite public and within the government). These two orientations have set the boundaries for the policymaking process and been the foundation for the continuity found in U.S. foreign policy since Vietnam.

Within these broad parameters, it must be made clear, that there was room for differences in the politics and behavior of U.S. foreign policy between and within administrations over time. Different administrations, for example, have had different foreign policy orientations—Republican administrations have tended to be more conservative internationalist in orientation and Democratic administrations have tended to be more liberal internationalist in orientation. Not surprisingly, with each new administration there usually has been a modification in the direction of U.S. foreign policy. Furthermore, different administrations have had to operate in a pluralistic domestic political environment where policy agendas and debates also fluctuated within a liberal to conservative orientation. This has often forced modern presidents to change or modify their foreign policies during their terms of office. In contrast to the cold war years, it became very difficult for any president or administration since Vietnam to devise an overall foreign policy that was successful in responding to changes in the global environment and obtaining substantial domestic support over extended periods of time. Therefore, the foreign policy continuity of the post-Vietnam era operated within a set of political parameters that allowed for more flexibility yet less consistency than found during the cold war years.

The modifications that have existed within the larger parameter of post-Vietnam foreign policy continuity are best understood by examining the foreign policy differences that have transpired, first between administrations and then within administrations over time. In the area of U.S. foreign economic policy, the differences have been less severe between administrations because American leaders continued to see the need for a stable international market economy and to espouse the value of free trade (see, e.g., Mingst 1982; Rohrlich 1987). Nevertheless, they have disagreed over the particular strategy and means to promote economic stability. Presidents Nixon, Ford, and Carter, for example, relied on more of a multilateral ad hoc approach to handle international economic problems as they developed. Each attempted to maintain the stability of the international market economy by obtaining the multilateral support of the major allies—Western Europe, Canada, and Japan—for stop-gap measures. United States' foreign economic policy under these administrations, in other words, tended to be more defensive and reactive to international economic problems as they have arisen since 1971. The Reagan administration took a different approach, relying on a laissez faire philosophy of minimal state intervention in the international political economy and emphasizing domestic economic growth as the key to expanding the global economy (see, e.g., Nau 1984–85; Spero 1991).

A similar fluctuation within the broad parameters of a conservative-liberal international orientation was even more visible in the national security area. The Nixon and Ford administrations represented the first real change from the cold war emphasis on the global containment of Soviet communism. Although operating within a conservative internationalist orientation, they relied more upon a ''Realpolitik'' tradition emphasizing the counterbalancing of the Soviet Union as a traditional great power to promote global stability and order. For Henry Kissinger, the national security advisor and the secretary of state under Presidents Nixon and Ford, the major threat was not communist expansion and Soviet hegemony but global instability, which Soviet interventionism could only exacerbate. Therefore, the key was not just to contain the Soviet threat through force, but both to contain the Soviet Union and encourage it to change from a revolutionary, expansionist global actor into a legitimate, status quo actor. This was to be done through a policy of détente based on the concept of linkage: accommodation (such as the provision of prestige through summit meetings and economic assistance through trade, technology, and financing) when the Soviet Union was acting in accord with American desires, or the threat and use of force when the Soviets were perceived as attempting to upset the existing balance of power (see Hersh 1983; Hoffmann 1978; Starr 1984; Walker 1977).[31]

Although U.S. foreign policy during the Nixon and Ford years of détente represented a significant change from the cold war policies of global containment, the real break with cold war policy came with the Carter administration in 1977, which initially rejected containment as the basis of its foreign policy. The people who staffed the Carter administration no longer saw a bipolar international system that pitted communism against the free world in a global cold war, or a traditional great power struggle between the Soviet Union and the United States. This cold war perception of international relations was replaced by a more liberal internationalist orientation that represented the first truly "post–cold war" vision in U.S. foreign policy since the end of World War II. The Carter administration saw a world of complex interdependence in which the United States would take the lead in building a cooperative global community. They downplayed the role of great powers (such as the Soviet Union), the utility of force and military intervention, and preoccupation with traditional security issues. Instead, Carter pursued a foreign policy of adjustment to international change based on moral leadership and preventive diplomacy, emphasizing human rights and negotiations instead of the use of force (see Rosati 1987; Smith 1986).[32]

With the coming of the Reagan administration in 1981, U.S. foreign policy fully returned to an emphasis on the global containment of Soviet communism through the threat and use of force in a policy reminiscent of the cold war era of the 1950s and 1960s. Its foreign policy called for a large military build-up and the restoration of cold war policies in order to deter and challenge the Soviet Union in world affairs. The Iran-Contra affair demonstrated the extent to which the Reagan administration was dedicated to fighting the cold war and "rolling back" Soviet-supported communism (Deibel 1989; Oye 1987; Tucker 1988/89). In sum, comparing the goals and strategies under Presidents Nixon, Ford, Carter, and Reagan demonstrates that, unlike the cold war years, the post-Vietnam period witnessed the initiation of different foreign policies by each new administration within conservative-liberal internationalist orientations.

Given existing international and domestic constraints, each administration also was forced to moderate its initial policies with time. In the area of foreign economics, it was easy for the Nixon, Ford, and Carter administrations to modify their policies since they had never actually devised a coherent strategy. However, the Reagan administration quickly found out that its planned free market approach did not sit well among allies abroad or many Americans at home, and was forced to modify many of its policies during the latter part of the administration. It is in national security policy, however, where changes in policy over time within the same administration were most obvious. For example, the Nixon and Ford administrations' détente policy walked a fine line between conservative and liberal internationalists: détente appealed to the liberals and containment appealed to the conservatives. However, it was not long before containment was under attack from the left, by liberal members of the Democratic Party angry at American intervention in Angola, and détente was under attack from the right, by conservatives within Ford's own Republican Party who characterized it as appeasement of the Soviet Union. President Carter came into office rejecting containment as the basis of its foreign policy, only to reinstate it by the last year of his administration in response to the Iran hostage crisis, the intervention of Soviet troops in Afghanistan, a growing domestic conservatism, and the 1980 elections. Finally, although President Reagan came into office as a cold war "hawk" ready to do battle with the "evil empire," he left office an arms control "dove," constrained by domestic and international criticism, meeting four times with Mikhail Gorbachev—the general secretary of the Soviet Communist Party—and signing the Intermediate Nuclear Forces Treaty. This modification of the early policies of each administration is indicative of the existence of a crisis of leadership that has prevailed in the making of U.S. foreign policy since Vietnam.

The Crisis of Leadership in the Politics of U.S. Foreign Policy. What accounts for these smaller patterns of policy inconsistency between and within administrations as they operate within the larger pattern of foreign policy continuity bounded by conservative and liberal internationalism? This is a function of the politics of U.S. foreign policy spawned by the Vietnam War as outlined above, especially the development of a more diverse and pluralistic domestic environment. Very simply, presidents have been unable to lead the government and the country in the making of American foreign policy. Republican administrations have tended to pursue more conservative internationalist foreign policies; Democratic administrations have tended to pursue more liberal internationalist foreign policies. However, no foreign policy has stood much chance of maintaining political support over an extended period of time because no new consensus and no set of groups have prevailed throughout society and the state. American foreign economic policy remained more consistent because the breakdown in consensus was not as severe here, though competing strategies of unilateralism and multilateralism existed.

Unlike the 1950s, presidents were no longer driven to pursue only an anticommunist policy of containment. This opened up new opportunities in foreign policy while also posing great risks. The fragmented nature of American beliefs, as well as competing domestic interests and institutions, made it increasingly unclear how far the president could go in pursuing a policy before he lost majority support. As Alexander George (1980, 236) has observed, "In the absence of the fundamental consensus that policy legitimacy creates it becomes necessary for the President to justify each action to implement the long-range policy on its own merits rather than as part of a larger policy design and strategy. The necessity for ad hoc day-to-day building of consensus under these circumstances make it virtually impossible for the President to conduct a long range foreign policy in a coherent, effective manner.''

Not surprisingly, all post-Vietnam presidents have failed to achieve a consensus and continuity in public support for their foreign policies (Melanson 1991). Nixon was forced to resign, Ford could not win election in 1976, Carter lost reelection in 1980, and Reagan, clearly the most popular and successful president in popular opinion, was not able to generate longterm mass support behind his policies. The nature of domestic politics, in other words, produced a crisis of leadership for the presidency and the country since Vietnam (Burns 1984; Destler, Gelb, and Lake 1976; Hodgson 1980; Lowi 1985; Mann 1990; Neustadt 1991; Pious 1979; Rosati 1993; Russett 1990; Smith 1988).

United States foreign policy in the post-Vietnam era has been one of initial change and then moderation for each administration within the legitimate political parameters of liberal and conservative internationalism. Although the interplay of the state, society, and environment have made it increasingly difficult for any administration to achieve successful policy outcomes, it has not resulted in any great and lasting policy failures that triggered change in the politics and substance of U.S. foreign policy. As Holsti and Rosenau have argued, ''perhaps the only constancy in American foreign policy since the Vietnam War has been the conspicuous lack of constancy in its conduct.''

The End of the Cold War and Foreign Policy Transition?

To sum up, the globalist era in U.S. foreign policy that began with American involvement in World War II has resulted in two general foreign policy periods separated by the Vietnam War. World War II and the rise of the cold war reflected international and domestic changes that produced twenty years of continuity in U.S. foreign policy. During this time, American national security policy was devoted to containing the threat of Soviet communism throughout the globe, supported by a foreign economic policy based on American leadership of the international political economy. The Vietnam War and the breakdown of the Bretton Woods system represented, and intensified, international and domestic changes that led to the questioning of the viability of the United States to promote a global containment policy and to maintain economic prosperity at home. During the post-Vietnam period, unlike the cold war years, foreign economic policy has been restored to a significant place on the foreign policy agenda, different foreign policy initiatives have been taken by different administrations, and each administration has eventually been forced by circumstances outside its control to moderate its initial policies—all within the domain of conservative to liberal internationalist political orientations, reflecting a crisis of leadership in U.S. foreign policy. Therefore, whereas U.S. foreign policy experienced a restructuring during the 1940s from a regionalist to a globalist orientation, the 1960s led to a broadening of the parameters of America's globalist orientation beyond the conservative internationalism that dominated the cold war years (see tables 11.1 and 11.2 for a summary of the eras and sources of U.S. foreign policy since the interwar years).

With the collapse of communism in Eastern Europe and the collapse of the Soviet Union, the United States may have entered a new "post–cold war era" in foreign policy (see, e.g., Rizopoulos 1990). Only time will tell, however, whether these profound global changes will result in a continuation of the

Table 11.1.   Eras of U.S. Foreign Policy

	Interwar Years	Cold War Years	Post-Vietnam Years
Scope	regionalist	globalist	globalist
Goals	1. economic expansion	1. political stability and security	conservative internationalist orientation
Strategy	mercantilism private investment	containment military force	versus
			liberal internationalist orientation
Goals	2. political stability	2. promote liberal economy	
Strategy	military force	free trade private investment	

Table 11.2.   Elements Explaining Historical Development of U.S. Foreign Policy

	Interwar Years	Cold War Years	Post-Vietnam Years
Environment	rising power	hegemonic power	declining power
Society	isolationist sentiment	anticommunist consensus	fragmentation of beliefs
		foreign policy establishment	collapse of foreign policy establishment
		national security infrastructure	rise of pluralism
State	weak	strong	weak
Critical Events Triggering Change		World War II Korean War	Vietnam War collapse of Bretton Woods

patterns which have prevailed in the post-Vietnam years or produce a politics of transition and foreign policy change. Most likely, it will intensify the post-Vietnam changes in the politics of U.S. foreign policy, resulting in an even more diverse and pluralistic domestic environment. Early evidence, for example, indicates that a noninternationalist orientation, in addition to conservative and liberal internationalism, has grown in visibility and influence throughout the policymaking process (Rosati and Creed 1992; Wittkopf 1990).

In this respect, the end of the cold war provided the Bush administration, and future administrations, with new opportunities and constraints in its conduct of foreign policy. Although more moderate than Reagan, Bush's foreign policy largely reacted to the profound changes in the new world order by relying on the legacy of the cold war past (Deibel 1991; Mead 1991). Considerable foreign policy continuity, in other words, prevailed in a world of great change. Yet, even with the sweeping success of the Persian Gulf War, the defeat of President Bush and the election of Democratic Party nominee Bill Clinton to be the next president symbolized the difficulty of governing since the Vietnam War. This is likely to reinforce the continuing crisis of leadership in U.S. foreign policy until a new period of transition and foreign policy change occurs.

Understanding Continuity and Change

An examination of the contemporary history of U.S. foreign policy illustrates that foreign policy tends to go through cycles of continuity and change as a result of the dynamics of state, society, and environmental interaction over time. The cyclical model developed is intended to contribute to both a better understanding of the dynamics of U.S. foreign policy since the interwar years and a general understanding of foreign policy restructuring. In this respect, brief reference to the strengths and weaknesses of the model of foreign policy restructuring is warranted. On the one hand, the model's fit with reality in explaining U.S. foreign policy is not as clean-cut as suggested—the politics of U.S. foreign policy are complex and messier than portrayed above. This is a problem with all models and conceptualizations, they must simplify reality in the process of capturing particularly essential patterns. On the other hand, the model does perhaps provide insight into the dominant patterns of continuity and change in U.S. foreign policy as it has evolved through different stages over time.

What about the model's generalizability beyond U.S. foreign policy? Although developed with the United States in mind, the model of foreign policy restructuring, or some variant of it, is intended to be generalizable to explain foreign policy change in other governments as well.[33] The comments by Niles Eldridge (1992, 118) on stability and change in social systems in general are quite relevant in this regard:

> The point is not that all sociocultural change should now be seen
> to come in brief spurts interrupting vastly longer periods of stasis.

. . . Rather, the point is to explore the possibility that social systems may be viewed as hierarchically arrayed stable entities—large-scale spatiotemporarily bounded entities. If so, then it must be true that a theory of evolution, even one that focuses exclusively on biological or cultural traits of organisms, cannot be complete if it addresses only mechanisms of stasis and change of such traits on a generation-by-generation basis.[34]

It may very well be, as David Skidmore (chap. 3) argues, that smaller powers with strong governments are more responsive to international change in accordance with a more evolutionary, as opposed to sporadic, pattern of change. In the language of Keohane and Nye (1977), small states are likely to be more sensitive and vulnerable to changes in the international system, and those with strong central governmental institutions are more able to adjust their foreign policies. Nevertheless, as Hermann (1991), Volgy and Schwarz (chap. 2), and much of the literature suggests, all governments face domestic and international constraints which promote resistance to change and support for foreign policy continuity. Put another way, the difference between the abilities of states in terms of size (small versus big) and type (strong versus weak governments) to adapt to the forces of change may be more a matter of degree than of kind (see Morse 1973; Sprout and Sprout 1968). Although the threshold for foreign policy change may be lower for smaller powers then great powers, the politics of continuity and change in foreign policy is still likely to involve a cyclical process (see, e.g., Biddle and Stephens 1989). Therefore, although adjustments to this model of foreign policy restructuring will be necessary to take into consideration differences in time and space, it does represent one approach for understanding the dynamics of foreign policy continuity and change.

Notes

1. Although part of a larger intellectual tradition, Masters (1992) reviews the thought of a number of political thinkers within the Western tradition and demonstrates that there is no logical or necessary relationship between the perception of gradual or sporadic biological change, on the one hand, and the perception of gradual or sporadic political change, on the other.
2. In their review of cyclical theories of American politics, Resnick and Thomas (1990, 19) arrive at the following conclusion: "Cyclical theories are not at the forefront of the study of American politics and are seldom found in conceptual frameworks based on pluralism, incrementalism, elitism, and the like. We maintain that cyclical theories have been neglected, to the detriment of understanding. They deserve more serious consideration in developing research strategies, if for no other reason than they make us more conscious of the impact of history and of the pattern and direction of our political and social development."
3. The cyclical model could just as easily be applied to subsystem politics and particular issues (see Baumgartner and Jones 1991; McFarland 1991).

4. For a discussion of the concept of cyclical change see Boulding (1970, chaps. 1, 3) and Sorokin (1947, chap. 45).

5. Ikenberry, Lake, and Mastanduno (1988) offer a framework for explaining U.S. foreign economic policy based on the interaction of state-centered explanations, society-centered explanations, and systemic-centered explanations. This is similar to the "frame of reference" originally suggested by Richard Snyder in his work on decision-makers and the decision-making process operating in an organizational context and affected by various elements of the internal and external setting (Snyder, Bruck, and Sapin 1962). For a revised version of the Snyder approach, see Brecher, Steinberg, and Stein (1969).

6. Dessler (1992) makes the epistemological distinction between correlational theory, embedded in positivism, and causal theory, representing a broader epistemology. He concludes that, whereas correlationally-oriented studies have resulted in considerable fragmentation and the development of theory which is at best "additive," the key to "integrative" theory is found in the development of theoretical causal models.

7. Wilbert Moore (1974, 5–6) distinguishes "between mere sequences of small actions, that in sum essentially comprise the pattern, the system, and changes in the system itself."

8. As Boulding (1970, 131) has both encouraged and warned, "One of the most fascinating tasks" is "that of identifying the dialectical and the nondialectical processes in human history and assessing their relative value and importance in the total picture of social dynamics and change. The task is by no means easy and in part may be impossible, simply because of the losses in the record and the difficulties of measuring and detecting the great, long, continuous, nondialectical changes."

9. According to Dessler (1991, 349), "To someone interested only in correlational knowledge, causal accounts are likely to appear to be empty, nonfalsifiable tautologies." However, it must be understood that "causal theory does not purport to identify the conditions associated with the occurrence of a specified type of outcome."

10. Theodore J. Lowi (1971), in *The Politics of Disorder,* distinguishes between the "politics of quiescence" and the "politics of moralizing."

11. Or in the words of Huntington (1981, 114), "the success of the new social force depends generally on the extent to which it is able to embody its interests in the existing political parties and existing governmental institutions. This struggle for access typically leads to a shift in the relations between social forces and political institutions, a political realignment, in which institutional constituencies and functions change."

12. According to Carlsnaes (1992, 246), "A social theory worth its salt must be able to account not only for particular changes but also for social change itself as an inherently dynamic phenomenon, in respect of which neither factor 'determines' the other but are both, in the final analysis, independent variables in an inextricably intertwined temporal process."

13. Resnick and Thomas (1990, 6) find that "even if cyclical theory does not meet the criteria which specify time phases very well, it can still be interesting and useful because it can bring together a number of phenomena which are interrelated and vary together."

14. Although realism in international relations traditionally has been based on the assumption of states as rational actors, Loriaux's (1992) study of the thought of Saint Augustine demonstrates that the intellectual foundations of realism have been, and should be, embedded in a more complex psychology. See also Waltz (1959, chap. 2).

15. "Any political theory in the United States—moral or political," states Lowi (1971, 53), "must begin with the recognition that our political system is almost perfectly designed to maintain an existing state of affairs—any existing state of affairs."

16. This is a position regularly advanced by political philosophers over the ages (see, e.g, Ferraro 1972; Machiavelli 1950)

17. Drawing on his earlier work, *Exit, Voice, and Loyalty* (1970), Albert Hirschman (1982) makes the significant point that individual disappointment will lead to political "underinvolvement" as well as to greater political activism.

18. As noted by Key (1964, 40), "It would be wrong to contend . . . that all political movements are set in motion by a change in objective external conditions or by material deprivation. Yet some new element must be introduced into a situation to stimulate resort to political action."

19. See, for example, Niccolo Machiavelli (1950) on "fortune" and Carl Von Clausewitz (1832) on the concept of "friction."

20. The outcomes of politics and history involve considerable uncertainty and usually unpredictability. Who would have predicted the triumph of Bolshevism during that transitional stage of Russian history. Likewise, who would have predicted the collapse of communism in Eastern Europe and the former Soviet Union in light of previous transitional outcomes, such as Hungary of 1956 and Czechoslovakia of 1968. According to chaos theory in physics, during what is referred to as "far-from-equilibrium situations," it is "inherently impossible to determine in advance which direction change will take" (Prigogine and Stengers 1984, xv).

21. Given the volume's focus on foreign policy restructuring, the focus is on macro-patterns in the foreign policy orientation of the United States as opposed to the specifics of particular foreign policies.

22. The political right shares this perspective, but argues that U.S. foreign policy has failed to stem the growth of communism as a result of the inadequacy of containment or, as more extreme elements argue, by conspiratorial design (see Holsti 1974; Melanson 1983).

23. This is consistent with conclusions arrived at by students of American politics (see, e.g., King 1978, 1990; Smith 1988).

24. It could be argued that the changes following Vietnam resulted more in the reform of U.S. foreign policy, than in its restructuring. Where reform ends and restructuring begins remains ambiguous and is open to reasoned debate.

25. Some scholars highlight President Roosevelt's idealism and commitment to democracy, human rights, and social welfare, emphasizing the role of the United Nations. Other scholars see him as much more pragmatic and concerned with restoring political and economic stability, concentrating on the role of power and spheres-of-influence. President Roosevelt, and the foreign policy that emanated from his administration, was very complex and, at times, contradictory—for he was both idealistic and pragmatic.

26. The origins and development of the cold war are topics of unending interest to

scholars. See Melanson (1983) and Walker (1981) for an overview of competing interpretations.

27. On the assumptions behind deterrence theory and the global strategy of containment, see Gaddis (1982), George and Smoke (1974), Jentleson (1987), and Mastanduno (1985).

28. Democracy as a foreign policy goal was primarily promoted in Western Europe and Japan, whereas capitalism was of greater global importance.

29. The origins of this attitude began with the rise of organized labor in the late nineteenth century (Goldstein 1977; Heale 1990).

30. Greater diversity of thought existed (see Rosati and Creed 1992), but these three perspectives nevertheless captured the thrust of the split in public beliefs.

31. There is much disagreement over the extent to which U.S. foreign policy changed during the Nixon and Ford administrations. One school argues that the Kissinger years were a period of continuity with earlier cold war policies because they continued to try to contain the Soviet Union, although not only through the use of force. Another school argues that this was a time of discontinuity in U.S. foreign policy because Kissinger downplayed the threat of communism, emphasizing traditional great power politics. Both schools shed light on the question, but tend to be incomplete. In fact, the Kissinger years represented a time of both continuity and change in U.S. foreign policy.

32. Although there was much disagreement during the early 1980s as to the nature of the Carter administration's foreign policy, a broad consensus on the Carter years has recently emerged that he entered office with an optimistic vision of global change and American world order policy. Disagreement exists, however, concerning to what extent the Carter administration's early foreign policy abandoned the containment strategy.

33. Huntington (1981, 114) disagrees on this point, arguing that "in America, ideological monism and institutional pluralism thus combine to produce a process of political change fundamentally different from that which has historically prevailed in the ideologically divided societies of Europe." But this is a view not shared by many students of American politics referred to in this chapter (see also Burnham 1976).

34. For variations on social change, see Moore (1974).

Part III

Conclusions

Chapter 12

Emerging Issues in Research on Foreign Policy Restructuring

Joe D. Hagan and Jerel A. Rosati

In this concluding chapter, Joe Hagan and Jerel Rosati discuss the key issues which have emerged from the volume that are important to the future study of foreign policy restructuring. Three significant questions are addressed concerning the study and dynamics of foreign policy that were initially raised in chapter 1. The first part addresses what, in essence, is the nature of foreign policy change and restructuring given the contributions made by the different chapters. This is followed by a discussion evaluating contending theoretical explanations of foreign policy change and assessing their complimentary nature. The chapter ends with a discussion of the wider theoretical implications of the study of foreign policy restructuring for contributing to an understanding of foreign policy and international relations in general.

The purpose of this volume has been to better understand the insufficiently explored phenomena of foreign policy change and restructuring. It has demonstrated that diverse theoretical logics and concepts are useful in attempting to discover the sources of change in foreign policy. It also has illustrated that the empirical application of these perspectives can produce useful insights into the dynamics and consequences of foreign policy restructuring. This concluding chapter, however, does not simply summarize the theoretical perspectives and empirical studies as laid out in the volume. Rather, the questions raised in the introduction are revisited in order to discuss how the chapters provide initial answers and contribute to further research on foreign policy restructuring.

The reader will recall that three basic questions were originally raised:

1. What is foreign policy change and restructuring?
2. What are the sources of foreign policy change? What bodies of theoretical knowledge and thought contribute to an understanding of foreign policy change?
3. To what extent does the study of change and restructuring contribute to an understanding of foreign policy and international relations?

The previous chapters collectively address these questions in at least two general ways. Most basically, in elaborating upon and illustrating specific theoretical perspectives, they have attempted to address these questions in greater detail than is often the case with more general theoretical frameworks. Second, and most importantly, these chapters draw attention to certain emerging issues that are likely to remain fundamental to more advanced research into the study of foreign policy and foreign policy change.

The Nature of Foreign Policy Change and Restructuring

As was indicated in the introductory chapter, one of the benefits of this volume's topic is that it forces students of foreign policy to confront and give greater thought to the phenomenon to be explained—foreign policy. It is not enough to concentrate and debate theoretical questions about the most powerful sources of foreign policy or methodological questions concerning how best to study foreign policy as has prevailed over the years. Instead, the concept of foreign policy itself deserves considerable attention and thought for its neglect "has been one of the most serious obstacles to providing more adequate and comprehensive explanations of foreign policy" (Hermann 1978, 25). Although no consensus has emerged, this volume does provide insights and raises significant issues for future scholarship concerning the nature of foreign policy change and restructuring.

All of the studies within the volume would subscribe to the view that foreign policy restructuring involves some kind of major or profound reorientation in the state's pattern of foreign policy. Yet, the diversity of foreign policy restructuring they consider is striking. Contrary to the familiar terrain of cold war realignment in the Holsti (1977) volume and various data-based studies (e.g., Andriole and Hopple 1986; Hagan 1989; Moon 1985), few of the analyses exclusively focus on restructuring in terms of realignment. While the McGinnis (chap. 4) and Sampson (chap. 5) analyses of Third World foreign policies focus primarily on alignments, the more general discussions of restructuring found in the Volgy and Schwarz (chap. 2) and Hagan (chap. 7) frameworks address realignment as well. The other studies emphasize nonrealigning forms of foreign policy change. The level of conflict and cooperation among established adversaries is the focus of Dixon and Gaarder's (chap. 9) examination of the level of American hostility toward the former Soviet Union. The level of flexibility in the formerly rigid and hostile relationship between long established adversaries is the primary focus of the Park, Ko, and Kim (chap. 8) and the Greffenius (chap. 11) analyses of East Asian and Middle Eastern foreign policies. The Skidmore (chap. 3) and Rosati (chap. 11) studies are concerned with the range and character of global involvement in the foreign policies of hegemonic powers such as the United States. While the selection of case studies is not meant to approach any kind of systematic sampling, it demonstrates that meaningful foreign policy change can take a variety of different forms.

In doing so, however, these studies do not resolve the matter of the essential features that define a "major change" in foreign policy. All of the cases of change discussed are substantively and theoretically meaningful, yet fail to conform to Holsti's (1982) conceptualization of foreign policy restructuring. Very few involve "the *dramatic, wholesale* alteration of a nation's pattern of external relations" across "*different* sectors" of the state's foreign relations (Holsti 1982, ix). Instead, the various studies indicate the possibility that there are degrees of change in foreign policy along the two dimensions Holsti raises: first, different levels of change may occur that are not necessarily always dramatic in nature and, second, the scope of change is not necessarily wholesale and may vary relative to specific issue areas or sectors of the state's foreign relations. Furthermore, the time frame in which change occurs—in terms of both its level and scope—does not always support the premise that restructuring necessarily marks a sharp, or clearly defined, break with the past.

Hermann (1990, 5) has described four graduated levels of foreign policy change and restructuring: international orientation change, problem/goal changes, program changes, and adjustment changes. Interestingly, as noted above in discussing Holsti's concept of realignment, most of the empirical studies in this volume do not highlight a change in a state's "international orientation" involving the "redirection of the actor's entire orientations toward world affairs." The empirical evidence cited in this volume instead points to the additional significance of the three less dramatic levels of restructuring, especially the second and third middle-range levels involving changes in the foreign policy goals and instruments of states over time. Schraeder's (chap. 6) analysis of U.S. policies toward Africa, for example, argues that successive presidential administrations have defined the region's problems as well as U.S. policy goals in different ways. In addition to changes in the foreign policy problems and goals of states, other analyses and frameworks presented have highlighted program changes involving shifts in the means or instruments used to address foreign policy goals. For example, the Park, Kim, and Ko (chap. 8) analysis of Korean and Taiwan foreign policies subtly centers around the question of the amount of accommodation with communist adversaries and the degree of flexibility in relations with third parties. While indicative of growing trade-offs between ideological confrontation and other foreign policy goals (e.g., trading opportunities), these new diplomatic postures also represent alternative strategies, or programs, for confronting or containing old adversaries.

Nor do these studies suggest that Hermann's adjustment changes should be entirely dismissed as unimportant and outside the realm of major change. These kinds of adjustment in the level of commitment or the scope of recipients, even though they do not affect "what is done, how it is done, and the purposes for which it is done" (Hermann 1989, 5), are evident in the gradual changes found in Sampson's analysis of Libyan foreign policy (chap. 5), and inherent in the policy effort underlying part of hegemonic adjustment and resistance in U.S. foreign policy (Skidmore, chap. 3; Rosati, chap. 11). Ironically, while these adjustments do not involve sharp or dramatic departures from earlier policy, their cumulative effect in shaping macro-economic and security policies has perhaps the most profound implications for the state's overall international orientation because it affects the balance between foreign commitments and national resources. Therefore, as virtually all of the empirical studies demonstrate, one needs to think in terms of multiple levels of foreign policy change and restructuring.

The question of what constitutes a major foreign policy change also concerns the *scope* of activity. For example, to what extent does change reflect a wholesale, comprehensive (i.e., intersector) reorientation of the state's foreign relations. Most of the changes this volume addresses do not conform to Holsti's (1982, 2) definition of restructuring in terms of "linking different sectors" of activity or Hermann's (1989, 6) concept of international orientation change in which "not one policy but many are more or less simultaneously changed." As depicted here, change is often limited to a narrower range of behavior in a state's foreign policies. While various frameworks presented in the volume allow for comprehensive change in foreign policy (e.g., Hagan, chap. 7; McGinnis, chap. 4; Rosati, chap. 11; Volgy and Schwarz, chap. 2), the empirical studies on the whole indicate that such comprehensive restructuring is rarely the case.

Sampson's (chap. 5) analysis of Libyan foreign policy across the Idris and Qadhdhafi regimes best reveals the possibility that elements of continuity and change can exist simultaneously across different sectors of a state's foreign relations. Although there was a fundamental reorientation in political relations with the West under Qadhdhafi, Libya's international economic relations remained largely unaffected. Most of the other studies within the volume also are bound by issue-area. One can rightly ask to what extent do changes in East Asian foreign economic policies (Park, Kim, and Ko, chap. 9), Third World regional rivalries (McGinnis, chap. 4), and U.S. security policies toward Africa (Schraeder, chap. 6) extend to other sectors of a state's foreign policies.[1]

Policy changes, furthermore, may not only be bound by issue but also by *time*. As Greffenius's (chap. 10) analysis of the Camp David Accords demonstrates, some changes are situationally specific and not generalizable to the entire issue area. Yet, if such changes occur at the peak of an international crisis or at a critical stage in negotiations, they are without question significant and should not be dismissed as substantively and theoretically unimportant. Hence, although it is difficult to equate restructuring with situationally specific policy shifts, it would appear somewhat restrictive to limit the notion of restructuring (at whatever level of change) only to cases where all major sectors of the state's foreign relations are simultaneously transformed.

What constitutes a major change or restructuring in foreign policy is perhaps at the heart of an anomaly in this book as well as an extensive literature involving whether or not United States foreign policy has experienced major change between 1945 and the so-called end of the cold war. A number of authors contend that American foreign policy has undergone significant shifts during this period. For example, Hagan (chap. 7) claims changes across certain regimes, Rosati (chap. 11) emphasizes the fundamental impact of the Vietnam War, and Skidmore (chap. 3) stresses the significance of the decline in American hegemony over the past two decades. In sharp contrast, Dixon and Gaarder (chap. 9) find that there was little basic restructuring during the cold war era in the centerpiece of U.S. foreign policy—hostility toward the Soviet Union—based on systematic evidence generated by events data. Their trend analysis, supported by more historical analysis such as conducted by Kegley and Wittkopf (1987), point to a basic continuity in U.S. foreign policy.

This brings the discussion to the core issue concerning what constitutes a major foreign policy change. It may be that the aggregation of behavior, such as compiling all of the events across the full range of U.S. activity toward the former Soviet Union, obscures important variations within specific areas of the relationship, such as arms control initiatives versus security conflicts in the Third World. It may be that aggregate measures of conflict do not reflect the contradictory patterns of continuity and change that are likely to coexist, as well as fail to indicate some of the subtlety in their levels of change since policy changes usually fall short of a full reorientation or even shift in goals. All this is an open question, of course, nonetheless the incongruity of findings suggests that care should be taken in executing aggregate data analyses of any nation's foreign policy.[2]

In sum, students of foreign policy need to give greater thought to the concept of foreign policy and to the implications this has for the development of theory and the cumulation of knowledge about foreign policy. With regard to the concepts of foreign policy change and restructuring, one needs to be precise with respect to at least three different dimensions: the level of change, the scope of change, and the time frame of change. Given the prevalence of diverse research agendas, different combinations of foreign policy change and restructuring are possible and likely as evident in this volume. This suggests that the study of foreign policy can be quite complex for both change and continuity are likely to coexist alongside each other as a state's foreign policy evolves throughout history. Therefore, turning to the next question, it is important to bear in mind that a careful characterization of the nature of foreign policy change is essential to theorizing about the sources of foreign policy restructuring.

Contending and Complimentary Explanations of Foreign Policy Change

A primary rationale for this volume has been to bring together a variety of different theoretical perspectives and empirically apply them so as to develop a better explanation of foreign policy change. The wide variety of theoretical approaches reflects the logics found in the literatures on rational choice theory, structural realism and hegemonic change, political economy, decision-making and organizational theory, nested games centering around internal politics, as well as state and political system structures. These efforts help to explicate various concepts useful for explaining the sources of foreign policy change—

leader belief systems, political opposition, democratic political patterns, international structures and hegemonic change, social change, political regimes and state structures, as well as other characteristics that mediate the influence of these various factors on foreign policy change, such as issue areas and situational conditions.

Despite their diversity, it is striking that across these explanatory perspectives there is a consensus on the need for *multicausal* explanations—that foreign policy reflects the complex interplay of governmental, domestic, and international factors. In fact, a broad synthesis emerges from the chapters in this volume which points to the existence of three sets of causal dynamics that underlie change—and affect continuity—in foreign policy: (1) change in global structures and the state's international position, (2) domestic political realignments, and (3) the policymaking process. The first two are essentially sets of conditions that pressure, or drive, governments toward restructuring. The third set refers to factors which often act to condition foreign policy responses to new international pressures and opportunities.[3]

Change in Global Structures and the International Position of the State. The view that foreign policy restructuring is essentially dictated by the constraints imposed on the state by the structure of the international system is common in such prominent literatures as neorealism, complex interdependence, and dependency theory. However, as explicated in several chapters here, these changes in systemic conditions actually reflect closely intertwined international and societal trends: first, rearrangements in the basic global and/or regional structures of the world and, second, changes in the societal resource bases of states (see, e.g., Sprout and Sprout 1965, 1968). The interaction of the international and societal environments, as they affect states' power in the international system and their proclivity for foreign policy change, is evident across the chapters that emphasize governmental responses to international constraints. Skidmore (chap. 3), for example, argues that broad trends in international structures (i.e., the emergence of rising powers) and the relative decline in each power's domestic resource base dictated U.S. and British hegemonic adjustments (see also Rosati, chap. 11). In McGinnis (chap. 4), dependence on foreign military suppliers drove the foreign policies of Third World rivals and thus were subject to restructuring when superpower policies changed.

Domestic Political Realignments. At perhaps the opposite end are explanations that posit foreign policy changes result from domestic political realignments— that is, a fundamental (more or less permanent) shift in the basic distribution of power and influence among contending political groups. While domestic processes are also central to the next type of explanation discussed—the policymaking process—their importance here is that realignments bring *new* sets of beliefs and/or interests into the foreign policymaking process. The realignment of political groups, including the emergence of new groups and interests, can occur at a variety of levels across the political system.[4] The most direct case of this exists when one leadership group replaces another group, which Hagan (chap. 7) argues may result in the redefinition of the national interest across successive regimes (see also Sampson, chap. 5; Volgy and Schwarz, chap. 2). Another conception of domestic political change focuses on the transformation of government processes and its impact on foreign policy, as in Taiwan and South Korea where democratization has bureaucratized decision-making and weakened state power vis-à-vis powerful domestic interests (Park, Ko, and Kim, chap. 8). Finally, as illustrated in Rosati's (chap. 11) cyclical analysis of American foreign policy, broad domestic trends and crises may lead to a restructuring of the domestic political environment, forcing leaders to engage in the "politics of adjustment" so as to respond to new kinds of political and societal groups outside the government. Each of these arguments involves a realignment of the basic domestic political context in which the ideas and interests of a new set of political actors drive foreign policy change.

The Policymaking Process.   This dynamic centers around the governmental and domestic political processes that condition the implementation of new policy initiatives developed by the central political leadership. These processes are usually relatively fixed and, as such, often operate as an important source of foreign policy continuity. Arguments of this sort are found throughout the volume. Dixon and Gaarder (chap. 8), Volgy and Schwarz (chap. 2), and Schraeder (chap. 6) stress bureaucratic incrementalism as a source of policy rigidity, although Schraeder further identifies how the politicization of issues will move them into the wider presidential and congressional arena thereby creating an opportunity for change. Hagan (chap. 7), McGinnis (chap. 4), and Rosati (chap. 11) consider broader kinds of *political* opposition which are able to block new policy initiatives, either by wielding a veto power or by threatening to withdraw support from the regime and its policies. Finally, Skidmore (chap. 3) distinguishes between weak and strong states' structures, arguing that leaders at the head of politically weak states are unable to institute foreign policy change because of their inability to override powerful domestic societal and economic interests. Across the discussion of these different governmental and societal actors is a common logic: opponents of change often occupy political positions in the policymaking process within the government and throughout society, and can block and resist initiatives flowing from either changed international circumstances or domestic political realignment.

Although these three sets of forces constitute alternative causal dynamics, this is not to say that they should be treated separately. The chapter authors, in fact, attempt at least a partial synthesis by integrating separate causal mechanisms. Almost all these chapters explicitly incorporate the internal decision-making structures and political constraints found in explanations developed from the policymaking process into their discussions of the other two types of explanations which stress governments' responses to changes in the global structures or domestic political realignments. This reflects the emergence of a growing consensus that comprehensive explanations of foreign policy change require a *synthesis* and the development of integrative theory.

Thus, as shown by McGinnis's (chap. 4) analysis of regional rivalries, leaders engage in a continuous "nested game" in which constraints and opportunities stemming from shifting international conditions must be balanced with domestic considerations (e.g., would a controversial initiative undercut the legitimacy and support of the regime?). Each of the studies that address the impact of leadership change in a regime (Volgy and Schwarz, chap. 2; Hagan, chap. 7; Park, Ko, and Kim, chap. 8) qualify the implications of such domestic changes with the argument that their full impact will be considerably diluted *if* the new leadership faces major opposition. In fact, one implication of Dixon and Gaarder's (chap. 9) empirical juxtaposition of the dynamics of elite change and decision-making is that bureaucratic incrementalism may have negated any differences in the various strategies of containment across administrations. Domestic political constraints are also central to the broader analyses of "hegemonic adjustment" found in the Skidmore (chap. 4) and Rosati (chap. 11) studies. Both argue that the role of domestic politics—e.g., weak state structures and various domestic oppositions—may undercut the leadership's adjustment of foreign (and domestic) policies which is necessary to confront the challenges to their state's hegemonic status.

Taken together, as diagrammed below, there is consensus (and emphasis) among the chapters that the third mechanism of foreign policy change, the policymaking process, is best viewed within the context of the other two sources of foreign policy (see figure 12.1). In other words, these political processes do not operate independently, but rather are important to the extent that they condition the impact of the broader domestic and international sources of foreign policy change. However, in relegating political explanations of foreign policy change to a supplementary theoretical status, these studies also make a broader claim that international and domestic sources of change are significantly modified by the state's policymaking apparatus. The theoretical and empirical conclusion emerging from this volume, therefore, lends considerable support to the view that understanding decision-making and political dynamics is essential in linking the deeper sources of change to governments' efforts to restructure foreign policy.

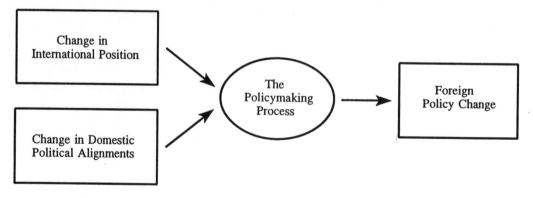

Figure 12.1   Causal Dynamics Underlying Foreign Policy Restructuring

If all this suggests an underlying logic to the chapters in this volume, it is not to say that this theoretical synthesis is complete or without problems. One problem throughout the volume is a bias toward treating the policymaking process as imposing only *constraints* on the implementation of new policies by leaders responding to domestic and international pressures for change in foreign policy. The chapters consistently emphasize that policymaking processes inhibit (or block entirely) a leadership's response to international changes and/or prevent a new leadership's implementation of policy changes—that is, bureaucratic and organizational processes ultimately marginalize the significance of a leadership's initiatives; political opposition dilutes the initiatives or precludes controversial policy proposals; and the structures of democratic systems and weak states enable societal groups to inhibit meaningful restructuring. This is not to say that all studies here consider such constraints as inevitable. Schraeder (chap. 6) carefully explicates situations that have permitted presidents and Congress to circumvent bureaucratic rigidity in U.S. policy toward Africa; similarly, Hagan (chap. 7) identifies conditions that mediate the constraints of regime fragmentation and other opposition. Yet, these illustrations still represent an emphasis on policymaking constraints as opposed to policymaking pressures and opportunities for foreign policy change.

What is missing, then, is the notion that policymaking dynamics may operate to "push" a leadership toward change. Although not apparent in the bureaucratic and organizational politics literature (see, e.g., Allison 1971), certain literature on group decision-making and domestic politics suggests that in some cases political pressure indeed does prompt leaders to initiate change in foreign policy. This may occur in a variety of settings. For example, in what is viewed as an alternative to bureaucratic politics, "groupthink" (Janis 1982) suggests that highly cohesive decision-making groups with conformist norms are often prone to forceful action (see Hermann 1993). Similarly, in some situations domestic opposition actually pressures leaders to initiate or favor change in foreign policy, particularly if the incumbent regime perceives a current policy to be undercutting its legitimacy (e.g., George 1980; Trout 1975). As leaders attempt to mobilize new support (or avoid the loss of allies) a dramatic shift in policy may be seen as an important means for enhancing their political situation. Finally, the accessible structures of democratic and weak states do not always assure the failure of a leadership's initiatives. Rather, it could be the opposition that is demanding a change in policy and therefore the state will be unable to maintain existing policies—in fact, just as weak states are often forced to respond to external pressures, they also are likely to respond to domestic political change (see for example, the discussion of challenging groups during a period of transition in Rosati, chap. 11).

Recognition that governmental and domestic politics may amplify leaders' predisposition toward change, as well as inhibit it, raises additional issues for future research on the sources of foreign policy restructuring. First, the simultaneous push and pull of the policymaking process indicates that, over the long term, the primary manifestation of domestic opposition is not that the government is completely unable to act (i.e., deadlock) but that it is able at best to only partially implement its new policies. Not only does this conform with analyses by Rosati (chap. 11) and Ikenberry (1988), it points to the importance of Goldmann's (1988) concept of administrative and political stabilizers as a means of containing domestic pressures undercutting desired policies. Second, there is a need to understand the conditions where the policymaking process throughout government and society promotes tendencies toward change as well as reinforces situations which dampen propensities for change. One needs to understand not only if leaders face domestic pressures but, if they do, how they respond to them. For example, at home, do they find political incentives or disincentives for pushing ahead with a new policy initiative? Finally, this does not suggest that leaders' motivations for changing policies are limited to the politics of the policymaking process. Other kinds of policymaking dynamics also operate to make leaders sensitive to international and domestic pressures for change. For example, the emerging political psychology literature on learning and leader perceptions points to cognitive processes that affect leaders' sensitivity toward international and domestic trends and the need for change (see Breslauer and Tetlock 1991; Rosati 1994). Although not a focus of this volume, psychological conceptions of leadership behavior are likely an essential complement to the political explanations of how leadership dynamics mediate the effects of domestic and international change on foreign policy restructuring.

In sum, three significant theoretical implications for explaining foreign policy change (and continuity) emerge out of this volume. First, all the contributors within the volume point to the existence of contradictory causal dynamics underlying foreign policy change. Some of these dynamics push and promote change while other dynamics constrain and hinder change. Second, there is a consensus that the making of foreign policy is complex and requires a synthetic and integrative approach. Focus on primarily one theoretical approach or set of causal factors is unlikely to lead to a comprehensive understanding of the reality of policymaking and foreign policy change. Finally, as most of the chapters make clear, the actual evolution of foreign policy is a function of politics. It is the political interplay between the government, society, and global environment that generate and affect foreign policy continuity and change.

Wider Implications of the Study of Foreign Policy Restructuring

The third, and most general, question addressed within the volume asks to what extent does the study of change and restructuring contribute to a broader understanding of foreign policy and international relations? The chapters in this volume suggest three general implications of the study of foreign policy change: (1) it lends itself toward a substantively richer theoretical focus in foreign policy studies, (2) it stimulates greater synthesis and integration between different explanatory approaches to foreign policy, and (3) it highlights the connections, and tensions, between the fields of international relations and foreign policy analysis.

The first implication is that the focus on foreign policy restructuring results in a more meaningful conceptual foundation for conducting research and cumulating knowledge in foreign policy. Contrary to many theoretical efforts in foreign policy analysis, the studies here are clearly organized around the dependent variable, "that which is to be explained" (see Hermann 1978).[5] This type of focus on foreign policy change has proven to have two major advantages. First, the foreign policy phenomena to be explained are not in question, but instead, are at the center of these theoretical efforts. In contrast to much of the systematic literature on foreign policy in which the primary concern has been to develop theories of foreign policy derived from particular sources (e.g., bureaucratic politics, leader belief systems, national attributes, etc.), the chapters in this volume concentrate explicitly on determining the effects of different theoretical approaches—and their interplay—on foreign policy change and restructuring. Second, the study of foreign policy change can lead to the development of theory and the generation of empirical studies at different levels of specificity and generality—at the broad-macro, middle range, and the more narrow-micro levels. This is because the focus on foreign policy change is less abstract theoretically and substantively more meaningful than the tendency, for example, in the comparative study of foreign policy to describe and explain the most general patterns in states' overall foreign policy behavior in terms of macro-level conflict or cooperation.

A second benefit of the focus on foreign policy restructuring is the stimulation of greater synthesis among different approaches which seek to explain foreign policy. Almost all of the authors in this volume consider multiple perspectives in explaining foreign policy restructuring. Instead of emphasizing separate, competing approaches (consistent with the longstanding levels of analysis debate; see, e.g., Singer 1961; Waltz 1959), attempts have been made to integrate multiple perspectives in an effort to better determine how various factors and processes combine to influence foreign policy restructuring. This synthesis is most clearly evident in the incorporation of the policymaking process as mediating the impact of broader kinds of domestic and international phenomena throughout the volume. How one goes about synthesizing the two exogenous sources of restructuring—changes in the state's international position and domestic political realignments—is less clear, but even here the theoretical efforts are more subtle than the conventional wisdom. For example, the traditional distinction between internal and external sources of foreign policy appears to have less utility than is generally believed. For example, the change in a state's international position makes sense only as a combination of external and internal dynamics, while domestic political change is at least partially driven by international considerations (see, e.g., Gourevitch 1978). Although efforts at synthesis can complicate research programs, it is consistent with the kind of theoretical and methodological diversity that permeates the study of foreign policy and can provide the basis for intellectual growth and knowledge (see, e.g., Lapid 1989).

Finally, explanations of foreign policy restructuring provide insights into better understanding several core issues in the study of international relations, including the power of neorealism and implications for the agent-structure debate. The study of foreign policy restructuring gets directly at the empirical power of structural approaches such as neorealism—the reigning theoretical perspective in international relations (see, e.g., Gilpin 1981; Waltz 1979). Structural approaches to the study of international relations tend to emphasize how states and, therefore, governmental foreign policy tend to be constrained and determined by the structures that prevail in the international environment. They tend to predict "evolutionary change" in which global structural change brings about governmental adaptation of foreign policy, an argument that assumes the inevitability and ease of governmental learning usually by downplaying domestic and societal sources of foreign policy and treating the state as a rational actor.[6] The value of the study of foreign policy restructuring is that it highlights the limits of neorealist views of international system dynamics by demonstrating the importance of either strong domestic resistance to, or domestic pressure for, change in foreign policy independent of change in the international environment. As all the contributors make clear, especially Skidmore (chap. 3), Sampson (chap. 5), and Rosati (chap. 11), such structural arguments, although parsimonious, are simplistic and incomplete if they fail to address the very basic ways in which societal and state factors shape government orientations in international affairs.[7]

The interaction of alternative causal dynamics of foreign policy change, as diagramed in figure 12.1, also puts the agent-structure debate into sharp clarity (see Wendt 1987; Dessler 1989; Carlsnaes 1992). At the heart of this issue "lies an increasingly widespread recognition that, instead of being antagonistic partners in a zero-sum relationship, human agents and social structures are in a fundamental sense intertwined entities, and hence that we cannot account fully for the one without invoking the other" (Carlsnaes 1992, 245–46). In this simple, three-part model (figure 12.1), the "agent" element is captured by the rise to power of a new set of leaders (or old leaders who now seek a change in course); their preferences constitute a political choice of one or another option in foreign relations. The political initiatives of these leaders are, however, usually conditioned by the two other structural elements of the model: the state's position in the global system and domestic political realignments. These structural dynamics constrain the emergence of new policy initiatives in two ways. First, well-defined global and domestic constraints on policy choices mean that certain foreign policy options are not even considered viable within domestic debates, and their advocates will not emerge as dominant within the political system. Second, structural constraints come into play when leaders find that international power relationships and/or domestic political alignments make impossible the implementation of new policies. In sum, where there are clear international (and domestic) constraints, there will likely be relatively little autonomy for independent agents of change (see, e.g., Volgy and Schwarz, chap. 2).

Yet there are situations in which government initiatives do dramatically override the constraints of international and domestic structures. In the early 1990s, the world is in the midst of precisely this kind of change. It stems from two kinds of intertwined dynamics. The first of these, which occurred in the former Soviet Union, takes place when domestic turmoil becomes so severe that it results in a political revolution and leads to the emergence of a new leadership that dismantles and transforms domestic structures and challenges (or ignores) conventional structures and norms of the international system (see, e.g., Rosati's discussion of cyclical change in chapter 11). Thus, as has happened in the past (e.g., following the 1789 French Revolution and in the aftermath of the Nazi's assumption of power in Germany in 1933), domestically driven, extreme choices (favoring radical change) ultimately override the established structures at home and abroad and lead to a radical reorientation of the state's foreign policy. The second dynamic is that a weakening of the structural constraints of the prior international system permits greater national autonomy in foreign policy so that political systems have a greater range of choice (see, e.g., Sampson's discussion of exploiting the seams in chapter 5). With the collapse of the Soviet threat, other powers now have options in foreign policy that would have had little domestic credibility during the cold war—e.g., a semi-isolationist retrenchment can be considered in U.S. politics, a Gaullist-style independence is viable for Germany and Japan, and neutrality has lost its meaning in Sweden. Of course, it remains an open question what choices will be taken, and how—and to what extent given domestic structural constraints—governments will redefine their foreign policies over the next few years. An understanding of the dynamics when domestic pressures override international constraints and/or when loosened international structures permit a wider latitude in foreign policy options provides important insights into how structural conditions operate to equip agents in international affairs.

The significance of all this is not simply limited to changes in foreign policy. The cumulative effects of foreign policy restructurings, especially among the major powers, will ultimately shape the structures of the emerging international system. That the current system is becoming increasingly complex, interdependent, and pluralist with numerous major powers is not in question; what remains to be seen is the nature of relations among these actors. Will all of the major powers remain essentially "status quo" powers willing to cooperate, as appears to be currently the case, or will there be a deterioration of relations among some players such that there is a return to the militancy which characterized the cold war system? In the transition to an increasingly multipolar system, there is likely to be an unusually wide scope of choice in the foreign policies of most states, and the process in which the push—and pull—of domestic politics determines those choices will provide insights into several theoretical issues. It will provide a laboratory in which the dynamic interaction between agents and structures determines how governments' foreign policies are developed to cope with international circumstances which, in turn, ultimately help to shape the emergence of new international structures.

In closing, the substantive significance of the study of foreign policy change and restructuring cannot be questioned—certainly not in the 1990s in light of the continuing transformation of foreign policies with the end of the cold war. Clearly, the study of foreign policy change is increasingly important in understanding the dynamics of continuity and change in world politics. In this respect, this book is intended to act as a stimulant to the evolving study of foreign policy and international relations. This remains an important endeavor, for progress on this scholarly front contributes to a more powerful understanding of the dynamics of world politics as the turn of the century approaches.

Notes

1. In the case of the Schraeder and Park, et. al., studies, it is also possible to ask whether the changes in internal decision processes apply to other sectors of foreign policymaking.
2. Note that Roeder's (1984) aggregate analysis of Soviet conflict behavior across successive leaders and factional alignments, for example, *does* capture important variation in foreign policy behavior.
3. Although our conceptual scheme is somewhat different, the three broad categories we identify are consistent with the general orientation found in Ikenberry, Lake, and Mastanduno (1988) involving the need to integrate system-centered, society-centered, and state-centered explanatory approaches. For a similar framework see Snyder, Bruck, and Sapin (1962). However, we are focusing not so much on different levels of explanations (i.e., the location of causality) but, instead, on the causal mechanisms by which these influences affect foreign policy.
4. Note that this cuts across the state-society distinction. Our concern is not whether the realignment of new powerful groups is within the state or regime, as opposed to the society. Our focus is on the fact that new groups have gained power or influence such that their beliefs and interests define the policy agenda and effect public policy in new ways.
5. Another example of foreign policy analysis cast at a more substantively meaningful level is the growing research on the origins of war, as illustrated by the work of Jack Levy (e.g., 1989) and the collection of essays in Rotberg and Rabb (1989).
6. At the same time, so-called neorealist scholars such as Gilpin (1981) recognize the inevitability and necessity of global war as a prelude to major change—a huge contradiction relative to their assumption about the independence, adaptability, and rationality of states which remains unresolved and largely inadequately addressed in much of their work.
7. This is, of course, a two-way street. Just as structural approaches are incomplete, the same can be said for foreign policy analyses that consider only societal or state sources of foreign policy. By emphasizing the role of international structure within a synthesis of systemic, societal, and state influences, foreign policy analysis is placed in its proper perspective. The works of Ikenberry (1988) and Lake

(1988), representing an international political economy and structure realist perspective, are beginning to grapple with this issue. For a more sophisticated and multicausal explanation of the change in Soviet foreign policy from this perspective, see Checkel (1993).

References

Abramson, Gary. 1992. "Rise of the Crescent." *Africa Report* 37:18–21.

Acheson, Dean. 1969. *Present at the Creation: My Years in the State Department.* New York: W. W. Norton.

Ajami, Fouad. 1981. *The Arab Predicament.* Cambridge: Cambridge University Press.

Akaha, Tsuneo. 1991. "Japan's Comprehensive Security Policy: A New East Asian Environment." *Asian Survey* 31:324–40.

Alavi, Hamza. 1972. "The State in Post-Colonial Societies: Pakistan and Bangladesh." *New Left Review* 74:59–81.

Alford, Robert R. 1975. "Paradigms of Relations Between State and Society." In *Stress and Confrontation in Modern Capitalism*, ed. Leon N. Lindberg, C. Crouch, and C. Offe, 145–60. Lexington, Mass.: D. C. Heath.

Alker, Hayward R., and Thomas J. Biersteker. 1984. "The Dialectics of World Order: Notes for a Future Archeologist of International Savoir Faire." *International Studies Quarterly* 28:121–42.

Alker, Hayward R., and C. Christensen. 1972. "From Causal Modelling Artificial Intelligence: The Evolution of a United Nations Peace-Keeping Simulation." In *Experimentation and Simulation in Political Science*, ed. J. A. Laponce and Paul Smoker, 177–224. Toronto: University of Toronto Press.

Allison, Graham T. 1969. "Conceptual Models and the Cuban Missile Crisis." *American Political Science Review* 63:689–718.

Allison, Graham T. 1971. *Essence of Decision: Explaining the Cuban Missile Crisis.* Boston: Little, Brown.

Almond, Gabriel A. 1965. *The American People and Foreign Policy.* New York: Praeger.

Alves, Dora. 1989. "The Changing New Zealand Defense Posture." *Asian Survey* 29:363–81.

Ambrose, Stephen. 1988. *Rise to Globalism: American Foreign Policy Since 1938.* 5th rev. ed. New York: Penguin Books.

Anderson, Lisa. 1985. "Assessing Libya's Qaddafi." *Current History* 84:502.

Andrews, William G. 1962. *French Politics and Algeria: The Process of Policy Formation, 1954–1962.* New York: Appleton-Century-Crofts.

Andriole, Stephen, and Gerald Hopple. 1986. "The Process, Outcomes, and Impact of Regime Change in the Third World, 1959–1981." *International Interactions* 12:363–92.

Appadorai, A. 1981. *The Domestic Roots of India's Foreign Policy, 1947–1972.* Delhi: Oxford University Press.

Arkhurst, Frederick S., editor. 1975. *U.S. Policy Toward Africa.* Garden City, N.J.: Praeger.

Aronson, Shlomo. 1982–1983. "Israel's Leaders, Domestic Order and Foreign Policy, June 1981–June 1983." *Jerusalem Journal of International Relations* 6:1–28.

Arrow, Kenneth J. 1963. *Social Choice and Individual Values.* New Haven: Yale University Press.

Arsenault, Raymond. 1972. "White on Chrome: Southern Congressmen and Rhodesia 1962–1971." *Issue: A Quarterly Journal of Opinion* 2:46–57.

Avery, William, and David Rapkin, editors. 1982. *America in a Changing World Political Economy*. New York: Longman.

Azar, Edward E. 1980. "The Codebook of the Conflict and Peace Data Bank." Mimeographed.

Azar, Edward E., and Thomas J. Havener. 1976. "Discontinuities in the Symbolic Environment: A Problem in Scaling." *International Interactions* 2:231–46.

Bachman, David. 1989. "Domestic Sources of Chinese Foreign Policy." In *China and the World: New Directions in Chinese Foreign Relations*, ed. Samuel S. Kim, 31–54. Boulder: Westview.

Baker, Pauline H. "The Sanctions Vote: A G.O.P. Milestone." *New York Times* 26 August 1986.

Baker, Pauline H. 1989. *The United States and South Africa: The Reagan Years*. New York: Ford Foundation and the Foreign Policy Association.

Ball, George. 1968. *The Disciples of Power*. Boston: Little, Brown.

Banton, Michael. 1965. *Roles: An Introduction to the Study of Social Relations*. London: Taistock Publications, Ltd.

Bar-Siman-Tov, Yaacov. 1983. *Linkage Politics in the Middle East: Syria Between Domestic and External Conflict, 1961–1970*. Boulder: Westview.

Barnds, William J. 1972. *India, Pakistan, and the Great Powers*. New York: Praeger.

Barnet, Richard J. 1971. *Roots of War: The Men and Institutions Behind U.S. Foreign Policy*. Baltimore: Penguin.

Barraclough, Geoffrey. 1964. *An Introduction to Contemporary History*. Middlesex, England: Penguin.

Baugh, William H. 1978. "Major Powers and Weak Allies: Stability and Structure in Arms Race Models." *Journal of Peace Science* 3:45–54.

Baumgartner, Frank R. 1989. *Conflict and Rhetoric in French Policymaking*. Pittsburgh: University of Pittsburgh Press.

Baumgartner, Frank R., and Bryan D. Jones. 1991. "Agenda Dynamics and Policy Subsystems." *Journal of Politics* 53:1044–71.

Baylis, Thomas A. 1983. Review of *Do New Leaders Make a Difference?*, by Valerie Bunce. *American Political Science Review* 77:230–31.

Bender, Gerald J., James S. Coleman, and Richard L. Sklar, editors. 1985. *African Crisis Areas and U.S. Foreign Policy*. Berkeley: University of California Press.

Bendor, Jonathan, and Thomas H. Hammond. 1992. "Rethinking Allison's Models." *American Political Science Review* 86:301–22.

Berkowitz, Morton, P. G. Bock, and Vincent J. Fuccillo. 1977. *The Politics of American Foreign Policy: The Social Context of Decisions*. Englewood Cliffs, N.J.: Prentice-Hall.

Bernstein, Thomas, and Andrew J. Nathan. 1983. "The Soviet Union, China, and Korea." In *The U.S.-South Korean Alliance*, ed. Gerald L. Curtis and Sung-joo Han, 89–127. Lexington, Mass.: D. C. Heath.

Berry, Jeffrey M. 1989. *The Interest Group Society*. Glenview, Ill.: Scott, Foresman.

Biddle, William Jesse, and John D. Stephens. 1989. "Dependent Development and Foreign Policy: The Case of Jamaica." *International Studies Quarterly* 33:389–410.

Blair, John. 1976. *Control of Oil*. New York: Pantheon.

Bolt, Ernest C., Jr. 1981. "Isolation, Expansion, and Peace: American Foreign Policy Between the Wars." In *American Foreign Relations: A Historiographical Review*, ed. Gerald K. Haines and J. Samuel Walker, 133–57. Westport, Conn.: Greenwood Press.

Boulding, Kenneth E. 1970. *A Primer on Social Dynamics*. New York: Free Press.

Bowles, Chester. 1956. *Africa's Challenge to America*. Westport, Conn.: Negro Universities Press.

Boyd, Gavin, and Gerald W. Hopple, editors. 1987. *Political Change and Foreign Policies*. London: Frances Pinter.

Brady, Linda. 1978. "The Situation and Foreign Policy." In *Why Nations Act*, ed. Maurice East, Stephen Salmore, and Charles F. Hermann, 173–90. Beverly Hills: Sage.

Braudel, Fernand. 1972. "History and the Social Sciences." In *Economy and Society in Early Modern Europe*, ed. Peter Burke, 11–42. New York: Harper Torch Books.

Brecher, Michael. 1972. *The Foreign Policy System of Israel: Setting, Images, Process*. New Haven: Yale University Press.

Brecher, Michael. 1975. *Decision in Israel's Foreign Policy*. New Haven: Yale University Press.

Brecher, Michael, Blema Steinberg, and Janice Stein. 1969. "A Framework for Research on Foreign Policy Behavior." *Journal of Conflict Resolution* 13:75–101.

Brecher, Michael, Jonathan Wilkenfeld, and Sheila Moser. 1988. *Crises in the Twentieth Century*, 2 vol. New York: Pergamon.

Breslauer, George W., and Philip E. Tetlock. 1991. *Learning in U.S. and Soviet Foreign Policy*. Boulder: Westview.

Bresnan, John, editor. 1986. *Crisis in the Philippines: The Marcos Era and Beyond*. Princeton: Princeton University Press.

Brito, Dagobert L. 1972. "A Dynamic Model of an Armaments Race." *International Economic Review* 13:359–75.

Brodin, Katarina. 1972. "Belief Systems, Doctrines and Foreign Policy." *Cooperation and Conflict* 11:97–112.

Broesamle, John H. 1990. *Reform and Reaction in Twentieth Century American Politics*. Westport, Conn.: Greenwood Press.

Brown, Seyom. 1983. *The Faces of Power: Constancy and Change in United States Foreign Policy from Truman to Reagan*. New York: Columbia University Press.

Brown, Seyom. 1988. *New Forces, Old Forces, and the Future of World Politics*. Glenview, Ill.: Scott, Foresman.

Brown, Michael, Gary Freeman, and Kay Miller. 1972. *Passing By: The United States and Genocide in Burundi, 1972*. Washington, D.C.: Carnegie Endowment for International Peace.

Brunk, Gregory G., and Thomas G. Minehart. 1984. "How Important is Elite Turnover to Policy Change?" *American Journal of Political Science* 28:559–69.

Brzezinski, Zbigniew. 1983. *Power and Principle: Memoirs of the National Security Advisor, 1977–1981*. New York: Farrar, Straus, Giroux.

Brzoska, Michael, and Thomas Ohlson. 1987. *Arms Transfers to the Third World, 1971–1985*. New York: Oxford University Press.

Bueno de Mesquita, Bruce. 1981. *The War Trap*. New Haven: Yale University Press.

Bueno de Mesquita, Bruce. 1983. "The Costs of War: An Expected Utility Approach." *American Political Science Review* 77:347–57.

Bueno de Mesquita, Bruce. 1985. "The War Trap Revisited: A Revised Expected Utility Model." *American Political Science Review* 79:156–77.

Bull, Hedley. 1977. *The Anarchical Society: A Study of Order in World Politics*. New York: Columbia University Press.

Bunce, Valerie. 1981. *Do New Leaders Make a Difference? Executive Succession and Public Policy Under Capitalism and Socialism.* Princeton: Princeton University Press.

Burke, S. M. 1979. *Mainsprings of Indian and Pakistani Foreign Policies.* Minneapolis: University of Minnesota Press.

Burnham, Walter Dean. 1976. "Revitalization and Decay: Looking Toward the Third Century of American Electoral Politics." *Journal of Politics* 38:146–72.

Burns, James MacGregor. 1984. *The Power to Lead: The Crisis of the American Presidency.* New York: Simon and Schuster.

Burns, James MacGregor. 1989. *The Crosswinds of Freedom.* New York: Alfred A. Knopf.

Burton, John. 1979. *Deviance, Terrorism, and War: The Process of Solving Unsolved Social and Political Problems.* Oxford: Martin Robertson.

Buzan, Barry, and Gowher Rizvi, editors. 1986. *South Asian Insecurity and the Great Powers.* New York: St. Martin's.

Callahan, Patrick. 1982. "Commitment." In *Describing Foreign Policy Behavior*, ed. Patrick Callahan, Linda P. Brady, and Margaret G. Hermann, 177–206. Beverly Hills: Sage.

Callahan, Patrick., L. Brady, and M. G. Hermann, editors. 1982. *Describing Foreign Policy Behavior.* Beverly Hills: Sage.

Calleo, David P. 1987. *Beyond American Hegemony: The Future of the Western Alliance.* New York: Basic Books.

Callinicos, Alex. 1988. *Making History: Agency, Structure, Change in Social Theory.* Ithaca, N.Y.: Cornell University Press.

Caporaso, James A., et al. 1987. "The Comparative Study of Foreign Policy: Perspectives on the Future." *International Studies Notes* 13:32–46.

Carlsnaes, Walter. 1992. "The Agency-Structure Problem in Foreign Policy Analysis." *International Studies Quarterly* 36:245–70.

Carr, Edward Hallett. 1964. *The Twenty Years' Crisis, 1919–1939.* New York: Harper and Row.

Carter, Jimmy. 1982. *Keeping Faith: Memoirs of a President.* New York: Bantam Books.

Catrina, Christian. 1988. *Arms Transfers and Dependence.* New York: Taylor and Francis.

Cecil, Lady Gwendolyn. 1921. *Life of Robert, Marquess of Salisbury.* 2 vols. London: Hoddes and Stoughton.

Challenor, Herschelle Sullivan. 1981. "The Influence of Black Americans on U.S. Foreign Policy Toward Africa." In *Ethnicity and U.S. Foreign Policy*, ed. Abdul Aziz Said, 143–82. New York: Praeger.

Chari, P. R. 1979. "Indo-Soviet Military Cooperation: A Review." *Asian Survey* 19:230–44.

Checkel, Jeff. 1993. "Ideas, Institutions, and the Gorbachev Foreign Policy Revolution." *World Politics* 45:271–300.

Choucri, Nazli, and Robert C. North. 1975. *Nations in Conflict.* San Francisco: W. H. Freeman.

Choudhury, Golam W. 1975. *India, Pakistan, and the Major Powers.* New York: Free Press.

Chung, Chin O. 1978. *P'yongyang Between Peking and Moscow: North Korea's*

Involvement in the Sino-Soviet Dispute, 1958–1975. University, Ala.: University of Alabama Press.

Cipolla, Carlos, editor. 1970. *The Economic Decline of Empires.* London: Methuen.

Clapham, Christopher. 1985. *Third World Politics: An Introduction.* Madison: University of Wisconsin Press.

Clausewitz, Carl Von. 1832. *On War.* New York: Penguin.

Clough, Michael. 1992. *Free at Last? U.S. Policy Toward Africa and the Cold War.* New York: Council on Foreign Relations Press.

Coates, James, and Michael Kilian. 1985. *Heavy Losses: The Dangerous Decline of American Defense.* New York: Penguin.

Cohen, Warren I. 1987. *Empire Without Tears: America's Foreign Relations, 1921–1933.* New York: Alfred A. Knopf.

Copper, John. 1988. *A Quiet Revolution: Political Development in the Republic of China.* Washington, D.C.: Ethics and Public Policy Center.

Cottom, Richard W. 1989. "Inside Revolutionary Iran." *The Middle East Journal* 43:168–85.

Crocker, Chester A. 1981. "The U.S. Policy Process and South Africa." In *The American People and South Africa: Publics, Elites, and Policymaking Processes,* ed. Alfred O. Hero, Jr. and John Barnett, 139–62. Lexington, Mass.: Lexington Books.

Crone, Donald K. 1988. "State, Social Elites, and Government Capacity in Southeast Asia." *World Politics* 25:253–68.

Crossette, Barbara. "U.S. Aide Calls Muslim Militants Concern to the World." *New York Times* 1 January 1992, A3.

Culverson, Donald. 1989. "The U.S. Information Agency in Africa." *TransAfrica Forum* 6:61–80.

Dahl, Robert A. 1967. *Pluralist Democracy in the United States: Conflict and Consensus.* Chicago: Rand McNally.

Dahl, Robert A. 1971. *Polyarchy: Participation and Opposition.* New Haven: Yale University Press.

Dallek, Robert. 1979. *Franklin Roosevelt and American Foreign Policy, 1932–1945.* Oxford: Oxford University Press.

Dallin, Alexander. 1981. "The Domestic Sources of Soviet Foreign Policy." In *The Domestic Context of Soviet Foreign Policy,* ed. Seweryn Bialer, 335–408. Boulder: Westview.

Dalton, Russell J., and Manfred Kuechler, editors. 1990. *Challenging the Political Order: New Social and Political Movements in Western Democracies.* New York: Oxford University Press.

Danaher, Kevin. 1985. *The Political Economy of U.S. Policy Toward South Africa.* Boulder: Westview.

David, Stephen R. 1979. "Realignment in the Horn: The Soviet Advantage." *International Security* 4:69–90.

David, Stephen R. 1991. "Explaining Third World Alignment." *World Politics* 43:233–56.

Davis, Nathaniel 1978. "The Angolan Decision of 1975: A Personal Memoir." *Foreign Affairs* 57:109–24.

Dayan, Moshe. 1981. *Breakthrough: A Personal Account of the Egypt-Israel Peace Negotiations.* New York: Alfred A. Knopf.

Deeb, Marius, and Mary Jane Deeb. 1982. *Libya Since the Revolution*. New York: Praeger.

Deeb, Mary Jane. 1991. *Libya's Foreign Policy in North Africa*. Boulder: Westview.

Deger, Saadet, and Ron Smith. 1983. "Military Expenditures and Growth in the Less Developed Countries." *Journal of Conflict Resolution* 27:335–53.

Deibel, Terry L. 1989. "Reagan's Mixed Legacy." *Foreign Policy* 75:34–55.

Deibel, Terry L. 1991. "Bush's Foreign Policy: Mastery and Inaction." *Foreign Policy* 84:3–23.

Dekmejian, R. Hrair. 1971. *Egypt under Nasir: A Study in Political Dynamics*. Albany: State University of New York Press.

Dessler, David. 1989. "What's at Stake in the Agency-Structure Debate?" *International Organization* 43:441–73.

Dessler, David. 1991. "Beyond Correlations: Toward a Causal Theory of War." *International Studies Quarterly* 35:337–55.

Dessouki, Ali E. Hillal. 1984. "The Primacy of Economics: The Foreign Policy of Egypt." In *The Foreign Policies of Arab States*, ed. Bahgat Korany and Ali E. Hillal Dessouki, 119–46. Boulder: Westview.

Destler, I. M., Leslie H. Gelb, and Anthony Lake. 1976. *Our Own Worst Enemy: The Unmaking of American Foreign policy*. New York: Simon and Schuster.

Destler, I. M., Priscilla Clapp, Hideo Sato, and Haruhiro Fukui. 1976. *Managing an Alliance: The Politics of U.S.-Japanese Relations*. Washington, D.C.: Brookings.

Deutsch, Karl W. 1974. *Politics and Government: How People Decide Their Fate*. Boston: Houghton Mifflin.

Deutsch, Karl W., and Richard L. Merritt. 1965. "Effects of Events on National and International Images." In *International Behavior*, ed. Herbert C. Kelman, 132–87. New York: Holt, Rineholt and Winston.

Dix, Robert H. 1982. "The Breakdown of Authoritarian Regimes." *Western Political Quarterly* 35:554–73.

Dixon, William J. 1983. "Measuring Interstate Affect." *American Journal of Political Science* 27:828–51.

Domhoff, G. William 1978. *The Powers That Be: Processes of Ruling Class Domination in America*. New York: Vintage.

Dominguez, Jorge I. 1989. *To Make a World Safe for Revolution: Cuba's Foreign Policy*. Cambridge, Mass.: Harvard University Press.

Doran, Charles, and Wes Parsons. 1980. "War and the Cycle of Relative Power." *American Political Science Review* 74:947–65.

Dower, John W. 1986. *War Without Mercy: Race and Power in the Pacific War*. New York: Pantheon.

Dowty, Alan. 1984. "Israel: From Ideology to Reality." In *The Arab-Israeli Conflict: Perspectives*, ed. Alvin Z. Rubinstein, 107–44. New York: Praeger.

East, Maurice A. 1972. "Status Discrepancy and Violence in the International System." In *The Analysis of International Politics*, ed. James N. Rosenau, Vincent Davis, and Maurice A. East, 299–319. New York: Free Press.

East, Maurice A. 1978a. "National Attributes and Foreign Policy." In *Why Nations Act*, ed. Maurice A. East, Stephen A. Salmore, and Charles F. Hermann, 123–42. Beverly Hills: Sage.

East, Maurice A. 1978b. "The International System Perspective and Foreign Policy." In *Why Nations Act*, ed. Maurice A. East, Stephen Salmore, and Charles F. Hermann, 143–60. Beverly Hills: Sage.

East, Maurice A., Stephen A. Salmore, and Charles F. Hermann, editors. 1978. *Why Nations Act: Theoretical Perspectives for Comparative Foreign Policy Studies.* Beverly Hills: Sage.

Easton, David. 1953. *The Political System.* New York: Alfred A. Knopf.

Eckstein, Harry. 1988. "A Culturalist Theory of Political Change." *American Political Science Review* 82:789–804.

Edelman, Murray. 1964. *The Symbolic Uses of Politics.* Urbana: University of Illinois Press.

Eldridge, Niles. 1992. "Punctuated Equilibria, Rates of Change, and LargeScale Entities in Evolutionary Systems." In *The Dynamics of Evolution,* ed. Albert Somit and Steven A. Peterson, 103–20. Ithaca, N.Y.: Cornell University Press.

Emerson, Rupert. 1967. *Africa and United States Foreign Policy.* Englewood Cliffs, N.J.: Prentice-Hall.

Etheredge, Lloyd S. 1985. *Can Governments Learn? American Foreign Policy and Central American Revolutions.* New York: Pergamon.

Everts, Philip P., editor. 1985. *Controversies at Home: Domestic Factors in the Foreign Policy of the Netherlands.* Boston: Martinus Nijhoff Publishers.

Faurby, Ib. 1982. "Decision Structures and Domestic Sources of Nordic Foreign Policies." In *Foreign Policies of Northern Europe,* ed. Bengt Sundelius, 33–71. Boulder: Westview.

Ferguson, Yale H., and Richard W. Mansbach. 1988. *The Elusive Quest: Theory and International Politics.* Columbia: University of South Carolina Press.

Ferguson, Yale H., and Richard W. Masbach. 1991. "Between Celebration and Despair: Constructive Suggestions for the Future International Theory." *International Studies Quarterly* 35:363–86.

Ferrero, Guglielmo. 1972. *The Principles of Power: The Great Political Crises of History.* New York: Arno Press.

Fingar, Thomas. 1980. "Domestic Policy and the Quest for Independence." In *China's Quest for Independence: Policy Evolution in the 1970s,* ed. Thomas Fingar and the *Stanford Journal of International Studies,* 25–92. Boulder: Westview.

Fitzgerald, Mary Anne. 1989. "The News Hole: Reporting Africa." *Africa Report* 34:59–61.

Foxley, Alejandro, Michael McPherson, and Guillermo O'Donnell, editors. 1986. *Development, Democracy, and the Art of Trespassing.* South Bend, Ind.: University of Notre Dame Press.

Franck, Thomas M., and Edward Weisband. 1972. *World Politics: Verbal Strategies Among the Superpowers.* New York: Oxford University Press.

Fraser, Steve, and Gary Gerstle. 1989. *The Rise and Fall of the New Deal Order, 1930–1980.* Princeton: Princeton University Press.

Friedberg, Aaron. 1988. *The Weary Titan: Britain and the Experience of Relative Decline, 1895–1905.* Princeton: Princeton University Press.

Friedlander, Melvin A. 1983. *Sadat and Begin: The Domestic Politics of Peacemaking.* Boulder: Westview.

Fukui, Haruhiro. 1970. *Party in Power: The Japanese Liberal-Democrats and Policy Making.* Berkeley: University of California Press.

Fukuyama, Francis. 1986. "Military Aspects of U.S.-Soviet Competition in the Third World." In *East-West Tensions in the Third World,* ed. Marshall D. Shulman, 181–211. New York: Norton.

Gaddis, John Lewis. 1972. *The United States and the Origins of the Cold War, 1941–1947*. New York: Columbia University Press.

Gaddis, John Lewis. 1978. *Russia, the Soviet Union, and the United States: An Interpretative History*. New York: Alfred A. Knopf.

Gaddis, John Lewis. 1982. *Strategies of Containment: A Critical Appraisal of Postwar American National Security Policy*. New York: Oxford University Press.

Galtung, Johan. 1971. "A Structural Theory of Imperialism." *Journal of Peace Research* 8:81–117.

Gamson, William A. 1975. *The Strategy of Social Protest*. Homewood, Ill.: Dorsey Press.

Garten, Jeffrey. 1989. "Trading Blocs and the Evolving World Economy." *Current History* 88:15–16, 54–56.

Garthoff, Raymond. 1985. *Detente and Confrontation: American-Soviet Relations from Nixon to Reagan*. Washington, D.C.: Brookings.

Gavshon, Arthur. 1981. *Crisis in Africa*. New York: Penguin.

Gelb, Leslie H., with Richard K. Betts. 1979. *The Irony of Vietnam: The System Worked*. Washington, D.C.: Brookings.

Gelman, Harry. 1984. *The Brezhnev Politburo and the Decline of Detente*. Ithaca, N.Y.: Cornell University Press.

George, Alexander L. 1980. "Domestic Constraints on Regime Change in U.S. Foreign Policy: The Need for Legitimacy." In *Change in the International System*, ed. Ole R. Holsti, Randolph M. Siverson, and Alexander L. George, 233–62. Boulder: Westview.

George, Alexander L., and Richard Smoke. 1974. *Deterrence in American Foreign Policy: Theory and Practice*. New York: Columbia University Press.

Gerner, Deborah J. 1991. "Foreign Policy Analysis: Renaissance, Routine, or Rubbish?" In *Political Science: Looking to the Future*, ed. William Crotty, vol 2. Evanston, Ill.: Northwestern University Press.

Gerner, Deborah J. 1991–1992. "Foreign Policy Analysis: Exhilarating, Eclecticism, Intriguing Enigmas." *International Studies Notes* 16/17:4–19.

Gervasi, Sean, Ann Seidman, Immanuel Wallerstein, and David Wiley. 1991. "Why We Said No to A.I.D." *Issue* 7:35–38.

Gibbs, David N. 1991. *The Political Economy of Third World Intervention: Mines, Money, and U.S. Policy in the Congo Crisis*. Chicago: University of Chicago Press.

Gigot, Paul A. 1987. "Glory Hallelujah: The Democratic Revolution Spread to Asia." *Policy Review* 40:56–60.

Gilbert, Ralph. 1967. "Legal Aspects of Doing Business in Libya." *The Libyan Economic and Business Review* 3:25–26.

Gill, Stephen. 1986. "U.S. Hegemony: Its Limits and Prospects in the Reagan Era." *Millenium: Journal of International Studies* 15:311–38.

Gillespie, John V., and Dina Zinnes. 1975. "Progressions in Mathematical Models of International Conflict." *Synthese* 31:289–321.

Gillespie, John V., and Dina Zinnes. 1977. "Embedded Game Analysis and International Conflict Control." *Behavioral Science* 22:22–31.

Gilpin, Robert. 1981. *War and Change in World Politics*. New York: Cambridge University Press.

Ginsburgs, George, and Roy U. T. Kim. 1977. *Calendar of Diplomatic Affairs: Democratic People's Republic of Korea 1945–1975*. Moorestown, N.J.: Symposia Press.

Gochman, Charles S., and Zeev Maoz. 1984. "Militarized Interstate Disputes, 1816–1976: Procedures, Patterns, and Insights." *Journal of Conflict Resolution* 28:585–616.

Goffman, Erving. 1961. *Encounters*. Indianapolis: Bobbs-Merrill Educational Publishing.

Goldman, Eric F. 1961. *The Crucial Decade—and After: America, 1945–1960*. New York: Random House.

Goldmann, Kjell. 1982. "Change and Stability in Foreign-Policy: Detente as a Problem of Stabilization." *World Politics* 34:230–66.

Goldmann, Kjell. 1988. *Change and Stability in Foreign Policy: The Problems and Possibilities of Detente*. Princeton: Princeton University Press.

Goldstein, Joshua S. 1988. *Long Cycles: Prosperity and War in the Modern Age*. New Haven: Yale University Press.

Goldstone, Jack A. 1980. "Theories of Revolution: The Third Generation." *World Politics* 32:425–53.

Goodenough, Ward. 1965. "Rethinking Status and Role." In *The Relevance of Models for Social Anthropology*, ed. M. Banton, 1–24. New York: Praeger.

Gould, Stephen Jay, and Niles Eldredge. 1977. "Punctuated Equilibria: The Tempo and Mode of Evolution Reconsidered." *Paleobiology* 3:115–51.

Gourevitch, Peter. 1978. "The Second Image Reversed: The International Sources of Domestic Politics." *International Organization* 32:881–912.

Greffenius, Steven. 1986. "The Foreign Policymaking Environment in Egypt and Israel." Paper presented at the annual meeting of the American Political Science Association, New Orleans.

Greffenius, Steven. 1987. "Patterns of Response in a Dyadic Relationship: Flexibility and Reciprocity in the Egyptian-Israeli Conflict." Ph.D. dissertation, University of Iowa.

Gross, Neal, Ward S. Masons, and Alexander McEarchen. 1958. *Explorations in Role Analysis*. New York: John Wiley and Sons.

Gurr, Ted R. 1974. "Persistence and Change in Political Systems, 1800–1971." *American Political Science Review* 68:1482–504.

Haas, Ernst B. 1970. *The Web of Interdependence: The United States and International Organizations*. Englewood Cliffs, N.J.: Prentice-Hall.

Haber, Eitan, Zeev Schiff, and Ehud Yaari. 1979. *The Year of the Dove*. New York: Bantam Books.

Hadar, Leon T. 1992. "The 'Green Peril': Creating the Islamic Fundamentalist Threat." Cato Institute Policy Analysis No. 177.

Hagan, Joe D. 1987a. "Regimes, Political Oppositions, and the Comparative Analysis of Foreign Policy." In *New Directions in the Study of Foreign Policy*, ed. Charles F. Hermann, Charles W. Kegley, Jr., and James N. Roseanu, 339–65. Boston: Allen and Unwin.

Hagan, Joe D. 1987b. "Political Regime Changes and Foreign Policy Restructuring in the Third World: An Interim Report." Paper presented at the annual meeting of the American Political Science Association, 3–6 September.

Hagan, Joe D. 1989a. "Domestic Political Regime Changes and Third World Voting Realignments in the United Nations, 1946–1984." *International Organization* 43:505–41.

Hagan, Joe D. 1989b. "Domestic Political Regime Changes and Foreign Policy Restructuring in Western Europe: A Conceptual Framework and Initial Analysis." *Cooperation and Conflict* 24:141–62.

Hagan, Joe D. 1993. *Political Oppositions and Foreign Policy in Comparative Perspective*. Boulder: Lynne Reinner.

Hagan, Joe D. Forthcoming. "What Role Does Domestic Politics Play in the Decision to Change Course?" In *Changing Course: When Governments Choose To Redirect Foreign Policy*, ed. Charles F. Hermann, Margaret G. Hermann, and Richard Herrmann.

Hagan, Joe D., Charles F. Hermann, and Margaret G. Hermann, editors. Forthcoming. *Leaders, Groups, and Coalitions: How Decision Units Shape Foreign Policy*.

Haggard, Stephan. 1986. "The Newly Industrializing Countries in the International System." *World Politics* 38:343–70.

Halberstam, Daniel. 1969. *The Best and the Brightest*. New York: Random House.

Haley, P. Edward. 1984. *Qaddafi and the United States Since 1969*. New York: Praeger.

Halperin, Morton H. 1974. *Bureaucratic Politics & Foreign Policy*. Washington, D.C.: Brookings.

Han, Sung-joo. 1983a. "South Korea and the United States: Past, Present, and Future." In *The U.S.-South Korean Alliance*, ed. Gerald L. Curtis and Sung-joo Han, 210–35. Lexington, Mass.: D. C. Heath.

Han, Sung-joo. 1983b. "North Korea's Security Policy and Military Strategy." In *North Korea Today: Strategic and Domestic Issues*. Berkeley: Institute of East Asia Studies, University of California.

Han, Sung-joo. 1986. "Political Institutionalization in South Korea, 1961–1984." In *Asian Political Institutionalization*, ed. R. Scalapino, S. Sato, and J. Wanandi, 116–37. Berkeley: The Institute of East Asian Studies, University of California.

Handel, Michael I. 1981. *Weak States in the International System*. London: Frank Cass.

Handrieder, Wolfram F. 1970. *The Stable Crisis: Two Decades of German Foreign Policy*. New York: Harper and Row.

Hanrieder, Wolfram F., and Graeme P. Auton. 1980. *The Foreign Policies of West Germany, France, Britain*. Englewood Cliffs, N.J.: Prentice-Hall.

Harary, Frank. 1961. "A Structural Analysis of the Situation in the Middle East in 1956." *Journal of Conflict Resolution* 5:167–78.

Harding, Harry. 1980. "The Domestic Politics of China's Global Posture, 1973–1979." In *China's Quest for Independence: Policy Evolution in the 1970s*, ed. Thomas Fingar and the *Stanford Journal of International Studies*, 93–146. Boulder: Westview.

Harkavy, Robert E. 1982. *Great Power Competition for Overseas Bases*. New York: Pergamon.

Harrison, Paul, and Robin Palmer. 1986. *News Out of Africa: Biafra to Band Aid*. London: Hilary Shipman.

Heale, M. J. 1990. *American Anticommunism: Combating the Enemy Within*. Baltimore: Johns Hopkins University Press.

Henderson, Gregory 1968. *Korea: The Politics of the Vortex*. Cambridge, Mass.: Harvard University Press.

Hermann, Charles F. 1969. "International Crisis as a Situation Variable." In *International Politics and Foreign Policy*, ed. James N. Rosenau, 409–21. New York: Free Press.

Hermann, Charles F. 1978. "Foreign Policy Behavior: That Which is to be Explained." In *Why Nations Act*, ed. Maurice A. East, Stephen A. Salmore, and Charles F. Hermann, 25–47. Beverly Hills: Sage.

Hermann, Charles F. 1982. "Foreign Policy." In *Encyclopedia of Policy Sciences*, ed. Stuart S. Nagel. New York: Marcel Dekker.

Hermann, Charles F. 1987. "Political Oppositions as Potential Agents of Foreign Policy Change: Developing a Theory." Paper presented at the annual meeting of the International Studies Association, Washington, D.C.

Hermann, Charles F. 1988. "New Foreign Policy Problems and Old Bureaucratic Organizations." In *The Domestic Sources of American Foreign Policy: Insights and Evidence*, ed. Charles W. Kegley, Jr. and Eugene R. Wittkopf, 248–65. New York: St. Martin's.

Hermann, Charles F. 1990. "Changing Course: When Governments Choose to Redirect Foreign Policy." *International Studies Quarterly* 34:3–21.

Hermann, Charles F. 1993. "Avoiding Pathologies in Foreign Policy Decision Groups." In *Force, Diplomacy, and Leadership: Essays in Honor of Alexander George*, ed. Dan Caldwell and Timothy McKeown. Boulder: Westview.

Hermann, Charles F., Charles W. Kegley, Jr., and James N. Rosenau, editors. 1987. *New Directions in the Study of Foreign Policy*. Boston: Allen and Unwin.

Hermann, Charles F., and Margaret G. Hermann. 1979. "Summary of the External Components in the CREON Project's Conceptual Framework for Explaining Foreign Policy." Paper presented to the Northeastern Political Science Association.

Hermann, Charles F., and Gregory Peacock. 1987. "The Evolution and Future of Theoretical Research in the Comparative Study of Foreign Policy." In *New Directions in the Study of Foreign Policy*, ed. Charles F. Hermann, Charles W. Kegley, Jr., and James N. Rosenau, 13–32. Boston: Allen and Unwin.

Hermann, Margaret G. 1980. "Explaining Foreign Policy Behavior Using the Personal Characteristics of Political Leaders." *International Studies Quarterly* 24:7–46.

Hermann, Margaret G. 1982. "Independence/Interdependence of Action." In *Describing Foreign Policy Behavior*, ed. Patrick Callahan, Linda P. Brady, and Margaret G. Hermann, 243–56. Beverly Hills: Sage.

Hermann, Margaret G., Charles F. Hermann, and Joe D. Hagan. 1987. "How Decision Units Shape Foreign Policy Behavior." In *New Directions in the Study of Foreign Policy*, ed. Charles F. Hermann, Charles W. Kegley, Jr., and James N. Rosenau, 309–36. Boston: Allen and Unwin

Herrmann, Richard. 1986. "The Power of Perceptions in Foreign Policy Decision-Making: Do Views of the Soviet Union Determine the Policy Choices of American Leaders." *American Journal of Political Science* 30:841–75.

Herrmann, Richard. 1988. "The Empirical Challenge of the Cognitive Revolution: A Strategy for Drawing Inferences About Perceptions." *International Studies Quarterly* 32:175–203.

Hersh, Seymour. 1983. *The Price of Power: Kissinger in the Nixon White House*. New York: Summit Books.

Higgins Benjamin. 1953. *The Economic and Social Development of Libya*. New York: United Nations.

Hilsman, Roger. 1964. *To Move a Nation*. New York: Doubleday.

Hinnebusch, Raymond A. 1984. "Revisionist Dreams, Realist Strategies: The Foreign Policy of Syria." In *The Foreign Policies of Arab States*, ed. Bahgat Korany and Ali E. Hillal Dessouki, 283–322. Boulder: Westview.

Hinton, Harold C. 1972. *China's Turbulent Quest: An Analysis of China's Foreign Policy since 1949*. New York: MacMillan.

Hirschman, Albert O. 1970. *Exit, Voice, and Loyalty: Responses to Decline in Firms, Organizations, and States*. Cambridge, Mass.: Harvard University Press.

Hirschman, Albert O. 1982. *Shifting Involvements: Private Interest and Public Action*. Princeton: Princeton University Press.

Hodgson, Godfrey. 1973. "The Establishment." *Foreign Policy* 10:3–40.

Hodgson, Godfrey. 1976. *America in Our Time*. New York: Vintage.

Hodgson, Godfrey. 1980. *All Things to All Men: The False Promise of the Modern American Presidency*. New York: Touchtone.

Hoffmann, Stanley. 1978. *Primacy or World Order: American Foreign Policy Since the Cold War*. New York: McGraw-Hill.

Hogan, Michael J., and Thomas G. Paterson 1991. *Explaining the History of American Foreign Relations*. Cambridge: Cambridge University Press.

Hogarth, Robin, and Melvin Reder, editors. 1986. *Rational Choice: The Contrast Between Economics and Psychology*. Chicago: University of Chicago Press.

Holbrooke, Richard 1986. "East Asia: The Next Challenge." *Foreign Affairs* 64:732–51.

Holloway, Anne Forrester. 1985. "Congressional Initiatives on South Africa." In *African Crisis Areas and U.S. Foreign Policy*, ed. Gerald J. Bender, James S. Coleman, and Richard L. Sklar, 89–94. Berkeley and Los Angeles: University of California Press.

Holsti, K. J. 1970. "National Role Conceptions in the Study of Foreign Policy." *International Studies Quarterly* 14:233–309.

Holsti, K. J. 1971. "Retreat from Utopia: International Relations Theory, 1945–1970." *Canadian Journal of Political Science* 4:165–77.

Holsti, K. J. 1977. "Restructuring Foreign Policy: A Neglected Phenomenon in the Theory of International Relations." Paper presented at the annual meeting of the International Studies Association, St. Louis, Miss., March.

Holsti, K. J., editor. 1982. *Why Nations Realign: Foreign Policy Restructuring in the Postwar World*. London: Allen and Unwin.

Holsti, K. J. 1982a. "Restructuring Foreign Policy: A Neglected Phenomenon in Foreign Policy." In *Why Nations Realign: Foreign Policy Restructuring in the Postwar World*, ed. K. J. Holsti, 1–20. London: Allen and Unwin.

Holsti, K. J. 1982b. "From Diversification to Isolation: Burma, 1963–7." In *Why Nations Realign: Foreign Policy Restructuring in the Postwar World*, ed. K. J. Holsti, 105–33. London: Allen and Unwin.

Holsti, Ole R. 1967. "Cognitive Dynamics and Images of the Enemy." In *Image and Reality in World Politics*, ed. John C. Farrell and Asa P. Smith, 16–39. New York: Columbia University Press.

Holsti, Ole R. 1969. "The Belief System and National Images: A Case Study." *Journal of Conflict Resolution* 6:224–52.

Holsti, Ole R. 1974. "The Study of International Politics Makes Strange Bedfellows: Theories of the Radical Right and the Radical Left." *American Political Science Review* 68:217–42.

Holsti, Ole R., and James N. Rosenau. 1984. *American Leadership in World Affairs: Vietnam and the Breakdown of Consensus*. Boston: Allen and Unwin.

Holsti, Ole R., and John D. Sullivan. 1969. "National-International Linkages: France and China as Nonconforming Alliance Members." In *Linkage Politics*, ed. James N. Rosenau, 147–95. New York: Free Press.

Hopple, Gerald. 1979. "Elite Values and Foreign Policy Analysis: Preliminary Findings." In *Psychological Models in International Politics*, ed. Lawrence Falkowski, 211–49. Boulder: Westview.

Horn, Robert C. 1982. *Soviet-Indian Relations: Issues and Influence*. New York: Praeger.

Howell, Llewellyn D. 1983. "A Comparative Study of the WEIS and COPDAB Data Sets." *International Studies Quarterly* 27:149–59.

Hughes, Anthony J. 1980. "Randall Robinson: Executive Director of TransAfrica." *Africa Report* 25:9–15.

Hughes, Barry, and Thomas J. Volgy. 1970. "Distance in Foreign Policy Behavior: A Comparative Study of Eastern Europe." *Midwest Journal of Political Science* 14:459–92.

Hunter, Helen-Louise. 1980. "North Korea and the Myth of Equidistance." *Korea and World Affairs* 4:268–79.

Huntington, Samuel P. 1968. *Political Order in Changing Societies*. New Haven: Yale University Press.

Huntington, Samuel P. 1981. *American Politics: The Politics of Disharmony*. Cambridge, Mass.: Harvard University Press.

Huntington, Samuel P. 1987–1988. "Coping with the Lippmann Gap." *Foreign Affairs America and the World* 66:453–77.

Hyland, William. 1987. *Mortal Rivals*. New York: Random House.

Ikenberry, G. John. 1986. "The State and Strategies of International Adjustment." *World Politics* 39:53–77.

Ikenberry, G. John. 1988. *Reasons of State: Oil Capacities of American Government*. Ithaca, N.Y.: Cornell University Press.

Ikenberry, G. John. 1989. *American Foreign Policy: Theoretical Essays*. Glenview, Ill.: Scott, Foresman.

Ikenberry, G. John, David A. Lake, and Michael Mastanduno, editors. 1988. "The State and American Foreign Economic Policy." *International Organization* 42 Winter, special issue.

Im, Hyug Baeg. 1987. "The Rise of Bureaucratic Authoritarianism in South Korea." *World Politics* 29:231–57.

Inglehart, Ronald. 1977. *The Silent Revolution: Changing Values and Political Styles Among Western Publics*. Princeton: Princeton University Press.

Isaacson, Walter, and Evan Thomas. 1986. *The Wise Men: Six Friends and the World They Made*. New York: Touchtone.

Ismael, Tareq Y., and Jacqueline S. Ismael. 1986. "Domestic Sources of Middle East Foreign Policy." In *International Relations of the Contemporary Middle East: A Study in World Politics*, ed. Tareq Y. Ismael, 17–40. Syracuse, N.Y.: Syracuse University Press.

Jaccard, James, Robert Turrisi, and Choi K. Wan. 1990. *Interaction Effects in Multiple Regression*. Newbury Park, Calif.: Sage.

Jackson, Henry. 1984. *From the Congo to Soweto: U.S. Foreign Policy Toward Africa Since 1960*. New York: Quill.

James, Patrick, Michael Brecher, and Tod Hoffman. 1988. "International Crises in Africa, 1929–1979: Immediate Severity and Long-Term Importance." *International Interactions* 14:51–84.

Janis, Irving. 1982. *Groupthink*. Boston: Houghton Mifflin.

Jensen, Lloyd. 1982. *Explaining Foreign Policy*. Englewood Cliffs, N.J.: Prentice-Hall.

Jentleson, Bruce W. 1987. "American Commitments in the Third World: Theory vs. Practice." *International Organization* 41:667–704.

Jervis, Robert. 1976. *Perception and Misperception in International Politics*. Princeton: Princeton University Press.

Joffe, Josef. 1989. "The Foreign Policy of the Federal Republic of Germany." In *Foreign Policy in World Politics: States and Regions*, ed. Roy C. Macridis, 72–124. Englewood Cliffs, N.J.: Prentice-Hall.

Johnson, Chalmers. 1966. *Revolutionary Change*. Stanford, Calif.: Stanford University Press.

Jordon, Donald. 1987. *Changing American Assessments of the Soviet Threat in Sub-Saharan Africa: 1975–1985*. Lanham, Md.: University Press of America.

Kahler, Miles. 1984. *Decolonization in Britain and France: The Domestic Consequences of International Relations*. Princeton: Princeton University Press.

Kalb, Madeleine. 1982. *The Congo Cables: The Cold War in Africa From Eisenhower to Kennedy*. New York: Macmillan.

Kaplan, Morton. 1957. *System and Process in International Politics*. New York: Wiley.

Katzenstein, Peter J. 1977. "Conclusion: Domestic Structures and Strategies of Foreign Economic Policy." *International Organization* 31:879–920.

Katzenstein, Peter. 1978. "Domestic Structures and Strategies of Foreign Economic Policy." In *Between Power and Plenty: Foreign Economic Policy of Advanced Industrial States*, ed. Peter Katzenstein, 295–336. Madison: University of Wisconsin Press.

Katznelson, Ira, and Kenneth Prewitt. 1979. "Constitutionalism, Class, and the Limits of Choice in U.S. Foreign Policy." In *Capitalism and the State in U.S.-Latin American Relations*, ed. Richard Fagen, 25–40. Stanford, Calif.: Stanford University Press.

Keesing's Contemporary Archives. 1964–1973. Bristol: Keesing's Publications, Ltd.

Kegley, Charles W., Jr. 1980. "The Comparative Study of Foreign Policy: Paradigm Lost?" Institute for International Studies Essays No. 10. Columbia: University of South Carolina Press.

Kegley, Charles W., Jr. 1987. "Decision Regimes and the Comparative Study of Foreign Policy." In *New Directions in the Study of Foreign Policy*, ed. Charles F. Hermann, Charles W. Kegley, Jr., and James N. Rosenau, 247–68. Boston: Allen and Unwin.

Kegley, Charles W., Jr., and Richard A. Skinner. 1976. "The Case-for-Analysis Problem." In *In Search of Global Patterns*, ed. James N. Rosenau, 303–18. New York: Free Press.

Kegley, Charles W., Jr., and Eugene R. Wittkopf. 1987. *American Foreign Policy: Pattern and Process*. New York: St. Martin's.

Kegley, Charles W., and Eugene R. Wittkopf. 1993. *World Politics: Trend and Transformation*. New York: St. Martin's.

Kennedy, Paul. 1987a. *The Rise and Fall of the Great Powers: Economic Change and Military Conflict from 1500 to 2000*. New York: Random House.

Kennedy, Paul. 1987b. "The Relative Decline of America." *The Atlantic Monthly* 260:29–38.

Keohane, Robert O. 1971. "The Big Influence of Small Allies." *Foreign Policy* 2:161–82.

Keohane, Robert O. 1982. "Hegemonic Leadership and U.S. Foreign Economic Policy in the 'Long Decade' of the 1950s." In *America in a Changing World Political Economy*, ed. William Avery and David Rapkin, 49–76. New York: Longman.

Keohane, Robert O. 1986. "Theory of World Politics: Structural Realism and Beyond." In *Neo-Realism and Its Critics*, ed. Robert Keohane, 165. New York: Columbia University Press.

Keohane, Robert O., and Joseph S. Nye, Jr. 1977. *Power and Interdependence.* Boston: Little, Brown.

Kerr, Malcolm H. 1971. *The Arab Cold War: Gamal 'Abd al-Nasir and His Rivals, 1958–1970.* London: Oxford University Press.

Key, V. O., Jr. 1961. *Public Opinion and American Democracy.* New York: Alfred A. Knopf.

Key, V. O., Jr. 1964. *Politics, Parties, and Pressure Groups.* New York: Thomas W. Crowell.

King, Anthony. 1978. *The New American Political System.* Washington, D.C.: American Enterprise Institute.

King, Anthony. 1990. *The New American Political System.* 2d ed. Washington, D.C.: American Enterprise Institute.

Kissinger, Henry A. 1966. "Domestic Structure and Foreign Policy." *Daedalus* 95:503–29.

Kissinger, Henry A. 1976. "Implications of Angola for Future U.S. Foreign Policy." *Department of State Bulletin* 74:174–82.

Kissinger, Henry A. 1979. *White House Years.* Boston: Little, Brown.

Kitchen, Helen. 1990. "Still on Safari." In *Centerstage: American Diplomacy Since World War Two*, ed. L. Carl Brown, 171–92. New York: Holmes and Meier.

Ko, Byung C. 1984. *The Foreign Policy System of North and South Korea.* Berkeley: University of California Press.

Kochanek, Stanley A. 1968. *The Congress Party of India: The Dynamics of One-Party Democracy.* Princeton: Princeton University Press.

Kogan, Norman. 1983. *A Political History of Italy: The Postwar Years.* New York: Praeger.

Kolko, Gabriel. 1988. *Confronting the Third World: United States Foreign Policy 1945–1980.* New York: Pantheon.

Kolodziej, Edward A., and Robert Harkavy, editors. 1982. *Security Policies of Developing Countries.* Lexington, Mass.: Lexington.

Koo, Youngnok, and Sung-Joo Han, editors. 1985. *The Foreign Policy of the Republic of Korea.* New York: Columbia University Press.

Korany, Bahgat. 1974. "Foreign Policy Models and Their Empirical Relevance to Third World Actors: A Critique and an Alternative." *International Social Science Journal* 26:70–94.

Korany, Bahgat. 1983. "The Take-Off of Third World Studies? The Case of Foreign Policy." *World Politics* 35:465–87.

Korany, Bahgat. 1984. "Defending the Faith: The Foreign Policy of Saudi Arabia." In *The Foreign Policies of Arab States*, ed. Bahgat Korany and Ali E. Hillal Dessouki, 241–82. Boulder: Westview.

Kotz, Nick. 1988. *Wild Blue Yonder and the B-1 Bomber*. Princeton: Princeton University Press.

Krasner, Stephen D. 1976. "State Power and the Structure of Foreign Trade." *World Politics* 28:317–37.

Krasner, Stephen D. 1978a. *Defending the National Interest: Raw Materials Investments and U.S. Foreign Policy*. Princeton: Princeton University Press.

Krasner, Stephen D. 1978b. "United States Commercial and Monetary Policy: Unraveling the Paradox of External Strength and Internal Weakness." In *Between Power and Plenty: Foreign Economic Policy of Advanced Industrial States*, ed. Peter Katzenstein, 51–88. Madison: University of Wisconsin Press.

Krasner, Stephen D. 1984. "Approaches to the State: Alternative Conceptions and Historical Dynamics." *Comparative Politics* 16:223–46.

Krasner, Stephen D. 1989. "Sovereignty: An Institutional Perspective." In *The Elusive State: International and Comparative Perspectives*, ed. James Caporaso, 80–88. Newbury Park, Calif.: Sage.

Kuhn, Thomas. 1962. *The Structure of Scientific Revolutions*. Chicago: University of Chicago Press.

Lake, Anthony. 1976. *The Tar Baby Option: American Policy Toward Southern Rhodesia*. New York: Columbia University Press.

Lake, David A. 1983. "International Economic Structures and American Foreign Economic Policy, 1887–1934." *World Politics* 35:517–43.

Lake, David A. 1988. *Power, Protection, and Free Trade: International Sources of U.S. Commercial Strategy, 1887–1939*. Ithaca, N.Y.: Cornell University Press.

Lancaster, Carol. 1984. "U.S. Aid to Africa: Who Gets What, When, and How?" *CSIS Africa Notes* 25:1–6.

Lancaster, Carol. 1988. *U.S. Aid to Sub-Saharan Africa: Challenges, Constraints, and Change*. Washington, D.C.: CSIS.

Lapid, Josef. 1989. "The Third Debate: On the Prospects of International Theory in a Post-Positivist Era." *International Studies Quarterly* 33:235–54.

Larson, Deborah Welch. 1985. *Origins of Containment: A Psychological Explanation*. Princeton: Princeton University Press.

Lasswell, Harold. 1971. *A Pre-View of Policy Sciences*. New York: American Elsevier.

Lebow, Richard Ned. 1981. *Between Peace and War: The Nature of International Crisis*. Baltimore: Johns Hopkins University Press.

Lefebvre, Jeffrey A. 1991. *Arms for the Horn: U.S. Policy in Ethiopia and Somalia 1953–1991*. Pittsburgh: University of Pittsburgh Press.

Lemarchand, Rene. 1989. "Burundi: The Killing Fields Revisited." *Issue* 18:22–28.

LePrestre, Philippe G. 1984. "Lessons of Cohabitation." In *French Security in a Disarming World*, ed. Philippe G. LePrestre, 15–47. Boulder: Lynne Rienner.

Levy, Jack 1989. "The Causes of War: A Review of Theories and Evidence." In *Behavior, Society, and Nuclear War*, ed. Philip E. Tetlock et al., vol. 1. Oxford: Oxford University Press.

Lewis-Beck, Michael. 1986. "Comparative Economic Voting: Britain, France, Germany, Italy." *American Journal of Political Science* 30:315–46.

Leys, Colin. 1976. "The Overdeveloped Post-Colonial Societies: A Reevaluation." *Review of African Political Economy* 5:39–47.

Lieberthal, Kenneth. 1984. "Domestic Politics and Foreign Policy." In *China's*

Foreign Relations in the 1980s, ed. Harry Harding, 43–70. New Haven: Yale University Press.

Lindbloom, Charles E. 1959. "The Science of Muddling Through." *Public Administration Review* 19:79–88.

Linden, Carl A. 1976. *Khrushchev and the Soviet Leadership, 1957–1964*. Baltimore: Johns Hopkins University Press.

Looney, Robert E. 1989. "Internal and External Factors in Effecting Third World Military Expenditures." *Journal of Peace Research* 26:33–46.

Loriaux, Michael. 1992. "The Realists and Saint Augustine: Skepticism, Psychology, and Moral Action in International Relations Thought." *International Studies Quarterly* 36:401–20.

Love, Janice. 1985. *The Anti-Apartheid Movement: Local Activism in Global Politics*. New York: Praeger.

Lowi, Theodore J. 1971. *The Politics of Disorder*. New York: Basic Books.

Lowi, Theodore J. 1972. "The Politics of Higher Education: Political Science as a Case Study." In *The Post-Behavioral Era: Perspectives on Political Science*, ed. George J. Graham and George W. Carey, 11–36. New York: David McKay.

Lowi, Theodore J. 1979. *The End of Liberalism: The Second Republic of the United States*. New York: Norton.

Lowi, Theodore J. 1985. *The Personal President: Power Invested, Promise Unfulfilled*. Ithaca, N.Y.: Cornell University Press.

MacFarlane, S. Neil. 1985. *Superpower Rivalry and 3rd World Radicalism*. London: Croom Helm.

Machiavelli, Niccolo. 1950. *The Prince and The Discourses*. New York: Modern Library.

Macridis, Roy C. 1989. "French Foreign Policy: The Quest for Rank." In *Foreign Policy in World Politics: States and Regions*, ed. Roy C. Macridis, 27–71. Englewood Cliffs, N.J.: Prentice-Hall.

Mahoney, Richard. 1983. *JFK: Ordeal in Africa*. New York: Oxford University Press.

Makinda, Samuel M. 1987. *Superpower Diplomacy in the Horn of Africa*. New York: St. Martin's.

Mann, Thomas E. 1990. "Making Foreign Policy: President and Congress." In *A Question of Balance: The President, The Congress and Foreign Policy*, ed. Thomas E. Mann, 1–34. Washington, D.C.: Brookings.

Mansbach, Richard W. and John A. Vasquez. 1981. *In Search of Theory: A New Paradigm for Global Politics*. New York: Columbia University Press.

Maoz, Zeev. 1989. "Joining the Club of Nations: Political Development and International Conflict, 1816–1976." *International Studies Quarterly* 33:199–231.

Marcum, John. 1972. "The Politics of Indifference: Portugal and Africa, a Case Study in American Foreign Policy." *Issue: A Quarterly Journal of Opinion* 2:9–17.

Mares, David R. 1988. "Middle Powers Under Regional Hegemony: To Challenge or Acquiesce in Hegemonic Enforcement." *International Studies Quarterly* 32:453–71.

Mastanduno, Michael. 1985. "Strategies of Economic Containment: U.S. Trade Relations with the Soviet Union." *World Politics* 37:503–31.

Mastanduno, Michael, David A. Lake, and G. John Ikenberry. 1989. "Toward a Realist Theory of State Action." *International Studies Quarterly* 33:457–74.

Masters, Robert D. 1992. "Gradualism and Discontinuous Change in Evolutionary

Biology and Political Philosophy.'' In *The Dynamics of Evolution: The Punctuated Equilibrium Debate in the Natural and Social Sciences*, ed. Albert Somit and Steven A. Peterson, 282–319. Ithaca, N.Y.: Cornell University Press.

May, Ernest. 1984. ''The Cold War.'' In *The Making of America's Soviet Policy*, ed. Joseph S. Nye, Jr., 209–30. New Haven: Yale University Press.

McConnell, Grant. 1966. *Private Power and American Democracy*. New York: Vintage.

McGinnis, Michael D. 1985. ''Arms, Aid, and Allies: A Formal Model of the Security Policies of Regional Powers.'' Ph.D. dissertation, University of Minnesota.

McGinnis, Michael D. 1990. ''A Rational Model of Regional Rivalry.'' *International Studies Quarterly* 34:111–35.

McGinnis, Michael D. 1991. ''Richardson, Rationality, and Restrictive Models of Arms Races.'' *Journal of Conflict Resolution* 35:443–73.

McGowan, Patrick J., and Howard B. Shapiro 1973. *The Comparative Study of Foreign Policy: A Survey of Scientific Findings*. Beverly Hills: Sage.

McFarland, Andrew S. 1991. ''Interest Groups and Political Time: Cycles in America.'' *British Journal of Political Science* 21:257–84.

Mead, Walter Rusell. 1987. *Mortal Splendor: The American Empire in Transition*. Boston: Houghton Mifflin.

Mead, Walter Russell. 1991. ''Saul Among the Prophets: The Bush Administration and the New World Order.'' *World Policy Journal* 4:375–420.

Mefford, Dwain. 1987. ''Analogical Reasoning and the Definition of the Situation: Back to Snyder for Concepts and Forward to Artificial Intelligence for Method.'' In *New Directions in the Study of Foreign Policy*, ed. Charles F. Hermann, Charles W. Kegley, Jr., and James N. Rosenau, 221–44. Boston: Allen and Unwin.

Melady, Thomas P. 1974. *Burundi: The Tragic Years*. New York: Orbis Books.

Melanson, Richard A. 1983. *Writing History and Making Policy: The Cold War, Vietnam, and Revisionism*. Lanham, Md.: University Press of America.

Melanson, Richard A. 1991. *Reconstructing Consensus: American Foreign Policy Since the Vietnam War*. New York: St. Martin's.

Mendelson, Sarah E. 1993. ''Internal Battles and External Wars: Politics, Learning, and the Soviet Withdrawal from Afghanistan.'' *World Politics* 45:327–60.

Merrill, John. 1989. *Korea: The Peninsular Origins of the War*. Newark: University of Delaware Press.

Midlarsky, Manus. 1981. ''The Revolutionary Transformation of Foreign Policy: Agrarianism and Its International Impact.'' In *The Political Economy of Foreign Policy Behavior*, ed. Charles W. Kegley, Jr. and Patrick McGowan, 39–62. Beverly Hills: Sage.

Milburn, Thomas W., Philip D. Stewart, and Richard K. Herrmann. 1982. ''Perceiving the Other's Intentions.'' In *Foreign Policy USA/USSR*, ed. Charles W. Kegley, Jr. and P. McGowan, 51–64. Beverly Hills: Sage.

Miliband, Ralph. 1969. *The State in Capitalist Society*. London: Quartet Books.

Mills, C. Wright. 1956. *The Power Elite*. London: Oxford University Press.

Mingst, Karen. 1982. ''Process and Policy in U.S. Commodities: The Impact of the Liberal Economic Paradigm.'' In *America in a Changing World Political Economy*, ed. William P. Avery and David Rapkin, 191–206. New York: Longman.

Modelski, George. 1978. ''The Long Cycles of Global Politics and the Nation-State.'' *Comparative Studies in Society and History* April:214–35.

Modelski, George. 1987. *Long Cycles in World Politics*. Seattle: University of Washington Press.

Moll, Kendall D., and Gregory M. Luebbert. 1980. "Arms Race and Military Expenditure Models: A Review." *Journal of Conflict Resolution* 24:153–85.

Moon, Bruce E. 1983. "The Foreign Policy of the Dependent State." *International Studies Quarterly* 27:315–340.

Moon, Bruce E. 1985. "Consensus or Compliance? Foreign Policy Change and External Dependence." *International Organization* 39:297–329.

Moore, Wilbert E. 1968. "Social Change." In *International Encyclopedia of the Social Sciences*, ed. David Sills, 365–75, vol. 14. New York: Crowell Collier and Macmillan.

Moore, Wilbert E. 1974. *Social Change*. Englewood Cliffs, N.J.: Prentice-Hall.

Morgan, T. Clifton, and Sally Howard Campbell. 1991. "Domestic Structure, Decisional Constraints, and War: So Why Kant Democracies Fight?" *Journal of Conflict Resolution* 35:187–211.

Morgenthau, Hans. 1973. *Politics Among Nations*. New York: Alfred A. Knopf.

Morgenthau, Hans, and Kenneth Thompson. 1985. *Politics Among Nations: The Struggle for Power and Peace*. New York: Alford A. Knopf.

Morrow, James D. 1989. "Capabilities, Uncertainty, and Resolve: A Limited Information Model of Crisis Bargaining." *American Journal of Political Science* 33:941–72.

Morse, Edward L. 1973. *Foreign Policy and Interdependence in Gaullist France*. Princeton: Princeton University Press.

Morse, Edward L. 1976. *Modernization and the Transformation of International Relations*. New York: Free Press.

Most, Benjamin A., and Harvey Starr. 1984. "International Relations Theory, Foreign Policy Substitutability, and 'Nice Laws.' " *World Politics* 36:383–406.

Most, Benjamin A., and Harvey Starr. 1989. *Inquiry, Logic and International Politics*. Columbia: University of South Carolina Press.

Nadel, Siegfried. 1957. *The Theory of Social Structure*. Glencoe, Ill.: Free Press.

Nau, Henry R. 1984–1985. "Where Reaganomics Works." *Foreign Policy* 57:14–37.

Nettl, J. P. 1968. "The State as a Conceptual Variable." *World Politics* 20:559–92.

Neuman, Stephanie G. 1986. *Military Assistance in Recent Wars: The Dominance of the Superpowers*. The Washington Papers/122. New York: Praeger.

Neuman, W. Russell. 1986. *The Paradox of Mass Politics: Knowledge and Opinion in the American Electorate*. Cambridge, Mass.: Harvard University Press.

Neustadt, Richard E. 1991. *Presidential Power: The Politics of Leadership from Roosevelt to Reagan*. New York: John Wiley.

Niou, Emerson M. S., Peter C. Ordeshook, and Gregory F. Rose. 1989. *The Balance of Power: Stability in International Systems*. Cambridge: Cambridge University Press.

Nisbet, Robert A. 1953. *The Quest for Community*. New York: Oxford University Press.

Nisbet, Robert A. 1969. *Social Change and History: Aspects of the Western Theory of Development*. New York: Oxford University Press.

Nye, Joseph S., Jr. 1988. "Short-Term Folly, Not Long Term Decline." *New Perspectives Quarterly* 5:33–35.

Nye, Joseph S., Jr. 1990. *Bound to Lead: The Changing Nature of American Power*. New York: Basic Books.

Nye, Joseph S., Jr. 1993. *Understanding International Conflicts*. New York: Harper Collins.

O'Donnell, Guillermo. 1973. *Modernization and Bureaucratic-Authoritarianism in Latin America*. Berkeley: Institute of International Studies.

O'Donnell, Guillermo. 1979. "Tensions in Bureaucratic-Authoritarian State and the Question of Democracy." In *The New Authoritarianism in Latin America*, ed. David Collier, 285–318. Princeton: Princeton University Press.

O'Donnell, Guillermo, Philippe C. Schmitter, and Laurence Whitehead, editors. 1986. *Transition from Authoritarian Rule: Prospect for Democracy*. Baltimore: Johns Hopkins University Press.

Ogene, F. Chidozie. 1983. *Interest Groups and the Shaping of Foreign Policy: Four Case Studies of United States Foreign Policy*. New York: St. Martin's.

Ohaegbulam, F. Ugboaja. 1988. "Containment in Africa: From Truman to Reagan." *TransAfrica Forum* 6:7–34.

Olson, Mancur. 1982. *The Rise and Decline of Nations: Economic Growth, Stagflation, and Social Rigidities*. New Haven: Yale University Press.

Oneal, John R. 1982. *Foreign Policymaking in Times of Crisis*. Columbus: Ohio State University.

Ori, Kan 1976. "Political Factors in Postwar Japan's Foreign Policy Decisions." In *Japan, America, and the Future World Order*, ed. Morton A. Kaplan and Kinhide Mushakoji, 145–74. New York: Free Press.

Ornstein, Norman J. 1984. "Interest Groups, Congress, and American Foreign Policy." In *American Foreign Policy in an Uncertain World*, ed. David P. Forsythe, 49–64. Lincoln: University of Nebraska Press.

Ostrom, Charles W., and Brian Job. 1986. "The President and the Political Use of Force." *American Political Science Review* 80:541–66.

Ottaway, Marina. 1982. *Soviet and American Influence in the Horn of Africa*. New York: Praeger.

Oye, Kenneth A. 1987. "Constrained Confidence and the Evolution of Reagan's Foreign Policy." In *Eagle Resurgent? The Reagan Era in American Foreign Policy*, ed. Kenneth A. Oye, Robert L. Lieber, and Donald Rothchild, 3–39. Boston: Little, Brown.

Oye, Kenneth A., Robert L. Lieber, and Donald Rothchild, editors. 1987. *Eagle Resurgent? The Reagan Era in American Foreign Policy*. Boston: Little, Brown.

Papadakis, Maria, and Harvey Starr. 1987. "Opportunity, Willingness, and Small States: The Relationship Between Environment and Foreign Policy." In *New Directions in the Study of Foreign Policy*, ed. Charles F. Hermann, Charles W. Kegley, Jr., and James N. Rosenau, 409–32. Boston: Allen and Unwin.

Parenti, Michael. 1989. *The Sword and the Dollar: Imperialism, Revolution, and the Arms Race*. New York: St. Martin's.

Park, Chang Jin. 1975. "The Influence of Small Powers Upon the Superpowers." *World Politics* 28:97–117.

Park, Jae Kyu. 1984. "North Korea's Political and Economic Relations with China and the Soviet Union: From 1954 to 1980." *Comparative Strategy* 4:273–305.

Park, Jae Kyu, Byung Chul Koh, and Tae-Hwan Kwak, editors. 1987. *The Foreign Relations of North Korea: New Perspectives*. Boulder: Westview.

Pellow, Deborah, and Naomi Chazan. 1986. *Ghana: Coping with Uncertainty*. Boulder: Westview.

Perlmutter, Amos. 1978. "Begin's Strategy and Dayan's Tactics." *Foreign Affairs* 52:357–72.

Perlmutter, Amos. 1982. "Begin's Rhetoric and Sharon's Tactics." *Foreign Affairs* 61:67–83.

Petterson, Donald. 1985. "Somalia and the United States, 1977–1983: The New Relationship." In *African Crisis Areas and U.S. Foreign Policy*, ed. Gerald J. Bender, James S. Coleman, and Richard L. Sklar, 194–204. Berkeley: University of California Press.

Pious, Richard. 1979. *The American Presidency*. New York: Basic Books.

Pipes, Daniel. 1983. *In the Path of God*. New York: Basic Books.

Plummer, Brenda Gayle. 1989. "Evolution of the Black Foreign Policy Constituency." *TransAfrica Forum* 6:67–82.

Polanyi, Karl. 1944. *The Great Transformation*. Boston: Beacon Press.

Porter, Bruce D. 1984. *The USSR in Third World Conflicts: Soviet Arms and Diplomacy in Local Wars, 1945–1980*. Cambridge: Cambridge University Press.

Powell, Robert. 1990. *Nuclear Deterrence Theory and the Problem of Credibility*. Cambridge: Cambridge University Press.

Prewitt, Kenneth, and Alan Stone. 1973. *The Ruling Elites: Elite Theory, Power, and American Democracy*. New York: Harper and Row.

Prigogine, Ilya, and Isabelle Stengers. 1984. *Order Out of Chaos*. Boulder: Random House for New Science Library.

Przeworski, Adam. 1986. "Problems in the Study of Transition to Democracy." In *Transition from Authoritarian Rule: Prospect for Democracy*, ed. Guillermo O'Donnell et al., 47–63. Baltimore: Johns Hopkins University Press.

Puchala, Donald J. 1981. "Integration Theory and the Study of International Relations." In *From National Development to Global Community*, ed. Richard L. Merritt and Bruce M. Russett, 145–64. Boston: Allen and Unwin.

Puchala, Donald J. 1990. "Woe to the Orphans of the Scientific Revolution." *Journal of International Affairs* 44:59–80.

Putnam, Robert D. 1988. "Diplomacy and Domestic Politics: The Logic of Two Level Games." *International Organization* 42:427–60.

Pye, Lucian W. 1985. *Asian Powers and Politics: The Cultural Dimension of Authority*. Cambridge, Mass.: Harvard University Press.

Quandt, William B. 1981. *Saudi Arabia in the 1980s: Foreign Policy, Security, and Oil*. Washington, D.C.: Brookings.

Quandt, William B. 1986. *Camp David: Peacemaking and Politics*. Washington, D.C.: Brookings.

Rabinovich, Itamar. 1972. *Syria under the Ba'th, 1963–66: The Army-Party Symbiosis*. New Brunswick, N.J.: Transaction Books.

Raiffa, Howard. 1968. *Decision Analysis*. Reading, Mass.: Addison-Wesley.

Rajmaira, Sheen, and Michael D. Ward. 1990. "Reciprocity and Evolving Norms in the Reagan and Gorbachev Eras." Paper presented at the annual meeting of the American Political Science Association, San Francisco.

Ramazani, R. K. 1989. "Iran's Foreign Policy: Contending Orientations." *The Middle East Journal* 43:202–17.

Rapkin, David P., William R. Thompson, and Jon A. Christopherson. 1979. "Bipolarity and Bipolarization in the Cold War Era." *Journal of Conflict Resolution* 23 (June): 261–95.

Ray, Ellen, William Schaap, Karl Van Meter, and Louis Wolf, editors. 1979. *Dirty Work 2: The CIA in Africa*. Secaucus, N.J.: Lyle Stuart.

Razi, G. Hossein. 1988. "An Alternative Paradigm to State Rationality in Foreign Policy: The Iran-Iraq War." *Western Political Quarterly* 41:689–723.

Resnick, David, and Norman C. Thomas. 1990. "Cycling Through American Politics." *Polity* 23:1–21.

Riker, William. 1962. *The Theory of Political Coalitions*. New Haven: Yale University Press.

Riker, William H. 1982. *Liberalism Against Populism*. San Francisco: Freeman.

Rioux, Jean-Pierre. 1988. *The Fourth Republic, 1944–1958*. Cambridge: Cambridge University Press.

Risse-Kappen, Thomas. 1991. "Public Opinion, Domestic Structure, and Foreign Policy in Liberal Democracies." *World Politics* 43:479–512.

Rizopoulos, Nicholas X., editor. 1990. *Sea-Changes: American Foreign Policy in a World Transformed*. New York: Council on Foreign Relations Press.

Roberts, Norman P. 1971. "The Changing Images of Africa in Some Selected American Media From 1930 to 1969." Ph.D. dissertation, The American University.

Robinson, Thomas W. 1982. "Restructuring Chinese Foreign Policy, 1959–1976: Three Episodes." In *Why Nations Realign: Foreign Policy Restructuring in the Postwar World*, ed. K. J. Holsti, 134–73. New York: Allen and Unwin.

Rodney, Walter. 1982. *How Europe Underdeveloped Africa*. Washington, D.C.: Howard University Press.

Roeder, Philip. 1984. "Soviet Policies and Kremlin Politics." *International Studies Quarterly* 28:171–93.

Rohrlich, Paul Egon. 1987. "Economic Culture and Foreign Policy: The Cognitive Analysis of Economic Policy Making." *International Organization* 41:61–92.

Rosati, Jerel A. 1981. "Developing a Systematic Decision-Making Framework: Bureaucratic Politics in Perspective." *World Politics* 33:234–52.

Rosati, Jerel A. 1984. "Congressional Influence in American Foreign Policy: Addressing the Controversy." *Journal of Political and Military Sociology* 12:311–33.

Rosati, Jerel A. 1987. *The Carter Administration's Quest for Global Community: Beliefs and the Their Impact on Behavior*. Columbia: University of South Carolina Press.

Rosati, Jerel. 1988. "Human Needs and the Evolution of U.S. Foreign Policy." In *The Power of Human Needs in World Society*, ed. Roger A. Coate and Jerel A. Rosati, 161–86. Boulder: Lynne Rienner.

Rosati, Jerel A. 1993. *The Politics of United States Foreign Policy*. Dallas: Harcourt Brace Jovanovitch.

Rosati, Jerel A. 1994. "A Cognitive Approach to the Study of Foreign Policy." In *Foreign Policy Analysis: Continuity and Change in its Second Generation,* ed. Laura Neack, Patrick J. Haney, and Jeanne A. K. Hey. Englewood Cliffs, N.J.: Prentice-Hall.

Rosati, Jerel A., and John Creed. 1992. "Extending the Three- and FourHeaded Eagle: Elite Beliefs in U.S. Foreign Policy During the Eighties." Paper presented at the annual meeting of the International Studies Association, Atlanta.

Rose, Arnold H. 1967. *The Power Structure: Political Process in American Society*. New York: Oxford University Press.

Rosenau, James N. 1966. "Pre-Theories and Theories of Foreign Policy." In *Ap-*

proaches to Comparative and International Politics, ed. R. Barry Farrell, 27–92. Evanston, Ill.: Northwestern University Press.

Rosenau, James N. 1967. "Games International Relations Scholars Play." *Journal of International Affairs* 21:293–303.

Rosenau, James N. 1968. "Comparative Foreign Policy: Fad, Fantasy, or Field?" *International Studies Quarterly* 12:296–329.

Rosenau, James N. 1975. "Comparative Foreign Policy: One-time Fad, Realized Fantasy, and Normal Field." In *International Events and the Comparative Analysis of Foreign Policy*, ed. Charles W. Kegley, Jr., Gregory A. Raymond, Robert M. Rood, and Richard A. Skinner, 3–38. Columbia: University of South Carolina Press.

Rosenau, James N. 1978. "Restlessness, Change, and Foreign Policy Analysis." In *In Search of Global Patterns*, ed. James N. Rosenau, 369–76. New York: Free Press.

Rosenau, James N. 1980. "Thinking Theory Thoroughly." In *The Scientific Study of Foreign Policy*, 19–31. New York: Free Press.

Rosenau, James N. 1981. *The Study of Political Adaptation: Essays on the Analysis of World Politics*. New York: Nichols Publishing.

Rosenau, James N. 1984. "A Pre-Theory Revisited: World Politics in an Era of Cascading Interdependence." *International Studies Quarterly* 28:245–305.

Rosenau, James N. 1990. *Turbulence in World Politics: A Theory of Change and Continuity*. Princeton: Princeton University Press.

Roskin, Michael. 1974. "From Pearl Harbor to Vietnam: Shifting Generation Paradigms and Foreign Policy." *Political Science Quarterly* 89:563–88.

Rotberg, Robert I., editor. 1988. *Africa in the 1990s and Beyond: U.S. Policy Opportunities and Choices*. Algonac, Mich.: Reference Publications.

Rotberg, Robert I. and Theodore K. Rabb, editors. 1989. *The Origin and Prevention of Major Wars*. Cambridge: Cambridge University Press.

Rothstein, Robert. 1968. *Alliances and Small Powers*. New York: Columbia University Press.

Rubinstein, Alvin Z. 1977. *Red Star on the Nile*. Princeton: Princeton University Press.

Rubinstein, Alvin Z. 1982. *Soviet Policy Toward Turkey, Iran, and Afghanistan: The Dynamics of Influence*. New York, Praeger.

Rusinow, Dennison. 1977. *The Yugoslav Experiment, 1948–1974*. Berkeley: University of California Press.

Russett, Bruce M. 1983. "International Interactions and Processes: The Internal vs. External Debate Revisited." In *Political Science: The State of the Discipline*, ed. Ada Finifter, 541–68. Washington, D.C.: American Political Science Association.

Russett, Bruce M. 1985. "The Mysterious Case of Vanishing Hegemony; or Is Mark Twain Really Dead?" *International Organization* 39:207–32.

Russett, Bruce M. 1990. *Controlling the Sword: The Democratic Governance of National Security*. Cambridge, Mass.: Harvard University Press.

Sadat, Anwar. 1978. *In Search of Identity: An Autobiography*. New York: Harper and Row.

Sadat, Anwar. 1984. *Those I Have Known*. New York: Continuum.

Safran, Nadav. 1978. *Israel: The Embattled Ally*. Cambridge, Mass.: Harvard University Press.

Salmore, Barbara G., and Stephen A. Salmore. 1978. "Political Regimes and Foreign

Policy." In *Why Nations Act*, ed. M. A. East, S. A Salmore, and C. F Hermann, 103–22. Beverly Hills: Sage.

Sampson, Anthony. 1975. *The Seven Sisters*. New York: Viking.

Sampson, Martin W. 1987. "Cultural Influences on Foreign Policy." In *New Directions in the Study of Foreign Policy*, ed. Charles F. Hermann, Charles W. Kegley, Jr., and James N. Rosenau, 384–405. Boston: Allen and Unwin.

Sanders, Jerry. 1983. *Peddlers of Crisis: The Committee on the Present Danger and the Politics of Containment*. Boston: South End Press.

Saul, John. 1974. "The State in Post-Colonial Societies: Tanzania." In *Social Register*, ed. Ralph Miliband and John Saville, 349–72. London: Merlin Press.

Scalapino, Robert A., and Jun-Yop Kim, editors. 1983. *North Korea Today: Strategic and Domestic Issues*. Korea Research Monograph 8. Berkeley: Institute of East Asia Studies, University of California.

Schattschneider, E. E. 1975. *The Semisovereign People*. Hinsdale, Ill.: Dryden Press.

Schlesinger, Arthur M., Jr. 1967. *A Thousand Days: John F. Kennedy in the White House*. Greenwich, Conn.: Fawcett Publications.

Schlesinger, Arthur M., Jr. 1973. *The Imperial Presidency*. Boston: Houghton Mifflin.

Schlesinger, Arthur M., Jr. 1986. *Cycles of American History*. Boston: Houghton Mifflin.

Schneider, William. 1984. "Public Opinion." In *The Making of America's Soviet Policy*, ed. Joseph S. Nye, Jr., 11–35. New Haven: Yale University Press.

Schneider, William. 1987. "Conservatism, Not Interventionism: Trends in Foreign Policy Opinion, 1974–1982." In *Eagle Defiant: United States Foreign Policy in the 1980s*, ed. Kenneth Oye, Donald Rothchild, and Robert Lieber, 33–64. Boston: Little, Brown.

Schraeder, Peter J. 1991. "Speaking with Many Voices: Continuity and Change in U.S.-Africa Policies." *Journal of Modern African Studies* 29:373–412.

Schraeder, Peter J. 1993. "The Study of U.S. Foreign Policy Toward Africa: From Intellectual 'Backwater' to Theory Construction." *Third World Quarterly* 14.

Schraeder, Peter J. 1994. *United States Foreign Policy Toward Africa: Incrementalism, Crisis, and Change*. London: Cambridge University Press.

Schrodt, Philip A. 1984. "Background to a Dynamic Model Using Artificial Intelligence Techniques." Paper presented at the US and Swiss National Science Foundation Conference on Dynamic Models of International Conflict, Boulder, Colo., 31 October to 3 November.

Schuler, G. 1976. "The International Oil Negotiations." In *The 50% Solution*, ed. I. William Zartman, 124–207. Garden City, N.Y.: Anchor Books.

Schumpeter, Joseph. 1949. *Theory of Economic Development*. Cambridge, Mass.: Harvard University Press.

Schwartz, Morton. 1975. *The Foreign Policy of the USSR: Domestic Factors*. Encino, Calif.: Dickenson.

Seale, Patrick. 1965. *The Struggle for Syria: A Study of Post-War Arab Politics, 1945–1958*. New York: Oxford University Press.

Seale, Patrick. 1988. *Assad: The Stuggle for the Middle East*. Berkeley: University of California Press.

Segal, Aaron. 1976. "Africa and the United States Media." *Issue: A Quarterly Journal of Opinion* 6:49–56.

Segal, David. 1988. "The Iran-Iraq War: A Military Analysis." *Foreign Affairs* 66:946–63.

Shalim, Avi. 1983. "Conflicting Approaches to Israel's Relations with the Arabs: Ben Gurion and Sharrett, 1953–1956." *The Middle East Journal* 37:180–201.

Shinn, Rinn-sup. 1973. "Foreign and Reunification Policies." *Problems of Communism* 22:55–71.

Shoemaker, Christopher C. 1981. "Dogs and Tails: Patron-Client State Relationships in the Nuclear Age." Ph.D. dissertation, University of Florida.

Shulman, Marshall. 1988. "Four Decades of Irrationality: U.S.-Soviet Relations." In *World Politics 88/89*, ed. Suzanne P. Ogden, 23. Gifford, Conn.: Dushkin Publishing.

Silberberg, Eugene. 1978. *The Structure of Economics: A Mathematical Analysis.* New York: McGraw-Hill.

Simmons, Robert R. 1975. *The Strained Alliance: Peking, Pyongyang, Moscow and the Politics of the Korean Civil War.* New York: Free Press.

Singer, J. David. 1961. "The Level-of-Analysis Problem in International Relations." In *The International System: Theoretical Essays*, ed. Klaus Knorr and Sidney Verba, 77–92. Princeton: Princeton University Press.

Singer, J. David. 1962. *Deterrence, Arms Control, and Disarmament.* Columbus: Ohio State University Press.

Singer, Marshall R. 1972. *Weak States in a World of Powers.* New York: Free Press.

Singer, Eric G. 1986. "Personality and Foreign Policy Behavior: A Study of Black African Leadership." Ph.D. dissertation, Ohio State University.

Singer, Eric G., and Valerie M. Hudson. 1987. "Role Sets and African Foreign Policy Behavior." In *Role Theory and Foreign Policy Analysis*, ed. S. Walker, 199–218. Durham, N.C.: Duke University Press.

Singh, S. Nihal. 1984. "Why India Goes to Moscow for Arms." *Asian Survey* 24:707–20.

Siverson, Randolph M., and Harvey Starr. 1990. "Opportunity, Willingness, and the Diffusion of War." *American Political Science Review* 84:47–67.

Skidmore, David. 1989. "The Carter Administration and Hegemonic Decline: Constraints on Policy Adjustment." Ph.D. dissertation, Stanford University.

Skidmore, David. Forthcoming. "The Politics of Decline: International Adjustment Versus Domestic Legitimacy during the Carter Administration." *Political Science Quarterly.*

Skocpol, Theda. 1985. "Bringing the State Back In: Strategies of Analysis in Current Research." In *Bringing the State Back In*, ed. Peter Evans, Dietrich Rueschemeyer, and Theda Skocpol, 3–43. Cambridge: Cambridge University Press.

Skowronek, Stephen. 1982. *Building a New American State: The Expansion of National Administrative Capacities.* New York: Cambridge University Press.

Small, Melvin and J. David Singer. 1973. "The Diplomatic Importance of States, 1816–1970: An Extension and Refinement of the Indicator." *World Politics* 25:577–99.

Small, Melvin, and J. David Singer. 1982. *Resort to Arms.* Beverly Hills: Sage.

Smith, Gaddis. 1976. *Morality, Reason, and Power: American Diplomacy in the Carter Years.* New York: Hill and Wang.

Smith, Hedrick. 1988. *The Power Game: How Washington Really Works.* New York: Ballantine.

Smith, Steve. 1983. "Rosenau's Contribution." *Review of International Studies* 9:137–46.

Snidal, Duncan. 1985. "The Game 'Theory' of International Politics." *World Politics* 38:25–57.

Snyder, Glenn H., and Paul Deising. 1977. *Conflict among Nations: Bargaining, Decision Making, and System Structure International Crises*. Princeton: Princeton University Press.

Snyder, Jack. 1991. *The Myths of Empire: Domestic Politics and International Ambition*. Ithaca: Cornell University Press.

Snyder, Richard C., H. W. Bruck, and Burton Sapin, editors. 1962. *Foreign Policy Decision-Making*. Glencoe, Ill.: Free Press.

Sofer, Sasson. 1988. *Begin: An Anatomy of Leadership*. Oxford: Basil Blackwell.

Somit, Albert, and Steven A. Peterson. 1992. *The Dynamics of Evolution: The Punctuated Equilibrium Debate in the Natural and Social Sciences*. Ithaca, N.Y.: Cornell University Press.

Sorenson, Theodore C. 1963. *Decision-Making in the White House: The Olive Branch or the Arrows*. New York: Columbia University Press.

Sorokin, Pitirim A. 1947. *Society, Culture, and Personality: Their Structure and Dynamics*. New York: Harper and Brothers.

Sorokin, Pitirim. 1957. *Social & Cultural Dynamics*. Boston: Porter Sargent.

Spanier, John. 1987. *Games Nations Play*. Washington, D.C.: Congressional Quarterly Press.

Spanier, John. 1988. *American Foreign Policy Since World War II*. Washington, D.C.: Congressional Quarterly Press.

Spero, Joan Edelman. 1991. *The Politics of International Economic Relations*. New York: St. Martin's.

Sprout, Harold, and Margaret Sprout. 1965. *The Ecological Perspective on Human Affairs*. Princeton: Princeton University Press.

Sprout, Harold, and Margaret Sprout. 1968. "The Dilemma of Rising Demands and Insufficient Resources." *World Politics* 20:660–93.

Sprout, Harold, and Margaret Sprout. 1969. "Environmental Factors in the Study of International Politics." In *International Politics and Foreign Policy*, ed. James N. Rosenau, 41–56. New York: Free Press.

Stanely, Peter W. 1986. "Toward Democracy in the Philippines." *Proceedings of the Academy of Political Studies* 36:129–41.

Starr, Harvey. 1984. *Henry Kissinger: Perceptions of International Politics*. Lexington: University of Kentucky Press.

Stein, Arthur. 1984. "The Hegemon's Dilemma: Great Britain, the United States, and the International Economic Order." *International Organization* 38:355–86.

Stein, Arthur A., and Bruce M. Russett. 1980. "Evaluating War: Outcomes and Consequences." In Ted R. Gurr, editor, *Handbook of Political Conflict: Theory and Research*. New York: Free Press.

Steinbruner, John D. 1974. *The Cybernetic Theory of Decision: New Dimensions of Political Analysis*. Princeton: Princeton University Press.

Stempel, John D. 1981. *Inside the Iranian Revolution*. Bloomington: Indiana University Press.

Stent, Angela. 1985. "Soviet-West German Relations Under Helmut Kohl: Continuity or Change?" In *Economic Relations with the Soviet Union*, ed. Angela Stent, 27–47. Boulder: Westview.

Stepan, Alfred. 1986. "Paths Toward Redemocratization: Theoretical and Comparative Considerations." In *Transition from Authoritarian Rule: Prospect for Democracy*, ed. Guillermo O'Donnell et al., 64–84. Baltimore: Johns Hopkins University Press.

Stockholm International Peace Research Institute (SIPRI). 1971. *The Arms Trade With the Third World*. London: Paul Elek.

Stockwell, John. 1978. *In Search of Enemies: A CIA Story*. New York: W. W. Norton.

Stoessinger, John G. 1985. *Why Nations Go to War*. New York: St. Martin's.

Stoler, Mark A. 1981. "World War II Diplomacy in Historical Writing: Prelude to Cold War." In *American Foreign Relations: A Historiographical Review*, ed. Gerald K. Haines and J. Samuel Walker, 187–206. Westport, Conn.: Greenwood Press.

Strange, Susan. 1987. "The Persistent Myth of Lost Hegemony." *International Organization* 41:551–74.

Stremlau, John J. 1977. *The International Politics of the Nigerian Civil War 1967–1970*. Princeton: Princeton University Press.

Sullivan, Michael P. 1976. *International Relations: Theory and Evidence*. Englewood Cliffs, N.J.: Prentice-Hall.

Sundelius, Bengt. 1989. "Das Primat der Neutralitatspolitik: Building Regimes at Home." *Cooperation and Conflict* 24:163–78.

Sundquist, James L. 1968. *Politics and Policy*. Washington, D.C.: Brookings.

Sutter, Robert G. 1978. *Chinese Foreign Policy after the Cultural Revolution, 1966–1977*. Boulder: Westview.

Sutter, Robert G. 1988. *Taiwan: Entering the 21st Century*. Lanham, Md.: University Press of America.

Sylvan, James. 1976. "Consequences of Sharp Military Assistance Increases for International Conflict and Cooperation." *Journal of Conflict Resolution* 20:609–36.

Tahir-Kheli, Shirin. 1982. *The United States and Pakistan: The Evolution of an Influence Relationship*. New York: Praeger.

Tamashiro, Howard. 1984. "Algorithms, Heuristics, and the Artificial Intelligence Modelling of Strategic Statecraft." In *Foreign Policy Decision Making: Perception, Cognition, and Artificial Intelligence*, ed. Donald A. Sylvan and Steve Chan, 197–226. Praeger: New York.

Tanaka, Akihiko. 1984. "China, China Watching, and CHINA-WATCHER." In *Foreign Policy Decision-Making: Perception, Cognition, and Artificial Intelligence*, ed. Donald A. Sylvan and Steve Chan, 310–44. New York: Praeger.

Taylor, Charles, and Michael Hudson. 1972. *World Handbook of Political and Social Indicators*. New Haven: Yale University Press.

Taylor, Alan R. 1982. *The Arab Balance of Power*. Syracuse, N.Y.: Syracuse University Press.

Teng, Chung-Chian. 1988. "Taiwan's Democratization and Foreign Policy Changes." Paper presented at the annual meeting of the International Studies Association, St. Louis, 30 March-3 April.

Thomas, Raju G. C., editor. 1983. *The Great Power Triangle and Asian Security*. Lexington, Mass.: D. C. Heath.

Thomas, Raju G. C., editor. 1986. *Indian Security Policy*. Princeton: Princeton University Press.

Thompson, W. Scott. 1969. *Ghana's Foreign Policy, 1957–1966: Diplomacy, Ideology, and the New State*. Princeton: Princeton University Press.

Thornton, Richard C. 1982. *China: A Political History, 1917–1980.* Boulder: West-view.

Thorson, Stuart J. 1984. "Intentional Inferencing in Foreign Policy: An Artificial Intelligence Approach." In *Foreign Policy Decision-Making: Perception, Cognition, and Artificial Intelligence,* ed. Donald A. Sylvan and Steve Chan, 280–309. New York: Praeger.

Thorson, Stuart J., and Donald A. Sylvan. 1982. "Counterfactuals and the Cuban Missile Crisis." *International Studies Quarterly* 26:539–71.

Thucydides. 1982. *The Peloponnesian War.* Crawley translation, revised by T. E. Wick. New York: Modern Library.

Touval, Saadia. 1972. *The Boundary Politics of Independent Africa.* Cambridge, Mass.: Harvard University Press.

Trout, B. Thomas. 1975. "Rhetoric Revisited: Political Legitimation and the Cold War." *International Studies Quarterly* 19:251–284.

Truman, David B. 1951. *The Governmental Process: Political Interests and Public Opinion.* New York: Alfred A. Knopf.

Tsebelis, George. 1990. *Nested Games.* Berkeley: University of California Press.

Tucker, Robert Tucker. 1988–1989. "Reagan's Foreign Policy." *Foreign Affairs America and the World* 68:1–27.

Tukey, John. 1977. *Exploratory Data Analysis.* New York: Addison-Wesley.

Tyler, Patrick. 1986. *Running Critical: The Silent War, Rickover, and General Dynamics.* New York: Harper and Row.

United Nations Statistical Yearbook. 1960–1973. New York: Publishing Services of the United Nations.

United Nations Yearbook of International Trade Statistics. 1982. New York: Publishing Services of the United Nations.

United States, House of Representatives. Committee on Foreign Affairs. Subcommittees on International Economic Policy and Trade, and on Africa. 1987. *Legislative Options and United States Policy Toward South Africa* Hearings and Markup, 9 April, 16 April; 4–5 June 1986, 99th Congress, 2nd Session. Washington, D.C.: Government Printing Office.

United States Arms Control and Disarmament Agency. 1973. *World Military Expenditures and Arms Trade.* Washington, D.C.: Government Printing Agency.

Vance, Cyrus. 1983. *Hard Choices: Critical Years in America's Foreign Policy.* New York: Simon and Schuster.

Vannicelli, Primo. 1974. *Italy, NATO, and European Community: The Interplay of Foreign Policy and Domestic Politics.* Cambridge, Mass.: Center for International Affairs, Harvard University.

Vasquez, John A. 1976. "A Learning Theory of the American Anti-Vietnam War Movement." *Journal of Peace Research* 13:299–314.

Vasquez, John A. 1983. *The Power of Power Politics: A Critique.* New Brunswick, N.J.: Rutgers University Press.

Vasquez, John A. 1985. "Domestic Contention on Critical Foreign-Policy Issues: The Case of the United States." *International Organization* 39:643–66.

Vasquez, John A. 1987. "Foreign Policy, Learning, and War." In *New Directions and the Study of Foreign Policy,* ed. Charles F. Hermann, Charles W. Kegley, Jr., and James N. Rosenau, 367–83. Boston: Allen and Unwin.

Väyrynen, Raimo. 1984. "Regional Conflict Formations: An Intractable Problem of International Relations." *Journal of Peace Research* 21:337–59.

Vengroff, Richard. 1976. "Instability and Foreign Policy Behavior: Black Africa in the U.N." *American Journal of Political Science* 20:425–38.

Vertzberger, Yaacov Y. I. 1984. *Misperceptions in Foreign Policymaking: The Sino-Indian Conflict, 1959–1962*. Boulder: Westview.

Vincent, Jack E. 1983. "WEIS vs. COPDAB: Correspondence Problems." *International Studies Quarterly* 27:161–68.

Vocke, William C. 1976. *American Foreign Policy: An Analytical Approach*. New York: Free Press.

Volgy, Thomas J. 1993. "Foreign Policy Restructuring: Comparing Change in the Third World." Paper prepared for the annual meeting of the American Political Science Association, Washington, D.C., September.

Volgy, Thomas J., and Henry C. Kenski. 1976. "Toward an Exploration of Comparative Foreign Policy Distance Between the United States and Latin America." *International Studies Quarterly* 20:143–64.

Volgy, Thomas J., and Henry C. Kenski. 1982. "Systems Theory and Foreign Policy Restructuring: Distance Change in Latin America, 1953–1970." *International Studies Quarterly* 26:445–72.

Volgy, Thomas J., and John E. Schwarz. 1989. "Does Politics Stop at the Water's Edge?" Paper presented at the annual meeting of the Western Political Science Association, March.

Volgy, Thomas J., and John E. Schwarz. 1991. "Does Politics Stop at the Water's Edge? Domestic Political Factors and Foreign Policy Restructuring in the Cases of Great Britain, France, and West Germany." *Journal of Politics* 53:615–43.

Volman, Daniel. 1984. "Africa's Rising Status in American Defense Policy." *Journal of Modern African Studies* 22:143–51.

Waddams, Frank. 1980. *The Libyan Oil Industry*. Baltimore: Johns Hopkins University Press.

Walker, Stephen G. 1977. "The Interface Between Beliefs and Behavior: Henry Kissinger's Operational Code and the Vietnam War." *Journal of Conflict Resolution* 21:129–68.

Walker, Stephen G. 1979. "National Role Conceptions and Systemic Outcomes." In *Psychological Models in International Politics*, ed. Lawrence Falkowski, 169–210. Boulder: Westview.

Walker, Stephen G. 1987. "Role Theory and the Origins of Foreign Policy." In *New Directions in the Study of Foreign Policy*, ed. Charles F. Hermann, Charles W. Kegley, Jr., and James N. Rosenau, 269–84. Boston: Allen and Urwin.

Walker, J. Samuel. 1981. "Historians and Cold War Origins: The New Consensus." In *American Foreign Relations: A Historiographical Review*, ed. Gerald K. Haines and J. Samuel Walker, 207–36. Westport, Conn.: Greenwood Press.

Wallerstein, Immanuel. 1986. *Africa and the Modern World*. Trenton, N.J.: Africa World Press.

Walt, Stephen M. 1987. *The Origins of Alliances*. Ithaca, N.Y.: Cornell University Press.

Walters, Ronald J. 1987. "African-American Influence in U.S. Foreign Policy Toward South Africa." In *Ethnic Groups and U.S. Foreign Policy*, ed. Mohammed E. Ahair. Westport, Conn.: Greenwood Press.

Waltz, Kenneth. 1959. *Man, the State and War: A Theoretical Analysis*. New York: Columbia University Press.

Waltz, Kenneth. 1979. *Theory of International Politics*. Reading, Mass.: Addison-Wesley.

Wander, Phillip. 1984. "The Rhetoric of American Foreign Policy." *The Quarterly Journal of Speech* 70:339–61.

Ward, Michael D. 1982. "Cooperation and Conflict in Foreign Policy Behavior." *International Studies Quarterly* 26:87–126.

Wariavwalla, Bharat. 1988. "Interdependence and Domestic Political Regimes: The Case of the Newly Industrializing Countries." *Alternatives* 13:253–70.

Weil, Martin. 1974. "Can the Blacks do for Africa what the Jews did for Israel?" *Foreign Policy* 15:109–30.

Weinstein, Franklin B. 1972. "The Uses of Foreign Policy in Indonesia: An Approach to the Analysis of Foreign Policy in Less Developed Countries." *World Politics* 24:356–81.

Weinstein, Franklin B. 1976. *Indonesian Foreign Policy and the Dilemma of Dependence: From Sukarno to Suharto*. Ithaca, N.Y.: Cornell University Press.

Weissman, Stephen R., and Johnnie Carson. 1981. "Economic Sanctions Against Rhodesia." In *Congress, the Presidency and American Foreign Policy*, ed. John Spanier and Joseph Nogee, 132–60. New York: Pergamon.

Wendt, Alexander E. 1987. "The Agency Structure Problem in International Relations Theory." *International Organization* 41:335–70.

Whiting, Allen S. 1983. "Assertive Nationalism in Chinese Foreign Policy." *Asian Survey* 23:913–33.

Whynes, David K. 1979. *The Economics of Third World Military Expenditure*. Austin: University of Texas Press.

Wilkenfeld, Jonathan, Gerald W. Hopple, Paul J. Rossa, and Stephen J. Andriole. 1980. *Foreign Policy Behavior: The Interstate Behavior Analysis Model*. Beverly Hills: Sage.

Williams, John T., and Michael D. McGinnis. 1988. "Sophisticated Reaction in the U.S.-Soviet Arms Race: Evidence for Rational Expectations." *American Journal of Political Science* 32:968–95.

Willis, F. Roy. 1971. *Italy Chooses Europe*. New York: Oxford University Press.

Wilson, Clifton E. 1991. "Diplomatic Expulsions: Law, Policy, and Norms." Paper presented at the 1991 International Studies Association Conference, Vancouver.

Wilson, James Q. 1973. *Political Organizations*. New York: Basic Books.

Wilson, James Q. 1989. *Bureaucracy: What Government Agencies Do and Why They Do It*. New York: Basic Books.

Winston, Patrick Henry. 1977. *Artificial Intelligence*. Reading, Mass.: Addison-Wesley.

Wittkopf, Eugene R. 1990. *Faces of Internationalism: Public Opinion and American Foreign Policy*. Durham, N.C.: Duke University Press.

Wriggins, W. Howard. 1987. "Pakistan's Foreign Policy After Afghanistan." In *The Security of South Asia: American and Asian Perspectives*, ed. Stephen P. Cohen, 61–80. Urbana: University of Illinois Press.

Wright, John. 1982. *Libya: A Modern History*. Baltimore: Johns Hopkins University Press.

Yergin, Daniel. 1977. *Shattered Peace: The Origins of the Cold War and the National Security State*. Boston: Houghton Mifflin.

Zagoria, Donald S. 1983. "North Korea: Between Moscow and Beijing." In *North*

Korea Today, ed. Robert A. Scalapino and Jun-yop Kim, 351–371. Berkeley: University of California Press.

Zagoria, Donald S. and Young Kun Kim. 1976. "North Korea and the Major Powers." In *The Two Koreas in East Asian Affairs*, ed. Williams J. Barnds, 19–59. New York: New York University Press.

Zartman, I. William. 1985. *Ripe for Resolution: Conflict and Intervention in Africa*. New York: Oxford University Press.

Zartman, I. William, and A. Kluge. 1984. "Heroic Politics: The Foreign Policy of Libya." In *The Foreign Policies of Arab States*, ed. Bahgat Korany and Ali Dessouki, 175–196. Boulder: Westview.

Zimmerman, William. 1979. "Crises and Crises Outcomes: Towards a New Synthetic Approach." *European Journal of Political Research* 7:67–115.

Zimmerman, William. 1987. *Open Borders, Nonalignment, and the Political Evolution*. Princeton: Princeton University Press.

Zinnes, Dina A. 1980. "Three Puzzles in Search of a Researcher." *International Studies Quarterly* 24:315–42.

Ziring, Lawrence, editor. 1982. *The Subcontinent in World Politics*. New York: Praeger.

Zylberberg, Jacques, and Miguel Monterichanrd. 1982. "An Abortive Attempt to Change Foreign Policy: Chile, 1970–1973." In *Why Nations Realign: Foreign Policy Restructuring in the Postwar World*, ed. K. J. Holsti, 198–219. London: Allen and Unwin.

Contributors

William J. Dixon, University of Arizona
Stephen M. Gaarder, University of Arizona
Stephen F. Greffenius, Olin Center for International Study, Boston
Joe D. Hagan, West Virginia University
Kyu-Ryoon Kim, Research Institute for National Unification, Seoul
Dae-Won Ko, Northwestern University
Michael D. McGinnis, Indiana University
Tong Whan Park, Northwestern University
Jerel A. Rosati, University of South Carolina
Martin W. Sampson III, University of Minnesota
Peter J. Schraeder, Loyola University of Chicago
John E. Schwarz, University of Arizona
David Skidmore, Drake University
Thomas J. Volgy, University of Arizona

Index